This book will no doubt be welcomed by all business men, lawyers, and judges interested in the application of the law to business, and of fundamental economic principles to the law, as well as by every citizen seeking a discussion of the monopoly problem that is at once readable and fundamental. It furnishes the first thoroughgoing examination, in the light of economic principles and by a competent economic authority, of the Sherman Anti-Trust Act and of the Clayton Act. The author, whose reputation in the field of economic theory is international, has had practical contacts with the problem of industrial monopoly, serving as adviser in the "Pittsburgh Plus" case against the United States Steel Corporation before the Federal Trade Commission. His investigations throw new light upon monopolizing practices unsuspected by the public; and his conclusions, while sanely constructive, are in many respects startling and revolutionary of popular opinions. Mr. Fetter is Professor of Political Economy at Princeton, and former President of the American Economic Association.

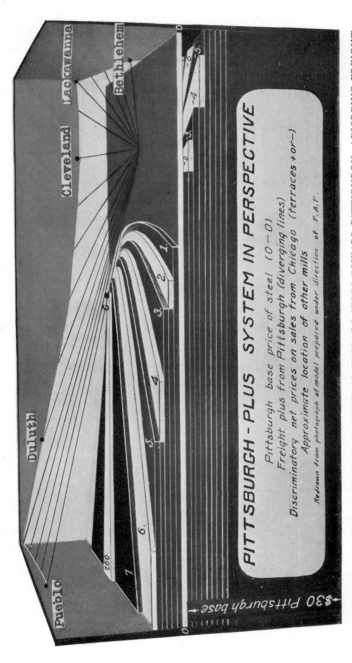

PITTSBURGH - PLUS SYSTEM IN PERSPECTIVE

Pittsburgh base price of steel (O – O)
Freight plus from Pittsburgh (diverging lines)
Discriminatory net prices on sales from Chicago (terraces + or –)
Approximate location of other mills

Redrawn from photograph of model prepared under direction of F.A.F.

FIG. I. SHOWING PUZZLING EFFECTS AS CHICAGO SELLS TOWARD PITTSBURGH, ABSORBING FREIGHT WITH CROSS SHIPMENTS TYPICAL OF ALL BASING-POINT DELIVERED PRICE SYSTEMS. COMPARE FIGS. 4, 5, 6, AND 26

THE MASQUERADE
OF MONOPOLY

BY

FRANK ALBERT FETTER

PH.D., LL.D.

PAST PRESIDENT OF THE AMERICAN
ECONOMIC ASSOCIATION

HARCOURT, BRACE AND COMPANY

NEW YORK

Typography by Robert S. Josephy

PRINTED IN THE UNITED STATES OF AMERICA

BY QUINN & BODEN COMPANY, INC., RAHWAY, N. J.

FOREWORD

THE realm of monopoly has remained, despite repeated attempts to penetrate it, a sort of *terra incognita,* a darkest Africa of our industrial life, where dwell wild beasts and monsters grim, and where strange commercial customs of discriminatory prices and illicit agreements flourish out of sight of the law and of the moral order. The courts, in their attempts to explore this dark wilderness, became lost a generation ago and have not yet been able to find their way out. Their forty years' wanderings are faithfully traced in the following pages.

Increasingly, even in legal circles, the truth has been recognized that economics must be the pathfinder. Legal precedents, precepts, and principles that were evolved in the days of handicraft production and ox-cart transport are absurdly inadequate when applied with rigid literalness to the magnified and complex commercial relations of modern industry. But without economic analysis and insight, even the best meant attempts of the courts to modernize the law of competition and commerce have gone, and must go, astray.

However, the records of important industrial cases that have been carried to the United States Supreme Court (together with inquiries by congressional committees and other governmental agencies) constitute rich storehouses of evidence on this subject. Utilizing these materials, we have approached the problem of contemporary monopoly in a concrete rather than an abstract manner. In our first seventeen chapters these official documents are freely drawn upon for illustrations of business practices in restraint of commerce, and for examples of the peculiar workings of legal minds of the old type, baffled in the midst of the new economic conditions. At each step these facts and opinions have been subjected to economic analysis and criticism.

Against this concrete background, and with real situations before the reader's eyes, the next six chapters (XVIII-XXIII) set forth the principles of market price, the norm of effective competition, and a consistent conception and definition of monopoly in the modern sense. Without such standards clearly in mind it is impossible to form valid judgments, economic or legal, about behavior in the sale of goods, or successfully to set up and administer rules for the regulation of interstate commerce.

The last five chapters (XXIV-XXVIII) revert to matters more concrete and immediately practical. Recent vigorous and persistent attacks upon the Clayton and the Sherman Acts are examined and appraised. In conclusion, is presented in the light of economic principles the simple and effective remedy for the evils, real and alleged, of the anti-trust laws, and for restoring and maintaining industrial freedom in domestic commerce. First, history and description of business practices, and of legal opinions showing the way the courts view these practices; second, economic analysis and the theory of markets and prices; third, practical application of the lessons of history and economics. The various parts may interest in different degrees lawyers, economists, business men, or merely public-spirited citizens, and each may be read understandingly without the other parts, but all converge upon the general subject, The Masquerade of Monopoly.

The author's obligations for information, help, and friendly criticisms are too numerous for detailed acknowledgment. However, a few cases are indicated in the notes, and he cannot refrain from mention of a few others. He is grateful for the stimulating contacts with Professors John R. Commons, of the University of Wisconsin, and William Z. Ripley, of Harvard University, his associates as economic advisers to The Associated States Opposing Pittsburgh-Plus; to Mr. Hugh E. White, who, linking practical insight with ideals of economic justice and zealous public spirit, collected and arranged so large a part of the more valuable statistical data and charts in that case and also in the Bethlehem-Lackawanna complaint, begun (but not pressed to a decision) by the Federal Trade Commission, which public records have been made still more useful by Mr. White's expert interpretations; to Mr. James E. Pope, President of the Pope Trading Company,

90 West St., New York City, for much technical information out of his lifetime of experience in the non-ferrous metals trade; to Princeton colleagues, Professors Frank H. Dixon, Leslie T. Fournier, and Frank Whitson Fetter, and Mr. Frank T. de Vyver, who have read and helpfully criticised the manuscript at various stages; and to Mr. Vernon A. Mund and Mr. John W. McBride, graduate students in economics, for their untiring assistance.

This essay in a much neglected field is hopefully dedicated to a nation of victimized consumers, and, not less sincerely, to a nation of victimized business men, many of whom are caught in the toils of vicious commercial practices not of their own making, practices wasteful of public and private wealth, and destructive alike of economic freedom, political justice, and business morals.

F. A. F.

Princeton, N. J.
April, 1931.

CONTENTS

PART IV

"NEW COMPETITION" AND OLD TRICKS

PART V

THAT ELUSIVE IDEAL—FREE MARKETS

PART VI

MARKETS—RESTRAINED AND LIBERATED

ILLUSTRATIONS

xi

THE MASQUERADE OF MONOPOLY

PROLOGUE

THE MASQUERADER

THE GENTLEMAN CROOK

A FAVORITE theme of romance is found in the adventures of the gentleman crook who reaps rich illicit rewards while eluding the officers of the law. Dressed in a clever disguise, he lives a life of thrilling danger but always escapes detection. The debonair Aristide even talks to the police who are on his trail, without their suspecting who he is. A special detective is engaged for the express purpose of running him to earth, but is so captivated by his engaging manners that he declares Aristide to be an estimable gentleman, an ornament to the community. A most narrow escape he had when, wearing his disguise, he was haled before an august court and the wise judges went so far as to agree that the evidence showed that Aristide may have violated the law some years before, but they could not bring themselves to believe that one of his attractive appearance could still be breaking the law. This incident served as a sort of vindication of good character, and Aristide went out to ply his profession more skillfully and easily than ever among the unsuspecting. Of course in the end the cruel Fates ought to overtake him and he ought to meet the punishment due to his misdeeds. But we dread to reach that sequel. Almost we have forgotten, as we follow the clever escapades of this lawless hero, that our sympathies belong on the side of law and order. We find it hard to sympathize with the slow-witted and blundering officials, and hard not to admire the ingenious way in which the hunted lawbreaker, apparently calm in the midst of every danger, puts their efforts to naught.

The astute reader has already discerned that this Story of the

Artful Aristide is merely allegorical. The very title of our book gave a clew to our meaning. The shifty gentleman criminal is Monopoly with its many shady practices in violation of the letter and spirit of the law; and the particular disguise that most successfully has concealed the identity of Monopoly is the basing-point practice. Unhappily for the cause of wise legislation and of good government, a plain impersonal account of business evils has not the fascinating interest of a detective story. When the public feels sure that it is suffering from some industrial ills such as monopolistic prices, it is ready to clamor for some kind of legislative remedy. But when the nature, extent, and even the existence of specific evils are in doubt, and when a clearer understanding of the subject would require patient and prolonged study, the public is likely to be merely bored. Besides, a description of impersonal economic forces and their action has not the romantic charm of personal adventure, although the results of such forces are incomparably more injurious to the general welfare than are the doings of any single supercriminal.

LEADING A CHARMED EXISTENCE

To citizens concerned with the solution of great public questions of an economic nature, no subject is of greater importance than is monopoly and its development in America since 1865. Discrimination was not unknown before, but the basing-point system of discriminations appears to have been as truly an invention of our own times as were the machine-gun, the aeroplane, and poison gas. The plain facts about it may seem at first incredible. For years it led a charmed existence, seeming to wear a magic cap of invisibility so that even those who were paying artificially enhanced prices usually did not know just what was being done to them. Local monopoly has seemed to be endowed with a strange hypnotic power that deluded the spectator. Buyers, like Titania on midsummer's night fondling the ass's head, have sworn upon the witness stand and before our high courts that they saw only economic beauty there. The buying public and the courts have looked upon the ugly face of monopoly and have seen in it only the friendly features of competitive price.

Even the masters of monopoly, or their very talented legal

advisers, have not always understood exactly the economic nature of the masquerader whose identity they were concealing. However, they have known full well that this practice of discrimination, which like a gift from the gods had been dropped into their laps, gave them a most effective power to restrain competition and to secure with their competitors agreements and common action that otherwise could not legally be secured. They knew it resulted in higher prices and larger profits, while deceiving the public and "getting by" in the courts.

THE INDUSTRIAL COMMISSION TRIES

Following the great business depression of the middle '90's, there began about 1897 a revival of business, and with this a rapid increase of the movement toward mergers, combinations, and agreements in restraint of trade, things which had begun to be noticed two decades earlier. Public opinion became much aroused on the subject, and discussion of "the trust problem" became more active than ever before. As a result of this, more than of anything else, Congress in June 1898 created an Industrial Commission to investigate and report upon the problems presented by labor, agriculture, and capital. This rather formidable body consisted of five Senators, five members of the House of Representatives, and nine other persons appointed by the President to "fairly represent the different industries and employments." It had the aid of numerous special experts and of a bevy of clerks, and before it finished its four-year task, expended several hundred thousand dollars and collected much interesting and irrelevant information on many topics.

Its first preliminary report (March 1, 1900), after two years of labor, was on the subject of *Trusts and Industrial Combinations*, a bulky volume of 1600 pages and of more than 1,000,000 words. It has something to say of the cruder form of predatory local price cutting, but from cover to cover not one word about the most subtle and dangerous practice of discrimination connected with delivered prices. Although the honorable commissioners and their staff of experts must have rubbed elbows many times with the mysterious masquerader, they had never penetrated his disguise. Almost two years later (December 1, 1901) another volume nearly as large appeared on the same subject (Vol. 13, of the Commission's Reports).

AFTER YOU, MY DEAR GASTON

Meantime great things had been happening in the field of industrial combinations. Under the very eyes of the Commission, and as if in contempt of its activities, the first billion-dollar corporation that the world had ever known was created as a holding company in February 1901. In the following May the Commission staged a dramatic event when Mr. Charles M. Schwab, the youthful president of this new giant in business, was introduced, was duly sworn, and took the witness stand. It was great newspaper copy, and the public eagerly read his testimony, to find that it was almost lacking in any facts not already known to the public. For the most part he was allowed, without embarrassing interruptions, to recite the prosy and familiar annals of the organization of the United States Steel Corporation. Most of the questions asked him were singularly considerate. An atmosphere of deference toward the genial young Colossus of the business world filled the room. This was a tribute to his frank and winning personality quite as much as to the staggering business power which he personified.

Many years later he said of himself: "Here I am, a not over-good business man, a second-rate engineer. I can make poor mechanical drawings, I play the piano after a fashion; in fact, I am one of those proverbial jacks-of-all-trades who are usually failures. Why I am not, I can't tell you." This is becomingly and sincerely modest, but those present on the day we are describing, though blind to the most significant incident in the whole day's events, could not but feel and acknowledge the very real qualities fitting him for business leadership. That day, by his disarming charm, he earned his salary for many years, when a less skillful handling of the situation might easily have altered the whole course of "trust-busting" history and have led within a short time to the dissolution of the greatest existing industrial combination.

The questions asked by the examiners served mainly to give

the witness occasion to express his personal belief that the formation of the combination had resulted in various ways only in good, and especially to the public. For a few critical moments, however, the spirits that preside over our economic destinies must have been thrilled with expectation as they listened to question and answer. The subject of prices being lightly touched upon, the witness thought that they were "largely regulated as a question of supply and demand," the magic phrase that banishes all doubts when monopoly is suspected.

THE PACK HITS THE TRAIL

The examination was nearing the end when, seemingly by accident, out of connection with anything that had gone before, the expert on transportation opened up a new line of inquiry and a long exchange of questions and answers ensued, of which the following brief verbatim sample may serve to show the character.

Q. (By Professor William Z. Ripley.) Are you familiar with the system of selling goods delivered by the constituent companies? A. Yes. It is simply the fixing of the price that you expect to receive for your goods at the central point plus tariff rates of freight.

Q. Are not the goods as sold and delivered all based on the rate from Pittsburgh? A. If Pittsburgh is the central point, yes. We have to sell at one central point at which deliveries can be collected, and I think Pittsburgh in most instances has been the central point.

Q. Would that be the system when you take in a number of factories or mills not located at Pittsburgh? A. Yes. I don't see any other plan of doing it; you must establish some central point.[1]

And the witness continued to recite a jumble of guesses and misunderstandings and misinformation, the nature of which is indicated in our further comments.

Here was the policy of local discrimination, more specifically that of basing-point delivered prices, stalking boldly through the room, but so disguised by the description that not an eye there saw it in its true character.[2] Never again was the subject referred to directly in the examination of this or of any other witness testi-

---

[1] *Report of the Industrial Commission*, Vol. 13, pp. 469-470.
[2] The frontispiece gives a (schematic) picture of the price system known as Pittsburgh-Plus, the curious qualities of which are to be carefully studied later.

fying before the Commission. This particular bit of evidence
appears in neither digest nor summary, and is strangely ignored in
all the conclusions and recommendations of the Commission and
in its 10,000,000-word report. While it was off on false trails,
a price policy that was to be for many years the most effective tool
of monopoly and was to cost the users of steel and of other basic
materials myriads of dollars, was made to appear to the eyes of
all present to be but an innocent agency of competitive business.

THE WINDINGS OF THE FOX

This extraordinary piece of testimony has valuable lessons for
the study of the trust problem in the first quarter of the twentieth
century. The witness declared that he was familiar with the
system of selling used by the constituent companies of his corporation, but it is charitable to believe that he was not. There
can be no doubt that he was describing the system of "delivered
prices" known as Pittsburgh-Plus. Even before the U.S. Steel
Corporation was formed, this system of discriminatory pricing
and charging for steel had already been used by its constituent
companies and by their competitors under agreements of now unquestioned illegality. It was to play an ever more important rôle
in the years to follow. But no one could get from the description
given by the witness a correct understanding either of what was
actually being done or of the real motives for doing it.

Look at the plausible expression, "the central point." The
central point of what? Of production or of shipment? The witness immediately gives the phrase the latter significance. "We
have to sell at one central point at which deliveries can be collected, and I think Pittsburgh in most instances has been the central
point." He could not "see any other plan." Here the central
point is a sort of jobbing or warehouse center, where various
grades and patterns of goods are actually, physically, brought
together from outside mills to make a single shipment (possibly
to save freight costs or trouble). Now it would be hazardous to
assert that this sort of thing had never been done in a single case,
but in studying thousands of pages of testimony collected in later
cases we have found no trace whatever of any such practice. If
it had occurred, it would have been lacking in the most essential

feature of basing-point prices, as then actually in practice, namely the charging of imaginary freight on goods not collected at a central point but shipped from some other point, the mills where they were produced.

WHERE IGNORANCE WAS BLISS

Was Mr. Schwab answering in ignorance of the real nature of the practice? Well, it is the duty of the sales department to attend to such minor matters. Perhaps it is the duty of the president of such a corporation not to know about them.

Other questions led the witness upon even more dangerous ground. His attention was called to complaints by customers that they were charged not the actual freight from the place of shipment, but more. Mr. Schwab replied, "If you will point out a method of avoiding that we will be very glad." Hence this book, to make glad the hearts of the monopolists. The witness appeared strangely ignorant of the usual practice in other lines of business (and a short time before in the steel industry) of selling at a uniform mill-base price. He felt this practice of making Pittsburgh the basing point for goods made in, and shipped from, mills not in Pittsburgh, to be a natural necessity in the steel business. But there was no such natural necessity before the various great combinations were formed, although the same thing had for some years been done intermittently by artificial agreement.

The witness evidently felt that he was on treacherous ground, so he proceeded warily. Replying to the question whether there was possibility of this policy developing still further by reason of the Steel Corporation's control of works in widely separated parts of the country, he hesitated and hedged, but opined "upon first thought that there is not much likelihood of any further extension in that direction." Perhaps he believed the plan to be already in operation in all the mills of his company. That seemed to be implied in his statement: "I do not see where it [any further extension] could occur at this moment."

He thought that most of the constituent companies published freight tariffs based on Pittsburgh like that of the National Tube Company, of which the examiner had a copy. But a moment later he hastened to deny this: "That has not been really the case," and he harked back to the idea that this one company (the National Tube) charged freight from Pittsburgh simply because "practically all goods sold by that company go from Pittsburgh, and it was perfectly fair, therefore, to say what the rates of freight would be from specific points." This implies that it would not be "perfectly fair" under other conditions. The witness left the final erroneous impression that (excepting the National Tube Company) the practice of "equalizing freights" was hardly in use at all. "Now, if you take the goods sold by two or more constituent companies, then no such list has been prepared," said he, and he quickly shifted the subject to rails.

THE ADVANTAGE OF LOCATION

Now rails, as every student of this remarkable price policy of Pittsburgh-Plus now knows, had been the one outstanding exception, the only great class of steel products, that had rarely if ever been sold in that way. It was a good attempt to cover the tracks of this policy; but the transportation expert who "knew his freight rate stuff" was hot on the trail, and in the end barely missed running the fox to cover. So back comes the question to the sale (at the Pittsburgh-Plus price) of steel shipped to Savannah from Birmingham, then a competitor. The witness admitted that competitors (as well as the U.S. Steel's mills) did this. Now the questioners were most eagerly seeking to discover some evidence that the big companies were trying to crush out the little companies. But the witness was able in this case to disclaim such a treatment of his competitors: "That was their advantage; they got a higher price; they reaped an advantage from their location . . . a natural thing for them to do." Again he declared "any manufacturing firm has the rights to all advantages of location."

This generous gesture of the Steel Corporation, like the flourish of a prestidigitator, served to distract attention from the other hand and what was up the sleeve, to wit, the fact that this same Pittsburgh-Plus price policy not only was tantamount to agreed prices followed by all the independents, but enabled every one of the numerous mills of the Corporation outside of Pittsburgh to get higher prices, and to "reap an advantage from their location"—an advantage greatly increasing in later years. This was not a *natural* advantage, as the witness asserted, but one created by the artificial system of pricing, built on the fiction that all goods, no matter where produced, were shipped from Pittsburgh.

The business which the witness thought entitled to the advantage of location was steel manufacturing, and the advantage consisted in exacting a higher net price and profit from buyers near mills than from those farther away. The advantage consisted in the power each mill not at the basing point has under the basing-point practice to "soak" the neighboring customer good and hard. But what about the advantage of location to the users of steel nearer to the place where steel is produced? Oughtn't they enjoy the "natural" advantage of their location? It used to be so, before the days of agreements, combinations, and Pittsburgh-Plus. If we can speak of what is natural, isn't it "natural" for oranges to be cheaper in California or in Florida than in Canada, and for wheat to be cheaper near the farm where harvested than in the distant city? Distance from the source of production and freight costs have seemed "naturally" to make a difference by increasing prices ever since commerce began, and nearness to reduce them. Fortunately for the witness such embarrassing questions were not raised then, or for many years later.

AN ERRORLESS FIELDING RECORD

In answer to the question whether "all parties producing for the market *agree* to deliver *as if* goods had been shipped from a single point," the witness made the oracular admission: "I think where such sales are made in that way that is substantially correct." As it was shown that sales were made in this way over a wide territory, the witness by implication admitted this was by agreement with competitors. But that was done in an unguarded moment, and it is hardly fair to chalk this up as an error to spoil a perfect fielding record for Mr. Schwab as a witness for his company on that day. Anyhow, the error let in no runs, and the opposing team made no tallies later.

The examination soon trailed off into harmless issues such as railroad building, control of ore supplies, etc., and never came back to local discrimination. The day ended with smiles and general good feeling, but if the American public which buys steel products had only understood what was happening, there would have been weeping and wailing in the land. Surely the young Mr. Schwab earned his salary that day; no one could have done it better.

ANOTHER DETECTIVE BUREAU

Several years had passed since that day of eminent testimony. One result, more or less directly the fruit of the Industrial Commission's work, had been the creation of the Bureau of Corporations in the Department of Commerce and Labor. This was in the vigorous days of Theodore Roosevelt's administration, proclaiming a new era in economic legislation and reform. A spirit of youthful optimism pervaded Washington. All things then seemed possible, for all things were untried. A member of the mythical tennis cabinet, high in the favor of the President, was a young lawyer from Cleveland. Taking office as Commissioner of Corporations in February 1903, with legal training, but innocent of any special knowledge of economics either theoretical or applied, he had, at the time of which we are now to speak, been nearly three years in office, energetically endeavoring, with the aid of a staff of nearly a hundred assistants and clerks, to perform the new task assigned to him. His chief duty as defined by the law was to investigate diligently the organization, conduct, and management of corporations engaged in interstate commerce. The purpose in collecting this information was not, as in the case of the Interstate Commerce Commission, to enforce the law, but rather to aid Congress in the making of new laws.[3]

A FRESH CLEW

In the closing days of 1905 economists from many universities were meeting in Baltimore, and a little group of them called by appointment upon the Commissioner of Corporations at his office in Washington. Their object was to learn how the work of the Bureau was progressing and to have an informal discussion. It was evident (and later confirmed by the published reports of the Bureau) that the Commissioner (as were his successors) was more interested in the legal aspects than in the more fundamental eco-

[3] See First Report, December 1904.

nomic aspects of the monopoly problem. One business practice, however, had particularly attracted his attention. It seemed to him to be new and interesting, and he asked his callers their opinion regarding it. He had found that some factories were accustomed to deliver their products to distant customers at a net price as low as that at which they sold to customers nearer to the mill, if not lower. What did the economists think of that? One of them ventured the opinion that this was discrimination against local buyers and was uneconomic, causing cross shipments and lost energy in mutual encroachment by producers upon each other's natural markets. From this the Commissioner dissented, showing that his question had been asked only in courtesy, as he already had made up his mind on the subject. He was inclined to think that it was only by thus cutting net prices or paying the freight that the benefits of competition could be extended to all parts of the country. He felt that when factories were large and widely scattered, this cutting of prices so that each would sell to the door of the other's mill was the only way that competition could be preserved. His view was the popular one, shared by Congress and later by a majority of the Supreme Court.[4]

BUT NO ARRESTS

Evidently, however, the Commissioner never felt confidence enough in his theory nor clear enough on his facts to publish them in his printed reports. Nor is it possible to be sure, from his brief mention of the practice, just what variety of local discriminatory prices had attracted his attention. It might have been one of several kinds or a mixture of them, according as sales were made from a single mill or from different mills and by different rules. We now know, however, that at that time and throughout that period these various forms of local discrimination were being practiced, and that they were, and continued to be, an important feature in monopolistic policy. The true nature and effects of these practices was never appreciated by the succession of legalistic Commissioners of Corporations, no one of whom referred to this question in the reports of the Bureau before it was merged into the Federal Trade Commission in 1914.

[4] See Ch. XXII.

The investigations of the Bureau into the economic aspects of corporations were mostly given to futile studies on costs of production, made without a clear conception of the economic meaning of "costs." After most of this work had been done, at an outlay of many hundred thousand dollars, the Commissioner holding office in 1912 claimed as a distinctive merit of the Bureau's work that it had shown (what competent economic theorists already knew) that book costs "are more or less meaningless," for various reasons.[5] Meantime the nearer, simpler, more hopeful task of regulating business practices to stop local discrimination was untouched by the Commissioners in their eleven years of service. When they were looking through their legalistic glasses directly at a discriminatory practice built on monopolistic power, they thought they were seeing true competition.

AN EVENTFUL CAREER

These are but glimpses of the elusive and deceptive practices of local discrimination before 1905. As our story proceeds, we shall see how the Supreme Court was misled in the greatest law suit ever involving an industrial enterprise; how a majority (though usually only a bare majority) of our highest court has been blind to this issue when important economic cases have come before it; how Congress has been confused in its attempts to frame new legislation to deal with the trust problem; how the Federal Trade Commission wavered and blundered, though at last it began to grope its way out; how the great patient public, long slumbering on this issue, began to waken, to comprehend, and to mutter discontent. All these things will be described in the following chapters in which will be traced the devious career of masquerading monopoly.

---

[5] *Report*, 1912, p. 8. It must be observed that if they had not been so, even if they could have been discovered, they could not have been of use in solving the problem of controlling industrial monopoly without direct price fixing, which, of course, was not possible under the law.

PART I

A GENTLE REPRIMAND TO OIL

CHAPTER I

OIL AND A PUZZLED COURT

AN EPOCH-MAKING CASE

IN MAY 1911 the Supreme Court of the United States handed down the most notable decision it had ever rendered on a case brought before it under the Sherman Anti-Trust Act of 1890. Confirming in all but certain "minor matters" the decision of the lower Federal Court, this decision decreed the dissolution of the then most notorious of the trusts, the Standard Oil Company of New Jersey.

This decision had been long awaited, both by defenders and by critics of this particular corporation, and by friends and enemies of the movement toward monopolistic organization. The attorneys for the Corporation had tragically warned the Supreme Court before its decision that "such a decree" (as that already rendered by the Court below) "if carried to its logical conclusion attacks the very foundations of the modern business world." [1] On the other hand the general public, with its fear of great combinations, was both dazed and elated at what at first view appeared to be the legal victory by unanimous decision on the major issue of dissolution. This decision was followed two weeks later by one dissolving the American Tobacco Company, supported by very much the same reasoning. The members of the Bar were much divided as to the significance of the two decisions, especially in respect to the so-called "rule of reason" there enunciated and christened for the first time.

The Standard Oil Company had, in the period of reckless busi-

---

[1] Brief on the law on part of appellants, by Messrs. Watson, Freeman, and Irwin, p. 127.

ness methods and "trust" formation between 1870 and 1901, incurred the greatest odium in popular opinion. A great sinner no doubt it had been, but in the public's thought it had become the scapegoat for the sins of all the other corporations grasping for monopolistic power and profits. The story of its great and noble deeds, as told by its promoters and by its lawyers, fills many volumes; the story of its misdeeds, as told by its competitors and victims, by prosecuting attorneys and by tribunes of the popular cause, is equally voluminous. In part these stories, amply documented with evidence taken from public hearings and court records, are real literature, warm with emotion and throbbing with moral fervor.[2]

THE ORIGINAL "TRUST"

It is not our purpose to relate this oft-told tale. Much of it has now merely an historical interest in the changed conditions which have developed since the notable decision of 1911—however much or little that decision contributed to bring about the changes. Indeed the Standard Oil Company or group of companies, in the last decade or more, has taken a very different position in respect to its business methods in its treatment of the public and its employees. In contrast with some business rivals in oil whose deeds became a public scandal especially after 1921, its titular spokesman has increasingly won the esteem of the once hostile public by standing for decency and right in business. For the purpose, however, of throwing light upon the subject of industrial price policies, we must recall the circumstances of the famous case.

The Standard Oil Company in some guise or other had been for forty years, since about 1870, almost continuously before the courts as well as before the bar of public opinion. After operating separately under various forms, forty different corporations had been in 1882, by a "trust" agreement, brought under a unified control. This fact doubtless was the main cause of the change that took place about that time in the meaning of the word "trust," making it both legally and popularly a synonym of the word "monopoly." [3] In 1892 this trust was declared by the Ohio

---

[2] Notably the works of Henry D. Lloyd, in *Wealth against Commonwealth,* 1894, and *Lords of Industry,* 1910; and by Ida Tarbell, in the *History of the Standard Oil Company,* 1904.

[3] Note the title of Anti-Trust Act, 1890.

Supreme Court to be void, and in 1897 proceedings were brought by the Attorney General of Ohio to show that the trust had not in fact been dissolved. Therefore in January 1899 the charter of the Standard Oil Company of New Jersey was amended so that it became a holding company for the stock of the companies formerly comprising the "trust."

THE LEGAL MILL BEGINS GRINDING

The Industrial Commission made the organization and methods of the Standard Oil Company one of the chief subjects of its inquiries between 1899 and 1901.[4] From 1903 to 1907 the newly created Bureau of Corporations carried on an extensive investigation of petroleum prices in all parts of the country. Before this was completed the Attorney General of the United States filed a bill of equity, November 15, 1906, in the Eastern Federal District of Missouri to enjoin the Standard Oil Company (together with about seventy subsidiary corporations and seven individuals who were the chief stockholders) from continuing the combination. November 20, 1909, the Circuit Court rendered a unanimous decision holding their combination to be "in restraint of trade" and "to have monopolized," and rendering a decree of dissolution against the seven individuals and thirty-eight of the corporate defendants. From this decision "the offending corporation" (words of the Supreme Court) appealed, and with a formidable array of legal talent carried the case before the Supreme Court. On the other side the case was prosecuted with greater vigor than ever had been shown by the Department of Justice in a trust case. An able trio assisted Attorney General Wickersham, consisting of Messrs. Frank B. Kellogg, C. B. Morrison, and Cordenio A. Severance, who greatly enhanced their reputations by their success in this case.

MOUNTAINS OF EVIDENCE

When the case at length reached the Supreme Court the record had grown to appalling magnitude. The Chief Justice described it as

inordinately voluminous, consisting of twenty-three volumes of printed matter, aggregating about twelve thousand pages, containing a vast

4 See especially Vol. 1 (1900) and Vol. 13 (1901) of its report.

amount of confusing and conflicting testimony relating to innumerable, complex and varied business transactions, extending over a period of nearly forty years.[5]

The Court despaired of studying for itself independently this mass of factual materials and legal briefs. It exclaimed:

Both as to the law and as to the facts the opposing contentions pressed in the argument are so numerous and in all their aspects are so irreconcilable that it is difficult to reduce them to some fundamental generalization, which by being disposed of would decide them all.[6]

And so, instead of following the usual practice of stating the facts as it sees them, the Court contented itself with paraphrasing the extreme contentions of either side and then wearily declaring:

to discover and state the truth concerning these contentions both arguments [of rival counsel] call for the analysis and weighing, as we have said at the outset, of a jungle of conflicting testimony covering a period of forty years, a duty difficult to rightly perform and, even if satisfactorily accomplished, almost impossible to state with any reasonable regard for brevity.[7]

Of any independent examination and analysis of the abundant evidence regarding the actual business methods and economic working of the enterprise before the Court (adjudged by it to be a monopoly), there is scarcely a trace here or elsewhere in the opinion.

The great mass of evidence, assembled at a direct cost of hundreds of thousands of dollars and at an indirect cost of many millions, was a storehouse of material never before equaled in any anti-trust suit. Here were presented in concrete form all of the crucial issues of the monopoly problem. It might have been said quite as truly of the Standard Oil case, as later it was said of another celebrated case (Pittsburgh-Plus), that the issues were fully 95 per cent economic, and not more than 5 per cent legal. But the Court did not use the opportunity to appraise the economic issues and clarify the whole business situation by indicating just which of these things were economically wrong, and just why. Aside from the noncommittal recital of conflicting statements of rival

---

[5] 221 U.S. 30-31 (1910).   [7] *Idem,* p. 48.
[6] *Idem,* p. 47.

counsel, there are in the main opinion [8] of 52 pages barely 2 pages that by liberal estimate relate to the economic issues. Even these few lines are so qualified, hesitating, and superficial, as to be useless for the guidance of future business practice.

IT WAS A CONSPIRACY

Hastily the Court, like an embarrassed speaker, changes the subject and shifts the discussion to more familiar ground, the legal aspects of the Act, in which alone it sees "the merits of the controversy." [9] The Court deliberately shuts its eyes as tight as possible to the economic (and consequent legal) nature of the specific acts of the defendant. So, after its opening cautious recital of the facts (not as it conceived of them, but as they were alleged by the two parties), the Court declares that it will give

no weight to the testimony adduced under the averments complained of except in so far as it tended to throw light upon the acts done after the passage of the Anti-Trust Act and the results of which it was charged were being participated in and enjoyed by the alleged combination at the time of the filing of the bill [1906]. [10]

Then after a learned discussion of the meaning of the Anti-Trust Act, [11] in the course of which discussion "the rule of reason" is more explicitly announced, the Court comes to the application of the statute to the case.

There it sees "no cause to doubt the correctness of these conclusions" of the lower Court to the effect

that the acts and dealings established by the proof operated to destroy the "potentiality of competition" which otherwise would have existed, and thus to make the transfer of stocks of January 1899 "a combination or conspiracy in restraint of trade" and "an attempt to monopolize." [12]

[8] Every one of the 24 pages of Justice Harlan's opinion, partly agreeing and partly dissenting, is concerned with the purely legal aspects. The opinion of the Circuit Court on the same case is little different in this respect, for of its 18 pages as printed, barely 19 lines (or less than 3 per cent) can be counted as a discussion of the economic issues.

[9] *Idem*, p. 47.

[10] *Idem*, p. 46.

[11] *Idem*, pp. 49-70.

[12] *Idem*, p. 74.

THE EVIL INTENT

As reasons for these conclusions the Court declares that the uniting of so many corporations,

aggregating so vast a capital gives rise, in and of itself, in the absence of countervailing circumstances, to say the least, to the *prima facie* presumption of intent and purpose to maintain the dominancy over the oil industry . . . the *prima facie* presumption of intent to restrain trade. to monopolize and to bring about monopolization . . . is made conclusive by considering [13]

the conduct and acts of the corporation both before and after the action of 1899.

If these acts are to be taken as "proof conclusive" it would seem that the Court had overcome its doubts both as to the results of the acts and as to the effectiveness in suppressing competition. But again the Court shrinks from committing itself on the nature (economic or legal) of the acts, in and of themselves, and while still disavowing "the purpose of weighing the substantial merit of the numerous charges of wrongdoing made during such period" it finds itself "irresistibly driven to the conclusion" that there was "an intent and purpose to exclude others . . . by acts" not in accord with the "usual methods" of business.[14]

The Court thus, by a tortuous line of reasoning, adopts substantially the prosecution's version of the facts. It decides that this particular company was guilty under both the first and second sections of the Act, not because the merger of 1899 was in and of itself illegal; not, either, because its acts after that date were in and of themselves clearly "in restraint of commerce" or gave proof of monopoly or attempt to monopolize; but only because in all the circumstances of the case, the Court (confessedly confused by the "conflicting testimony") felt that the combination of 1899 manifested an "intent and purpose" to restrain trade (unreasonably) and to accomplish a monopoly.

ESTABLISHED DOCTRINE OF INTENT

Thus the Court, though shrinking from an analysis and appraisal of the separate acts and dealings of the combination, at

[13] *Idem*, p. 75.   [14] *Idem*, p. 76.

length, "solely as an aid for discovering intent and purpose," gave them indirect significance, and pronounced them "wholly inconsistent" with the "usual methods" of business.[15] A legalistic habit of throwing every question of plain fact into a séance for mind-readers seems to have been bred of the practice of criminal law. No word resembling "intent" or "purpose" occurs in the Anti-Trust Act, though it is true that the idea is implicit in the words "attempt" and "conspiracy."[16] But each of these words is used in the statute in addition to other words indicating objective behavior, acts, and conditions,[17] and, surely, not to weaken or displace, but rather to make the statement of causes of illegality clearer and more inclusive. Now the general policy of the courts in determining the existence of monopoly under the Sherman Act seems to follow the same order as the statute: that is, the courts inquire into purpose only in a supplementary way—only when the restraining or monopolistic character of the acts considered singly is doubtful. Some leading cases are cited in the notes.[18]

Nothing could seem simpler than the doctrine in this line of decisions. Proof of intent is not an additional barbed-wire entangle-

[15] *Idem*, p. 76.

[16] Conspiracy is defined in various decisions as "an agreement . . . to do, by concerted action, something criminal or unlawful, or, it may be, to do something lawful by criminal or unlawful means." U.S. v. Debs, 64 Fed. 748 (1894). Conspiracy in restraint of trade is itself an offense under the Sherman law and no overt acts are necessary. 173 Fed. 825 (1909).

[17] Contract, combination in the form of trust or otherwise, monopolize, attempt to monopolize, combine, etc.

[18] A Circuit Court declared in 1903, "It has now been settled by repeated decisions of the Supreme Court that this question [restraint of trade] must be tried, not by the intent with which the combination was made . . . but by the necessary effect which it has in defeating the purpose of the law." (125 Fed. 457, 1903.) The Supreme Court said soon after the Oil case: "Of course, if the necessary result is materially to restrain trade between the States, the intent with which the thing was done is of no consequence." (U.S. v. Reading Co., 226 U.S. 370, 1912.) A Circuit Court said: "The defendants are presumed to know the law . . . and . . . to intend the consequences of their acts." (U.S. v. Patterson, 201 Fed. 715, 1912.) But here is the use of "intent": "Intent . . . would convert what on their face might be no more than ordinary acts of competition or the small dishonesties of trade into a conspiracy of wider scope . . ." (Justice Holmes in Nash v. U.S., 229 U.S. 378, 1913.) In another oft-cited opinion by Justice Holmes, he said to the same effect: "It is suggested that the several acts charged are lawful and that intent can make no difference. But they are bound together as the parts of a single plan. The plan may make the parts unlawful . . . Intent is almost essential . . . to such an attempt." U.S. v. Swift (Meat Packers' Trust Case), 196 U.S. 396, 1905. See further on intent, below, Ch. XXVIII.

ment provided for the defense; it is not an additional burden imposed upon the government to add to its difficulties in prosecutions under the Anti-Trust Act. Lack of proof of intent cannot be set up by the defense to qualify or mitigate the illegality of combinations, of monopoly *as a fact*, or of specific acts of restraint of commerce; but evidence by the prosecution of intent to monopolize may enable the prosecution to prove the existence of monopoly when without it the acts viewed singly would look quite innocent. Consideration of intent is a safeguard for the public, but it is an additional hazard for the defense.[19]

WERE THE ACTS INNOCENT PER SE?

If that is the true doctrine of the law, the great emphasis in the Oil case upon intent could but imply that neither the Company's formation nor its acts seemed to the Court to be clearly illegal. Indeed the most ostensible need of the "rule of reason" in the Oil and Tobacco cases, as announced by Chief Justice White, was that a literal construction rendered it impossible to apply the law to a multitude of acts which would come within its scope by resort to a "reasonable" construction.[20] If we are to attribute any influence in later decisions to the new "rule of reason," it is an influence in just the opposite direction, causing the Court to excuse behavior of unquestioned illegality, taken by itself, when the Court in its wisdom (or not perceiving the real economic results) thinks that the public welfare on the whole warrants it. So far as this is done the Court makes itself, not Congress, the lawmaking power. It was the implication of the innocence of the particular acts that made the decision in the Oil case in its economic aspects such a futile and fatal victory for the public, for notorious and scandalous as had been the price policies in the oil business, the Court had declined to condemn them "in and of" themselves, and thus had greatly increased the difficulties of enforcing the Act in the future.

In truth the determination of the real nature, and effect upon

---

[19] Though no proof of intent is necessary to establish a monopoly in fact, there can be no finding of an *attempt* to monopolize without proof of intent. U.S. v. Quaker Oats, 232 Fed. 500 (1916). Here intent is connected with the attempt, not with the actual monopolizing. The conspiracy itself and the unlawful combination are distinct offenses. U.S. v. Cassidy, 67 Fed. 698 (1895).

[20] 221 U.S. 178 (1911).

prices, markets, and competition, of these acts and dealings, is essentially an economic task, for the performance of which the Court had no adequate training, and in which it had no competent economic advice. It may be well, therefore, to consider now some of the allegations and evidences of more glaring practices, especially those of unfair competition and of local price cutting, whose real economic nature must be clearly understood before there can be any hope of solving the problem of monopoly.

—————

CHAPTER II

ALL'S FAIR IN LOVE AND THE OIL BUSINESS

SUCCESSIVE LINES OF DEFENSE

NUMEROUS allegations were made by the prosecution in the Oil case regarding various acts grouped under the term "unfair competition." The defense at various stages in the briefs took various positions regarding it: (1) that monopoly itself is not illegal; (2) that it is only certain definite acts of exclusion that constitute monopoly, and these must be explicitly defined by the law and the courts; (3) that there is no such thing as unfair competition; (4) that the particular form and method of unfair competition, the local price cutting alleged, rarely occurs, yet (5) that on the other hand it is quite the usual and normal form of competition.

The defense at one point maintained that no matter what the "size, domination, and control of the market or prices," in other words, no matter how complete *in fact* the monopoly, this situation does not constitute a "monopoly in the legal sense," in the absence of specifically prohibited "means and agencies of exclusion." [1] Here, as repeatedly, the defense tried to show that a monopoly is not a monopoly. Both courts in their decisions are silent as to this particular argument, but the Supreme Court implies a rejection of it. Notably the Supreme Court repeatedly shows that it is trying to look through the form to the substance, "the baneful result," "the evils," which monopoly produces, whatever be the means employed, to see the "evil consequences which might arise from the acts of individuals producing or tending to produce the

[1] Brief in the Circuit Court, Johnson and Milburn, pp. 170, 174.

26

consequences of monopoly."[2] Yet finally it rather vaguely assumes, too, that the means and agencies of exclusion were of a nature prohibited and illegal.

ARE THESE ACTS ILLEGAL?

The defense protested that to make monopolizing a criminal offense without any standard for judging the means by which the exclusion of others is effected, which is essential to monopolizing, would be an "intolerable situation." This protest, uttered before the case was decided, surely had much justification.[3] It was the function of the Courts to provide such a standard, but the decision left these matters in as great a haze as before.

Counsel for the Company, however, at this point executed an about-face and sought to throw doubt upon the whole idea of unfair competition, and attempted to muddy all the waters of discussion by denying the possibility that any one (or any court) could draw a line between business acts in respect either to their ethical or their legal quality of fairness or unfairness of competition.

Nowhere is to be found a better statement of the record of misdeeds which, taken as a whole, without analysis, was virtually accepted by the Court as true, than that contained in the painstaking brief of the prosecution. A few extracts from the vast collection of evidence in the record may serve to indicate its salient features:

The testimony in this case shows that the various defendants have pursued a system of unfair competition against their competitors, whereby the independent companies selling and marketing petroleum have either been driven out of business or their business so restricted that the Standard Oil Company has practically controlled the prices and monopolized the commerce in the products of petroleum in the United States. This system has taken the form of price cutting in particular localities while keeping up high prices, or raising them still higher, in other localities where no competition exists; of paying rebates to customers as a part of said system of price cutting; of obtaining secret information as to competitive business largely through bribing railway

---

[2] 221 U.S. 56-57 (1911).
[3] Brief, Johnson *et al.*, p. 170. Note, however, that exclusion is not the valid test of monopoly; see below, Ch. XXIII.

employees, and using said secret information to procure the countermanding of orders of said independents, and to facilitate the price-
cutting policy; of the use of so-called bogus independent companies—
that is, companies held out by the Standard Oil Company as independent which are engaged in price cutting, while the Standard Oil Company maintains the prices through its well-known companies—and other
abusive competitive methods against the independents.[4]

SPIES AND BRIBES

We desire here to describe briefly the various devices to which the
Standard has resorted in the pursuit of its methods of unfair competition. The Standard Oil Company keeps a secret department in New
York, known as the statistical department. Through this department it
has a complete system of espionage upon its competitors all over the
United States. It was with great difficulty that the Government succeeded in finally uncovering this system. Many of the leading men connected with the Standard Oil Company were placed on the stand and
denied knowing anything about the department until they were confronted with certain reports and statements which had come into the
Government's hands. It appears by this testimony that the Standard Oil
Company has a system of reports whereby every salesman and local
agent procures information as to shipments of oil by independents into
his district. These are procured by bribing railway employees to report
competitors' shipments; by keeping men around railway stations to learn
the shipping directions on barrels or cars; by following the tank wagons and salesmen of independents; by employing detectives to procure
the information from the independents' employees, and by various other
equally disreputable means. These reports are sent in immediately to
the head office of the Standard's marketing division. From such reports
the local salesmen and agents throughout the country are informed of
the shipments made into their territory. This information is also reported to the head sales agents of the several Standard marketing companies at their New York headquarters and is preserved in the statistical department at 26 Broadway, to which we have referred. The greatest secrecy is maintained in regard to this entire system. For instance,
railroad employees who furnish a large part of this information do not
sign their names to the reports which they furnish or use stationery
either of the Standard Oil Company or of the railroad company.

On the basis of this information regarding competitive shipments the
Standard Oil Company at this central statistical department keeps com-

[4] Brief for the U.S. (1909), Vol. 1, pp. 187-188. This testimony is fully summarized in Vol. 2 of the brief, pp. 427-641.

plete records showing the percentage of the business done by independent concerns in each of its large territories and in each of its smaller subdivisions and in individual cities. The Government put in evidence from the records of the statistical department at New York such tables showing the percentage of independent business throughout the country, and also put in evidence numerous reports obtained from railroad employees and summarized reports of individual competitive shipments. This information is obviously of the greatest advantage to the Standard in determining where and how far it will cut prices in order to destroy competition. Moreover, it appears that the information of competitive shipments is often used in advance of the arrival of the shipments to secure the countermanding of orders and to facilitate other methods of unfair competition.[5]

MACHIAVELLIAN BUSINESS MORALS

The counsel for defendants, having throughout the hearings and in their briefs sought first to deny absolutely the reality of these acts, next, to raise doubts regarding their frequent occurrence, and third, to minimize their importance when they have occurred, at length, in the face of the overwhelming evidence, virtually admitted the truth of the allegations and in the retreating battle fell back upon a fourth and final line of defense, a bold-faced justification of any and all methods that could be employed in competition, in fact a denial of the possibility of any such quality as "unfairness" in business. This shameless doctrine is expressed in part as follows:

The conduct of a trade consists of a multitude of acts varying in their ethical quality. Competition is a state of war. One man may push it to the extreme limits, whilst another may draw the boundary line clear inside of them. Price cutting and rebating, collecting information of the trade of competitors, the operation of companies under other names to obviate prejudice or secure an advantage, or for whatever reason, are all methods of competition. Who knows where the line is that separates "fairness" in these methods from "unfairness"? What legal standard determines what is "fair" and what is "unfair"? . . . What legal rules or standards has a man to guide him in determining when his methods cross an imaginary line between fair and unfair, so that his success thereby becomes a criminal offense? Those who stand upon an

[5] Brief for the U.S., Vol. i, pp. 189-191.

Act which encourages competition cannot complain of the extermination which competition involves.[6]

The law libraries may be searched in vain for expressions more Machiavellian than these. The champions of monopoly incautiously betray their contempt for the Anti-Trust Act itself as aiming to "encourage" competition, and flout any attempt to preserve by any means a wholesome conception of business practices.

LAWYERS DEFY MORALITY

In the briefs of the same leaders of the American Bar before the Supreme Court this argument is quite as brutal:

Price cutting and rebating, collecting information of the trade of competitors, the operation of companies under other names to obviate prejudice or secure an advantage or for whatever reason, are all legal methods of competition whatever moral criticism they may justify. There is no rule of fairness or reasonableness which regulates competition.[7]

By other defendants' counsel this argument is somewhat softened or muddled:

Competition knows no limit except that the means used must be lawful . . . How could the law measure and define what was fair, what reasonable, and what undue? . . . He may use any means which does not infringe upon the legal rights of his fellow citizens . . . But aside from this limitation, the choice of weapons and of means, is his own; the war is on, and each competitor may use all means which his wealth, his connections, his study, his superior skill or knowledge may give him.[8]

The change of phrasing somewhat cloaks the cynicism of the contention, but the use of the word "legal" evades or begs the question whether certain acts, alleged and proved by the evidence, were unlawful. The question is: are the acts not unlawful because unfair? [9]

[6] 173 Fed. Rep. 177; brief of the law for defendant in Circuit Court, Johnson and Milburn, pp. 170-171.

[7] Brief of Johnson *et al.*, Vol. 1, p. 90.

[8] Brief, Watson *et al.*, pp. 190-191.

[9] The three sets of briefs for the defendants in the Supreme Court, while developing most elaborate legalistic arguments regarding the final acts of combination, have less to say on the specific charges of alleged unfair methods and practices than had the briefs in the Circuit Court; in the appeal most of the

SOPHISTICAL EPIGRAMS

At this point any true economist must voice his protest against the proposition that "competition is a state of war," certainly not the competition contemplated and to be permitted in our system of private industry. This proposition belongs in the class with those sophistical epigrams invented as tools for use in social propaganda, such as Proudhon's dictum that "Property is theft." These catch-phrases to deceive the unwary confuse under one designation things that are extreme opposites. War between nations means the negation of all ordinary processes of trade between them. It means an end for the time of commercial competition and of commercial dealings between the citizens of the warring states. It means the suspension of all the normal peacetime rules of commerce, contractual relations, moral codes, and legal safeguards in business, so painfully built up through centuries of experience in the peaceful arts of commerce. It means, in the relation of the armed forces of the two warring states, abandonment of the normal practices of humanity and a reversion to primitive acts of physical violence and destruction to accomplish the overthrow of the nation's enemies.

Competition in trade and commerce, on the other hand, is, in every essential feature which could have any significance in discussions of monopoly and of restraint of trade, at the opposite pole of human conduct from war. It is peacetime rivalry of fellow citizens or between citizens of two nations at peace. Civilized nations at peace mutually extend to alien traders the humane protection of the civil and criminal law.

RULES OF THE GAME

In the true ideal, trade is to be likened rather to a friendly game than to deadly war. The game is, or in accord with sound public policy should be, carried on within the limits sanctioned by the rules of the game, of old by "the law of merchants," and today by the best prevailing business practice, as this has been modified, corrected, and strengthened by statute and by judicial interpretation. These rules are designed to make the game of

testimony as to "unfair" competition is passed over in silence. This evidences greater tact, if not better morals, in treating a rotten case.

business competition subserve the one great aim of increasing the common welfare. From time to time they must be revised to meet new conditions. Competition, to be sure, may be likened to war in one respect, but in one respect only: it is rivalry. But within the rules of the game it is not a rivalry that destroys the physical wealth of the rivals, does physical violence to them, or transgresses the normal rules of morals and the civil law. Its social ideal in domestic trade is rivalry of peaceful, and even friendly, fellow citizens in productive service for the general good. The buying public, if free to choose between rival producers, in the conditions of a real market, awards thus the prize for quality of goods, service, or prices by the democratic method of popular election, each dollar of purchasing power giving one vote.

It is also a false idea of true competition in trade that it necessarily or usually leads to the business destruction of competitors. This notion, repeatedly suggested in the confused pleadings [10] of lawyers, has appeared also in the confused opinions of the courts. In a market where goods at hand are offered for sale at the same time, the normal result of sellers' competition is a uniform price at which all of the goods are sold. This price, being lower than one where competition between sellers is inactive or absent, is to the advantage of the buyers, and, to be sure, may either at the time or eventually exclude from the market other would-be sellers who are more distant or less efficient. By this very process of selection under *fair* competition, the more efficient have a chance to succeed, and less successful competitors are led to confine themselves in the long run to other territory where they show that they can excel, or to other lines of effort and enterprise for which their talents and resources fit them better.

COMPETITION AND SOCIAL SERVICE

There may be much tragic mischance in fair competition, and many personal disappointments through mistaken judgments, but its ideal throughout is that of a process in harmony with social justice, not one shot through with heartless enmity. The more vital operation of competition is to be thought of rather in terms

[10] E.g., brief for the defendants, on the law, in the Circuit Court, Watson *et al.,* pp. 65 ff., giving numerous citations on competition.

of service to society than in the injury of competitors. Its normal
effect is positive not negative, creative not destructive. It is testing,
classifying, and rewarding economic agents for the things they
can do, and are doing best. There is a great and essential truth in
the thought of "the economic harmonies" (however much it may
have been at times exaggerated) which is at the very heart's core
of the public policy favoring competition and of the laws maintaining it. That truth is twisted into an ugly error when the
apologists for monopoly darken the counsels of the courts with
confusion of commerce with war.

The careless legal dictum that every act of competition is an
attempt to monopolize and every successful act of competition
results (in so far) in monopoly, is closely related to this confusion
regarding fair competition. It, too, appeared in the arguments of
counsel for the Oil trust, and has been joyfully cited by every
apologist for monopoly ever since. Its fuller discussion may better
be undertaken later in connection with the theoretical analysis of
the competition concept.[11]

SHIRKING ITS JOB

The Supreme Court failed to pass either a scientific or a clear
legal judgment upon perhaps the most shocking business practices ever brought with abundant evidence to its attention. It failed
to clarify the distinction between fair and unfair methods of competition which would have set forward by a generation the belated
treatment and solution of the "trust" problem. Thus this notable
case ended May 15, 1911, with a decision spelling wasted opportunity. The Court, lacking clear convictions on the essentially
economic issues involved, side-stepped its responsibilities. It
thereby contributed to the enactment, three years later, of the
Federal Trade Commission Act with its fifth section declaring
unlawful "unfair methods of competition in commerce," an act
passed in an attempt by an aroused public to put an end to an intolerable situation. The Supreme Court has been thought at times
to display a somewhat jealous spirit toward this rival created by
the new legislation of the early days of the Wilson administration;

[11] See below, Ch. XXIII.

but viewed with the philosophic eye, it is seen to be the Court's own child, born of its neglect.

Who, be he jurist or layman, can doubt that through the Anti-Trust Act of 1890 (if not by the common law) the Federal Courts were endowed with well-nigh plenary power not only to pronounce upon and specify these particular acts as "contracts" or "conspiracies" in restraint of trade; not only (by sections 1 and 2) to punish them by fine and imprisonment; but also (by the fourth and succeeding sections) to prevent, restrain, enjoin, and prohibit each and every one of them? In the most richly documented case relating to industrial monopoly that had come before the Supreme Court, the Court did none of these things, but instead gave to an anxious public a nearly futile decree of dissolution.

CHAPTER III

LOCAL PRICE CUTTING—SAINT OR SINNER?

AN UNANSWERED QUESTION

THE "unfair methods of competition" denounced by the prosecution were of widely various kinds and characters. Though the defense in turn denied all these acts, evaded responsibility for them, and sought to justify them, most of them have since been outlawed by public opinion and by Federal legislation. Such are discriminatory railroad rates and rebates, the use of pipe lines not as common carriers, espionage, bogus companies, etc. We may dismiss this part of the subject as *res adjudicata.* But as regards "local price cutting," the verdict is even yet not so clear. Indeed the term "local price cutting" was then and often still is used so ambiguously as to make impossible a clear conception of its real legal and economic character. The decision in the Oil case as regards this matter doubtless had great influence in determining the main features of the Clayton Act (of 1914) in respect to discrimination, and in other ways also helped to continue and even to increase the confusion surrounding public policy in respect to the regulation of industrial prices. The purpose of our work being to clear away this confusion, no better object lesson can be found than the Standard Oil case, in which most concretely are presented the salient features of this practice.

COMPETITION AND PRICES

The main facts as summarized in the Government's brief were these:

This same statistical department at New York keeps records showing the prices at which the Standard sells oil at each town throughout the United States, together with the margin of profit of the marketing company on such oil. Summaries of these records were introduced by the Government. They show in a most startling manner the practice of local price cutting and price discrimination, the widest possible differences appearing in the prices and profits per gallon at different towns even in the same general vicinity, to say nothing of still greater differences between different parts of the country. These statistics corroborate the testimony of numerous witnesses for the Government regarding local price cutting.

The statistics show that in many places where there is a large percentage of independent business and sharp competition, the Standard Oil companies sell oil at a loss, and in most places where there is any considerable competition at low prices with a small margin of profit, whereas throughout the larger percentage of the territory where competition is substantially or entirely eliminated the Standard companies sell at very high prices with a large margin of profit. The tables contain the prices and the profit per gallon in all the leading main stations throughout the United States and many of the substations, and the averages for the several marketing districts.[1]

Again, to illustrate the extreme differences in the prices in individual cities, it appears that during 1904 in Los Angeles the price of oil was 7.5 cents per gallon, while there was a large amount of competition, 33.4 per cent. At the same time in Seattle, where there was no competition, the price was 15.5 cents, and in Portland, where there was also no competition, 15 cents. The Standard Oil Company lost 3.41 cents per gallon in Los Angeles, while it made a profit of 5.30 cents in Seattle and of 3.87 cents in Portland. Similar conditions exist in various other parts of the United States.[2]

MAN OF A THOUSAND FACES

Through these (bogus independent) companies and also through its openly controlled companies the Standard pursued a system of cutting prices in places where the independents were doing business, in many cases below the cost and to a point which caused loss to competitors. The oral testimony of representatives of independent concerns on this subject of price cutting confirms the evidence from the tables of prices obtained from the records of the Standard and shows clearly the motives for the wide differences in prices at different places. A large amount of testimony was offered by the defendants to show that the independents usu-

[1] Brief for the U.S., Vol. 1, pp. 191-192.
[2] *Idem*, Vol. 1, p. 193. Further illustrations of such price discrimination with the statistics are presented in Vol. 2 of the brief, especially pp. 428-500.

ally cut prices first. This testimony is in many cases contradicted by the Government's witnesses and in other cases the apparent cuts by independent concerns were explained clearly. It is shown that while in many cases the Standard's well-known companies nominally maintained prices the secret companies were cutting prices, and also that the Standard companies often departed from their public prices by means of secret rebates, and prices openly made by independent concerns to meet these secret prices were what the defendants' witnesses called cut prices. In other cases where oil was selling at very high prices and there was no competition the independents would establish a price the same as the Standard had in other surrounding towns, whereupon the Standard would continue to lower prices until there was no profit in the business.[3]

CHAOTIC PRICES RESULT FROM MONOPOLY

The evidence and exhibits in this case show plainly that there is no uniform price of refined oil and naphtha in the United States. . . . As already stated, even after making allowances for the difference in cost of transportation and cost of marketing, the prices in those areas and towns where the Standard has little or no competition are generally much higher than in places where it has a large degree of competition. This appears clearly by the fact that the profit per gallon of the marketing companies is far higher in noncompetitive than in competitive territories and places. This means obviously that the Standard Oil Company arbitrarily fixes the price of oil in all places where it has little or no competition without regard to any competitive market value. Even in places where there is a considerable degree of competition the evidence of independent oil dealers and manufacturers indicates that the price is in nearly all cases fixed by the Standard and that the competitors merely follow that price and seldom if ever go below it, for the reason that to do so simply invites further cuts by the Standard, until there is no profit in the business.[4]

While therefore it is true that in certain sections of the country and certain towns there is a sufficient degree of competition to lead the Standard to sell oil at what properly may be called a competitive price, it is still the fact that the Standard determines the prices throughout the country. At times, indeed, the Standard sells oil at less than the normal competitive price, and even at less than cost. In so doing, however, it is just as truly fixing the price arbitrarily as where it charges an exorbi-

[3] *Idem*, Vol. 1, pp. 194-195. Various other means used by the Standard were then described.

[4] *Idem*, Vol. 2, pp. 64-65.

tant profit, for it employs such extreme price cutting as a means of destroying the business of independent concerns in order that, having driven them out, it may subsequently charge monopoly prices.[5]

Such local price cutting in various lines of business was already an old story in the public's ears. In the period of the '70's and '80's fairly evenly matched enterprises had struggled to attain dominance by crippling or crushing their rivals. It was a real rough-and-tumble fight, no ring rules, nothing barred—hitting below the belt, eye-gouging, kicking and knifing until the weaker adversary was left dead or helpless on the field. Out of such mêlées a few larger concerns emerged a bit battered but with a greater dominance over some portion of the territory in some lines of trade. After that, aided by discriminatory freight rates and the advantage of greater size and financial power, the maintenance, in a large degree, of their control of the situation was not difficult. In these practices (popularly assumed to be "competitive") the Standard Oil Company had been the outstanding example and had achieved the most marked success.

PRACTICE OF LOCAL DELIVERIES

But was this because other groups of men in other lines of business were by nature more moral or less willing and desirous of attaining dominance each in its own line? Surely that is too simple a view of the subject. Quite incidentally the true answer was nearly hit upon by Government counsel. They do not see any broad significance in the facts, but they do see that the system of local delivery by tank wagons which early, as a matter of convenience, became a practical necessity, gave "the Standard Oil Company an opportunity to attack the district" as would not have been possible if oil had been sold at uniform f.o.b. prices at central markets. Here is the fuller statement of this situation:

The Standard Oil Company is particularly able to carry on this predatory competition for the reason that it does not sell its product at central markets or through ordinary channels like most other large manufacturers. It markets its product to the retailer in every village and community in the United States and often directly to consumers.

[5] *Idem,* Vol. 2, p. 65.

It does from 85 to 90 per cent of the business in the United States, leaving about 10 or 15 per cent to all its competitors. It is perfectly obvious, therefore, that if all the balance of the trade in the United States were in one concern it could not afford to have marketing stations and facilities in every part of the United States. In order to market in effective competition with the Standard Oil Company the independents must of course ship by tank cars, which is much cheaper than shipping by barrel, especially in less than carload lots, and they must also have stations for unloading where tanks are available, and tank wagons to meet the trade in competition with the Standard. It would be obviously impossible for such a concern to afford to spread its product over the whole United States. Even if all the balance of trade were in the hands of one concern it would have to confine itself to particular districts where it could have adequate facilities equal to the Standard's, and therefore since the 10 or 15 per cent is in the hands of a large number of independents these independents must all the more confine themselves to small districts. This gives the Standard an opportunity to attack the particular district, as it does, and either to keep the independent concern down to a minimum of business or to destroy it entirely. It has undoubtedly been the policy of the Standard Oil Company to permit the independents to do a small percentage of the business, and this percentage has run from 10 to 15 per cent for many years. By thus keeping the independents within reasonable bounds it may control the prices, permit them to make a moderate profit and not allow their competition to get beyond control, and in most parts of the country make enormous profits itself. There is no question that if this court holds the Standard combination to be a legal organization and not guilty of monopoly—in other words, gives it carte blanche to pursue its own methods—it can eliminate every competitor within two years.[6]

The system of local deliveries is again referred to in these words:

Oil is not sold to the trade in appreciable quantities at central markets from which the purchaser pays the transportation charge to destination. Instead, through the marketing system of the Standard Oil Company, which has already been described, the oil is transported by the Standard itself, through one or another of its marketing concerns, to the towns throughout the entire United States, and is there, for the most part, delivered directly to retail dealers. The result is that the price of oil may be, and actually is, widely different in different towns.[7]

---

[6] *Idem*, Vol. 1, pp. 188-189. [7] *Idem*, Vol. 2, p. 64.

RESULTS OF DELIVERED PRICES

One must have in mind the condition of true markets (described more fully in Chapters XVIII-XX) to appreciate the radical nature of the change that local deliveries by distant large producers to isolated small buyers had quickly wrought in the very nature of the trading process. The local buyers no longer had access to a market where competition among sellers, in accordance with the principle of indifference, resulted in a uniform price to all buyers. The seller no longer sold to all buyers at one place, leaving it to each buyer to transport the goods, or to have them transported, to their destination. The seller sold two commodities at once, the physical goods which he produced, and their transportation to destination. The transportation, also, the Standard partly produced by the use of its own pipe lines and tank wagons, but mainly bought from the common carriers. (The unlawful rebates it obtained are a different story.) Now, if, in fact, the goods continued to be sold at a uniform base price, and the seller then delivered them, charging the regular freight rate, the change would have been a mere matter of words and of putting two items on one bill. It is this which discriminators by means of delivered prices always first explain that they are doing—merely, in the kindness of their hearts, saving their customers the trouble of looking up the freight rate. But the real trouble is that this practice of quoting and selling at delivered prices enables the seller to evade quoting a *general* price open to all at a definite base or origin of shipment. This destroys even the semblance of a market and gives rise to local price cutting.

QUIBBLING ON TERMS

The prosecution declared:

The practice of unfair competition by means of local price cutting is alleged in the petition and is denied by the answer.[8]

Counsel for the Oil company objected to every bit of testimony about local price cutting as "incompetent" (usually as based on hearsay). Nevertheless the record contains a great mass of evi-

[8] *Idem,* Vol. 2, p. 428.

dence on this subject and tables of figures which, even in summarized form, cover 160 pages.[9] Defendant's counsel professed
that by analysis they showed that "all towns specified by the Government's witnesses where instances of local price cutting are
claimed to have occurred number 37," seemingly insignificant when
the company sold oil by tank wagons in more than 37,000 towns
in the U.S.[10] In this conflict, not so much of the evidence as of its
significance, there is heard a veritable Babel of tongues as to the
meaning of local price cutting. The prosecution treated as evidence
of local price cutting (and quite rightly, from the economic standpoint) the hundreds of varying "margins" of profits per gallon
(net, after making allowance for freight and marketing costs)
which had been shown by the investigation of the Bureau of Corporations to have occurred in thousands of cases, varying by localities somewhat inversely with the percentage of competition. The
defendants in reply entered upon some ingenious distinctions between local price reductions that still yield a profit, and those that
are unprofitable (three varieties of the latter being recognized).
At some points in the briefs they justify local price cutting only
when it is profitable, and by implication confess its unfairness when
it is unprofitable. Such a passage is the following:

It is obvious, however, that local reductions in price which leave the
market on a profitable basis, . . . can only be construed, in the absence of other evidence to the contrary . . . [as] nothing more than
competition within the limits of that freedom to trade . . . open to
the defendants equally with all other persons.[11]

In their briefs in the Supreme Court they still pretended at times
to understand the charge of price cutting as an unfair method of
competition to mean:

Cutting the price in that community below cost with the purpose and
effect of driving out such independent and destroying his business.[12]

It would usually be impossible to prove what was the cost of
production of the seller. "Cost" is a very evasive notion and it can

[9] *Idem,* pp. 427-588.
[10] Brief, Johnson *et al.,* Vol. 2, p. 175.
[11] Rosenthal brief in Circuit Court, p. 627.
[12] Johnson brief in Supreme Court, p. 173.

be even approximated only by those having access to all the documents of the business.

PUTTING ON A BOLD FACE

But evidently fearing that this defense could not be maintained in the face of the abundant evidence of slashing cuts in local prices, the Oil company generally sought to justify without qualification both profitable and unprofitable local price cuts, declaring both to be normal methods of competition. So, beginning with the denial of the practice and opposing the introduction of any evidence of it, the defense ends by not only admitting it, but by justifying it most broadly as a normal and desirable method of competition. They said:

In fixing different prices for sales of the same commodities in different localities or to different persons a trader is using one of the important instruments of competition, and the freedom to do this for the purpose of holding or increasing his trade is one of the equal rights which all traders enjoy and which this statute cannot have been intended to impair.[13]

Specifically of unprofitable local price cutting, they said:

Nor can it be doubted that [local] reductions in prices . . . [on an unprofitable basis, . . . made to meet prices initiated by the competitor in that locality] are similarly legitimate. There is nothing illegal in selling at an unremunerative price, nor is such a practice in conflict with the rights of others to be free to trade,[14]

And it is declared that if such local discrimination is taken as indicative of a purpose

to monopolize trade, then competition in any locality under such circumstances must cease and all trade be handed over to the latest comer who is willing to take it at an unremunerative price.[15]

BUT ''HE BEGAN IT''

While thus in the broadest terms justifying all forms of price cutting, defendants sought to show that in most cases where prices were reduced to an unprofitable level it was the independents (not

---

[13] Rosenthal, *op. cit.*, pp. 625-6.   [15] *Idem*, p. 628.
[14] *Idem*, p. 627.

they) who began the cutting (a quite innocent act, as they had just claimed, but if any one was guilty, it was the other fellow).

In every case it appeared that the decline in the Standard's prices was forced by the price cutting of the competitor.[16]

In doing this the defending lawyers gave another twist to the notion of (local) price cutting by making it mean prices below those *previously* existing in a locality—not prices below those charged by the same seller contemporaneously in other localities. By this confusion of time differences (fluctuations), with place differences, they were able plausibly to accuse their competitors of being local price cutters when the latter were simply charging uniform base prices at certain bases or sources of supply.[17]

A PROSECUTION CONFUSED AND HESITANT

Throughout the conduct of the case the prosecution seemed weakly to imply that local price cutting (the real discriminatory sort) might be all right under ordinary conditions (as between competitors of fairly equal strength or even by a very strong competitor if the result was not to create a monopoly, even though it drove the weaker competitor out of business). The prosecution in hesitating expressions explained to the Court its attitude toward local price cutting, revealing its lack of firm grasp of any underlying theory:

We do not wish to be understood as discouraging enterprise or as taking a position against legitimate competition, but if the Sherman Act means anything in this country it means a monopoly acquired by such methods of competition as this. Unless it is enforced, the small corporation or individual who wishes to engage in business will have absolutely no opportunity at all. This testimony is valuable as showing the intention of the Standard Oil Company to monopolize the commerce in oil throughout the United States. In many districts it has an absolute monopoly. We mean by absolute monopoly that in those districts it does all of the business and has eliminated every competitor. Practically this is the case throughout the Rocky Mountain country and most of the Pacific Coast States. The percentage of independent busi-

[16] Johnson brief, in Supreme Court, p. 179.
[17] E.g., Rosenthal brief, p. 628, and generally pp. 609-623. Further details are given in the Appendix to Ch. III.

ness throughout the entire Southern States is very small. Moreover, where there is competition the competitors are usually strictly under the control of the Standard, in that they must, in order to be allowed to do business, sell oil at practically the price the Standard dictates and confine themselves to a small percentage of the trade.[18]

BEFOGGED BY INTENT

There is therefore evinced in the argument of the Government no thought of condemning local price cutting (or any other of the market and price practices of the defendant) *per se*. The prosecution was maintaining only that local price cutting was unfair under all the proved circumstances of the case, that is, when done with intent to achieve and with the result of actually achieving a complete (or almost complete) monopoly of the business in that territory. Thus it was the prosecution that first advanced the theory of "intent" and "purpose" which unfortunately was adopted by the Court in its decision. It and the Court chose to place the chief emphasis throughout upon the feature of conspiracy, although in the Sherman Act, to make assurance doubly sure, "conspiracy" and "combination" are both proscribed. Not only are combination and monopoly declared illegal, but conspiracy with other persons to do these things, even if without result or success, is brought under the same ban and penalty. It can, however, hardly be maintained that this theory on which the case was prosecuted completely bound the hands of the Court, so that it could not place its stamp of disapproval upon these uneconomic practices. Can this be so, in view of the wide range of the Court's discretion, jurisdiction, and powers?

PUBLIC WELFARE FALLS BY THE WAYSIDE

A word in this connection regarding the public interest at stake in local price cutting. If a strong company charges monopolistic prices and makes monopolistic profits in any territory, the only way usually that the public can get the benefits of competition is for some independent to reduce prices in that locality. Now if this lower price (freight figured) is the independent's general price at its own mill base point, this is not "local" price cutting. But if a

[18] Brief for the U.S., Vol. 1, pp. 382-383.

company cuts its price in one area, while maintaining its price elsewhere, that is local price cutting. The one is competition, the other is evading competition. The latter so-called competition, not directed against all competitors in a real market area, but only against certain isolated competitors, is only pseudo-competition. (This point will be further treated in connection with the discussion of the nature of competition and monopoly in Part V.)

This famous Oil case thus ended without throwing any light upon the fundamental economic issues; rather, just because issues so plainly presented were ignored, it left them in greater haze and confusion. From a record that still is a great mine of evidence regarding business practices of the large enterprises of that day, not one nugget or grain of precious principle was extracted by the bungling processes of the law to enrich judicial wisdom on the economic nature of monopoly. Such a failure alone is perhaps sufficient to prove that success cannot be achieved by the law without assistance from economic analysis.

CHAPTER IV

THUS THE LAW DECREES

CRIME GOES UNPUNISHED

PROSECUTION and defense alike, each for its own purposes, had repeatedly called attention throughout the trial of the Standard Oil case to the fact that the Anti-Trust Act was a criminal statute, providing penalties of fine or imprisonment, or both, for the guilty. The decree, however, that was issued by the Circuit Court, and confirmed "except as to minor matters" by the Supreme Court, merely "commanded the dissolution of the combination, and therefore in effect, directed the transfer back to the share-holders" of the stock to which they were entitled in the various subsidiary corporations.[1] As the stock of the holding company was very closely held in the hands of a few men who had been continuously in control of the enterprise since its beginning, this disposition of the matter was generally viewed by the public as futile.

If the penal clauses of the statute were ever to be applied, they must have been in this case. Justice White seems to have forgotten his own mildly sarcastic comment upon the closely parallel decree in the Northern Securities case, of which, in dissenting, he had said in 1904:

the evil sought to be remedied is the restraint of interstate commerce and the monopoly thereof, alleged to have been brought about, through the acquisition by [certain individuals] of a controlling interest in the stock of both roads. And yet the decree, . . . authorizes its return [the stock] to the alleged conspirators, and does not restrain them from exercising the control resulting from the ownership. If the conspiracy and combination existed and was illegal, my mind fails to perceive why

[1] 221 U.S. 78 (1911).

46

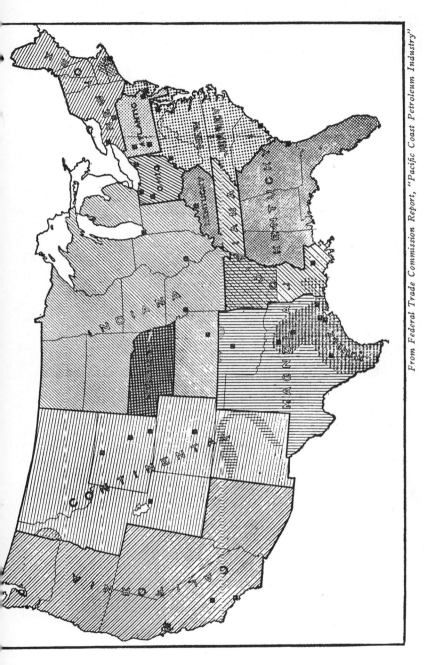

FIG. 2.   CHIEF GASOLINE MARKETING TERRITORIES OF THE STANDARD COMPANIES.

it should be left to produce its full force and effect in the hands of the individuals by whom it was charged the conspiracy was entered into.[2]

WAS THE VERDICT FUTILE?

Counsel for the Standard, when trying to convince the Court that the agreement of 1899 was really of little importance, had urged that in the period from 1892 to 1899 there "was no actual competition in the legal sense between any of the Standard Oil companies." The stock was held in the same proportionate relations by a certain few people. And, as if warning of the futility of such a decree as later was entered in this case, they declared: "There was also no possibility of competition because of the continued common ownership of all the companies." [3]

Without multiplying legal comments on this remarkable outcome of the case, it may suffice to note these words of a distinguished lawyer, now a justice of the Supreme Court, as follows:

Q. In the Standard Oil we now have 28 corporations, but a mutual ownership of stock? A. (by Mr. Brandeis) Yes.

Q. And they are not common directors, but the evil persists just the same? A. The evil does persist, and I think the great evil that was done there was to have the decree in the form in which it was. I should most strongly have contended, and, in fact, in arguing the Tobacco case did contend, that there was a dissolution which did not dissolve.

Q. You think the Supreme Court has the power to order the dissolution of stock ownership, but that the mere matter of preventing common directors will not accomplish the dissolution? A. It will not.[4]

A student of the economic aspects of the oil industry since the decree makes this restrained comment upon it:

However commendable the law and its interpretation may have been, in its application to the oil industry, it seems to have been practically vitiated at the outset by the method of dissolution agreed upon. . . . Thus, the holders of a majority of the stock in the Standard Oil Company of New Jersey now became the holders of a majority of the stock in each of the constituent concerns, and as such exerted a controlling influence in all. But the Court had done its duty, and the Department

[2] 193 U.S. 373 (1904).
[3] Brief, Johnson *et al.*, Vol. 2, p. 67.
[4] *Hearings on Trust Legislation*, 1914, p. 691.

of Justice seemed satisfied with the dissolution. . . . Meanwhile, the oil industry, notwithstanding its rather frequent investigation at the hands of governmental agencies, has been free from active Government regulation.[5]

OLD EVILS PERSISTED

The majority opinion of the Supreme Court in its brief preliminary discussion of "the remedy to be administered" mentioned, besides dissolution, the need "to forbid the doing in the future of acts like those which we have found to have been done in the past which would be violative of the statute."[6] The opinion further approved the decree of the court below as respects enjoining the owners of stock "from in any way conspiring or combining to violate the act or to monopolize or attempt to monopolize in virtue of their ownership of the stock. . . ."[7] This seems to be nothing more than a superfluous general statement that they must not conspire to violate the law, without any specific indication as to what they were to refrain from doing.

The Court's decree presumably aimed at the restoration of competitive conditions in the oil industry. How far was it successful? An unqualified answer is not easy to give, and careful consideration of the history of the industry since the decree leads to a moderate judgment, inclining neither to the one extreme of denying any effect nor to the other of affirming that success was complete. For a good many years prophecies by the more pessimistic critics of the decree seemed to be verified. There appeared to be little change for the better and "obviously a genuinely competitive situation was not immediately established."[8] Each of the Standard's subdivisions no doubt continued to exercise a considerable measure of monopolistic control after the decree. It was observed that because of the conditions as to quantity, etc., that are placed upon the shipment of oil by pipe lines, "neither the Court's decree nor the legislation of Congress has yet served to make the pipe lines of the country common carriers *de facto*,

[5] G. W. Stocking, *The Oil Industry and the Competitive System*, 1925, p. 48.
[6] 221 U.S. 77-78.
[7] *Idem*, p. 79.
[8] A judicious examination of the facts bearing upon this question is found in Stocking, *op. cit.*, pp. 49-82 (1925), whose words (p. 54), are here quoted.

though they are common carriers *de jure*." [9] The fact that the pipe lines were largely in the hands of the Standard group hampered the starting of small competing plants. In some regions, notably in mid-continent and in the Rocky Mountains, the dominance of the Standard was much greater than in others.[10]

STILL LOCAL MONOPOLIES

Federal investigations [11] have shown that at times, as in 1921, if not always, the Standard has been able to exercise a local monopoly power in Montana and Wyoming, both by paying there lower prices for crude and by charging higher prices for refined products than it did in near-by territory, due account being taken of cost of freight. That is, the company sold only at delivered prices, and not at refinery base prices, and netted more on sales within the territory nearest its plants. Too lenient a judgment of this practice is expressed in the words: "It may be that no logical objection can be offered to such a policy on business grounds." But the same student suspects that monopoly is masquerading in the disguise of competition when he says:

But obviously any claim that such a practice results from the free working of competitive influences is fictitious and untrue.[12]

The same geographical relationship of (net realized) prices varying nearly inversely with freight differences has pretty regularly prevailed in other cases, as, e.g., between the mid-western States and New York. The Standard has maintained higher discriminatory prices in the regions nearer the wells and refineries (non-competitive), while dumping its excess production two thousand miles away to be disposed of in a more competitive area, where supply and demand operated to lower prices. An economic paradox, and a sure sign of a local monopoly!

---

[9] *Idem*, p. 99.

[10] For details of ownership in this and other fields see John Ise, *The United States Oil Policy* (1928), p. 227 ff.

[11] E.g., Report of Federal Trade Commission, *Petroleum Trade in Wyoming and Montana*, July 1922.

[12] Stocking, *op. cit.*, p. 92.

STILL FEAR OF "REPRISALS"

A more subtle and pervasive sort of domination or control of price policies seems to have been continued by the Standard (i.e. by the branch operating in each region) by virtue of its being the most important company, even where competitors have been numerous in the field. This, too, can be shown by economic analysis to involve the element of local monopoly. A "follow-the-leader-policy" takes the place of the older, cruder, cutthroat competition and works just as effectively. The Standard takes the lead in naming a price in a particular locality, and others as a rule adhere to it. In many places and over long periods the prevailing practice (as described by the Federal Trade Commission around 1915) was this:

The market price was that named by the Standard Oil Company, which established and maintained fixed differentials for different classes of customers. The members of the Marketers' Association agreed to maintain and follow the retail prices and the differentials allowed by the Standard for the different classes of customers.[13]

Public bids from widely separated refineries to supply municipalities are, when opened, found to name identical delivered prices, and identical delivered prices prevail in the wholesale and retail trade. This docility of all the so-called independents in following the leader may be seen, on more careful scrutiny, to be the result of competitors' fear of cutthroat competition, more artfully and sparingly exercised than in the old days, united with the hope of reward in being allowed to live and obtain higher prices by acting with tacit if not explicit agreements.

The smaller independents seem to have a genuine fear of the Standard's ability to force them out of business should a price-cutting campaign be inaugurated.[14]

An untiring delver after the facts of the situation comments as follows:

No one who has talked much with independent oil men needs to be told that only a man of much courage or of little sense will try to "buck

---

[13] *Report on Pacific Coast Petroleum Industry*, Part 2, p. 7.
[14] Stocking, *op. cit.*, p. 95.

the Standard Oil Company," or, in other words, to set a price differen:
from that which the Standard has set. Some independents have done
that in the purchase of crude oil, and even in the sale of gasoline,
but it is generally regarded as a dangerous policy.[15]

The President of the National Marketers' Association (not producers but jobbers) said in 1923:

> If you start real competition—and by that I do not mean multiplying
> the opportunities we have today to buy stuff, but I mean competition
> that bases its price on cheaper delivery cost—you are up against a sys-
> tem of reprisals that rather deprive you of a desire to try the experi-
> ment more than once.[16]

SYSTEMATIC COLLUSION

In citing these passages we do not mean to imply that like prices
asked by two or more sellers in a real market is a sign of conspiracy, collusion, or restraint of trade. On the contrary, "one price
in a market" is the normal result of true market conditions. But
observe, this whole régime of follow-the-leader is an artificial
system of delivered prices calculated with reference to an arbitrarily selected point. The crux of the situation is implied in the phrase
used above by the official of the Marketers' Association, who no
doubt knew what he was talking about: "real competition—and by
that . . . I mean competition that bases its price on cheaper
delivery cost." That means that the independents who are bullied,
coaxed, or rewarded (or induced in all three ways) into a tacit
agreement to conform to this system of delivered prices are able
(and required) to charge more to near-by customers than to those
farther away.

THE HAPPY FAMILY

Before the dissolution decree this policy was practiced in the oil
industry boldly and baldly; it continued to be practiced in a more
artful way thereafter in the oil as in many other industries. It
escaped the attention of the courts both in the Oil and in the Steel
dissolution suits and was very vaguely understood by the public

[15] John Ise, *op. cit.*, p. 252, date 1928, supported by numerous references to
trade journals and governmental investigations of date 1923-1924.
[16] Senate Report No. 1263, March 3, 1923, Committee on Manufactures, p. 572.

until the movement began in 1919 which resulted in bringing the Pittsburgh-Plus complaint before the Federal Trade Commission. Restraint of competition took on a form so tolerant in outer appearance as to pretty well deceive the public and the courts as to what was really happening. No longer was the slogan "extermination"; it became "coöperation." A policy of live-and-let-live took the place of a war of prices. Monopolists no longer tried to look and act like pirates, but like Sunday school superintendents. All efforts now were bent toward maintaining prices, so that all sellers alike might flourish, not cutting prices, either locally or generally, to kill off the weaker. So long as the little independents were "good," the big company would, in the then new phrase, "hold the umbrella over them and they could stay in out of the rain." If the little fellows began to misbehave, did not stay in their places, became too greedy, tempted by generous and stable prices, then at last it might be necessary for the market leader to teach them to keep their places.

THE PUBLIC PAYS THE FLORIST

So far as the public is concerned, this live-and-let-live policy in its immediate workings is not better but worse than the older, cruder methods of cut-throat competition. The lion of monopoly no longer devours the independent lambs on sight. For long periods they lie down together, but the public "is the goat." Prices remain high for longer periods, and the intervals when they are low become rarer and briefer, reversing the rule of the old régime when frequent periods of low prices to the public were followed by occasional brief periods of pretty complete monopoly control. It pays the market leader to be a gentle missionary rather than a bold bad man. This milder policy of collusive maintenance of prices had, for years before the decision of the Oil suit, been tested by the Standard in alternation with the policy of local price-cutting. Rewards were sometimes bestowed upon competitors in place of blows. Monopoly had learned to "say it with flowers" and make the public pay the florist's bill. This policy had become quite as important likewise at this time with other large corporations such as U.S. Steel.

But not a suspicion of all this appears to have crossed the minds in the Department of Justice. Learned in the law but innocent of economic training, their thought on these matters still was of the vintage of the '80's, and they continued to present to the Court indictments based on the naïve assumption that the only price policy by which a powerful corporation could accomplish a "restraint of trade" was that of cutthroat competition. On this assumption great masses of evidence in the Oil and other important cases were collected in the effort to prove an intention to destroy smaller competitors—and of course with meager results. The evidence had little pertinence to the economic and legal issues regarding the policy actually in operation. The joke was on the public. While it continued to watch at one hole, the sly fox Monopoly was running in and out at another.

THE STARS IN THEIR COURSES

In the long run, however, conditions may change, and even the weak dissolution decree may help to change them and may become more effective through them. Such appears to have been the course of history in the eighteen years after 1911. Too much significance must not be attached to certain figures showing the decline of the *proportion* of the whole oil business of the country done by the eleven Standard companies, from approximately 85 per cent (about 1905) to 50 per cent of the total by 1923.[17] The oil business as a whole, largely as a result of the increase of gasoline engines, of automobiles, and of good roads, was advancing by leaps and bounds in the years following the dissolution decree. At the same time there occurred a rapid westward shift of the industry to the newly discovered fields in the mid-continent, California, Rocky Mountain and Gulf regions, some of them offering tempting opportunities and favorable conditions for independent, decentralized investment and enterprise.

Moreover, delivery by auto-truck tanks was probably a development favorable to competition by smaller companies in restricted districts near the wells. Independent competition was favored also (as compared with conditions before 1910 and quite apart from any influence of the dissolution decree) by the almost complete vic-

[17] See, on the fallacy of declining percentages, the case of the Steel Corporation, below, Ch. VIII.

tory of Federal control of railroads in the legislation of 1903, 1906, and 1910, over the old and long-continued abuses of freight rebating and of local and personal discrimination in freight rates and service which had been most effective agencies in building up the Standard Oil monopoly. The new trust-curbing legislation of 1914 and the activities of the newly created Federal Trade Commission visibly increased the courage of smaller enterprisers and the caution of market leaders.

THE DECREE MAY HAVE HELPED

These circumstances help to explain both the decrease in the Standard's percentage of the total oil business of the country and an appreciable improvement in competitive conditions, more marked in some areas and in some respects than in others. But this explanation does not rob the dissolution decree of all significance in bringing about this result. The long and expensive lawsuit had brought to the promoters and owners of the Standard an undoubtedly distasteful notoriety. New forces (reflections of public opinion and the new legislation) were moving in the business world, making for better ideals and practices. With the lapse of years, a new generation of leaders, animated by this better spirit, was coming into control. Then, most directly, the outcome of the suit was a condemnation, even though vague and unspecific, of the illegal practices of the company, and gave some assurance of fair play to independents and of protection by the government against a renewal of the abuses.

The Standard became by the decree not one but eleven companies, legally separate and legally warned to continue to act separately. No longer was there a strong central control. Even the personal and sentimental ties were weakened by time. Relentless fate removed one after another of the notable men who, working together with one mind, had built up the great organization. Large blocks of the capital stock were sold on the exchanges and came into the hands of widely scattered investors. Each separate organization had its own officers, largely working within its own territory, each with its separate problems, policies, and ambitions. Profits accrued to separate treasuries, out of which dividends were separately paid. At length around 1922 the customary relationships of the various Standard companies began to be more gravely disturbed. With large production and price reduction on the Pacific coast, the crude oil of California "literally pushed its way into the refinery markets of the East." "Eastern Standard companies, unrestrained by sentiment, suspended in part their purchase of crude from the Prairie Oil and Gas Company" (of the Standard), which long had limited itself largely to buying and selling mid-continent crude. This, with other similar happenings, "indicates strongly that the old Standard Oil Company is crumbling from within." [18]

The Standard Oil Company of Indiana has especially allied itself since 1925 with various non-"Standard" oil enterprises and has come more directly into competition with several of the other Standard companies by entering their territory.[19] As these words were first written, the battle of the proxies was on between the titular head of all the Standard companies and the chief executive of the Standard Oil of Indiana for control of that organization. The result was a victory of the former, in March 1929. The sympathies of the country were strongly with the victor because of his fine plea for higher norms of business ethics in respect to the pending Fall and Sinclair oil scandal suits.

LIVE-AND-LET-LIVE LIMITED

Each of the Standard companies is usually the largest company operating in its main territory, though it may have several large rivals. Brief and bitter local price wars have been frequent in the past few years, evidently to chastise the little fellows. The Standard could not now, if it would, crush its larger competitors without a very costly war of prices. They are no longer weak in finances and poor in equipment. So far as any one of the Standard companies acts "in restraint of trade" it must do so chiefly by "conspiracy" (in fact if not in name) with others, and that means some form of live-and-let-live policy, some device of delivered prices to disguise monopoly. This policy tends to degenerate into chaotic local price cutting if the power of the dominant leader relatively decreases greatly. The problem of insuring truly competitive conditions in the oil industry thus is now much the same as that in

---

[18] Stocking, *op. cit.,* pp. 110-112.
[19] *Idem,* pp. 112-113.

numerous other industries where the same tactics are employed. The final solution is to be attained only by putting an end to discrimination. The weak dissolution decree at last, however, in ways unforeseen, has partially justified itself by its results. In strengthening in some ways the struggling forces of competition it has ceased to be a mere scrap of paper.

PART II

STEEL MAKES ITS THRILLING ESCAPE

_____

CHAPTER V

ENTER THE GOOD TRUST, CLAD IN STEEL ₹ ARMOR

THE GUESSING CONTEST CONTINUES

THE masked ball goes merrily on. Now enters one disguised as a good trust, all clad in steel armor.

One capable student of the problem commented as follows upon the outcome of the Oil and Tobacco suits:

> It is one of the disappointing aspects of the decisions that they fail to answer clearly the question which just now most vitally concerns the business community, namely, how far does the statute as interpreted by the court go in its condemnation of great industrial combinations? To present the problem concretely: is the United States Steel Corporation a combination in restraint of trade in the statutory sense or not? I have read with care the reasons given in the decisions . . . and I must confess my inability to give a confident answer to this question. [And he speaks of the suspense and dread that result from this situation.] [1]

The Court had failed to give a clean-cut answer to either of the two chief questions, legal and economic: first, whether such a merger as that of 1899 was illegal in itself, or secondly, whether the acts leading up to and in furtherance of it were in themselves illegal, and if so in what the illegality consisted. The Oil decision gave little if any guidance for the future either to business or to the legal profession. Virtually it said to the country: Keep on guessing; we cannot now tell you what weight we propose to attach, in adjudicating the Anti-Trust Act, to the various contracts and business policies evidenced in this case; we really do not know

_____

[1] H. R. Seager in *Political Science Quarterly*, Vol. 26, p. 611, December, 1911.

ourselves. However, the Court implied that if any other combination were brought before them that seemed to them, all things
considered, to be as bad as the Standard Oil Company, it would
be declared illegal. Little help that was toward predicting what
the Court would do, as the country learned with a shock not many
years later in the Steel dissolution suit.

POLITICS SPURS ACTION

The Oil decision with its dissolution decree was rendered March
15, 1911, and, as if by unanimous consent, public thought turned
to the U.S. Steel Corporation as next to be haled into court in this
new and more vigorous policy of enforcing the Anti-Trust Act.
It was, indeed, rather generally assumed that the Department of
Justice had simply been awaiting the outcome of the Oil case to
decide just what would be its next step in regard to the Steel
Corporation. That great combination, formed in 1901 under the
very eyes of the Industrial Commission then in session, had
brought under unified control more numerous and varied concerns and plants and probably a considerably larger capital than
had the Standard Oil Company. For ten years, in a period of most
active discussion of "trust busting," it had pursued its way somewhat defiantly and unhindered by Federal prosecution. However,
by direction of Congress in 1905, it had been extensively investi-
gated by the Federal Bureau of Corporations.

The campaign of 1912 was approaching, in which, as every one
foresaw, the "trust issue" was destined to play an important part.
President Taft was preparing to stand in the next campaign for
the *status quo* in legislation and a more vigorous enforcement of
the Anti-Trust Act, with the emphasis on dissolution. The Oil dissolution decree lent new plausibility and hope to that method, but
the "rule of reason" had raised new doubts and fears in many
minds. The politicians at Washington were looking for issues, and
by June 1911 the so-called Stanley Committee of the House had
put on the witness stand the astute Mr. Elbert Gary, who, after an
interval, had succeeded the genial Mr. Charles M. Schwab as
president of the Steel Corporation. The Committee continued its
hearings with many witnesses well into the early weeks of 1912,
compiling 4,000 printed pages of testimony relating almost en-

tirely to the steel industry. Meantime, on October 26, 1911, the
Attorney General of the United States made a vigorous gesture on
behalf of the Administration by filing a petition in the Federal
District Court of New Jersey, praying that the Corporation and
its constituent companies be held to be unlawful monopolies and
be decreed to be illegal and be dissolved. For nine years the case
dragged through the courts.

A CLOSE CALL

The long-awaited final decision in 1920 verified the jubilant pre-
dictions of the corporation lawyers after the Oil decision. The
Court now, by a bare plurality, with three vigorously dissenting
and two taking "no part in the consideration or decision of the
case," exonerated the defendant U.S. Steel Corporation from the
charge of being a monopoly.

The plurality consisted of Justices McKenna (who delivered the
opinion), White, Holmes, and Van Deventer, all four of whom
had voted for conviction in the Standard Oil case. The minority
consisted of Day (the only other justice holding over since 1911,
and the writer of the vigorous dissenting opinion in this case) and
Clark and Pitney, two more recent appointees. Justice McReynolds
took no part, presumably because for a year and a half, while the
Department of Justice was prosecuting this suit, he had been
Attorney General (March 1913-August 1914); nor did Justice
Brandeis, who, as a practicing attorney before taking his seat on
the bench, had expressed his opinion that the Steel Corporation
was in fact a trust. It was generally believed that in view of the
very reasons for their non-participation, these two justices were
in sympathy with the view of the minority. Never has there been
a more paradoxical situation and a closer decision in an important
case in our highest court.

The Corporation was declared to be a good trust, or at least a
reformed sinner, and considerably shaken in nerve and much
bedraggled, it marched out of court as proudly as it could, bearing
a certificate of good character signed by four of the seven—or to
speak more accurately, by four of the nine—members of the
Supreme Court. It had won, no doubt, in terms of counsel fees, a
costly victory, but cheap at the price. A miss is as good as a mile,

and for practical purposes five more votes would have been a sheer waste of good ballots. Ever since then, whenever (as in the Pittsburgh-Plus hearings) by some careless phrase any one has intimated that in any way the Steel Corporation might be monopolistic, its counsel, like mercenary lions of Lucerne, would shake their shaggy manes and roar, defying all the world to imply a questioning of this verdict by a plurality of the Court in vindication of their worthy clients.

THE ISSUES IN THE CASE

It is not essential for our purpose to give an extended account of the formation and history of the Steel Corporation. That will be found set forth in testimony collected in many public hearings and in numerous writings, critical or otherwise. It may suffice to recall a few salient points, letting the other facts appear in turn as the economic issues come under discussion. This great industrial combination, proclaimed as the first billion-dollar corporation in the history of the world, was formed in 1901 by means of a holding company which brought together into one super-combination a number of combinations which had been formed mostly between 1898 and 1900, in various branches of the iron and steel industry. After the beginning of the suit in 1911 the voluminous record grew for four years until the Circuit Court rendered its decision June 3, 1915, four judges participating, two (Judges Buffington and McPherson) uniting in one opinion, and two (Judges Woolley and Hunt) in another, but all four concurring in the conclusion to dismiss the bill.

The issues both in the Circuit and in the Supreme Court, briefly expressed, were these: (a) Was the combination formed for the purpose (with the expectation) of achieving a monopoly? (b) Has it in fact succeeded at any time in achieving a monopoly or (not treated as just the same question) in restraining trade? (c) (If the answer to (b) is in the affirmative): Does the corporation now possess monopoly power, or (not just the same question) have the illegal practices been continued to the present? (d) (If the answers to (a) and (b) are in the affirmative and the answer to (c) is in the negative): Does the original expectation of, and temporary success in, achieving monopoly warrant a present dissolution decree when all illegal practices have been discontinued and the combination has now no monopoly power? [2]

GILDING THE HALO

The two opinions in the lower Court differed absolutely in their answer to the first question and somewhat in details and emphasis as to the others, but agreed as to the one important practical point, their refusal to dissolve the combination. Judges Buffington and McPherson, both natives and lifetime residents of Pennsylvania, answered emphatically in the negative all the questions. They united in an ardent vindication, at times mounting to a glorification, of the Steel Corporation as a law-abiding enterprise making (with slight exceptions) for perfect competition and for higher ethical standards in business. The combination was the natural and inevitable result of economic evolution. Every claim of merit was conceded, every complaint denied in a manner which left to the Corporation counsel nothing to desire.

SOME DOUBTS OF SANCTITY

Further comment may be given in Justice McKenna's own words.

The other opinion [by Judge Woolley and concurred in by Judge Hunt, 223 Fed. Rep. 161] was in some particulars, in antithesis to Judge Buffington's. The view was expressed that neither the Steel Corporation nor the preceding combinations, which were in a sense its antetypes, had the justification of industrial conditions, nor were they or it impelled by the necessity for integration, or compelled to unite in comprehensive enterprise because such had become a condition of success under the new order of things. On the contrary, that the organizers of the corporation and the preceding companies had illegal purpose from the very beginning, and the corporation became "a combination of combinations, by which, directly or indirectly, approximately 180 independent concerns were brought under one business control," which, measured by the amount of production, extended to 80 per cent or 90 per cent of the entire output of the country, and that its

[2] Numerous other minor, and some quite important, matters were given much attention in the four opinions written in the two courts, but they were significant only because of their bearing upon these four questions, (b) and (c) being each really two questions, or at least presenting two somewhat differing aspects.

purpose was to secure great profits which were thought possible in the light of the history of its constituent combinations, and to accomplish permanently what those combinations had demonstrated could be accomplished temporarily, and thereby monopolize and restrain trade.[3]

After this and further comparisons of the two opinions in the Circuit Court, Justice McKenna says: "We concur in the main with that of Judges Woolley and Hunt." The only difference indicated by him is that he hesitatingly suggests that Judge Woolley underestimated, "it may be," the influence of the "tendency and movement to integration" which made the formation of the Corporation "a facility of industrial progress" "though it cannot be asserted it had become a necessity." This is an economic question to which we must later revert.

MORE DOUBTS

The dissenting minority, Justices Day, Pitney, and Clark, quite agreed with Judge Woolley's view that the original purpose of the combinations was illegal.

It is the irresistible conclusion from these premises that great profits to be derived from unified control were the object of these organizations.[4]

And they agreed with Judge Woolley rather than with Judge Buffington that

The contention must be rejected that the combination was an inevitable evolution of industrial tendencies compelling union of endeavor.[5]

Therefore, agreement was expressed by nine judges (two district and seven Supreme Court) that the original formation of the corporation was in violation of the law, and by the same nine that it was not a necessity of economic evolution—though four of the nine hesitatingly called it a tendency, a movement, and a facility of industrial progress and appear elsewhere in the opinion to assume that it was necessary for the public welfare.

DID IT ACHIEVE MONOPOLY?

We pass on still hopeful to the second question, and here we find another and quite different ground on which the dissenting

---

[3] 251 U.S. 438-439.   [4] 251 U.S. 459.   [5] *Idem.*

minority would have based a decree of dissolution. They believed that the combination not only was born in illegality, but succeeded for a time in illegally achieving a monopoly and continued for a time acting in restraint of trade. The minority declared that "this unlawful organization exerted its power to control and maintain prices" and thus violated the law "by its immediate practices." [6] They believed therefore that

if the Sherman Act is to be given efficacy, there must be a decree undoing so far as is possible that which has been achieved in open, notorious, and continued violation of its provision.

Justice McKenna and his three colleagues of the plurality adopted a different view, that of Judges Woolley and Hunt, which turns on a technical legal distinction between the fact of possessing monopoly power and the derivation of that power from the very formation of the merger. They believed that the testimony did

not show that the corporation *in and of itself* ever possessed or exerted sufficient power when acting alone to control prices of the products of the industry.[7]

Its organizers therefore did not achieve monopoly *by the very fact* of the combination. They had "underestimated the opposing conditions." They did, however, succeed in restraining trade in that

at the very beginning the Corporation instead of relying upon its own power sought and obtained the assistance and the coöperation of its competitors (the independent companies) . . . it concerted with them in the expedients of pools, associations, trade meetings, and finally in . . . "the Gary Dinners" [between 1907 and 1911] . . . "They were pools without penalties" and more efficient in stabilizing prices.[8]

A SHOW OF INDIGNATION

Judge Woolley, whose views Justice McKenna and the plurality accepted, had declared with a show of indignation:

By the proceedings at the Gary Dinners, and at the meetings of the dinner committees, the fixing and maintaining of prices were as suc-

---

[6] *Idem,* 460.
[7] *Idem,* 440 (italics ours).
[8] 251 U.S. 440. Words of Justice McKenna in summary of Judge Woolley's opinion, which was followed by the Supreme Court.

cessfully accomplished as by meetings called for that purpose during the period from 1904 to 1907, and by the pools created for that purpose from 1901 to 1904. It therefore appears that from the organization of the corporation in 1901 until the Gary Dinners were discontinued in January, 1911, the corporation, first by one method, and then by a second method, and then by a third method, employed means to procure the establishment and maintenance of uniform prices for its diversified products, and by these means the Steel Corporation, with its competitors, did combine and control prices, and in controlling prices restrained trade. If by the three methods pursued, in the three periods named, prices were not artificially and successfully maintained, as shown by the history covering those three periods, I am at a loss to know by what means it would be possible to fix and maintain prices that would unduly restrain trade in the sense of violating the Anti-Trust Law.[9]

GUILTY MONOPOLY BUT NO ONE GUILTY

It appears therefore that Judges Woolley and Hunt as well as the entire Supreme bench, agreed that the Corporation was, from its formation until a few months before the inception of the suit, for ten years openly, flagrantly, and continuously violating the Anti-Trust Act. That is a penal statute, for whose violation are prescribed as penalties fines or imprisonment or both, and as remedies, under the equity powers of the Court, either dissolution or any other measure that the Court in its wisdom might deem effective. What is the Court going to do about it? Just here, where the opinion has reached the climax of condemnation, it abruptly changes to palliation of the offenses and explanation of the surprising decision to do nothing whatever about it.

This apology contained two reasons for treating the Corporation as guiltless. The first rested on a sharp distinction drawn by the Court between acts by the Corporation in illegal restraint of trade performed with the connivance of others, and the exercise of monopoly powers by the Corporation itself. So far from deeming such conspiring in restraint of trade to be an evidence of monopoly (power) by the Corporation, the Court takes it to be conclusive proof that the Corporation was not a monopoly—for otherwise it

[9] 223 Fed. Rep. 175-176.

would not have had to secure the coöperation of others. It is therefore held (in the words of Judge Woolley, p. 178) that "the corporation, in and of itself, is not now and has never been a monopoly or a combination in restraint of trade." The emphasis is strongly on the phrase "in and of itself," and the distinction strongly insisted upon is that taking part in the creation of a monopolistic condition or "a combination in restraint of trade" does not constitute the corporation itself "a monopoly" or make it a combination in restraint of trade. The thought is that its power and guilt are no greater than those of any little independent. The complaint did not include the independents, but if they had been included, they surely could not have been more guilty than was the Corporation; so it seemed to follow that, although "a monopoly" and "a combination in restraint of trade" had been formed, nobody was guilty. O wise judge! A Daniel come to judgment!

A CALL FOR COMMON SENSE

It is well to recall here Chief Justice White's conclusion, after his learned survey of the history of the law in the Standard Oil case, that

In this country also the acts from which it was deemed there resulted a part if not all of the injurious consequences ascribed to monopoly (which originally could arise only from an act of sovereign power) came to be referred to as a monopoly itself. In other words, here as had been the case in England, practical common sense caused attention to be concentrated not upon the theoretically correct name to be given to the condition or acts which gave rise to a harmful result, but to the result itself and to the remedying of the evils which it produced.[10]

Where now was "the practical common sense," and upon what was the attention of the Court concentrated? Was it upon the acts and facts that constituted restraint of trade and thus monopoly? The argument seems to be merely a quibble about the difference between "a combination in restraint of trade" and "a monopoly" in the sense of a single corporation able by itself alone to "restrain trade."

The minority disagreed very emphatically with this conception

[10] 221 U.S. 56.

of a monopoly, and clearly recognized the relative and limited character of monopoly. Justice Day said:

> Nor can I yield assent to the proposition that this combination has not acquired a dominant position in the trade which enables it to control prices and production when it sees fit to exert its power . . . That the exercise of the power may be withheld, or exerted with forbearing benevolence, does not place such combinations beyond the authority of the statute which was intended to prohibit their formation, and when formed to deprive them of the power unlawfully attained.
>
> It is said that a complete monopolization of the steel business was never attained by the offending combinations. To insist upon such result would .be beyond the requirements of the statute and in most cases practicably impossible . . .[11]

THE COURT GRANTS IMMUNITY

Another reason in the minds of the plurality of the Court for not dissolving the Corporation seems to have been the belief that the accused had reformed his ways and that therefore, on grounds of public policy, he should be pardoned for past offenses. The minority believed (here in accord with the plurality) that the combination was illegally formed, but maintained *on principles of law* alone (as opposed to the plurality) that the combination should be dissolved regardless whether its conduct had been exemplary since, and regardless of what ends of public welfare the Court might think would be served by allowing it to continue. Justice Day, with the concurrence of Justices Clark and Pitney, said with severity:

> As I understand the conclusions of the Court, affirming the decree directing dismissal of the bill, they amount to this: that these combinations, both the holding company and the subsidiaries which comprise it, although organized in plain violation and bold defiance of the provisions of the act, nevertheless are immune from a decree effectually ending the combinations and putting it out of their power to attain the unlawful purposes sought, because of some reasons of public policy requiring such conclusion. I know of no public policy which sanctions a violation of the law, nor of any inconvenience to trade, domestic or foreign, which should have the effect of placing combina-

[11] 251 U.S. 464-465.

tions, which have been able thus to organize one of the greatest industries of the country in defiance of law, in an impregnable position above the control of the law forbidding such combinations. Such a conclusion does violence to the policy which the law was intended to enforce, runs counter to the decisions of the Court, and necessarily results in a practical nullification of the act itself.[12]

These are scathing words, not used by reckless and radical critics of the Supreme Court, but spoken in the presence of all the world by three most able and respected Justices of the Court, while Justices McReynolds and Brandeis sit silently by, thinking we know not what unutterable thoughts.

LAW A MERE ''ABSTRACTION''

Justice McKenna's reply to the bitter accusations uttered by the dissenters was an implied admission of their truth, but he seems to be appealing to some occult reason (whether or not it be the rule of reason) as elevating the Court above the obligation of literally enforcing the statute. He says:

But there are countervailing considerations. We have seen whatever there was of wrong intent could not be executed, whatever there was of evil effect, was discontinued before this suit was brought; and this, we think, determines the decree. We say this in full realization of the requirements of the law. [How clearly we hear in these words the echoes of the heated debate within the judicial chambers!] It is clear in its denunciation of monopolies and equally clear in its direction that the courts of the Nation shall prevent and restrain them (its language is "to prevent and restrain violations of" the act), but the command is necessarily submissive to the conditions which may exist and the usual powers of a court of equity to adapt its remedies to those conditions. In other words, it is not expected to enforce abstractions and do injury thereby, it may be, to the purpose of the law. It is this flexibility of discretion . . .[13]

and more on this line to the bewilderment of the lay mind—and to the equal bewilderment of the three dissenting members of the Court. If this is the rule of reason, it ceases to be a mere *obiter dictum* and is used now in interpreting the Anti-Trust Act. A law

---

[12] *Idem*, p. 463.   [13] *Idem*, p. 452.

whose specific application Justice McKenna did not favor became *ipso facto* an "abstraction," not to be enforced.

THE GOOD BISHOP FORGIVES

This much is clear to common intelligence, unillumined by any supernatural light; also it is clear that the Court has improvised for the occasion a new statute of limitations to nullify the operation of the Anti-Trust Act. Although a corporation in its very creation and for years thereafter may be a violator of the law, it somehow has its guilt all wiped away by time. The intervening years are viewed as a period of probation in which the sinner, without "reforming" legally the form of organization illegally assumed, may show by his good deeds that he will henceforth be a blessing and not a curse to society (as Congress in its ignorance had supposed). It is as if an incorporated Jean Valjean had stolen a suit of clothes—yes, a whole storeful of clothes—and, being caught with the goods, was not only let go scot-free but allowed to keep the loot because it would help make him a good citizen. This is easy for any one to understand without special legal training. But the good Bishop forgave for the theft of his own goods, not those of the public.

PROFITING BY OFFICIAL TORT

Warming to his task, Justice McKenna imputes to the Department of Justice not so much a neglect of duty as a sort of dispensing and pardoning power to be exercised merely by neglect of its duty to enforce the Act promptly at the time it is violated. He says:

it is certainly a matter for consideration that there was no legal attack on the Corporation until 1911, ten years after its formation and the commencement of its career. We do not, however, speak of the delay simply as to its time—that there is estoppel in it because of its time— but on account of what was done during that time—the many millions of dollars spent, the development made, and the enterprises undertaken, the investments by the public that have been invited and are not to be ignored. And what of the foreign trade . . .[14]

[14] *Idem,* pp. 452-453.

"A matter for consideration." Why, and by whom? As he has just said: "by a court of equity to determine what is the appropriate relief" to be granted. That, as the Justice says, is "not . . . to advance a policy contrary to that of the law, but in submission to the law and its policy, and in execution of both." [15] The Biblical phrases used by Chief Justice White twenty-two years before seem to have undergone a transformation so that they now read something like this: The rule exacts that the spirit which killeth a law of Congress, and not the letter which vivifies it, is the proper guide by which to interpret a statute correctly.[16]

THE SUPPRESSED TRUTH

The issues presented in the Steel case differed in important ways from those in the Oil case, and on these differences, emphasized and magnified, hung the opinion of the four who now voted to acquit a combination in steel, whereas the same four had all voted eight years before to convict a combination in oil. But equally certain does it appear today in a careful study of the economic aspects of the two cases, that in quite as important ways the issues were alike, and the likenesses were overlooked and misinterpreted by the Court. Such a study reveals a remarkable negligence in developing and presenting to the Court the economic aspects of this case, and a no less remarkable astuteness of the defense in suppressing pertinent evidence regarding the real nature of the selling devices used by their clients. The defense enlisted economic experts to make an expensive *ex parte* study of the case, testimony which the defense was unprepared to combat. The Supreme Court, learned in the legal rather than in the economic phases of the problem, was confused and misled by this *suppressio veri et suggestio falsi.*

A decade is a brief period in the history of nations and of the law, but even this short time has served to throw new light upon the facts of this case and upon principles that were then obscure. It would, of course, be rash to assert positively that had these matters all been well and truly set forth, any one of the four Justices

[15] *Idem,* p. 452.
[16] Compare words in the Freight Association case, March 22, 1897, 166 U.S. 354.

in the plurality would have voted differently. This is not, however, an unreasonable guess, inasmuch as the Court was so evenly balanced that a hair might have tipped the scales, whereas the suppressed evidence and arguments were ponderous. This famous suit has gone into history, but it is not without hope and prospect of future service in this field of public policy that, after this brief outline of its legal aspects, we now subject to a critical examination its neglected economic features.

———

CHAPTER VI

AN EMPIRE OF STEEL

THE STEEL ARMADA

THROUGHOUT the progress of the Steel dissolution suit the question constantly recurs whether the very existence of such an enormous aggregation of steel plants and resources did not constitute in effect a "continuing violation" of the Anti-Trust Act. The facts were such that they suggested to every mind the same thought, that this enormous combination must in the very nature of things possess great power to "restrain trade." Here are some extracts from a description dated 1907, after some further additions had been made to the combination, but referring mainly to the year 1901, all written in an admiring, not in an adverse, spirit: [1]

To escape from its bewildering statistics let us imagine that the United States Steel Corporation is a combination of the navies of the world. Let us suppose that we are standing upon some lofty promontory where we can see the mighty fleet pass in review before us. It consists of 213 squadrons, some with few vessels and some with many. After years of warfare, these squadrons were organized into eight powerful navies: and now, finding that it is better to combine than to compete, they have decided to come together under one admiral and one flag.

Leading the way come the Carnegie war ships, the most formidable steel navy in the world . . . It is practically thirty fleets under one control . . . Next comes the Federal Steel Navy, commanded by Admiral Elbert H. Gary. . . . It is a strong aggregation of five large fleets . . . and now . . . come the American Steel and Wire vessels, 126 in all. . . . Most of the ships are gay with fresh paint. Flags

———

[1] H. N. Casson, *The Romance of Steel, the Story of a Thousand Millionaires,* 1907, p. 215.

are flying, bands are playing, and all is spick and span . . . Another
two year old fleet follows—the American Tin Plate. Its ships are noticeably smaller but more numerous. It is an aggregation of 38 squadrons with 278 vessels in all . . . Next the National Tube, a thirty
vessel fleet . . . It was upon this fleet that Carnegie was about to
make such a fierce onslaught when Morgan, the peacemaker, inter-
fered . . . The sixth fleet flies the well-known Rockefeller flag. It
was picked up, here a vessel and there a vessel, by its dreaded com-
mander. It cost him little but he is selling it for something like fifty
million dollars . . . In the rear come two smaller fleets—the National
Steel and the Steel Hoop. . . . As if this immense aggregation were
not enough, four other large squadrons are soon to be added—the
American Bridge, in which was Carnegie's old warship, the Keystone,
the Clairton Steel, the Union Steel, and the Shelby Steel Tube.

AN INDUSTRIAL EMPIRE

Evidently this was written before the notorious purchase of the
Tennessee Coal and Iron Company, in 1907. The writer then
presents what he calls a "feast of statistics," of which here are a
few morsels:

The United States Steel Corporation owns as much land as is contained in the three states of Massachusetts, Vermont, and Rhode Island.

It owns and operates a railroad trackage that would reach from New
York to Galveston.

It has nineteen ports and owns a fleet of one hundred large ore ships.

It makes more steel than either Great Britain or Germany, and one
quarter of the total amount made in all the countries of the world. Its
stock and bonds outstanding were $1,400,000,000 at the date of its
first annual report. St. John in the wonderful vision with which the New
Testament concludes . . . pictures it as a "city of pure gold." But this
was Heaven, not earth. Nothing terrestrial, whether past or present, fact
or imagination, equals the wealth of this single American Corporation.
And not even this stupendous total expresses the full power of this industrial empire. Behind it stood Morgan, Rockefeller, and Carnegie,
representing about two billion dollars of well-handled and aggressive
capital. Said the Wall Street men: it means unity, coöperation, assured
profit.[2]

Stripped of all rhetoric, the cold unadorned facts are staggering
in their seemingly necessary implication of unified irresistible

[2] *Idem,* pp. 218-225.

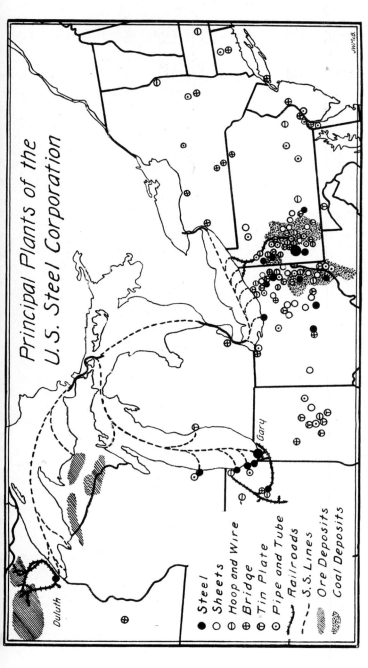

FIG. 3. PRIMARY PRODUCTION, CHIEFLY AT PITTSBURGH, CHICAGO, AND REGION BETWEEN; FABRI-CATING PLANTS SCATTERED MORE WIDELY. NEARLY FIFTY OTHER PLANTS, MOSTLY INTEGRATED WITH THOSE SHOWN (BUT INCLUDING BIRMINGHAM AND OTHERS OFF THIS MAP) ARE NOT SEPARATELY MARKED

power to dominate in essential ways the steel business of the country. Before 1901 this one combination had been some twelve combinations, and not many years before some 200 or more independent plants and managements.[3]

NEW REALITIES OF PRICE CONTROL

Looking at realities and not at abstractions, would any one for a moment maintain that an ironclad agreement among either these several hundred concerns or these twelve groups to act as one as to prices would not have given them collectively far more power over prices than could possibly be exerted by any one of them or by all of them acting as separate units? Would not such an agreement and conspiracy, so long as it continued in force, have been flagrantly illegal and a continuing violation of the Anti-Trust Act?

Mr. Gary admitted after some hesitation that the ultimate power as to price policies for all subsidiaries was vested in one central management. Can any one doubt then that the unified power of the United States Steel Corporation in restraint of trade was far more effective and continuous in its operation than any mere pool or secret conspiracy of the constituent parts could have been—always unstable and difficult to maintain? Looking at the realities rather than at legal formalities, did not the very creation of the Corporation therefore put under a single control a power over price policies far greater than any that had or ever could come before the Court in the form of a complaint against a group of independents for conspiracy in restraint of trade? The patient ultimate purchaser of steel may here see the highest Court perform the mathematical and economic miracle of showing in the light of reason that in matters monopolistic the whole is less than any of its parts. Learned judges will demonstrate to their own satisfaction that while it was grossly illegal for independent corporations to have a merely partial agreement to control prices, it became perfectly legal for the same hundred-or-more once independent companies to follow absolutely unified price policies after they had been financially merged into one. Such to the legalistic mind is the mystic power of legal incorporation to transform into a single

[3] Variously estimated (see quotations above) not including the Tennessee Coal and Iron Company, purchased 1907, and the Gary and Duluth plants, built later.

"person," incapable of conspiracy with himself, scores of separate corporations which in turn control hundreds of separate plants and comprise thousands of individual owners and a billion of capital. Could any more effective means have been taken to make impossible over a large part of the industrial field the continued existence of truly independent industries of moderate size? Surely, here too is some explanation of the quick growth of a new swarm of mergers after the remarkable decision in the Steel Dissolution suit.

"THE NATURAL THING TO EXPECT"

The reasonable answer to these questions was promptly given by Judges Woolley and Hunt in the lower court. After some scandalized comments on the way in which many "competitive producing concerns" were acquired, Judge Woolley said:

The immediate, as well as the normal effect of such combinations, was in all instances a complete elimination of competition between the concerns absorbed, and a corresponding restraint of trade.[4]

This referred to the several constituent combinations which were formed before 1901. Of the power of the United States Steel thereafter, the same Judge says:

by the power resulting from the increased elimination of competition, the Steel Corporation would be enabled to fix and regulate the production and prices of all commodities in the industry. Such would seem to be a natural thing to expect of a combination of competing corporations which in themselves were combinations of competing corporations. . . .[5]

The dissenting minority of the Supreme Court summarized in the following words the views *first* held by all four judges of the lower Court, and approved them as expressing the truth of the situation:

the constituent companies of the United States Steel Corporation, nine in number, were themselves combinations of steel manufacturers, and the effect of the organization of these combinations was to give a control over the industry at least equal to that theretofore possessed by the constituent companies and their subsidiaries; that the Steel Corporation

[4] 223 Fed. Rep. 168 (1915).   [5] *Idem*, p. 168 (1919).

was a combination of combinations by which directly or indirectly 180 independent concerns were brought under one control. . . .[6]

AN ASTONISHING REACTION

Judge Woolley, however, later contradicted his own propositions and shifted his view, saying of the period before 1911:

Without the coöperation of independent producers, prices of steel products could not have been raised and maintained by the corporation alone.[7]

And of the period after 1911 he declares:

the corporation, in and of itself, is not now and has never been a monopoly or a combination in restraint of trade. . . .[8]

If the "immediate and normal effect" of the forming of each of the subsidiary corporations was "in all instances, a complete elimination of competition between the concerns absorbed and a corresponding restraint of trade" (i.e. among the individual concerns of each group), how is it possible for a rational mind to maintain that a further supercombination of these combinations would suddenly nullify all this accumulated monopoly power? Is not rather the conclusion inevitable that supercombination would further extend this monopoly power by the elimination of competition among the several groups at certain other places and in certain other areas?

But no; the weasel phrase "in and of itself" served to shift the Judge's thought from the elimination of competition between and among the hundreds of concerns formerly owned and operated separately, to the continuance of competition between these same concerns (collectively) and whatever independents there were remaining. And lo! this giant corporation suddenly found it "impossible" to exercise *any* "restraint of trade" whatever "if not combined with its competitors" (the independents remaining).[9] Because the elimination of competition among some 200 combined concerns did not at the same time eliminate competition with the remaining independents, it did not restrain trade at all!

---

[6] 251 U.S. 458 (1919).
[7] 223 Fed. Rep. 176.
[8] *Idem,* p. 178.
[9] *Idem,* p. 176.

LOST IN THE MAZES

No logical connection is discoverable between Judge Woolley's two conflicting propositions. He simply gets lost in the mazes of his own argument, and because the Corporation between 1901 and 1911 coöperated with the independents so as to fix prices *more* effectively, he leaps to the *non sequitur* that it had acquired *no* power by reason of its size and consolidation *to fix them at all* as among its own members or to force or induce the smaller independents to conspire with it to fix them.[10] In this and the other opinions that favored the Corporation is implied the assumption that unless the great combination had *complete* monopoly power to fix prices *by itself* it had no power whatever more than would have been possessed by its two hundred parts acting separately. Between absolute monopoly and absolutely free competition these judges see no possible gradation!

Even Judge Buffington has to wrestle with his doubts on this *prima facie* absurdity:

> The vast size of the Steel Corporation they formed, the influence and control incident to such size, its seeming power to crush competition, its ability to absorb business through its systematized organization are all factors so associated with monopoly to restrain trade and crush out competition that we may say that, standing alone as a mere isolated fact, this great company gives one such an impression of monopoly that we feel we may in this inquiry place the burden upon it and its formers to satisfy us by affirmative proof that monopoly was not the purpose for which it was formed.[11]

Yet Judge Buffington concludes after an examination of the plausible explanations given by the "formers" that they have sustained this burden of proof and have convincingly shown not only that monopoly was not the purpose for which it was formed, but also was not a result attained by its formation. He concludes that the Corporation was a "normal, regular, and natural outcome" of a gradual, sustained evolution of the iron and steel industry. But neither he nor Judge Woolley nor Justice McKenna gives further thought to the economic problems of what is the normal, regular,

[10] *Idem.*   [11] 223 Fed. Rep. 121 (1915).

and natural and inevitable effect upon prices of such a vast merger of formerly competing companies.

NEW TWISTS OF LOGIC

Justice McKenna in the prevailing opinion followed the devious windings of Judge Buffington's reasoning in the lower Court. At first he had to struggle against serious doubts. He says:

> The Corporation is undoubtedly of impressive size and it takes an effort of resolution not to be affected by it or to exaggerate its influence. But we must adhere to the law and the law does not make mere size an offense or *the existence of unexerted power* an offense. It, we repeat, requires overt acts. . . .[12]

The thought here plainly is that the Corporation has great powers of a sort to influence prices and restrain trade, but that it is not guilty, because it does not exert them. But this is soon shifted, following the fallacious reasoning of the lower Court, to the different thought that this enormous aggregation of steel producers "neither attempted *nor possessed* the power alone" (Judge Woolley's words) to restrain trade or influence prices in any way. Justice McKenna gives a new curve to the twisting logic, beginning with these words:

> It is greater in size and productive power than any of its competitors, equal or nearly equal to them all, but its power over prices was not and is not commensurate with its power to produce.[13]

A loose proposition from which is drawn a lame conclusion! For this does not say what Justice McKenna at once assumes that it does. It does not say that the combination has *no greater* power over prices either *than had any one of its uncombined competitors,* or *than its constituent concerns would have had* if acting separately without illegal conspiracy. It says merely that its power over prices "is not commensurate with" "its power to produce." The power of the Corporation to produce was at least tenfold greater than that of its nearest competitor and about two hundredfold greater than that of any one separate plant; Justice McKenna's declaration amounts merely to saying that "its power over

[12] 251 U.S. 451. (Our italics.)   [13] *Idem,* p. 445.

prices" "was and is not" tenfold greater than that of its nearest competitor, or two hundredfold greater than any single plant would have. But he illogically twists this into the proposition (upon which he then based the decision) that the great combination has, by virtue of its size and combination of formerly competing companies, no power whatever to influence prices or to restrain trade.

ALL DOUBTS FLUNG ASIDE

A moment more the leap to the fallacious conclusion is halted by a doubt in the mind of the Justice:

It is true there is some testimony tending to show that the Corporation had such power . . .

But he brushes this aside and adopts completely the (revised, not the first) view of the lower Court on this point.

The conflict was by the judges of the District Court unanimously resolved against the existence of that power, and in doing so they but gave effect to the greater weight of the evidence.[14]

He adds, to the same effect: "whatever there was of wrong intent could not be executed." [15] He fully accepts certain testimony and the interpretation put upon it by Corporation counsel,

that no adventitious interference was employed to either fix or maintain prices and that they were constant or varied according to natural conditions.[16]

He sarcastically rejects any suggestion "that this testimony be minimized or dismissed" by any consideration of the power and influence of the Corporation. Now this plainly asserts that the Corporation *acting by itself alone* (a thought often repeated in the friendly opinions) was not "a monopoly," had no monopolistic power, and could not act successfully to restrain trade.

"MERE SIZE" AND PRICE LEADERSHIP

The fact that the Corporation assumed the leadership in price agreement was undisputed and is repeatedly assumed in the opinions as a matter arousing no curiosity and calling for no ex-

[14] *Idem,* p. 445.   [15] *Idem,* p. 452.   [16] *Idem,* p. 449.

planation. It is treated as a mere accident, a mere quirk of Fate. The Court assumes that the great size of the Corporation gave it no greater power to assume this leadership in conspiring and in securing (either compelling or attracting) the coöperation of the independents than any one of its constituent companies would have had if acting separately! This applies to the period of admitted agreements between 1901 and 1911, and *a fortiori* to the period after 1911 when, the judges believed,[17] no common action as to prices was taken and no leadership exercised. Of course, if the size of the combination enabled it to take a leadership as to prices which otherwise would have been impossible, then "mere size" would be the source of "restraint of trade," no less because exerted indirectly than if exerted directly.

Only a singular ignorance of the history of the American trust movement as well as of the theory of monopoly could make it possible for any one, judge or layman, to believe that monopoly is monopoly only when acting without the compliance and coöperation of smaller competitors. If a corporation controls less than 100 per cent of the product within a certain territory, it can, to be sure, exert monopoly power for a time and within limits merely by restricting its own output; but this is neither so effective nor so profitable a method as that of securing by hook or by crook the coöperation of its competitors. Indeed the failure of a large combination either to drive independents out of business or to bring them into conspiracy with it (by pools, agreements, etc.), though not necessarily depriving it of all its power, must cost it large profits. Economic analysis makes the reasons for this very clear. Let the fear of prosecution deprive the big corporation of the power to drive its competitors out of business, and there is left to it still the very effective method of bringing them into coöperation (conspiracy in restraint of trade), the policy followed by the Steel Corporation.

EQUALITY IN GUILT MAKES INNOCENCE

The opinions in this case both in the District and in the Supreme Court imply a very different and mistaken understanding. Said Judge Woolley:

[17] See further on this belief, below, Ch. X.

The raising and maintaining of prices of steel products from 1901 to 1911 cannot be attributed to the dominancy by the corporation over the industry, because of its size. It was due to coöperation between it and nearly all other producers in a joint effort to raise and maintain prices, in which they persisted and succeeded. Without the coöperation of independent producers, prices of steel products could not have been raised and maintained by the corporation alone. The offense of the corporation, therefore, was . . . an offense *precisely similar* [18] to that of which every independent and coöperating producer was guilty, and consisted in the act of *combining with its competitors*,[19] to produce an unlawful result. If it had not combined with its competitors, or if they had not combined with it, restraint of trade, due to the fixation of prices, would in my opinion have been impossible . . . The corporation dominated only in the sense of contributing substantially to what was done and making attractive what it desired to be done, and the others yielded cheerfully. Their offense was no different from that of the corporation, and the offense of the corporation was distinguished from theirs only in the leadership it assumed in promulgating and perfecting the policy.[20]

"Their offense was no different" and the Corporation's offense "was distinguished" . . . "only in the leadership," and the Court detected in this "only" neither any hint of a guilty conspiracy nor any result of the superior size and financial power that was of any significance whatever. The Court could detect no evidence (though it was baldly patent) that the Corporation exercised any coercion ("others yielded cheerfully") to force others into a conspiracy to raise and maintain prices before 1911. This conclusion is at variance with the first reasonable presumptions of the Judges themselves as well as with the most elementary knowledge of monopolistic methods.

BLAMELESS LIFE AND NEGLECTED EVIDENCE

Another and perhaps even stronger reason that the Court declined to dissolve the billion-dollar corporation was that it believed that the objectionable practices, after being continued for ten years, had been abandoned nine months before the institution of the suit. Greater weight was given to this belief by the further belief that this change came not from fear of prosecution, but "from a conviction of their futility, from the operation of forces

---

[18] Our italics.   [19] Italics in original.   [20] 223 Fed. Rep. 176.

that were not understood or were underestimated" at the formation of the combination—this again implying that the Corporation
proved to have no power whatever to affect prices.

The Court declares that "since 1911 no act in violation of law
can be established against (the Corporation) except its existence be
such an act." [21] This pronouncement marked the success of the
counsel of the Corporation in presenting, but far more in skillfully
suppressing, evidence, while it marked the failure of the Government counsel either to comprehend or to present to the Court the
real situation. The Court was deceived as to the essential facts and
as to their economic meaning.

For this result the prosecution seems the most blameworthy.
Much neglected evidence which would have cast a different light
on many features of the case was readily available, but its significance was overlooked. Defendants' counsel were much more awake
to some important economic aspects of the case than were the attorneys for the Government, and they had taken the precaution
to engage economic experts to make an *ex parte* study of the case
for nearly two years before it came to trial in the Circuit Court
(in 1915), at which time was closed the record on which the case
was later carried to the Supreme Court. The prosecution on the
contrary ignored economic advice.[22] Throughout the tens of thousands of pages of printed testimony that one may read today, it is
patent that Government counsel were in respect to the economic
issues groping their way in a labyrinth without any guiding thread
of principle.

NEW FASHIONS IN MONOPOLY

Government counsel were in the main conducting the case along
the lines laid down in the Standard Oil suit, seeking the same kind
of evidence, hoping to obtain the same sort of decree of dissolution. They failed to sense the great change in the conditions and
circumstances. The Oil decision was based largely on evidence of
price wars and cutthroat competition of an earlier date designed to

[21] 251 U.S. 451.
[22] It called one unwilling witness, a government official and competent
economist, to present, doubtless against his better judgment, one piece of economic evidence as to average prices compiled by the Bureau of Corporations,
which had no real pertinence to the issues in the case.

put smaller competitors out of business. The Steel Corporation, however, had used mainly the method of agreement with its smaller competitors, the policy of live-and-let-live, and of the maintenance and stabilizing of (local discriminatory) prices as high as possible. Fashions in "trusts" and trust methods had changed between 1900 and 1920 as much as those in women's dress. Even before the dissolution of the Standard in 1911, ruthless cut-throat price wars in the oil industry, as in other leading industries, had largely ceased. They had mostly given place to a policy of live-and-let-live, with common understanding and action in a scheme of basing-point prices, while cutthroat competition was only a concealed weapon for occasional though effective use. Most of the more spectacular and damaging evidence of the older, cruder methods in the Oil case antedated 1901, and that case would have presented a very different aspect if the evidence presented to the Court in 1911 had been confined to the acts of the preceding ten years. The Standard was made a scapegoat for popular resentment against corporation excesses. It had to bear the odium of its older practices, while the Steel Corporation succeeded well in disassociating its record after 1901 from that of the constituent companies before that date, so that it suffered scarcely at all from the hang-over of prejudice in the minds of the judges against the unbridled violation of the law in the '90's when the constituent combinations were formed. Thus, starting with a clean slate, it succeeded first in convincing the Court that while it "conspired" between 1901 and 1911 with smaller competitors, it in no sense dominated their actions, but dealt with them purely as co-equals; and finally in making the Court believe that after 1911 its policies and prices had completely exemplified conditions of free competition, the ideal operation of supply and demand in true markets. Government counsel failed to comprehend the new situation and the need of a new legal attitude toward it.

HOODWINKING THE SUPREME COURT

A tangle of facts and confused interpretations must be cleared away to uncover the real situation. Let us for the present dismiss the conditions of the ten years preceding October 1911, except such of them as continued in effect after the suit was undertaken.

It was conceded, in Justice McKenna's words, that "the activities and offendings" of the accused in the period from 1901 to 1911 "have illustrative periods of significant and demonstrated illegality." [23] It was to the events after 1911 that the judges voting to exculpate the Corporation attached a controlling significance, which led them, with slight exceptions, to pronounce the Corporation's record to be spotless in respect to the issues of the suit.[24]

As we reread the evidence and opinions in the case with the aid of economic analysis and of facts that have later come to light, it is clear that the prosecution and the Court were both off on the wrong trail. Needless to say, the defendant, so far from setting them right, led them off further into the jungle of confusion. It was in respect to the prosecuting counsel a case of the blind leading the blind; in respect to defendants' counsel, a case of hoodwinking the Supreme Court—helping to darken its blindness.

[23] 251 U.S. 437.
[24] E.g., see in Judge Buffington's opinion, 223 Fed. Rep. 82, 89, 161; in Judge Woolley's, 171, 172, 178; in Justice McKenna's, 251 U.S. 445, 447, 449, 451.

CHAPTER VII

INTEGRATION WITHOUT INTEGRITY

UNCOVERING THE HIDDEN

WE HAVE seen how strong and clear was the first impression of all the judges that such a gigantic merger of steel enterprises must gain a large measure of unified influence over prices. But only the three dissenting in the Supreme Court adhered to this reasonable view, while the other judges (eight in all) emerged from a welter of arguments gripping the contrary conclusion. In truth the power was being constantly exercised and therefore existed. The main facts in this remarkable chapter in the masquerade of monopoly came to light years later (1920-1923) in the hearings on the Pittsburgh-Plus complaint before the Federal Trade Commission. With slight interruptions, from the time of its formation in 1901, the Corporation was the ringleader in a gigantic conspiracy in restraint of trade and in an artificial system of price maintenance. This was continuing under the eyes of the Court as it was pronouncing its pardon for past errors and exonerating the accused from all charges of present power or efforts to restrain trade. While lacking in part the cruder features of the methods followed in earlier price wars, this method was as effective in giving substantial results. The Standard Oil in its balmiest days never got better ones. Results—that was what business wanted; how it got them was to it "merely an academic question."

COMPETITION AMONG VARIOUS GROUPS

What has economic theory to say as to the effect a vast combination of formerly competing concerns may have in restricting trade? Is it in effect "a continuing violation of the statute"—as the

judges unanimously thought on first glance it must be? The full
answer (which is in the affirmative) is a part of the general theory
of market prices and market areas. This chapter will seek to indicate merely how in some concrete ways the Steel Combination
must effectually have altered the formerly operating forces of
competition.

The some hundreds of steel plants composing the Combination
were of different sorts and produced a variety of steel products,
some plants only one main class, other large plants several classes
of products. The main classes of steel products (while there are
great numbers of patterns, sizes, and varieties in each class) are:
rails, plates, shapes, bars, tubes (pipe), and wire. The Combination
included also a number of cement plants, as well as numerous
fabricating plants for turning out such products as bridges, steel
cars, and tin plates.[1]

Now the question of competition divides into as many special
questions as there are main classes of steel plants; for, except in
some remote way, rail mills cannot be said to be competitors of
plate, bar, tube, or wire mills, or tin-plate mills with bridge factories. So it is chiefly, if not solely, with the mutual competition
of plants of each general class that we are concerned in a consideration of the effects of the merger of separate plants under the
single control of the Corporation. However, in the testimony and
in the briefs and opinions, only the faintest traces (if any) of such
a distinction appear.

AGAIN SEEKING INTENT

In the prevailing opinions little time is spent on the question
whether the effect of the merger was to give monopolistic power
to the Corporation.[2] Even that little is merely an "inquiry whether
it was formed *in order to* so monopolize or restrain trade," [3] or to
answer the question, "Was an intent to monopolize or to unduly

---

[1] It had, besides, many plants producing pig iron, which is in large measure
a raw material for the steel business; but our subject now is steel prices, and
as the sale of pig iron has been conducted and determined by very different
policies from the sale of steel—much more in accord with normal market conditions—we leave out of consideration pig-iron price policy.

[2] See Judge Buffington's opinion, 223 Fed. Rep. mostly pp. 114-154; Justice
Woolley's, *idem*, pp. 166-170; Justice McKenna's, 251 U.S. 452-454.

[3] Judge Buffington, 223 Fed. Rep. 114. Our italics.

restrain trade shown by the circumstances which led up to and surrounded the organization of the Corporation?" [4] Here again, as
in the Standard Oil case, the legal mind is engrossed with the
question of "intent" to monopolize, almost completely disregard-
ing the question of actual economic power to monopolize. An
enormous amount of evidence had been introduced regarding the
conversations and negotiations of Messrs. Morgan, Schwab, Carnegie, *et al.*, preceding the first merger in 1901, and with President
Roosevelt regarding the purchase, in 1907, of the Tennessee Coal
and Iron Company. The two opinions in the lower court analyzed
these *ex parte* statements at length but arrived at opposite conclusions. Judge Buffington (Judge McPherson concurring) found
the "formers" of the Corporation guiltless of any intent to
monopolize:

we cannot but feel, in the light of the proofs, that (the various purchases) were made in fair business course, and were, to use the language
of the Supreme Court in the Standard Oil Case, "the honest exertion
of one's right to contract for his own benefit, unaccompanied by a
wrongful motive to injure others." [5]

Judge Woolley (Judge Hunt concurring), from the same evidence, drew the opposite conclusion as to intent, or purpose:

I am of opinion that the circumstances which led up to and surrounded the organization of the Steel Corporation show that those who
organized the Steel Corporation intended it to monopolize and unduly
restrain trade. [6]

INTEGRATION WITH HONEST FACE

In examining the evidence as to intent, Judge Buffington was
greatly impressed with "the tendency of the steel business (from
the '80's on) towards concentration, combination, rounding up, or
continuity of operation (p. 123). "From these figures the insistent
necessity of integration in the steel business will be seen" (p. 125).
These ideas reënforced his conviction, earlier expressed, that "the
iron and steel trade of the United States has been a gradual sustained evolution" (p. 121). As proofs of this he saw the "rapid
and widespread fever of integration by consolidation that took

---

[4] Judge Woolley, *idem*, p. 166.   [5] *Idem*, p. 150.   [6] *Idem*, p. 171.

place toward the close of the century," notably the formation of
the constituent companies, the Carnegie Steel and the Illinois Steel,
which then formed the Federal Steel (pp. 127-131). By integration
is here meant carrying the process of manufacture continuously
under one ownership and management "back to the base of supply
and also into more diversified and extended finished product" (p.
131). If integration was the motive, then monopoly was not—so
ran the judicial thought. But if we find that integration was not the
motive—what then as to monopoly?

Mr. Gary had plausibly advanced this view of the purpose of
the formation of the Federal Company:

in this whole plan, . . . there was an effort made to acquire property
that would be useful to each other, and by that I mean to acquire a plant
that furnished certain commodities to another plant which we were acquiring and to acquire—the latter because it could, at good advantage,
secure the products which it needed for its uses, and so all through the
line, from the ore down to the conversion from one product into another and the final distribution of the finished product.[7]

Judge Buffington said of this and other similar testimony:

All of which seems to strengthen and confirm the conclusion of the
insistent requirement of integration in the steel trade at the close of the
century.[8]

Further he said:

That this plan of integration in varied products—and nothing in excess of the required integration—was carried out is also shown by the
proofs.[9]

The "proofs" consist of assertions in manifest conflict with the
facts, made by officials of the Corporation. The Judge therefore
believed "that integration along manufacturing lines" was one of
the important "avowed purposes of those who formed the Steel
Corporation," and this combines with other testimony to convince
him "that monopoly of the steel and iron business was not the
purpose for which that corporation was formed." [10]

[7] 223 Fed. Rep. 141, citing Testimony, Vol. 12, p. 4751.
[8] *Idem*, p. 129.
[9] *Idem*, p. 138, and see especially pp. 138-141.
[10] *Idem*, pp. 141-142.

THE HONEST FACE DECEIVES THE COURT

Judges Woolley and Hunt are more suspicious. They are impressed in the explanations of Messrs. Schwab, Morgan, *et al.*, with respect to the objects in view, by such

conspicuous features . . . [as] overcapitalization, and the elimination of competition, . . . in seeking the purposes for which the corporation was organized. That evidence, as against the testimony to the contrary, impels me to the opinion that the primary purpose of the organization of the Steel Corporation was not integration.[11]

Justice McKenna concurred "in the main" with the views of Judges Woolley and Hunt "except" on this very point:

it may be, that they underestimated the influence of the tendency and movement to integration, the appreciation of the necessity of value of the continuity of manufacture from the ore to the finished product. And there was such a tendency; and though it cannot be asserted it had become a necessity, it had certainly become a facility of industrial progress.[12]

Justice McKenna, agreeing rather with Judge Buffington in this matter, approvingly summarized his conclusions in these words:

The corporation, in the view of the opinion, was an evolution, a natural consummation of the tendencies of the industry on account of changing conditions, practically a compulsion from "the metallurgical method of making steel and the physical method of handling it," this method, and the conditions consequent upon it, tending to combinations of capital and energies rather than diffusion in independent action . . . The tendency of the industry and the purpose of the corporation in yielding to it were expressed in comprehensive condensation by the word "integration," which signifies continuity in the processes of the industry from ore mines to the finished product.[13]

BEHIND THE MASK

Thus it is plain that belief in the economy, value, facility, and *probable* necessity of integration tipped the scales heavily to the final decision not to dissolve the Corporation. It appreciably confirmed the plurality in the view that dissolution would check a natural evolution of industry toward greater efficiency and lower

[11] *Idem,* p. 169. [12] 251 U.S. 442. [13] *Idem,* pp. 437-438.

costs, which, given complete competition, which was assumed, eventually would lead to lower prices to the public. The Court was attempting to justify in the name of integration something essentially different and was postulating competition where it was a contradiction in terms. In the course of the discussion the economies of integration become confused with two quite different ideas: first, with the advantages of large production in a single plant; second, with the advantages (indeed the supposed necessity) of horizontal merger under one ownership of numerous like plants in diverse localities.

By this confusion, the virtues and evolutionary necessity of technical integration are transferred as an economic halo to the graceless head of the combination of competitors in restraint of trade.[14]

There are no doubt technical and resulting economic advantages of (vertical) integration of processes within a single plant, in some cases. To show them, much testimony was collected, of which many extracts appear in the opinion.[15] Greatest stress is laid upon inventions (such as the Jones mixer) by which the fluid pig iron could be used in Bessemer converters or open-hearth furnaces without cooling and remelting. This is real technological integration in a single plant, but most of the remainder of the evidence relates to vertical financial merger of physically separate plants— the advantage on the one hand of steel fabricators' being able to produce for themselves a regular supply of crude (or partly fabricated) material, and on the other hand of steel producers at stages of the process nearer the ores having, without uncertainty or selling costs, a more regular outlet for their products. All this evidence is irrelevant to the question whether the formation of the gigantic combination by horizontal financial merger of *like* plants in 1901 was a necessity and a great technical economy, though the Court assumes that it is relevant.[16]

---

[14] Further details are given in Appendix A to Ch. VII.

[15] E.g., 223 Fed. Rep. 117-145 *passim.*

[16] Other reasons for its irrelevancy are: First, the evidence related almost exclusively to the period from 1880 to 1900 (particularly the '90's), during which time vertical integration had been almost completely realized in the much smaller constituent companies which were merged into the Corporation. Second, integration could be attained and perfected with apparently as great completeness by concerns much smaller than the great Corporation; as further discussed in the text.

JUDICIAL SOMERSAULTS

In discussing integration each Court contradicts itself in different parts of the same opinion. Most of the discussion bears on the question whether large size and apparently overshadowing power are necessary conditions of evolution toward efficiency, and the answer both of the Circuit and of the Supreme Court in substance is in the affirmative (by Judge· Buffington explicitly so, and by Justice McKenna and his colleagues, so in effect). But when the question under consideration is whether genuine, active, effective competition has existed after the formation of the Corporation, the argument of the witnesses, of defendant's counsel, and of the Court, is reversed with eagerness to show that so-called competitors only a fraction of the size of the Corporation are as thoroughly integrated and quite as efficient. This leads to the conclusion that the Corporation, even if it had the purpose, has not the power "to throttle the growth" of competitors which, though much smaller, are quite as efficient as it is. In hundreds of pages of testimony "competitors" emphatically assured the Court that they were, by virtue of thorough integration, and their resulting technical efficiency, abundantly able to meet the great Corporation on any plane of competition.

These witnesses, skillfully selected and guided, succeeded in convincing the more impressionable judges in the lower Court of two directly contradictory propositions; the formation of the Combination *did*, and at the same time *did not*, lead to greatly increased technical efficiency. The illogical shift from the notion of the necessity of "integration" to that of its futility is, at some points in the opinion, swift and startling! [17]

FALSE INFERENCE

What becomes of the notion that the formation of the Corporation was a great, and the only possible, step forward in technical efficiency? Judge Buffington forgets this issue and goes on to argue that inasmuch as efficiency was not the result of the formation of the Corporation, monopoly was not the purpose. Is there any logical connection between the premise and this conclusion? None

---

[17] Further evidence of this shift is given in Appendix B to Ch. VII.

whatsoever, except as disproof. If Judge Buffington's revised view was correct, that the Corporation was not more efficient technically, and as these shrewd practical men may be assumed to have known what they were about, is not the more probable inference that their real reason was something else than the one they professed? That it was to gain greater control of prices was the view taken sanely by the three dissenting Justices. It was also the view taken by Judges Woolley and Hunt who (as to this point) more consistently held that the "purpose" was monopoly; but they mistakenly believed it failed for lack of power; "the constituent companies absorbed by the corporation were strongest at their birth." [18] The plurality of the Supreme Court, however, in this instance, preferred to loop the loop with Judge Buffington.

A FANTASY OF MASS SPECIALIZATION

Confused also throughout the discussions of the advantages of integration was the idea of plant specialization—that is, the advantages of large production of a single product at a single plant. This idea showed itself in the oft-cited version of the siren song in which Mr. Schwab lured the financial affections of the willing Mr. J. P. Morgan. Mr. Schwab said in that fateful address in New York on December 13, 1900, to which Mr. Morgan listened with such entrancement:

I believed that the next great step in economical manufacture was to so regulate the business and plants of the business in manufacturing on a larger scale than had ever been attempted heretofore; that instead, as was then the practice, of having one mill to make 10 or 20 or 50 products, the greatest economy would result from having one mill make one product, and make that product continuously.[19]

The examples given show that by one product is meant not merely a general class such as steel products, or a somewhat narrower class such as "structural steels," but an extremely narrow class such as "angles exclusively," "beams exclusively," "and so forth," also

bridges and other fabricated materials . . . steel cars, and one kind of steel cars . . . passenger cars, for example, as being different from

[18] 223 Fed. Rep. 170. [19] 223 Fed. Rep. 117.

freight cars, two separate works, as following out this general line of policy, would have to be built and so operated.

Incidentally thrown in, is the suggestion

that great economies would result from locating mills [evidently each one of these fabricating mills] at the point of consumption, by which the cost of transporting the finished material to the point of consumption would in many cases be reduced or saved.[20]

MASS PRODUCTION VS. FREIGHT COSTS

Now despite the authority of Mr. Schwab as a master ironmaker, he has here confused two opposite economic aspects of the problem of large production, one its technical advantages at the plant, the other its limits and disadvantages in marketing the product. His doctrine of the marvelous efficiency of large production to be developed without limits ignores the simple principle that specialization is limited by "the extent of the market," that is, by the amount that can be sold profitably from one plant. Decreasing unit-cost of manufacture by mass production at one place is offset by steadily rising cost of shipment to points of consumption over wider areas. In producing heavy products especially the limit of net advantages in mass production at one plant is quickly reached. At that point it becomes more efficient, not less so, to produce some variety of products nearer the consumers rather than in plants more narrowly specializing. When Mr. Schwab incidentally later recognized "the advantages of scattered duplicate mills" he was refuting his main argument. He was following the Biblical injunction—literally though not in spirit—not to let his left hand know what his right hand doeth. But his evidence "went over great" with the Court, which hearkened trustfully to the words of the oracle of big business.

DOES MERGER "SAVE FREIGHT"?

The argument on integration turns at some points on the (supposed) economic necessity, in order to save freights, of uniting, under one ownership, plants turning out *like* products, but in different territory:

[20] Cited by Judge Buffington, 223 Fed. Rep. 117.

The proofs also show it is necessary to have structural plants in different localities. In that regard and referring only to the Middle West equipment, the proof is that the American Bridge Company has in the West [here quoting from defendants' testimony, Vol. 10, p. 3961] "a plant at Toledo, one at Ambridge (Pittsburgh), one at Gary, Ind., a large plant and a comparatively new plant; one at Chicago, one in Minneapolis, one in St. Louis, and one in Detroit . . . It is a zone business more or less." A zone business is a "business within 300 or 400 miles of where the plant is located. It is a question of freight rates." [21]

All of this is in its economic analysis and implications a veritable welter of half truths, untruths, and distorted truths, pervaded with the belief, developed for the purpose, and leading to the conclusion, that these mergers of like plants were part of a process of integration, and that integration was a natural economic and commendable evolution of industry and justified the formation of the U.S. Steel Corporation, and in no way influenced or diminished the forces of competition. These statements so exaggerate the effect of stabilizing freight rates and abolishing rebates that this alone must falsify the conclusion. Of course, the need to pay any freight whatever to that extent locally restricts "the market" (more accurately, the profitable sales area) of any factory. Every business, but particularly one whose products are heavy, to some degree is a "zone business." Illegal rebates had only partly modified this restriction to the plants whose owners were thus favored, enabling them to sell farther away from their mills on a delivered price and to ship into territory where otherwise their smaller competitors would have been able to survive.

BETTER STOP DISCRIMINATION

It is a dangerous half truth that the only way of "overcoming the regular freight rate" is by horizontal merger, for its true meaning can be only this: either that goods have been sold at discriminatory prices or that illegal rebates have enabled a mill to sell in territory where otherwise it would have been unable to sell profitably. When these rebates are stopped, the only way the mill can "overcome" the new (that is, return to the old illegally created) condi-

[21] *Idem*, p. 132.

tions is to acquire a mill in that territory! Or discrimination may
have been practiced by local price cutting, and such merger to
reduce this discrimination is called a natural "tendency to integration"! But the advantage resulting from this is quite different from
that of integration; it is often spoken of in the testimony as "a
saving of freight." But clearly the "saving of freight" is there,
whoever owns the duplicate plant before the merger. The so-called
"saving" is the result merely of the nearness of the mill to the
customer (point of delivery)—a geographical fact, not a technological fact of greater efficiency resulting from merger. The
freight is in no way "saved" to the public when two or more competing plants which have been cutting prices locally are merged
into a single corporation. The "saving" is simply added to monopolistic profits. If all discrimination were stopped by legal action,
the "saving" would come to the public in lower prices.

THE MARVELS OF LOGICAL CATALYSIS

The use of the integration argument in the suit was analogous to
that of a catalyst in a chemical process, helping to transform and
energize other arguments which would have been inert but for
its presence, but in the end forming no part of the product. Thus
the supposed need of integration (of the kind and on the scale
occurring in this combination) strongly helped to persuade the
judges to accept at face value the flimsy explanation of the
"formers" of the Corporation and to acquit them of any purpose or
intent to control prices and restrain trade. It invested this mainly
horizontal merger with a halo of merit and sanction as a great
and needed advance step in technical efficiency and in social
economy. This merit and sanction was, in the process of confused
thinking, diffused over the essentially different process of the
merging of great numbers of like plants in scattered locations, and
this too became (in the minds of the judges) a great and necessary
advance step in technical efficiency, assumed to be without any
effect whatever in the direction of restraint of competition. Particularly the great economies of "integration" (plus gigantic
merger) appeared to the judges to have been the necessary condition for the large development of foreign business in steel (mostly
through dumping) and to have had this (as it seemed to the

judges) admirable and beneficial result. These remarkable illogical transformations being completed, the notion of the great technical benefits and need of integration (plus merger on so large a scale and in this particular case) drops out of the reasoning. The judges make the discovery through other evidence (or think they do) that the "integration" of this corporation (even with its overtowering financial power and alliances) had somehow left it weaker competitively than many of the smaller independents, unable to stem their steady growth at a greater *rate* than its own, unable without their willing coöperation to restrain competition in any manner whatever. These opinions should necessitate a revision of the earlier arguments on integration, but the sophistical catalyst had done its work and forms no part of the final judgment.

OTHER INFLUENCES IN THE ARGUMENT

These later conclusions are mainly inconsistent deductions from a quite different line of evidence. This now, in its turn, it is our task to examine. This evidence was all directed to persuading, and did persuade, the judges who voted for vindication to accept the astonishing proposition that during the nineteen years of its existence (1901-1920) the accused Corporation and its subsidiaries had never, by reason of size, integration, and combination of formerly competing plants, possessed any power or exercised any influence over prices. These judges conceded that in the first ten years (1901-1911) there had been numerous restraints of trade by agreement in which the Corporation acted only with the same power and in the same way as did any of its smaller competitors. But these old lapses were to be forgiven and forgotten. Since 1911 "no adventitious interference was employed to either fix or maintain prices and . . . they were constant or varied according to natural conditions," [22] apparently meaning: in the way prices would behave if the great steel combine had never been formed, or if it were dissolved into its constituent elements. Thus was completely evaded the question whether, by the merger, competition was restricted among the constituent plants of the Corporation. We have in the next chapter to examine the reality of its competition with the independents.

[22] 251 U.S. 449.

CHAPTER VIII

THE GIANT WEAKLING

MORE DRAFTS ON CREDULITY

IT TAKES some credulity to believe that the units in the steel combine went on competing just as fully as if they had not been combined. After that, Baron Munchausen must sound as tame as a Rollo book, and *Gulliver's Travels* be but a bedtime story. After that, the proposition that the members of such a combination would go on competing as fully with the remaining independents and they as fully with each other as if no combination had been formed, should present hardly more difficulty than the axiom that the greater includes the less. But the lawyers of the Steel Corporation took no chances, and not anticipating how easily their victory would be won, they skillfully marshaled a mass of evidence to convince the Court of the truth of these propositions. The testimony was mainly of two kinds, or from two sources: first, from independents (supposedly free to compete); second, from customers (supposedly free to testify). Against such testimony the prosecution made a truly pitiable showing, in view of the real situation as it is now known. This evidence was supplemented by some other. In a negative way of rebuttal were presented statistics as to the relative upward trends of steel prices and other prices after 1901, and further, some opinions from professed experts to the effect that the Corporation had no power by itself to restrain trade in any manner or degree. Various other matters were touched upon in this connection, but most of them were of minor importance.

FIGURES DON'T LIE, BUT—

Very impressive, no doubt, were statistics of the rate of the Corporation's growth relative to that of all others taken together. They were appealed to repeatedly and confidently by the defense, and cited trustingly in the vindicating court opinions. This evidence weighed heavily in the scales of judgment. There is no need to burden the reader with masses of statistics. The bare figures are not in dispute, but only their significance. The salient facts are these: The Corporation had grown (absolutely, in tonnage produced) 34 per cent, but all other companies combined had grown 59 per cent. (The opinion says, at one point, 40 per cent.) Certain independents had increased their own production by much greater percentages, two between 63 and 91 per cent, four between 153 and 463 per cent, one (the Inland Steel) by 1,496 per cent, and one (the Bethlehem Steel) by the startling figure of 3,780 per cent. The Corporation's proportion of the total national output (relative growth), however, had declined. The Corporation's proportion of the total in 1901 was 50.1, but in 1911 had fallen to 45.7. Conversely, all other (so-called) competitors in 1901 produced 49.9 per cent of the total, and in 1911 54.3 per cent.

WHAT DO THEY PROVE?

These figures were accepted in the prevailing opinions as very significant. What were they taken to signify? The disproof of any monopolistic power residing in the Corporation or of any participation by it in restraint of trade; nothing less.[1]

Yet this idea must in the light of economic analysis of the situation be rejected. It results from ignoring the simple truth that monopoly is always a limited and relative power, shading off in various directions, according to freight-costs, as well as to other conditions, such as styles, patterns, service, financial resources, etc. A fuller elucidation of this problem is a part of the theory of markets and market sales-areas but it is worth our while to look at some aspects of the subject in the present connection.

It is obviously illogical to infer from the growth of competitors in outlying regions of the country, where the Corporation has no

---

[1] See Appendix A to Ch. VIII on the false conclusions drawn from these statistics.

plants, that it has no power whatever to restrain trade in the region where its plants are located. In principle this is as false as it would be to infer from the growth of plants in Germany or in Belgium that a corporation controlling the entire product of the United States had no monopoly power. The difference is one of degree and not one of principle. Such plants as the Bethlehem Steel, the Colorado Company at Pueblo, the Lackawanna Steel at Buffalo, are separated by hundreds or by thousands of miles from the nearest plant of the Corporation producing the same kind of goods. The most notable exception to this statement is Jones and Laughlin at Pittsburgh, whose coöperation with the Corporation in price policies has been notoriously harmonious.

THE CENTER OF MONOPOLY

It was said in 1907 of the geographical distribution of the some two hundred plants in the Corporation:

> Its iron-works and steel-works are mainly in Pittsburgh and twenty-five smaller steel cities within a hundred miles' distance; but it also owns large plants in Chicago, Joliet, Milwaukee, St. Louis, Worcester, and elsewhere. It is about to create a new industrial center (Gary) at the southern end of Lake Michigan.[2]

The year this was written the Corporation acquired also the Tennessee Coal, Iron and Railroad Company, whose plants were at or near Birmingham, Ala. After the building of Gary the Corporation's production of steel of the more basic forms was in a measure approximating 95 per cent confined to the two districts, Pittsburgh and Chicago, with small outlying plants at Duluth and Birmingham; at the other outlying cities mentioned it had fabricating plants (whose products were not so fitted for standardization either as to quality or prices). Within this great elliptical empire of steel, with Pittsburgh at one focus and Gary at the other, the predominance of the Corporation in capacity and output was overwhelming. Outside that area, either at Chicago and westward or eastward in the old middle States (eastern Pennsylvania, New York, Maryland) protected or safeguarded by a broad zone of costly freights, occurred much the largest increase of its com-

---

[2] Casson, in 1907. *Op. cit.,* p. 219.

petitors' output, both absolutely and relatively. Nowhere in the evidence, hearings, and opinions in this suit is there any hint of any significance to these facts other than that they were taken to prove that the Corporation was "not a monopoly"!

ZONES OF RELATIVE MONOPOLY

The fact that "the steel business is a zone business" bobs in and out of the discussion; you see it when it can be used to becloud the issue (as to make it appear that a horizontal merger of like plants is necessary for "integration"), and you do not see it when it would enlighten the issue (as to show, truly, that monopoly is relative to place and limited by distance). The growth of the competitors in the aggregate all over the country does not prove the general impotence of the Corporation to dominate price policies. By the use of these percentage figures the Corporation is pictured as a comparative weakling, unable to cope with its more vigorous independent competitors, ignoring the fact that most of them are located in parts of the country where the Corporation had either no plants at all or none of the same kind.

The Courts thought it pertinent to enter into an extended inquiry to show the possibility of independents drawing ore supplies from Cuba and Brazil to plants on the Atlantic Coast where they have "in many cases substantial freight advantage over the Steel Corporation," and to show that other eastern, southern, and western companies, as the Colorado, etc., have large ore supplies of their own. Judge Buffington concludes from these facts "that the steel and iron business of this country is not being, and indeed cannot be, monopolized by the Steel Corporation." [3]

Judge Woolley also sees in these facts a proof that "the Corporation has not a monopoly of the raw materials of the steel industry," [4] implying that monopoly is absolute, therefore nonexistent unless it extends in equal degree to every portion of the national territory.

ABSOLUTE VS. RELATIVE GROWTH

The feat of convincing the Court of this economic absurdity was performed by defendants' counsel with virtuosity. The main fal-

---

[3] 223 Fed. Rep. 68-75.   [4] *Idem*, p. 163.

lacy is the rather superficial confusion of a decrease relative to competitors with an absolute decrease of size and of monopoly power. It is a statistical trick to cite as significant that in twelve years a small plant at Bethlehem increased 3780 per cent of its size in 1901, whereas the Steel Corporation, which already in 1901 was producing more steel than all Great Britain or than all Germany, increased less than 40 per cent! Start the comparison only a little earlier, and the increase at Bethlehem can be shown to be infinite! It is usually a mathematical impossibility for any older enterprise to increase at as great a *rate* per cent in a certain period as can an enterprise in its beginning years.[5]

A MYSTERIOUS PARALYSIS

Closely connected with this phase of the general argument was the notion that the Corporation lacked the power to put any one competitor out of business by local discrimination (price cutting). No specific attempt to substantiate this notion appears in the prevailing opinion of Justice McKenna, for he waves this and related matters aside with the words, "our consideration should be of not what the Corporation had power to do or did, but what it has now power to do and is doing." [6] This was but a superfluous remark, for in the next few pages he concluded that the Corporation neither was doing nor had the power to do by this or any other method anything unlawful that could put competitors out of business. Thus tacitly, the Supreme Court adopted a view which had been presented by defendants frequently throughout the hearings and which had been accepted by the lower Court, to wit, that the Corporation had no economic power to cut prices locally (at least, not enough to cripple any selected competitor seriously). It expresses the truth far better to say that because of the fear of prosecution under the Anti-Trust Act, the Corporation did not think it safe to cut prices locally though it might have had the power.

[5] Ample evidence of this confusion between absolute increase and relative increase, in the form of statements from each of three opinions, is given in Appendix B to Ch. VIII.
[6] 251 U.S. 444.

A DISASTROUS DOCTRINE

Intertwined in the reasoning of the Court's decision is the implication that "a combination in restraint of trade" is not illegal under the statute unless or until the power thus attained could be shown, by specific evidence of its results, to have been exercised. Justice McKenna said:

> The law does not make mere size an offense or the existence of unexerted power an offense. It, we repeat, requires overt acts . . . It does not compel competition nor require all that is possible.[7]

To say that "mere size" is not an offense surely ought not to mean that "unexerted power" *attained by combination of formerly competing plants* is not an offense under either the first or second section of the Anti-Trust Act. Such a doctrine is fraught with peril to the statute and disaster to the public interest. It grants immunity from prosecution to any combination not only at the time of its formation but so long as (in this case ten years), from fear of prosecution, it refrains from exerting its power. Then, by the plurality opinion, the combination may continue to enjoy immunity later, if it can convince the Court that although formed for that purpose, it is not at the moment exerting its thus acquired monopolistic power. At least that was what happened in this case, the Court being further confirmed in the justice of this conclusion by the odd notion that although the constituent combinations undoubtedly had great monopolistic powers, these collective powers vanished the moment the supercombination had been formed! If the real ground of the decision was that the combination had no monopoly power, is not the proposition about "unexerted power" a mere *obiter dictum* in this case? Yet it has been repeatedly cited in later briefs to justify monopoly attained by merger.

A CONFIDENT INDEPENDENT

The groundwork for the reasoning and conclusion that the Corporation had not the power to cripple its competitors by local price cutting was carefully laid by defendants' counsel by means of opinions that in the very nature of market conditions and relations in the industry the Steel Corporation could have no such power,

[7] *Idem*, p. 451.

and of statements by leading independents (who obviously had not been put out of business) that they "thought" the Corporation could not put them out of business if it tried. These pseudo-practical opinions of "independents" are, however, all expressed in nearly the same words used in the testimony of the chief theoretical expert witness, as if they were reciting an agreed formula. The Court feels the hairy hand of the practical Esau but hears the dulcet voice of the academic Jacob. The evidence and argument on this point are discussed at length only by Judge Buffington, but his conclusions are implied and embodied in the two other prevailing opinions. The conclusions, as we shall show, are thoroughly unsound in economics.

The president of the Cambria Steel Company of Johnstown, Pa., goes upon the stand and gives testimony which the Court said was "enlightening as showing that his and other companies in the steel business feel that the Steel Corporation has no power, even if it disposes, to monopolize, restrain, or stop their business." The witness made sweeping and confident claims that any one of a number of smaller companies, including his own, could compete successfully with the U.S. Steel because "fully the equal" in efficiency and experiencing "absolutely no difficulty in producing the various products at practically the same cost."

The witness assented to the proposition that the Steel Corporation has no such advantage.

as would enable it to put its competitors out of business . . . impossible to do so without committing suicide . . . could not confine destructive warfare to any one competitor . . . because the markets are all affected in sympathy, and, if the price was made below cost in one market only . . . we would seek other markets . . . You cannot affect the price in one market without affecting it in all the other markets in the country.[8]

This testimony, if correct, was an obvious disproof of the claims that the great combination was a technical necessity of progress. The industrious but brain-fagged Judge Buffington first cited this evidence impressively to prove that the Corporation was no more efficient than its small competitors, and then ignored it when a few pages later he came to examine the evidence which led him

[8] 223 Fed. Rep. 71-72.

to his erroneous opinion regarding the "necessity" of the integration.

ZONE BUSINESS MARKETS "ALL OVER"!

Comes, too, the president of the Republic Iron and Steel Company, of Youngstown, Ohio, which, the Court says, had "practically eliminated all its scattered iron mills and concentrated them in operation at a few points of production," producing now little iron but about a million tons of steel per annum. His testimony (which the Court pronounces "instructive") announces with a bang an astonishing doctrine of "markets" for a zone business. He affirmed that the "market" for his product is

all over the United States and Canada. The Steel Corporation has not power to put the Republic out of business . . . or its competitors generally, or any of its principal competitors . . . [because], one, it has not the physical ability, and secondly, it would involve its own market . . . [and] suffer equally with us.[9]

He then explained that by physical ability he meant technical efficiency, through integration, together with management and financing, and explained that all "markets" are involved because every company is compelled to sell steel to every one of its customers as cheap as to every other, for if it did not it "would probably soon hear from" the one charged more, "because these two men would naturally compete in the general market of the United States with their machinery."

This leaves the impression that any customer who found that he was paying more to a factory for steel than another customer had but to call the seller's attention to the fact to have the discrimination corrected—a preposterous statement. In fact, for twenty years many enterprising customers had vainly sought in a variety of ingenious, legal, and justifiable ways to escape from the consequences of such discrimination. The witness continued with a mingling of truth and error:

the markets are interrelated and interlaced to such an extent that you cannot reduce prices, in my judgment, in one market, without affecting in a short time the market elsewhere for the same commodity.[10]

[9] 223 Fed. Rep. 73-74.   [10] *Idem,* p. 74.

The attempt of counsel to get a stronger statement elicited only a reiteration from the witness that the Steel Corporation could not localize a destructive warfare against its competitors.

MR. SCHWAB PROUD AND CONFIDENT

To the same effect spoke Charles M. Schwab, once president of the Steel Corporation, now the head of one of the largest independents, the Bethlehem Steel Company. He went even further and developed the paradoxical idea that the size and strength of the giant Corporation made it even weaker than a small independent in this sort of competition. Secure in his protective zone of freight rates, he replied proudly and confidently, "It could not put me out of business, even if it desired."

Judge Lindabury, chief counsel for the Corporation, explained that he was "speaking, of course, of power, not of inclination," and Mr. Schwab finally replied:

I think it would be easier for a large independent to attack a smaller manufacturer in his district than it would for the Steel Corporation to do so . . . Because the business of the independent is so circumscribed to the locality within which his competitor would be located; while if the Steel Corporation expected to do it they would have to extend their operations over a greater field, following the same policy that they always have followed.[11]

Observe, the witness referred to this as indicating merely the "policy," not the limited power, of the Corporation. (This no doubt referred to the basing-point policy.) The examining lawyer, however, sensed the danger in this suggestion and therefore quickly shifted his questions so as to bring out the contrast between those wicked old days when the old constituent companies spanked the babies so hard that they died, with these gentle times when the Corporation runs a children's hospital. Mr. Schwab's answer is quoted in another connection in the following chapter.

SOME BAD ACADEMIC THEORY

From so-called practical witnesses there is more testimony to the same general effect, that the Corporation had no more power

[11] See Transcript of Record, Defendants' Testimony, Vol. 11, p. 4191.

over price policies than any little independent. Most of it implies a complete ignoring of freight limitations in the steel business. It pictures the steel industry as not a "zone business"—its products can be sold from each mill everywhere as, indeed, under the basing-point conspiracy to sell at identical delivered prices was the case. But there was nothing in the statement of this theory to limit its application to steel; it applies equally well—or by the same bad logic—to every conceivable business. But the completest formulation of this paradoxical argument was made by the academic witness who no doubt had supplied counsel with the model on which all the like testimony was patterned. He declared that although local price cutting against particular competitors was easy to practice in other businesses, it was simply impossible in the steel business. The interested reader may consult in the Appendix a summary of this astounding testimony.[12]

This academic version of the doctrine thus expounded is even more confused than that of the practical witnesses. They, as a result of wide experience, of course knew well that the "market" (sales-territory) for the products of a steel mill does not extend equally all over the country except as the result of agreed restraint of competition from other mills. If the cross-examination had been guided by an understanding of the real economic situation, it must have elicited from these witnesses the admission of certain simple facts which would have exploded the hydrogen in this argument. The sale of any standardized product such as steel to all parts of the country from one mill is impossible except under a policy of artificial identical delivered prices, and this involves an agreement, tacit or open, among sellers, and a restraint of trade. The net realized prices are very far from uniform, being highest near the mill. It is not economic normalcy, it is economic absurdity, for mills to sell and make cross shipments into each other's "natural" territory. This that was happening in the steel industry was the result of the Corporation's domination, not the proof of its powerlessness.

[12] See Appendix C to Ch. VIII.

WHY LACKING "INCLINATION"

Undoubtedly the Corporation had the "power" to kill off many of its smaller competitors in various parts of the country. Then why did it not do so? That it did not, for more than brief periods, employ the old cutthroat methods was pretty certain. By the courts this fact was referred to as if it banished from their mind any lingering doubts as to the powerlessness of the Corporation. The lenient attitude of the Corporation can be simply explained by its fear of the law. The leaders of the combination were shrewd men: they knew that with the Anti-Trust Act in force, and an aroused public resentment, the day of such strong-arm tactics was past. They feared the legal consequences. The Anti-Trust Act was so far effective that it put the fear of the law into the Steel Trust so that it hesitated to slay its smaller competitors with a club. This change in the situation was more promptly and clearly recognized by the founders of the Steel Corporation than by most other trust magnates (though likewise by the Standard Oil, for the violent deeds for which it was condemned in 1911 had mostly occurred before 1900). Even with its ostensible policy of benevolence toward competitors the Corporation barely squeaked through with an acquittal.

A FAMOUS VICTORY

But this new fear of the law did not mean the assurance of free competition and of unrestrained trade, as the public and the courts had believed it would. Far from it. By other means the combination was able to attain in large measure, if not completely, the purpose of its organization, and it proceeded to make prompt use of them. It is hardly doubtful that if the judges had known the truth as to the basing-point practice, they would have pronounced a different verdict. The plurality voted to vindicate the giant combination because they were persuaded that it was not only innocent of all attempts to control prices after 1911 and up to the moment of the decree of 1920, but because they believed it to be powerless to do so or even to bring any pressure upon the independents (by penalty or reward) to enter with it into any form of agreement, explicit or tacit. The Corporation was an amiable

Gulliver, bound and helpless among the Lilliputians. It was giant in size but a pigmy in strength. How the successful litigants must have roared with laughter over these naïve economic views as they got together—corporation lawyers, Steel Trust officials, and fellow conspiring-independents—to celebrate and revel in their famous victory.

PART III

THE MILLENNIUM OF METAL MONOPOLISTS

CHAPTER IX

BE GOOD AND YOU'LL BE HAPPY

FAITH AND INNOCENCE

THE keystone in the arch of reasoning over which the Court passed to a verdict of vindication for the Corporation at the bar was belief in the absence (at least after 1911) of any means or acts of restraint of competition in the steel industry. It was a belief in the prevalence, complete and unconfined in area, of a régime of real markets and market prices determined by the workings of "demand and supply." Let us examine further the evidence and reasoning on which this faith of the Court was built. The evidence was of both an affirmative and a negative nature— affirmative in the direct testimony of numerous supposed competitors and of customers that in their opinion competition was real and active in the steel industry, and negative in that the prosecution (if it even tried) did not succeed in getting any independents or customers to testify to the contrary.[1]

It is now known that both the affirmative testimony and the inferences from it were false. There was in fact among the sellers to all intents and purposes an understanding and agreement as to price policy—the Pittsburgh-Plus plan—though a loose use of words doubtless relieved their consciences from a sense of guilt for misstatements made under oath. There was on the part of buyers (customers) generally a misunderstanding of the real nature of the price policy in operation, and also in the case of many of the fabricators testifying (who seem to have been skilfully selected)

---

[1] See Appendix A to Ch. IX for the testimony that impressed the Courts.

a selfish bias in favor of the price policy in force as against their competitors.

ARTFUL MINGLING OF TRUTH AND ERROR

The government's case was built upon the assumption that the Corporation had a dominating power, not that it was merely one co-equal conspirator among the others. Government counsel suggested in accord with this view that the general acceptance by the independents of the Corporation's prices was but another evidence of its power, but the Court rejected this view in favor of its opposite; namely, that it was rather an evidence of weakness—the Corporation "did not have power in and of itself, and the control it exerted (i.e. before 1911) was only in and by association with its competitors." [2] Justice McKenna referred unfavorably to government counsel's suggestion thus:

In one [paradox] competitors (the independents) are represented as oppressed by the superior power of the Corporation; in the other they are represented as ascending to opulence by imitating that power's prices which they could not do if at disadvantage from the other conditions of competition; and yet confederated action is not asserted. If it were this suit would take on another cast. The competitors would cease to be the victims of the Corporation and would become its accomplices. And there is no other alternative. [3]

The failure of the prosecution to assert confederated action was one of the worst of its many blunders—but this was not Justice McKenna's thought. He sees in the admitted fact of confederated action (before 1911) only a proof of the weakness of the Corporation, and he refers to the suggestion of confederated action after 1911 with the implication of its self-evident absurdity. It is true, he says, that if confederated action were asserted the suit would have taken on "another cast." But it is clearly not true, as he assumes, that there is "no other alternative" between being victims or willing, co-equal accomplices. Surely both common experience and court records daily disclose situations where accomplices are also in a measure victims—are more or less coerced into becoming accomplices. Many an Oliver Twist is victim of some Fagin.

[2] 251 U.S. 441, 446, 448; see also on this point above, Ch. VI.
[3] *Idem*, p. 449.

Further, is not an artful mingling of fear and reward, of force and favors, usually a more effective way than force alone for a leader—though the stronger—to secure compliance with his will? Accomplices may be in a measure victims, and fear may be mingled with rewards to enforce coöperation. Here are alternative explanations which the Court dismisses summarily, either of which would have given the case a very different cast. The Court was in the dark as to the real nature of the prices charged. They were not, as the Court was led to believe, general uniform market prices, but rather a complex system of discriminatory prices, which involved concerted action by all the independents to conform with (and to abstain from competing to reduce) the delivered prices named by the Corporation.

STICKING TO SO-CALLED MARKET PRICES

The Court was impressed by the testimony (as set forth, for example, by Mr. Schwab) that it was the practice of the Steel Corporation to name its prices openly in the trade journals and to "stick to these prices, throughout the trade." It was not observed by the Court, however, that these published prices were not uniform mill-base prices, but Pittsburgh base prices which, by the addition of freight, immediately became a national system of Pittsburgh-Plus delivered prices, identically quoted by all the independents as well as by all the mills of the Corporation wherever located (at Birmingham partially modified). The Court attached much importance to the expressions of the witnesses representing six different independents.[4]

There is no mystery to us today in what was a sealed book to the Court. It meant in the case of rails a "tacit" understanding as to uniform price at all mills, unvarying over long periods of time; it meant in the case of other steel products that each independent was adhering to a system whereby its prices *at* its mill were the Pittsburgh mill-base price plus freight cost to its mill—while its *delivered* prices everywhere else were determined by the mere announcement of the Corporation's Pittsburgh price. Observe too that this meant that every independent mill (not at Pittsburgh) was systematically discriminating among its own customers as to

[4] Examples are quoted in Appendix B to Ch. IX.

its mill prices, and faithfully abstaining from lowering its prices to all that sales-territory where it had a natural freight advantage. If that was not the negation, denial, and defeat of real price competition, there never could be such a thing as restraint of trade.

WHAT IS PITTSBURGH-PLUS?

It is not quite the time or place for the systematic discussion of the nature and the history of the Pittsburgh-Plus practice, but it will help the understanding of what follows if we here define it. Pittsburgh-Plus is the term used first for a certain *method* of delivered price quotation in the steel industry, next for the actual *delivered price* at which a particular shipment of steel is sold, and finally for the *system* of prices resulting, in their territorial relations.

Pittsburgh-Plus as a *method of quotation* is the quoting to their customers by mills outside of Pittsburgh of delivered prices made up of a Pittsburgh base price for goods, plus the freight that would have to be paid on those goods if they actually had to be shipped from Pittsburgh to their destination. The Pittsburgh-Plus *system* of steel pricing is used to embrace, together with the system of actual prices, the whole complex of explicit and tacit understandings bringing about and maintaining prices more or less closely in accord with this method of quotations.[5]

THE REAL SITUATION

We here find the explanation of the ever-recurring assertion of the all-too-friendly independent witnesses that their "markets"

---

[5] In Figure 4 are shown the main features of the plan of pricing on a simple profile, and in the frontispiece these features are shown more elaborately in perspective. All mills at Pittsburgh sell at the base price announced by the Steel Corporation, plus actual freight to destination. The *net realized price* of Pittsburgh mills is always exactly the *base price* (here assumed to be $30 a ton, as it often has been on some kinds of steel). All mills elsewhere, as at Bethlehem or Chicago, sell at exactly the same *delivered price* (Pittsburgh base, plus imaginary freight), which makes their *net realized price* near their own mills higher than the *base price* by the full amount of the freight, here shown as $7.60 at Chicago and $7 at Bethlehem. But if they sell toward Pittsburgh they absorb freight and their *net realized price* is reduced. Approximately halfway to Pittsburgh the *net* of outside mills falls to just the Pittsburgh base, and on sales into Pittsburgh and beyond, falls below that amount. Figures 5, 6, and 26 help further to make clear the curious and complicated results of the workings of the simple formula.

extended over the entire United States. In respect to a "zone" business limited by freight (which under natural conditions the business of steel, or any heavy standardized product, is in high degree), such a statement as applied to competitive markets is an absurdity.[6] Indeed it can only be made to describe a situation where all real markets everywhere (even that at the basing point, Pittsburgh) are destroyed and, by widespread collusion among steel sellers, the customers are deprived of the right to bargain be-

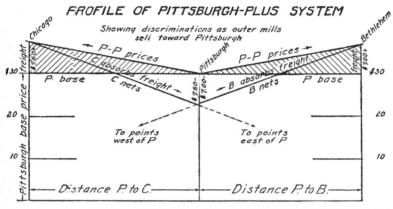

FIG. 4. CROSS SECTION OF PITTSBURGH-PLUS PRICE SCHEME SHOWN IN FRONTISPIECE. FURTHER EXPLANATION IN FOOTNOTE 5

tween the nearer and the distant mill. Of this, more in connection with customers' testimony.

The establishment of this system of artificial prices was just what had been accomplished by open conspiracy through pools before and after the formation of the Corporation down to 1904, just what was continued by common action reflecting a tacit illegal agreement down to 1907, and continued further by the Gary dinners, admittedly illegal, down to 1911 (with a brief interruption in 1909). Most astonishing of all, in view of the trustful innocence of the Court (excepting the three dissenting justices), this was just what continued in actual operation after 1911 down to the very day of the decision in 1920 and for fully four years

[6] See Ch. XX.

thereafter. Indeed, despite the Federal Trade Commission order of 1924, this system of pricing, somewhat modified, persists even to this day. For nearly twenty years under the very eyes of the Department of Justice this practice had continued. As the Court was gravely declaring that prices were everywhere being determined by local demand and supply, in fact they were everywhere being automatically determined by the Corporation's committee on Pittsburgh base prices. The Corporation, by using its dominating position to enforce a follow-the-leader policy in industry, was accomplishing even better results to its own profit and that of the independents than had been accomplished by illegal pools and agreements. The beauty of the arrangement was that whereas the old methods would pretty certainly have brought a decree of dissolution and have defeated the purposes of its founders, the new method brought encomiums and a laurel wreath from the highest Court of the land.

VESTED RIGHTS AT PITTSBURGH

What were to the Corporation the other advantages of this arrangement, as compared with either the old periodic price wars or a system of local markets and genuine competition? The advantages were of several sorts, all eventuating, of course, in pecuniary profit. First, this system artificially insured to Pittsburgh its continuance as the dominating center of the steel industry long after the conditions had passed that once had naturally made it so. Most of the basic plants of the Corporation were, we may recall, at the time of its formation, in and near Pittsburgh (the Pittsburgh district). Many of these plants were technically inferior to Gary and to those of many younger independents. In naming the Pittsburgh base price for steel products, the Corporation had initially the greatest assurance that that price (being a net receipt to all mills in that district) which set the minimum that it would get at any of its mills would contain an ample margin of profit above cost at Pittsburgh's obsolescent mills. Next, this price by the Corporation's own action and tacit agreement and practice of the independents determined automatically the delivered price (Pittsburgh steel price plus freight) in every part of the United States. Thus all Pittsburgh mills (so long and so far as this price policy was in force) were insured of entry, on a basis of exact delivered price equality with all independents, without higgling, to every distant hamlet in the country. This gave to the Corporation for its originally enormous capacity near Pittsburgh a sort of vested right and assurance against having its sales-territory gradually narrowed by the underselling of plants in the outlying areas. The aging beauty had her face lifted. The basing-point practice effected an artificial increase and prolongation of Pittsburgh's power to sell anywhere and everywhere without having to meet a local cut in competitive prices and without having to scrap her antique hunks of junk. This was heaven in the realm of Vulcan and Pluto. One magical effect of this was manifest in periods of increasing freight rates (as in 1918-19), the normal effect of which would have been to have at once cut off Pittsburgh from a large sales-area, whereas, instead, the result was merely an automatic increase of delivered costs of steel products to consumers in almost every part of the country.

BOOSTING PROFITS ELSEWHERE

Further, not all the Corporation's plants were at Pittsburgh, and every one of its mills outside that district could charge the same delivered price as the Pittsburgh mill, inasmuch as the independents playing the game did not cut it. This, of course, gave the mill at any distance from Pittsburgh a (net) price on all sales at its doors greater by the amount of the freight than the price received at Pittsburgh. At mills as far away as Chicago the imaginary freight addition to the base price (on steel not shipped at all) was about 12 to 30 per cent; at Duluth it was over 40 per cent of the base price. If the Pittsburgh mills' price gave a fair profit, the profit (in dollars) at the outlying mills was certain to be greater by the amount of the freight, unless their cost of production was higher. Such figures as have, despite the watchfulness of the Corporation officials, filtered through to the public, agree with other evidence in indicating that the newer mills built after 1901, taking advantage of the great technical inventions, were much more efficient than the older ones at Pittsburgh. If, with real competition, prices had in time come into accord with costs (plus a "fair" profit, say as much as at Pittsburgh) the mill price at these newer mills would have to become much lower than at Pittsburgh, and the delivered prices in a large area would have fallen. But under the Pittsburgh-Plus price policy the building and enlargement of the mills at Gary meant a continually widening and deepening of the vein of gold from which profits could be mined after 1907. At the same time the growth in the total production and use of steel in the country was such that this increase at Gary and else-where in the Chicago district could occur without cutting into the production at the mills in the Pittsburgh district. But these events —never forget—were occurring while Pittsburgh-Plus was in oper-ation, which undoubtedly was artificially retarding a still greater growth in the consumption of steel that would have occurred if lower prices had prevailed at the outlying mills and over a large part of the country. Such a growth of mills in outlying areas would have occurred partly because of displacing Pittsburgh products there, and partly because of a stimulation, by lower prices, of new demand in those areas.

"INDEPENDENTS FOLLOW CHEERFULLY"

The system of pricing in operation had in it certain elements of instability and weakness, being, as it was, in defiance of a more natural adjustment of prices geographically relative to mills and market areas, and maintained, as it was, only by a widespread con-formity of action by many independents. The immediate interest of each of these independents was often—indeed, in some ways, steadily—such as to tempt them to break away from this prac-tice; but their long-run interest (in view of the dominating power of the Corporation) was such as to prevent them, except at times of overwhelming pressure, from yielding to this temptation. Let us see by what means the Corporation made it to the interest of the independents to conform, and virtually to conspire with it thus in restraint of commerce.

The Corporation could work upon its competitors through two motives, fear and favors. First, as to the favors. For the inde-pendents in the Pittsburgh district (greatest of whom was the firm of Jones and Laughlin), what could be more agreeable than to secure all the benefits of a generous price (generous at least to

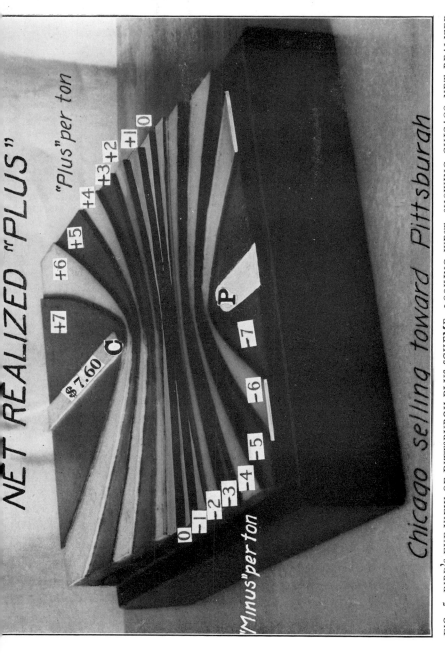

FIG. 5. BIRD'S-EYE VIEW OF PITTSBURGH-PLUS SCHEME, LOOKING WEST, SHOWING CHICAGO NET REALIZED PRICE TERRACES

the sellers, though not to the buyers) insuring an ample margin
of unit-profit, together with the advantages of stability of prices
and entrance on equal price terms to the most distant destinations
in the country? Here were large rewards for conformity. For
when has it ever been a painful task for sellers to conspire to
secure from the public higher prices with ample profit?

Even more luscious was the reward of independents at some
distance from the Pittsburgh base, on sales for near-by delivery
and in a direction away from Pittsburgh. To mills at Youngstown,
Chicago, Johnstown, Philadelphia, Buffalo, and Bethlehem, many
of them even better situated than Pittsburgh in relation to ore
supplies and some of the other essentials for efficient production,
and to deliveries, came with every weekly announcement of the
Corporation's Pittsburgh price the glad tidings that they could
add to this amply profitable base price the full amount of freight
from Pittsburgh to their mill and in their territory. They did not
need to expose themselves to the danger of detection by entering
into a pool, or even by attending Gary dinners. If these methods
had not been illegal, it still would have been silly to use them
when exactly the same result could be reached through the simple
method of not acting the fool by cutting the Corporation's prices.
No more killing the goose that lays the golden egg! The day of
miracles had returned. The steel industry had found the pot of
gold at the end of the rainbow. Agreeable? Well, rather! But
agreement? Who could prove it? They had "agreed" to nothing—
but they did just what they would have done if a definite contract
in restraint of trade had been drawn up in black and white, and so
did the Corporation in its turn. And so in a growing country, where
steel mills multiplied, fortunes were made at the price only of
playing the game according to the plan and leadership of the
Steel Corporation—very different from the purpose and plan en-
visaged in the Anti-Trust Act. Could they "get by with it" if it
came to court? At least it was worth the attempt—with little to
lose and hundreds of millions to gain even if the courts eventually
got wise and put an end to it.

A BLISSFUL CONSPIRACY

On the witness stand in 1922 Henry P. Bope, a veteran of the steel trade, commented as follows upon the use of the Pittsburgh base by the Bethlehem Steel Company:

to my knowledge [Mr. Schwab] has always used the Pittsburgh basis in order to get all the money he could out of the freight . . . I would not say that Mr. Schwab was a philanthropist, at least not in business.[7]

Another reward to the independents for entering into this tacit conspiracy was not only the implied promise but the actual security it gave them from attack by the Corporation, either through local price cutting directed against any one of them, or through a general "price war" extending to all parts of the country. This reward, therefore, is but the positive aspect of the fear on the part of smaller competitors of these dreaded reprisals. Despite the assertions that the Corporation lacked the economic power to employ these measures effectively, assertions coming both from practical and theoretical so-called experts, there could have been no illusions in the minds of these practical officials of the independents that such a power could be exercised in both these ways. As for the Corporation, it shrewdly chose the course that was best for itself under the circumstances, best in the long run for its treasury, and best for its legal self-preservation. At the same time it gave the blissful assurance to every competitor that he had only to "play the game" to be secure against attack by a competitor who could, when he would, wield the club of Hercules. The benevolent giant, however, never would begin a cut of prices, local or general, that was not in the common interest of all producers. There could be no price war anywhere unless some rash independent began it. The Corporation would never strike the first blow. Stable prices maintained at a generous level, peace and security, these were the positive aspects of reward to independents for entering upon and helping to maintain the most effective conspiracy in restraint of competition in prices that, perhaps, the world has ever seen.

[7] Pittsburgh-Plus hearings, F. T. C. Docket 760, pp. 10992-10993, in excerpts of case, p. 3191.

THREAT OF THE BIG STICK

Let us now look at the grimmer reverse side of the shield, the motive of fear that must have been ever present in the minds of independents. The Corporation was following the maxim of our one-time President: Speak softly and carry a big stick. Let us again recall that the prosecution in the steel suit attempted to follow the pattern set in the Oil case and to marshal its evidence toward the discovery of those cruder practices toward competitors proved in that and in other successful prosecutions under the Anti-Trust Act.[8] This doubtless was a serious mistake in the tactics of the prosecution. Times and manners in the steel business had changed since 1901 and largely and necessarily because of the formation of the Corporation. That changed the situation, not because it was a new force for business morals, but because now, as the great market leader, it had such power and dominance that it rarely needed to use violence to enforce its price policy. Formerly, before 1900, in the period of formation of the earlier combinations, which became subsidiaries of the great "combination of combinations," ruthless price wars and local price cutting against particular independents were frequent. But little if any of this was true competition, and surely it was not legal after 1890, if before. It was merely a pseudo-competition—a use of discriminatory local prices as an offensive weapon to create or to strengthen monopoly. It was thus that the earlier monopolistic combines were formed, which later became the super-monopolistic combine, formed too, be it noted, under the threat of "ruthless" competition.[9]

It is therefore mere persiflage to say, as Judge Buffington did, that

no testimony has been produced in this record that a return to the old trade war system of ruinous competition would, as a matter of fact, benefit the public interests.[10]

Surely not. Why should any one try to prove that such methods would be to the public interest? What a travesty of reason to imply

[8] Notably, in the Tobacco, Keystone Watch, and Powder cases.
[9] See testimony in brief, *Amici curiae*, Vol. 2, p. 644; and below in this chapter.
[10] 223 Fed. Rep. 95.

that such an orgy of illegality was really competition! How absurd to imply that the one alternative to dissolving the combination was a return to "the old trade war system of ruinous competition" while Justice sat helplessly by, watching the destruction wrought by this flouting of the Anti-Trust Act!

THE FRIGHTFUL ALTERNATIVE

These distorted views, whose belief is implied in the final verdict of the highest Court, were trustingly taken by the courts from the lips of the leading officials of the Corporation, who at every opportunity on the witness stand pictured the new peaceful régime of ethical business relations among steel producers, in contrast with the wicked old days which, they artfully implied, would inevitably return if the Corporation were to be dissolved. Such utterances had marked the hearings of the Stanley Committee in 1911, of the Cummins Committee of the U.S. Senate in 1913, and many public expressions of such men as Messrs. Gary and Schwab. Mr. Gary was asked by Congressman Martin Littleton in the hearings of the Stanley Committee of the House of Representatives (June 2, 1911, p. 79):

Q. Is it your position that [the Sherman Anti-Trust Act] practically orders a continuance of the old warfare of competition? A. I am afraid it does. I do not know that it does, but I fear it does.

This thought was industriously and in the end successfully played up by the skillful corporation lawyers in this case. To take one example: Mr. Schwab was on the stand, giving expression to the remarkable views before noted, concluding with the assertion that the Steel Corporation would, in order to cripple or destroy any one selected independent, "have to extend their operations over a greater field, following the same policy that they always have followed." [11] The examining lawyer here gave the testimony an adroit turn to bring out the evils of the old days whose return only the continuance of the combination could prevent:

Q. That is, destruction of the small and weak was a practice not unknown to them in the old days, was it? A. It was.

[11] See above, Ch. VIII.

Q. And quite extensively carried on? A. [Stage directions should read, "grimly"] Rather, yes.

Q. And with quite effective and marked results? A. [Stage direction, "In a suggestive tone"] At times, yes;

Q. What percentage of them emerged from the different steel wars in the old days, these small fellows? A. Not many.

Q. There were more gravestones than there were live competitors? A. Yes. [Stage directions should read, "All look silently and significantly at each other a moment, then smile."] [12]

Other similar statements by independents are quoted by Judge Buffington,[13] expressing satisfaction that the old days of indiscriminate price cutting were no more. But note that these are exactly the sentiments that would be expressed by fellow conspirators in restraint of trade who were enjoying their share of the positive rewards plus the no less valuable negative reward of immunity from local price cutting by their giant competitor so long as they played his game. But the judges saw no possibility of such an interpretation—engrossed as they were with the thought that the giant weakling had somehow lost its *power* (not merely the inclination or the motive) to cripple or destroy its competitors as was done in the wicked old days.

EVEN MR. SCHWAB TREMBLES

But Mr. Schwab has no such judicial illusions, and when he drops his guard he tells in another connection how even he, as president of the Bethlehem Steel Corporation, does not dare, for fear of precipitating a war of prices, to "vary by 10 cents a ton" the price announced by the Steel Corporation. Judge Buffington quotes this testimony with the naïve and inconsistent comment that "we can readily see how rail manufacturers simply followed that basic price to prevent the ruinous rail wars of the past." Mr. Schwab was speaking of the remarkable fact that rails all over the country had for many years been sold at the unvarying price of $28 (a mill-base price in contrast with the Pittsburgh-Plus prices on most other steel products):

[12] Transcript of Record, Defendants' testimony, Vol. 11, p. 4191.
[13] 223 Fed. Rep. 93.

if I were to vary that [price] 10 cents a ton today I would precipitate a steel war . . . that would result in running my works without any profit . . . I would not vary the price of my rails under any circumstances, not if I knew it was to get 100,000 tons in orders, for the reason that my competitor next door would put the price down to (sic) $1 a ton, or $.50 a ton even, and we would all be in a position where we would be running without any profit at all.[14]

Leaving aside the artful or humorous suggestion that so small a reduction as 10 cents or even 50 cents a ton would wipe out all profit, here evidently is an utter paralysis of competition in price, a paralysis of fear, as Mr. Schwab describes it. And who is the competitor that is "next door" to everybody else? Who but the market leader who names and maintains the unvarying price? Would small competitors at a distance be able to come in and take away the "zone business" of rails at Bethlehem if prices were 10 cents or 50 cents a ton lower? Rather would they not be less able to do so than before? How, indeed, is there ever to be anything resembling real competition and a real market price at any producing center when the strongest independent in the country dares not name at his own mill and in his own sales territory a price less by 10 cents a ton than that sanctioned by the great market leader? We are sure that a "ruinous steel war" (both general and local price cutting) would be illegal, but as those causing it contest this interpretation and never have been punished by the law, it is just as effective a threat for them to hold over their small competitors as if it were legal. Indeed, the decision in this suit went further than the courts had ever gone before to legalize an occasional use of price wars, the very thought of which is enough to paralyze would-be competitors with fear.

SURVIVAL OF THE FITTEST

However, after the formation of the Steel Corporation in 1901 the rule was a continued adherence of all to a scheme of prices based on Pittsburgh, not on their own mills, and the exception was an occasional period in which reductions of prices went to the extreme, as in 1908, 1909, and 1911 (and again in 1921, the

---

[14] Transcript of Record, Vol. 11, p. 4387; quoted in 223 Fed. Rep. 154 with small clerical errors.

year after the decision in this case). The unanimity of action in the period before 1907 was mainly secured by pools and agreements unquestionably illegal, and from 1907 to 1911 by "understandings" furthered by the Gary dinners, likewise illegal.[15] At intervals, however, as in 1909, the Corporation was forced "to declare for an open market," and then, as it declared with grim humor, it "permitted natural laws to take their course." [16] The Court believed that in the periods of agreement "the Corporation dominated only in the sense of . . . making attractive what it desired to be done, and the others yielded cheerfully." [17] That is, the judges admit that the Corporation has sought to sway the action through offering rewards, but they deny that it has used the motive of fear.

Now, just what was "an open market"? Ought it not to be just what the Anti-Trust Act intended as the ideal? Alas, that the sober judges missed the humor in the droll remarks of Mr. Elbert Gary which were included in the record of this case! In February, 1908, in conference assembled with the competitors of the Corporation, he counseled them

to assist one another by the friendly interchange of views rather than a resort to unreasonable and destructive competition, which would ultimately result in the application of the law of the survival of the fittest.[18]

A BILLION PLUS IS SPEAKING

When 1500 million dollars was talking at 10 and 20 millions, could there have been any doubt in the mind of any one present who was (financially) the fittest to survive, or just what Mr. Gary meant? What in fact happened was told by himself a year later, with certain decorative dictums to assure the public that all was done within the law. As a result of various meetings in the first half of 1908, said he,

stability of prices, as distinguished from wide and sudden fluctuations, existed until about the beginning of 1909, although no agreements were made to maintain prices, and notwithstanding a small percentage of

---

[15] See Judge Woolley's description, 223 Fed. Rep. 175.
[16] *Idem.*
[17] *Idem*, p. 176.
[18] *The Iron Age*, February 6, 1908, p. 443.

manufacturers stood aloof from the conferences . . . It appears that for one reason or another . . . many of the smaller concerns . . . have been selling their products at prices below those which were generally maintained [that is, Pittsburgh-Plus as announced by the Corporation] . . . In view of the circumstances . . . the leading manufacturers of iron and steel have determined to protect their customers, and for the present at least, sell at such modified prices as may be necessary with respect to different commodities in order to retain their fair share of the business. The prices which may be determined upon and the details concerning the same will be given by the manufacturers to their consumers direct as occasion may require.[19]

"Modified" prices to be known only by each customer! *The Iron Age* complacently calls this a "temperate and even amiable declaration," but it plainly means that the prices of the Corporation are no longer to be either public or uniform at Pittsburgh, and that such special prices are to be made to each customer in each case as will undersell the independents that dare to offer lower prices. It is a plain announcement of a punitive expedition against independents who have dared to reduce prices in their own neighborhoods.

GENTLEMEN, FRIENDS, NEIGHBORS

With the temporary abandonment of the Gary dinners as a result of public criticism, competition again became active, and nearly two years later Mr. Elbert Gary, having assembled about him in one room 95 per cent of the steel trade, made to them a statement in which he reached the highest level of his peculiar humor, artfully intermingling cajolery and veiled threats, expressions of respect for the law, and suggestions of the way in which it might be evaded. Thus he spoke, in part:

in view of the fact that we have no right legally to enter into any arrangement by direct or indirect means which enables us to maintain prices, to divide territory, to restrict output, or in any way to interfere with the laws of trade or to stifle competition, and in view of the fact that we cannot legally directly or indirectly do anything which may be construed to be in restraint of trade, and, therefore, are relegated to the one position of treating each other on the basis of fair, just and

[19] See *The Iron Age,* February 25, 1909, pp. 648-9.

equitable treatment, it behooves us to use the greatest care in the exercise of our rights, and in the transaction of our business so as to make it absolutely certain that day by day, and with reference to every transaction, we are certain to recognize the rights of our competitors or friends, and the obligations which we are under toward them . . . we have something better to guide and control us in our business methods than a contract which depends upon written or verbal promises with a penalty attached. We as men, as gentlemen, as friends, as neighbors, having been in close communication and contact during the last few years have reached a point where we entertain for one another respect and affectionate regard.[20]

What could be lovelier and more gentle than these words? But how is respect and affection better to guide in their business methods, and to what end are these methods directed? Surely not toward even "indirectly" entering into an "arrangement" to maintain or control prices, for that is "illegal"—and the good Mr. Gary would not suggest that!

MR. GARY AN EASY MARK

So we get a shock, as the spokesman of $1,500,000,000 continues speaking as follows to the small-fry millionaire inpendents:

At the present time the question of maintaining or changing the prices of the commodities in which we deal is uppermost in our minds.

Then, after further discussion of this topic, comes again this ironical disavowal that his words mean what every listener there knew they did mean:

if by my conduct or by my language I have induced any of you to suppose that I believe our corporation has any advantage or is disposed to take any advantage, or has intended to urge you to fix or to maintain prices concerning your commodities which are not in accordance with your own views, I do not hesitate to ask your pardon.

Alas for the foolish belief of Messrs. J. P. Morgan and Charles Schwab in 1901 that merger—artfully christened integration— would bring any advantages to the giant corporation! The humble Mr. Gary not only makes no suggestions to the competitors of

[20] *The Iron Age,* January 19, 1911, pp. 208-210.

the Corporation regarding maintaining prices, but he turns to them for suggestions—but of course only about lowering prices—not about raising them; that would be illegal.

If any of you desire to lower prices at any time, and will make the fact known to me, you will find that I am a follower and not a stubborn opposer. I shall always beg leave to express my opinions in regard to what I think are fair prices, but I will do it not for the purpose of expecting you to adopt my views, nor for any purpose except the same purpose that you have in mind when you express to me your opinions. We deal in the open, we deal fairly, and, as I have frequently said, you will always find me an easy mark. If a majority of you shall be of the opinion that I am making a mistake in advocating the maintenance of prices you will have no difficulty in getting me to change my opinion.[21]

Isn't that delicious? Mr. Gary—Judge Gary—an easy mark! And what could be more legally, sarcastically, vaguely explicit than the warning of what he, backed by $1,500,000,000 of capital, intended to do if any one rashly continued to sell to any of the Corporation's customers at prices lower than its announced figures?

DISARMING SUSPICION

Nearing the end of his remarks, the cautious old lawyer thought it well to disavow again any evil intentions. The world is so suspicious! *Honi soit qui mal y pense.*

You may read in the newspapers hints that we are actually making agreements to maintain prices or that we are indirectly or by inference making arrangements which are in restraint of trade and so we must make it certain that the contrary is true. I would not make an agreement under any circumstances to maintain prices or to do or refrain from doing anything which would prevent me from being absolutely independent from all others in every respect concerning every department of our corporation, or in regard to the conduct of our business, and I would not ask for any different conclusion from others. As I said before, the very fact that it is understood we have this right; that we are independent; that we can go out of this room and do exactly as we please without violating any agreement or understanding, and that all must depend upon the belief that as honorable men we are desirous of conducting ourselves and our business in such a way as not to injure

[21] *Idem.*

our neighbors, must make each of us much more careful in regard to the conduct of our affairs.[22]

These words were spoken in 1911, but seventeen years later Mr. Gary's successor was believed by hardheaded observers to be disposed worthily to preserve the Corporation's traditional policy, if not to sharpen it. A despatch of January 2, 1928, from Pittsburgh commented on the opening of several new mills for the manufacture of sheets and strips to supply partly rolled material to regular tin mills, and indicated the likelihood that, with this increased output, prices might have to be reduced. As to the attitude of the new Corporation chief it said:

Designation of Mr. Farrell as the chief executive of the Steel Corporation confirms expectations that his policies as to sales competition will prevail. This does not mean that there will be more disposition to seek orders by the price-cutting route. Rather it means that independent producers will be more careful, realizing that Mr. Farrell could be aggressive on occasion.[23]

There you have it—the mailed fist in the silk glove.

[22] *Idem.*
[23] The New York *Times,* January 3, 1928, p. 43.

CHAPTER X

CAMOUFLAGING A CONSPIRACY

OF THE period from 1901 to 1911, Judge Woolley's view, adopted by the majority of the Supreme Court, was thus expressed:

It therefore appears that from the organization of the corporation in 1901 until the Gary Dinners were discontinued in January 1911, the corporation, first by one method [the pools created for that purpose, from 1901 to 1904], and then by a second method [by meetings called for that purpose during the period from 1904 to 1907], and then by a third method [the Gary dinners], employed means to procure the establishment and maintenance of uniform prices for its diversified products, and by these means the Steel Corporation, with its competitors, did combine and control prices, and in controlling prices restrained trade. If by the three methods pursued, in the three periods named, prices were not artificially and successfully maintained, as shown by the history covering those three periods, I am at a loss to know by what means it would be possible to fix and maintain prices that would unduly restrain trade in the sense of violating the Anti-Trust Act.[1]

Judge Woolley's disapprobation here reached its climax, sweeping aside Mr. Gary's pretenses and condemning these dinners as "in effect pools," as "pools without penalties." Justice McKenna believed them to be "more efficient in stabilizing prices." [2] Even the most trustful Judge Buffington declared

the conclusion inevitable that the result of these meetings was an understanding about prices that was equivalent to an agreement . . . We

[1] 223 Fed. Rep. 176, June 3, 1915.   [2] 251 U.S. 440, October 1919.

cannot doubt that such an arrangement or understanding or moral obligation—whatever name may be the most appropriate—amounts to a combination or common action forbidden by law. The final test, we think, is the object and the effect of the arrangement, and both the object and effect were to maintain prices, at least to a considerable degree.[3]

Here, too, Judge Buffington reaches his climax of disapproval, making results the test. Despite this record of illegality, all four Circuit judges, followed closely in this by Justice McKenna and three of his colleagues, found it possible to let the Corporation go scot-free. After a superficial show of differences of opinion in details, Judges Woolley and Hunt face about abruptly and unite with their more lenient colleagues in their surprising verdict. Surely Justice McKenna misstated the views of the judges in the lower Court (while agreeing with them in dismissing the case) when he said:

We have seen that the judges of the District Court unanimously concurred in the view that the Corporation did not achieve monopoly, and such is our deduction.[4]

The Corporation *together with* its fellow conspirators did, even on the Court's own statement, achieve a monopoly before 1911, but the Court makes everything hang on the verbal technicality that the Corporation was not "a" monopoly (that is, did not have un-limited power), and although it entered into a combination in violation of the Anti-Trust Law, it did not achieve monopoly "in and of itself," but only by persuading the independents to conspire with it.

THE PRODIGAL SON

Confusing as are the reasoning and conclusion of the Courts regarding the period before 1911, they are lucidity itself compared with its view of the situation thereafter. The lower Court believed that all illegal conduct ceased

January 11, 1911, and the bill in this suit was filed on October 26, 1911. The testimony does not show that since the date of the last Gary dinner the corporation, either alone or in coöperation with others, has

[3] 223 Fed. Rep. 160-161.   [4] 251 U.S. 444.

fixed or maintained prices of the products of the steel industry, or attempted so to do.[5]

This view was adopted in its entirety by Justice McKenna and three of his colleagues:

the illegal practices have not been resumed, nor is there any evidence of an intention to resume them.[6]

CONSPIRACY BEFORE 1911, AND AFTER

In 1909 and 1910 Chicago mills partially, then fully, adopted a "mill base Chicago" for a time, but in November 1910 the return to the Pittsburgh basing plan was announced. A notable temporary change of this sort occurred in February 1921 in the territory east of Pittsburgh, after the conclusion of this suit. But between 1911 and 1920 came the most remarkable decade of prosperity and harmony the steel business had ever known. It was in this Golden Age of peace in the steel business when the lion and the lamb were lying down together, during the four years 1911 to 1915, that the testimony was taken and the record in this case was compiled. The next five years, 1916-1921, witnessed the Great War, its end, and two prosperous years following. Never was a decade so completely lacking in periods of "open markets," never was the system of Pittsburgh basing-point prices all over the country maintained so near to perfection. There were merely slight ripples to disturb the calm, and a short time (1917-18) when the War Industries Board partially modified the plan by establishing a Chicago base.

The most that the prolonged conspiracy before 1911, branded by the courts as illegal, could do when it was most successful, was partially and temporarily to attain a follow-the-leader scheme of delivered prices, with Pittsburgh as the basing point; yet after 1911 the same plan almost *continuously and perfectly* functioned without the open appearance of meetings and agreements. Judge Buffington applied the test of "the object and the effect of the arrangement" to the means by which the Pittsburgh-Plus plan before 1911 was realized, and even he declared that both object

[5] Judge Woolley's opinion, 223 Fed. Rep. 178; Judge Buffington *a fortiori*.
[6] 251 U.S. 445.

and effect were to maintain prices. But he and the other majority judges, seeing that in the period after 1911 these same *means* were no longer employed, decided with great positiveness that their *effect*, a restraint of competition, could not possibly exist. Judge Buffington in the eager advocacy of his opinion accepts as a "fact" the claim of witnesses

that the iron and steel trade in the various products of the Steel Corporation is and has been open, competitive, and uncontrolled, and that all engaged therein have free will control in selling at their own prices.

And he forgets his own previous belief when he concludes

that the prices of the product sold by the Steel Corporation have been the result of the joint action of the law of supply and demand and of that vigorous rivalry which has *at all times* [italics ours] existed between the Steel Corporation and its competitors.

Judge Woolley more guardedly and consistently limited his statement to the period after 1911:

the testimony does not show that *since the date of the last Gary Dinner* the corporation, either alone or in coöperation with others, has fixed or maintained prices of the products of the steel industry, or attempted so to do.[8]

And Justice McKenna, likewise observing this limitation, declares:

since 1911 no act in violation of law can be established against it.[9]

On this vulnerable belief turned the verdict.

CUSTOMERS GIVE THEIR OPINIONS

This belief was based not only on the testimony of supposed competitors, as described in the last chapter, but upon that of customers, which made upon the judges an even greater impression. The defense called 200 of its customers as witnesses to declare that they believed competition had been active, a number which "seems fairly representative," as the Court said. The prosecution attempted to belittle this testimony by remarking that nearly

[7] 223 Fed. Rep. 82.   [9] 251 U.S. 451.
[8] *Idem*, p. 178. (Italics ours.)

40,000 others had not been called, but Justice McKenna taunts it with its failure to produce a single customer to testify to the existence of "the sinister dominance of the Corporation." The Supreme Court said:

Not having done so, is it not permissible to infer that none would testify to the existence of the influence that the Government asserts? [10]

In the light of the facts now known we must say, however, that the inference was erroneous and therefore not "permissible." Although the great masses of evidence on this phase of the case covered a large portion of ten volumes of the printed hearings, the opinions disposed of this phase of the evidence somewhat summarily, Judge Buffington's opinion being the only one in which any specific testimony was repeated. Even that cited only fifteen of the customer-witnesses, and this inadequate survey was accepted without amendment by the other majority judges. Of the expressions chosen as most representative regarding the existence and prevalence of competition, nearly all involved an economic interpretation of what was happening, rather than a recountal of the happenings themselves. They were opinions, not facts. The question whether the prices quoted and the system of prices were a proof of real competition was in this case the very crux of the controversy, and its answer on any agreed statement of facts called for interpretation by experts, economic or legal, respectively. As to the real significance of what was occurring under their very eyes, these "practical" witnesses were almost wholly in the dark.[11]

A JUGGLE OF DATES

When the Department of Justice, other public officials, and the Supreme Court itself all failed to penetrate this masquerade of monopoly, how can it be thought that these lay witnesses understood the real economic and legal situation? Recall certain conditions which we have already observed. The testimony in this case nearly all related to the period from 1901 to about 1913, and the larger part of this particular testimony was taken in 1912. The record was closed in 1914 and necessarily went to the Supreme

[10] *Idem,* p. 448.
[11] Some illuminating details are discussed in Appendix A to Ch. X.

Court as of that date (the District Court decision being rendered in 1915). Undoubtedly further evidence relating precisely to the years from 1914 to 1920 (and until February 1921) would have shown a pretty steadily increasing adherence to the "official" formula, and a pretty constant reduction in the number and range of "varying" quotations (of delivered prices) that could be obtained by a buyer from different mills. The "formula" of identical delivered prices had worked rather haltingly in the period 1901 to 1911, when the means employed to make it work were flagrantly illegal, but paradoxically worked more and more perfectly in the succeeding decade when the Court believed no such illegal methods were used and competition was complete and perfect. Note, however, that the testimony about competition which impressed the Court, while all taken after 1911, was put in general phrases and mostly relates plainly to the whole preceding period back to 1901. Some specifically say "since 1901"; others say "always" (or negatively, "never"); and only rarely a more cautious statement is confined to the period after 1904. It is this evidence from customers relating to this period before 1911 which is the main and (together with that of competitors for the same period) the only basis of positive testimony for the Court's conclusion that after 1911 there was no restraint of competition. The Court's conclusion was influenced largely also by the negative fact that no customers or competitors testified to the opposite effect.

A CURIOSITY IN JUDICIAL REASONING

We are thus confronted with this curiosity in judicial reasoning: that the Court accepted as proof of perfect competition, in the period after 1911, witnesses' belief as to practices and prices before 1911; yet the Court had itself concluded from other evidence that the earlier period had been marked by the flagrant and repeated use of illegal means of restricting competition. The Court saw no inconsistency in this juggle of dates and of testimony.

If the judges were right, as no doubt they were, in their recognition and condemnation of the illegality of the earlier period, are we to conclude that the witnesses were consciously misrepresenting? No, the very looseness of their language, which should have stamped their testimony as worthless, gave a thousand loopholes for misunderstanding. This was so in respect to almost every phrase in the testimony, as quoted by the Courts, that involved a denial of an agreement as to prices. In all this testimony, when witnesses denied knowledge of any agreement they were assuming that the various meetings before 1911 did not evidence an agreement (though the Courts held that they did). When therefore the Courts declared (in 1915 and 1920 respectively) that these actions did amount to an agreement, all this testimony automatically took on a meaning different from that which the judges trustingly continued to give it. This is so as to the testimony both of competitors and of customers.[12]

THE AFRICAN IN THE WOODPILE

A further comment upon this ambiguity in the meaning of "agreement." We now know very well what was the mode of quotation of prices and what was the general scheme of relative local prices that was in operation (with some interruptions) in the steel industry during most of the period embraced by the evidence. The Pittsburgh-Plus system was not recognized, understood, or passed upon in this case by the courts, unless indirectly and as it were unwittingly in their condemnation of the particular means of attaining it by open agreement between 1901 and 1911. But in interpreting the evidence it must always be remembered both that the customers very vaguely understood how this plan worked and what was being done to them, and that the sellers always strenuously denied that conformity with this formula of pricing and selling steel would involve any understanding, agreement, or conspiracy as to prices. This was the position maintained by the Corporation also throughout the Pittsburgh-Plus hearings and arguments from 1919 until 1924. Therefore, when (for example) the salesmanager of the Lackawanna said of the years 1901 to 1910 that "there was no time during that period when the prices he either quoted or fixed were quoted or fixed in agreement with any of their competitors," this did not, as he used the words, deny the entire conformity of his prices with the Pittsburgh basing-point scheme. This was the African in the woodpile. The witness and the Courts were simply begging the question by excluding any

[12] See further data in Appendix B to Ch. X.

such practical conformity of action from the meaning to be attached to the word "agreement." [13]

Almost the first judicial utterance on the issues of this case had been Judge Buffington's remark: "This case—a proceeding under the Sherman Anti-Trust Law—is largely one of business facts." And he had continued:

"The construction of that statute has been settled by the Supreme Court . . . It follows, therefore, that our duty is largely one of finding the facts and to those facts applying settled law.[14]

How easy it sounded! But how complete the failure of the Court, through lack of economic insight, to understand the true state of facts, and how unsettled the law which it applied—further unsettled by this application.

THE BIAS OF LOCATION

Another circumstance further weakening this customer testimony in which the Courts placed implicit trust is the limitation of the business concerns represented to locations in the territory known as the Pittsburgh district (or to cities adjacent to it, or in a comparatively few cases to points eastward). Witnesses from areas west of central Ohio or farther south are almost wholly lacking. Was this pure accident, or was it the result of design? These witnesses were 200 in number, estimated to be one-half of 1 per cent of all customers, of whom the Court cites specifically 15 (or about one-twenty-fifth of 1 per cent of all) as most significant. These were hardly a fair statistical sample, and they appear to have been carefully hand-picked for the defense. It is now well understood that the Pittsburgh-Plus scheme of prices in operation when most of this testimony was being taken was to the advantage of the fabricators in the Pittsburgh district. They bought their steel materials at the flat Pittsburgh basing price, without freight plus, while fabricators at a distance from Pittsburgh were compelled to pay the full Pittsburgh-Plus rate, although they might be at the very door of the mill from which they bought. The disadvantage to competitors was felt little if at all in the

[13] The extent of conformity is treated below in Ch. XII, "Sharpshooting at a Formula."
[14] 223 Fed. Rep. 58.

fairly neutral zone of freights in Ohio (as far as Cleveland, Toledo, Canton, etc.), and relatively little eastward, where freight hauls from Pittsburgh even to the coast were not so great. The disadvantage was greatest to the fabricating plants as far west as Chicago, or farther. (Certain technical conditions, such as freight on waste and cuttings in fabrication, increased this disadvantage.) Likewise jobbers of steel in the Pittsburgh and adjacent districts had an advantage over competing jobbers in outlying areas. Direct consumers, such as local gas and coal companies (buying pipe, rails, etc.) in the Pittsburgh district did not directly compete with concerns at a distance, but at least enjoyed the lowest prices possible under this plan (that is, the net Pittsburgh base) and had every reason to be satisfied. Finally, railroads, because able to accept delivery at any point on their lines, were largely relieved of any disadvantage of the freight-plus burden at a distance from Pittsburgh (and rails, it will be recalled, were sold at a base price uniform at all mills, in exception to the general scheme).

INTERESTED WITNESSES

With these facts before him, let the reader scrutinize this list of fifteen witnesses whose testimony was selected by the courts as most strikingly proving the satisfaction of the whole body of consumers with the existing scheme of prices. The list comprised 7 fabricators, 4 jobbers, and 4 direct consumers. Ten of the 11 fabricators and jobbers were located in the Pittsburgh district or as near as Cleveland, and the other one was a small firm to the east, at Brooklyn. Two of the four direct-consumer witnesses were in the Pittsburgh district, one being the president of a local coal company, the other the president of the largest local gas company (and at the same time a director of the Steel Corporation—a fact which the Court manifestly overlooked). The other two witnesses were purchasing agents of railroads, both of which had interlocking directors with the Steel Corporation.[15] Thirteen railroads which, through their officers (usually the purchasing agents), testified to their satisfaction with the fairness of the Steel Corporation, had interlocking directors with it, and three others were closely affili-

---

[15] George F. Baker on the C. B. & Q. and George F. Baker and J. P. Morgan on the New York Central.

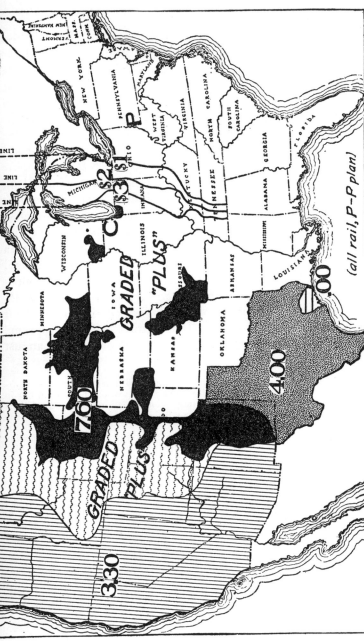

Composite of several exhibits in F.T.C. Docket 760 (P-P complaint). Witness, H. E. White

FIG. 6. EXTRA PROFITS TO CHICAGO MILLS. SIMILAR SURPLUSES WERE ENJOYED BY MILLS AT BIRMINGHAM, DULUTH, AND PUEBLO. COMPARE FIG. 26. MAP SHOWS MILL DISCRIMINATION BETWEEN BUYERS FROM CHICAGO (SEE CHS. XX–XXII) BUT NOT ABSOLUTE PRICES PAID BY CONSUMERS

ated with companies likewise so connected. Fourteen of the fifteen witnesses who most impressed the Court were, because of their location, either directly profiting by the system or not subject to its disadvantages. Counsel for the prosecution, after eight years spent on the case, failed to sense the real nature of this evidence, and had failed to bring a single customer-witness to rebut this testimony, as could easily have been done.[16]

THE MISSING ACTOR

It is, in our present understanding of this problem, indeed an incredible thing that such an important influence as the basing-point system should have been entirely ignored in the greatest industrial lawsuit the world had ever seen. This perhaps justifies the consideration we have given to this feature of the case at a length which might else seem unwarranted. The trial of the steel dissolution case was the play of *Hamlet* with Hamlet left out— it may be a more accurate comparison to say, the play of *Othello* without Iago. The masquerade of monopoly had been carried off successfully even in and through the chambers of the Supreme Court of the United States, in virtual contempt of that august tribunal.

[16] Indeed, six of the firms which in the dissolution suit testified for the Corporation, declaring their satisfaction with its price policies, testified against it in the Pittsburgh-Plus complaint a few years later, quite reversing the tenor of their evidence. Perhaps in 1912 they really did not fully understand what was being done to them, and further the pressure upon them to comply with the Corporation's wishes was undoubtedly great. These firms were: Illinois Steel Bridge Company, Jacksonville, Ill.; Deere and Company, agricultural implements, Moline, Ill.; Sykes Company, sheet metal workers, Chicago, Ill.; Pressed Steel Tank Company, Milwaukee, Wis.; Wisconsin Bridge and Iron Company, Milwaukee, Wis.; Western Wheeled Scraper Company, Aurora, Ill. And see further, on discontented customers, next chapter.

CHAPTER XI

THE PITTSBURGH-PLUS PRACTICE

VICTIMS BECOME VOCAL

THE mills of justice like the mills of the gods, grind slowly. Not until ten years after the formation of the Steel Corporation was a suit begun to attack its legality. Not until another nine years had passed was the case decided.[1] Most of the evidence contained in the record on which the final decision was based related to a state of facts seven or eight years earlier. Meantime the world had experienced the greatest war in history and the steel industry in all its branches had enjoyed in the United States the most phenomenal growth and prosperity. When the venerable Justice McKenna was delivering his opinion, March 1, 1920, the steel industry, together with general business, was at the height of the after-war boom, destined to collapse a few months later. How confidently he pointed to the fact that from 40,000 customers "not one was called" by the prosecution to complain against the price practices of the Corporation, and he exclaimed: "Is it not permissible to infer that none would testify?" Alas for the fallibility of human judgment! As these words were uttered, the mutterings of discontent, for many years increasing, were beginning to swell into a loud chorus of complaint. In 1918 numerous individual protests had been made against the price policy of the Corporation, culminating in January 1919 in the formation of the Western Association of Rolled Steel Consumers for the purpose of bringing

[1] A decision was handed down in June 1915, by the lower Federal Court in favor of the Corporation, whereupon the government appealed to the Supreme Court. The case was argued before the Supreme Court in March 1917, restored to the docket for reargument in May 1917, reargued in October 1919, and finally decided March 1, 1920.

about the abolition of the price system known as Pittsburgh-Plus. In the legal proceedings which followed in the next five years, not one customer but scores went upon the stand to testify, not in praise of the Corporation, but in protest against the unfairness and illegality of its price practices. The number of discontented customers who had now found their voices ran into the tens of thousands. True it is that great difficulty was experienced in persuading the first witnesses to testify, for all but a few braver spirits were seized with panic at the very suggestion of appearing against the all-powerful Corporation. But as the ranks of the protestants grew, and therewith their confidence in earnest action, so grew their courage and eagerness to testify. The thing complained against, be it noted, was no new thing, but was the very condition secured and the practice enforced between 1901 and 1911 by various methods of pools, agreements, and meetings pronounced by the courts to be illegal, but, *mirabile dictu*, a condition which when even more regularly and completely maintained after 1911 without any visible machinery of illegal agreement, the majority of the Supreme Court mistook for a normal system of competitive market prices.

HOW PITTSBURGH-PLUS STARTED

Until the Pittsburgh-Plus complaint before the Federal Trade Commission, beginning in 1920, some months after the decision in the dissolution suit, no effort was made by any public agency to inquire into the history of this much-used practice in selling steel. In the hearings on that complaint, however, many witnesses were questioned, most of whom displayed a surprising ignorance of the practice or a strange inability to tell, in their wordy and obscure answers, anything really definite about it. One witness called by the Government, however, a man of unequaled experience in this field, told the whole story in a fairly connected way that may be fitted together with all the other clear bits of evidence on the subject. He was, to be sure, at times evasive in his interpretations, which he confused with his statement of facts. But listen to the tale of the birth and youth of Pittsburgh-Plus, as told by Colonel Henry P. Bope, a veteran of the steel industry. He was testifying in November 1922.

When a mere boy, in 1879 he entered the employ of the Carnegie Steel Company as its first stenographer, and later for many years was its salesmanager until 1918, when he became connected with the American Steel Corporation. Asked what was the practice before 1880 as to price quotation for steel, he answered:

A. The practice was to quote f.o.b mills. Every mill was a law unto itself.

Q. And the difference in prices between the mills, did that amount to the freight rate, or was it entirely independent? A. Each mill made whatever price seemed necessary to take the business. . . .

Q. Was this time you speak of, in 1880, the first time, as far as you know, that the Pittsburgh basing system was established? A. As far as I know, the first time.[2]

History is still silent regarding any earlier use of this device. Its use for many years after 1880 was confined to beams (structural materials). Prior to 1900 or 1901, there were few Pittsburgh-Plus prices on plates, shapes, bars, sheets, tin plate, or wire.[3] The first step taken to introduce Pittsburgh-Plus prices in structural materials had been the formation in the spring of 1880 of the first beam association, including the Carnegie Company and three others, all three located east of Pittsburgh, in New Jersey or Pennsylvania, (the Passaic Rolling Mills, the New Jersey Steel and Iron Company, and the Phoenix Iron Company). The Carnegie Company, having no competitors west of it, simply named the Pittsburgh price, and the other conspirators used that price, plus freight, as their price delivered to customers, a highly convenient and profitable arrangement for everybody but the consuming public.

EXPERIMENTS IN MONOPOLY

It surely is not an insignificant coincidence that the invention, the earliest successful application, and for nearly twenty years the

---

[2] Federal Trade Commission, Docket 760, Pittsburgh-Plus Complaint, Record, pp. 10861-10862, reprinted in brief, *Amici Curiae*, p. 639. Question and answer above, it is made clear by the context, refer, in the accurate sense of our definition, to the practice of mills outside of Pittsburgh using the Pittsburgh base price. The witness carefully adds: "except that the Pittsburgh mills always quoted the Pittsburgh price, of course."

[3] References in brief, *Amici Curiae*, p. 88.

only considerable use of this system of basing-point delivered prices was in that branch of the steel industry where monopolistic conditions earliest appeared, and where the territorially limited monopolistic control by a dominant leader could most readily be strengthened by agreements with smaller competitors in the outlying sales territory. But even with the Carnegie Company in this dominant position, as the most experienced witness testified, the structural steel producers could not maintain "uniform" (delivered) prices without having a basing point. As he said, they tried to do so once, much later, in 1909, but with such poor success that in a short time that they were glad to go back to the Pittsburgh base. This example would have been instructive to the judges who had curiously argued that agreement between the dominant corporation and smaller competitors effectually proves that it is "in and of itself not a monopoly."

After a few years, about 1884, the Beam Association decided to try a zone method of fixing prices. They parceled out the country, taking an average freight rate and using Pittsburgh as a basing point. As a result of this system the various producers of beams reached the customers in each zone at the same delivered prices (which were discriminatory prices net to the mill). The straight Pittsburgh basing-point plan, rather loosely observed, alternated in use in the selling of structural materials with the zone plan, which predominated between 1897 and 1904. After 1904, beams usually were sold (except in brief periods of the breakdown of the .practice) on the straight Pittsburgh-Plus plan, and the zoning plan was abandoned.

Some time in the '90's the Pittsburgh-Plus plan was adopted by the wire-nail manufacturers. The first specific mention in the record is a notice of the reaffirmation of prices on the Pittsburgh basis in 1895.[4] Abundant evidence appears of its continued use for wire thereafter, though sometimes (just when does not appear in the record) this was considerably modified by making what was called an "arbitrary" plus for Chicago over the Pittsburgh base, regardless of the freight rate.

Steel billets, too, as early as 1896 were sold for a time at de-

---

[4] *The Iron Age,* October 31, 1895, cited in government's brief, p. 20.

livered prices on a Pittsburgh base, fixed, of course, by a pool,[5] but this arrangement appears to have been short-lived, and in November 1900 the basic steel makers met and again chose Pittsburgh as the basing point for the delivered prices which they fixed by agreement.

MONOPOLY FULL GROWN

It was shortly before and during the year 1900 that large numbers of steel plants were combined to form the various large companies which were destined to be merged in turn within another year to form the United States Steel Corporation. Evidencing the new-found powers of these mergers to restrict competition, a veritable epidemic of the use of Pittsburgh-Plus began. Mr. Charles M. Schwab, then with the Carnegie Steel Company, and long experienced in practicing the gentle art of monopoly in beams, looking upon his handiwork and finding it good, organized in 1900 a Plate Association and fixed the price of plates on the Pittsburgh base, a scheme that then operated successfully, with slight interruptions, for a quarter of a century. It was, however, for a time (between 1901 and 1904), modified somewhat by exceptions and by a zoning plan in which the whole country was divided into seventeen districts, in each of which the price (delivered) of structural steel was the same, regardless of differences in freight costs from Pittsburgh.[6]

The same year (1900) most, if not all, of the sheet and tin mills of the country were absorbed by the American Sheet Steel Company and the American Tin Plate Company, these two being later combined in the American Tin Plate Company, this in turn becoming a part of the United States Steel Corporation. The American Sheet Steel Company "took in nearly all of the sheet producing mills," and at once inaugurated the Pittsburgh-Plus plan.[7]

A MUSHROOM CUSTOM

Until that time, the most experienced witness testified, the price of sheets and of tin plates had never been made on a Pittsburgh

[5] *Idem,* p. 50.
[6] Government's brief in the Pittsburgh-Plus complaint, p. 17, with references to exhibits.
[7] *Idem,* p. 15, with references to evidence.

base, but generally had been sold f.o.b. mill, although in 1899 either a New York or a Chicago basing point was used.[8] There was testimony specifically as to one new mill, started in Ohio in March 1901, that it continued until 1903 to sell f.o.b. and then "started selling on the Pittsburgh base because it then became the 'custom' of steel mills to do so." [9] Likewise other new mills for a time shaded the Pittsburgh-Plus price, "what was known as the market," but soon, about 1903, began "to adhere to Pittsburgh-Plus." [10] Ah, how brief the time needed—in this case, three years—for an illegal practice, maintained by continual acts of illegality, to be transformed into an immemorial business custom, which unsuspecting jurists may be made to believe is the result of a natural evolution, to be respected and protected by the courts as a necessary exercise of that "freedom of competition" which alone can preserve the rights of the public! [11]

A NON-PRODUCING BASING POINT

Observe a peculiar condition of the sheet and tin plate industries —a "striking" fact we should say, if it had not failed ever to strike the dim sight and the dull ears of all the official investigators and the courts. There were no mills for the manufacture of sheets or tin plates either in Pittsburgh or in the Pittsburgh switching district, and the Ohio mills produced a greater tonnage in sheets than those in Pennsylvania (all of which were outside the Pittsburgh district). Now the fairy tale of the origin of Pittsburgh-Plus, oft told to show the simple convenience and "naturalness" of the plan, was that Pittsburgh was the great center of steel production from which most steel products were actually shipped when the Pittsburgh basing-point practice came into use. In the case of some kinds of steel, largely produced in the Pittsburgh district, the use of Pittsburgh as a basing point had a deceptive appearance of naturalness, though in principle it is artificial for all kinds of products alike. But such an explanation of the use of Pittsburgh as a base for pricing sheets and tin plate is peculiarly fantastic.

[8] *Idem*, p. 25.
[9] *Idem*, p. 24.
[10] *Idem*, p. 25.
[11] See below, Ch. XXII, especially discussion of the Fairmont Creamery Case.

NOW FOR A MERRY LIFE!

Now Pittsburgh-Plus was off and away on its merry life, bringing joy to the hearts of monopolists, and levying its rarely remitted toll from that patient burden bearer, the American people. For the formation of the giant steel corporation saw the all-but-universal adoption in the steel industry of this plan of bringing independents into conformity with the prices named by the Corporation, and of securing identity of delivered prices quoted to and paid by consumers. This whole movement had gone on under the very eyes of the Industrial Commission—Argus-eyed it should have been with its great corps of "experts" and investigators, but blind to the real significance of these occurrences.

It was at this historic point of time in May 1901 that Mr. Charles Schwab appeared on the witness stand and gave utterance to the serio-comic opinions which were related and interpreted in our opening pages. No doubt the reader would now find new interest and significance in perusing again that dialogue in which Mr. Schwab, who undoubtedly knew every turn and winding of the devious trail, so effectually threw his questioners off the scent and made them look as foolish as a pack of hounds sniffing the air and baying the moon, not knowing where they are or how they got there. Perhaps this was what, after all, the "formers" of the Corporation meant by "integration," a word by which they later hypnotized the courts. It was integration of prices, the delivered prices of the Corporation and of its former competitors becoming one and the same to each customer, regardless of their own diverse conditions of production, location, freights, and customers' nearness to the mills—a unity from which the buying public, except with rare and brief respites, was to have henceforth no appeal to the saving grace of competition. What is such integration but monopoly? Was it not the vision of this kind of integration which so inspired the youthful wizard of Pittsburgh when he wove his spell over the great House of Morgan?

A PLAN WITH A PURPOSE

When the simple facts are narrated regarding the early history of Pittsburgh-Plus up to that day of May 1901, as these facts now may be gathered from sworn testimony given for the first time twenty years later, can there be any uncertainty regarding the purpose and real nature of the practice? It is so plain that it calls for no Sherlock Holmes to unravel it. But no more than did the Industrial Commission, did the various Commissioners of the Bureau of Corporations down to 1914, see and comprehend just what was happening. Neither did the Department of Justice in its blundering attempts, after ten years of unaccountable delay, to prosecute the giant merger for violation of the Anti-Trust Act, open its eyes to the real situation and make these facts an essential part of the incriminating evidence. Nor did the courts, unaided by the prosecuting counsel, succeed any better in appreciating the real nature of this practice, whose existence was barely mentioned through the course of the Steel dissolution suit, and to which no significance was attached in the attempt to determine the existence of monopoly. The courts were concerned solely with the *means* employed to circumvent the law and not with the *end* itself; or it may be more accurate to say, they were concerned only with superficial means, and neither with the more ultimate means nor with the end itself. The pools, agreements, and meetings between 1901 and 1911 (which the judges in both courts unanimously held were illegal) were mere secondary means directed toward establishing and maintaining the Pittsburgh-Plus practice. This was the immediate means used to bring about an illegal restraint of trade, monopoly, the real aim and end of all these practices.

SILENCE IS GOLDEN

So the courts (without truly having before them any considerable evidence relating to anything after 1912) concluded, in the absence of evidence of formal agreements with independents, that after 1911 a state of ideal competition began and continued until 1920; whereas, in truth, the Pittsburgh-Plus system, to create and enforce which was the sole object of these illegal practices, had never been so completely successful in its results as it was in this very period. It was as if the courts, having declared that any agreement to accomplish the illegal end (restraint of trade) was illegal, had then assumed that no such agreement could possibly be made unless the court could see the conspirators' lips or fingers moving to speak or spell the forbidden words. The illegality consisted not in actually restraining trade, but only in talking about it. The courts were interested only in symptoms and not in the disease, for the real disease, the real offense against the Anti-Trust Law, was the maintenance of Pittsburgh-Plus, itself the proof and exercise of monopoly power.

A PATRIOTIC RECESS

For years after the Steel dissolution suit had begun in 1911, few ripples of true competition in prices disturbed the calm surface of the waters of monopoly. From 1914 until 1917, with enormous sales to the warring powers, the American steel industry was enjoying a feast of rising prices paid alike in foreign and in domestic sales, a large part of the latter with a bonus of Pittsburgh-Plus prices thrown in for good measure, heaped up and running over. Then the waters began to be troubled. In April 1917 the United States entered the war, and for a time, in the first wave of patriotic enthusiasm, selfish private considerations were swept aside on behalf of national necessity. In September 1917 the War Industries Board as a war measure established Chicago as a basing point for steel prices, on a parity with Pittsburgh, thus for the time eliminating the Pittsburgh-Plus practice as applied to mills in the Chicago district. This necessarily changed the territorial price relationships of the sales areas not only near Chicago but for great distances westward. The manufacturers (called fabricators) are middlemen in the sense that they purchase rolled steel as the "raw" (partly finished) material which they make into more elaborate forms, such as steel buildings, boilers, automobiles, windmills, hardware, and thousands of other articles. Western fabricators, not having now to pay the artificial Plus for their materials, enlarged their plants and extended the sales territories of their products.

THE GODS ON OLYMPUS

But suddenly, July 21, 1918, after ten months, while the war was at its height, Pittsburgh-Plus was restored on the suggestion of Mr. Elbert Gary, president of the Steel Corporation, at a meeting of the War Industries Board, on which he was serving without pay. This action dramatically illustrates the ways in which the gods on the industrial Olympus sometimes dispose of the fate of the mere mortals down on earth who must pay the bill. The action was taken at the most intense stage of military operations, without public knowledge or the slightest opportunity for a hearing being given to the fabricators or to the general public.

Mr. Brookings, the chairman of the War Industries Board, who had previously confessed with evident regret that he did "not know what the change means to the purchaser or consumer," began with a cheerful pun:

"That leaves the one basic question for us to discuss, I believe. Is it understood that the steel people now feel that it is necessary and wise to change the basic price of Chicago?"

Mr. Gary: "I think our Committee agrees generally as to what Mr. Replogle has said on the subject."

Mr. Brookings: "Mr. Replogle has stated that in his opinion it would be a good thing to do." Then turning to Mr. Replogle (well known in the steel industry): "Will you write this up so there will be no question about it?"

And it was done.[12] Yet even now there is some question about it. Within less than a week the Illinois Steel Company (the great Chicago and Gary subsidiary of Mr. Gary's corporation) had raised to the Pittsburgh-Plus rate the prices to its customers who had contracts under the Chicago base, and simultaneously, with one heart and one mind, the independents "cheerfully" followed this patriotic example.

At once arose protests from many business concerns that were adversely affected. These being futile, the Western Association of Rolled Steel Consumers for the Abolition of Pittsburgh-Plus was organized in January 1919 and engaged an eminent attorney, the late John S. Miller, who was in correspondence and in conference with Mr. Gary until July 1919.

THE COMMISSION DRAWS BACK

It seems to have been Mr. Gary's suggestion (perhaps sparring for time, as the dissolution suit was still pending) that the subject

---

[12] Minutes of the War Industries Board, June 21, 1918, read into the Pittsburgh-Plus record during the examination of Mr. Gary, November 15, 1922, Record, pp. 11700-11713, especially pp. 11706, 11713.

should be brought to the attention of the Federal Trade Commission, and together these two had a meeting with the Commission. Acting on this line, the Association on August 1, 1919, made application for a complaint to be issued against the Steel Corporation and certain independents. Likewise applications were made by the City of Duluth, by the State of Minnesota, and by many organizations of business men in the west and south. The Supreme Court having meantime delivered its opinion in the dissolution suit, the Commission, four months later, in July 1920, denied the application for a complaint by a vote of three to two. Mr. Gary's legal staff had vigorously combated the application. The individual statements made by each of the five Commissioners and given to the press make instructive reading today, showing, as they do, the widest divergence of reasoning even among those voting on the same side and the hopeless bewilderment of the Commission as a whole in the face of issues which most of them were unfitted by their training to analyze and resolve. Commissioners Murdock, Colver, and Gaskill voted against, and Thompson and Pollard for, the issuance of the complaint. Commissioner Huston Thompson in dissent showed fullest appreciation of the issues involved. However, the main ground on which he based his vote was simply that, in view of the large public interests involved, of the many applicants for a complaint, and of the insufficiency of data thus far collected by merely *ex parte* methods, other evidence was necessary before the Commission could properly determine whether to dismiss the application.

The opinions show that the Commissioners were somewhat chastened by recent decisions of the Supreme Court in which the Commission's actions had been rather sharply rebuked and limited, e.g., the Gratz case, and were in awe of the recent decision in the dissolution suit, in which, as the most legalistic of the Commissioners believed and declared:

The United States Supreme Court has established the validity of such [the United States Steel Corporation's] existence and ownership. Under the law it may fix a price for the product of all its mills on a common basis. It does so, using Pittsburgh as the base.[13]

13 Federal Trade Commission press release, July 24, 1920.

Thus this legal mind drew from that decision (taken in connection with an implied minor premise of the unqualified private property

American Farm Bureau Federation, Weekly News Letter,
January 24, 1924

FIG. 7. PHANTOM FREIGHT. ONE OF MANY CAR-
TOONS SHOWING POPULAR UNDERSTANDING AND
RESENTMENT IN THE WEST. CAPTION READ,
"WHAT'S WRONG WITH THIS PICTURE?"

rights of a corporation) what seemed to him the simple (though it is truly a preposterous) conclusion, that the Pittsburgh-Plus practice was recognized and sanctioned by the Supreme Court, despite the fact, as shown in our foregoing chapters, that even its existence was ignored throughout the dissolution suit.

THE COMMISSION MOVES

Such widespread resentment as was then felt against the Corporation's prices and practices, especially in the west and south, by thousands of its customers, so recently before described by Justice McKenna as happy and content under its benign rule, was not to be easily put down by this first rebuff from the Commission. On September 1, 1920, the advance of freight rates by 40 per cent automatically increased the Plus (this being also the difference in net realized price) at Chicago from $5.40 to $7.60 a ton, and made corresponding differences in price throughout the country, in accordance with the Pittsburgh-Plus scheme of pricing. Protests redoubled and a new petition for the issuance of a complaint was filed. Mr. H. G. Pickering of Duluth now ably presented the case for the Western Association in place of Mr. Miller, whose health had failed and who soon after died. On September 20, 1920, by a vote of three to two the Federal Trade Commission granted a rehearing, which began December 6. The increasing public interest was evidenced by the appearance, by attorney, of the American Farm Bureau Federation and, by representatives, of other organizations. April 30, 1921, again voting three to two,[14] the Commission issued a complaint against the Steel Corporation (no independents being included). The gathering of evidence and taking of testimony in many parts of the country was begun promptly and was continued for two and a half years.

PITTSBURGH-PLUS CONDEMNED

Meantime, early in 1923, was organized The Associated States opposing Pittsburgh-Plus, by the four States of Illinois, Iowa, Minnesota, and Wisconsin, which appropriated various sums totaling $55,000 and were joined by twenty-eight other States through executive action. Eleven of these States through their legislatures passed resolutions condemning or protesting against Pittsburgh-Plus. The Associated States largely superseded and took over the activities of the Western Association of Rolled Steel Consumers, and later submitted a brief as *amici curiae*. On its petition the final

---

[14] Commissioners Murdock and Gaskill in the negative, and Nugent, who had replaced Colver on the Commission, in the affirmative with Thompson and Pollard.

hearings in the case were postponed from May to December 1923 to permit the employment of economic advisers to study the economic issues which had been given such a dominant place in the respondents' defense. Dismissal of the complaint was generally expected. The testimony of three economists regarding the price theory involved was given in December 1923, the oral arguments of counsel were concluded June 24, 1924, and the decision of the Commission (voting four to one, Commissioner Gaskell dissenting) was given July 21, 1924, ordering, in substance, that the Corporation cease and desist from the Pittsburgh-Plus practice.

Within the sixty days allotted, the Corporation filed its answer, half evasive and contemptuous, promising to comply with the decision so far as this was practicable (whatever that may mean). The Commission, still thrilling with its own temerity in rendering a decision that a few months before scarcely any one had expected, was as much pleased as it was surprised to escape the unpleasant prospect of another long contest before the Supreme Court, the outcome of which must ever be doubtful, and the more so in the light of then recent litigation. It was therefore not prepared to take affront at the flippant manner of the Corporation, and prudently refrained from demanding a more specific answer. It has not courted trouble since by inquiring too closely through its field agents what has really been done in compliance with the order "to cease and desist." So here, in a matter of the greatest moment in the field of trade practices, the Commission has given to the public little information about actual conditions.

SO FAR AS IT PLEASED

From the press and other unofficial sources, however, it may be learned that the Corporation soon put into effect a Chicago base price $2 above the Pittsburgh base (on the plan of the Birmingham differential which had been in force some years, as a modification of Pittsburgh-Plus in southern territory). This action was at once followed by all the independents. After the temporary collapse of the basing-point system in the crisis of 1921, prices on plates, shapes, and bars at the Chicago mills had never been returned to the Pittsburgh base, but had been quoted on a Chicago base generally $2 above Pittsburgh. This seems to have been just what was now, as a show of partial compliance with the order, made the rule as regards other classes of steel products. At the same time this action gave a measure of assurance that full Pittsburgh-Plus on plates, shapes, and bars would not be suddenly

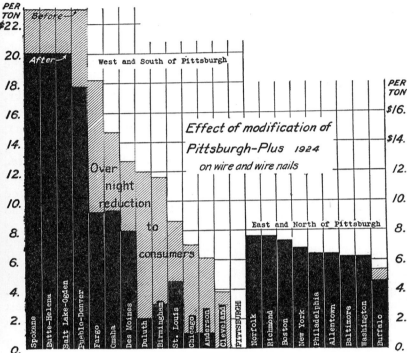

FIG. 8. EFFECTS PRONOUNCED BY A WESTERN U. S. SENATOR TO BE ALONE SUFFICIENT TO JUSTIFY THE EXISTENCE OF THE FEDERAL TRADE COMMISSION. CHART BASED ON DATA IN DOCKET 962 (BETHLEHEM-LACKAWANNA MERGER). WITNESS, HUGH E. WHITE.

restored, as had several times happened before. As a Chicago $2 differential was $4.80 a ton less than the full Plus, the result of the change was to reduce the cost (relative to the Pittsburgh base) of steel to fabricators and to other users of steel in Chicago and in western territory by that amount below what it had been or would have been under the old system of prices. Colorado, Duluth,

Birmingham, and other mills adjusted their prices to this new base.

The "overnight effect" of the partial abrogation of the Pittsburgh-Plus plan, September 16, 1924, is shown on the accompanying diagram. It was greatest ($10 a ton) at Duluth, nearly as great at Birmingham, about $6 at Chicago and near by, and as much as $3 at many points westward. East of Chicago, Pittsburgh-Plus rates remained in full force, excepting at Buffalo, where the rate (slightly adjusted with the new rate at Cleveland) was reduced about $.60 a ton. This demonstrates the falsity of the contention of witnesses and of attorneys for the Corporation that the Pittsburgh-Plus method of *quotation* had no influence whatever on prices. Even this substantial modification of it altered at once the whole complex of territorial relationships of prices, and the interests of great numbers of fabricators and of ultimate consumers.

SUBSTANTIAL RESULTS

Three years after the order went into effect one of the leading steel trade journals could say editorially:

Those who attacked the Pittsburgh-plus method have thus far been victorious. Their prime motive was cheaper steel and they have obtained it . . . As with the 8-hour day in the mills, what is roundly scored today as revolutionary is the accepted practice of tomorrow. The current method of quoting has become commonplace and there is no agitation for revision from either producers or consumers [15]

The prosperity of many of the western fabricators was indeed phenomenal. They were from $3 to $10 a ton stronger than before in their bidding against mills fabricating in the Pittsburgh district, who by the old plan were on a plan of price equality or better with mills in the uttermost parts of the country. Western fabricators were now able, in a more normal way, to underbid and thus to exclude the fabricated products of the Pittsburgh district from a larger part of this western territory. The steel mills too, in the Chicago district, have ever since been able to run at a higher percentage of their capacity than before, relative to those in the Pittsburgh district. Even this partial alteration of the rule of pricing

[15] *Iron Trade Review,* September 29, 1927.

(which the spokesman of the Corporation had strenuously maintained was "merely" a mode of quotation and had no effect on prices) had worked something of an economic revolution in the territorial distribution of the steel industry.

FOLKS STILL BELIEVE IN FAIRIES

A year later the journal just quoted made the further comment:

Four years ago this month the federal trade commission's decree of banishment against Pittsburgh as a basing point for . . . products produced in the Chicago district became effective. . . . The practical intent of the commission's order was to make Chicago independent of Pittsburgh in the pricing of steel. The East was not a party to the Pittsburgh basing point proceeding. This intent has not wholly become fact. Chicago base prices today are usually a differential . . . over the Pittsburgh base. Consumers, however, have benefited because delivered prices even on this basis are less than would be the sum of the Pittsburgh base plus a freight rate of $6.80 per ton. While Pittsburgh today still wields an influence not only on Chicago but also on all markets, its disintegration as a base is pronounced.

Birmingham as well as Chicago is a base for many finished products.[16] Many of the smaller middle western wire mills are their own basing points. . . . It may be that these changes would have evolved naturally, but undoubtedly some impetus emanated from the federal government's mandate.[17]

Evidently the writer of this editorial even then only vaguely understood the purely arbitrary character of the Pittsburgh basing practice, and still put faith in the childish tale of the "natural evolution" of this business practice. In truth it was the result of artificial agreement, or of simultaneous action tantamount thereto, and could be put down only by the strong arm of the law. Otherwise his comments, so far as they go, probably indicate pretty well the actual situation at the time.

MULTIPLE BASES

After 1924, Chicago did not truly become an independent basing point, nor did the independent mills determine their own

[16] This was true of Birmingham before the decision; in the same way it had a differential base.
[17] *Iron Trade Review*, September 20, 1928, p. 709.

prices on a mill base in a freely competitive market. The Chicago base (a fixed differential of about $2 above the Pittsburgh base) is announced by the Corporation for its own mills, and automatically with every such announcement other prices everywhere,

Chicago Tribune Survey, November 20, 1928

FIG. 9. WESTERN STEEL PRODUCERS BENEFIT BY MODIFICATION OF PITTSBURGH-PLUS. CARTOON ENTITLED "HOW THE MAGNET WORKS WITH THE SHIELD REMOVED"

quoted by everybody, Corporation and independent mills alike, follow these announced prices. For a time no one made any pretense of abandoning or of modifying the Pittsburgh basing plan in its application to mills east of Pittsburgh, and eastern mills selling to the west simply adjusted their prices in conformity with the new schedule in western territory. On December 7, 1927, however, the

Bethlehem Steel Company announced a series of mill bases for several of its recently merged mills in the eastern territory. The merger was at the time under attack by the Federal Trade Commission, with the certainty that the basing-point policy would be made an important issue. The *Daily Metal Trades Service* declared the importance to the trade of this change took "second place only to the announcement several years ago of the abandonment of Pittsburgh-Plus." The *Service* declared that it "appears to relate to far deeper causes than merely temporary sales policies" and broadly hinted at growing "tightening of the territorial" competition between the Bethlehem mills and "the Cleveland-Pittsburgh district." In view of this, the Youngstown-Bethlehem merger (pending at this writing) takes on more significance as against law and public interest; but the Department of Justice at Washington lifts not a finger.

NO FREE STEEL MARKETS

There is a woeful lack of specific information available to the public regarding the adjustment of prices to various delivery points in relation to the various basing points. What has been established appears to be a system of multiple basing points with identical delivered prices (similar to that long used in the cement industry),[18] involving denial of freedom of access at each mill and discriminatory treatment of customers, absorption of freights, cross shipments, virtual conspiracy, and the other uneconomic incidents of a single basing-point system.

The formal acceptance by the Corporation of the Commission's order seemed at the time to bring to a close another chapter in the long history of the artificial control of steel prices in America. But those best informed on the subject know well that this subtle device in restraint of trade, "conceived in sin and born in iniquity," had not really ended its career as an accomplice of monopoly in circumventing the laws of trade and of the nation, either in the steel or in numerous other industries.

[18] See below, Ch. XVII.

CHAPTER XII

SHARPSHOOTING AT A FORMULA

THE SPECTER AT THE BOARD

IT IS an intriguing question why the Steel Corporation, acting as always "under advice of counsel"—and they were the best to be had—should, in 1924, to the surprise of all the legal and the business world, have decided to accept, at least in form, the order to desist from the Pittsburgh-Plus practice, and even partially put the order into effect. For twenty-three years the maintenance of Pittsburgh-Plus had been the object of the Steel Corporation's utmost solicitude. While the complaint was pending, Mr. Gary had declared that the case was destined to be the greatest law-suit of all time; and counsel had often implied or uttered the threat that appeal would be taken to the Supreme Court from any adverse decision of the Commission. Was this mere bluster and bluff "to get on the nerves" of the Commission? Able counsel had fooled the courts before; could they not hope to do it again? No, apparently hope gave place to fear. The Corporation shrank from entering again the portals of the Court from which it had so recently escaped with a doubtful vindication by an ambiguous majority.

The full explanation of this change of front the public may never learn from any one of that little inner group of astute counselors who alone could give it, but we may venture a guess. The specter of monopoly had disconcertingly appeared at the banquet board. Repeatedly that forbidden name had been reëchoed in the later stages of the hearings and even in the final briefs of complainants. To appeal now from the Commission to the Courts would involve the disagreeable chance that the whole question of the nature of the Corporation and of its practices as involved in the dissolution suit might be opened up again, and with a whole new fund of facts and interpretations that before had been successfully concealed.

The suit had been brought in 1911 for violation of Sections One and Two of the Anti-Trust Act of 1890, alleging monopoly and restraint of trade as shown by the very facts of its formation and of its continuing existence. Conspiracy was not alleged, and the independents thus were not included in the action. The Pittsburgh-Plus price policy as used by the Corporation itself was not referred to in the complaint, and the prosecution ignored it completely in the marshaling of evidence to prove restraint of trade.

A TIME FOR CAUTION

A year after the conclusion of the dissolution suit, the complaint in the Pittsburgh-Plus case was issued by the Federal Trade Commission (April 30, 1921) against the use of the Pittsburgh-Plus plan of pricing for violation both of Section Two of the Clayton Act, forbidding discrimination, and of Section Five of the Federal Trade Act, forbidding unfair methods of competition. Of these two counts in the complaint the more essential one was that charging discrimination; the charge of unfair competition was thrown in merely for luck, loading the legal blunderbuss with extra slugs in the hope that by accident they might hit something. In neither the dissolution nor the basing-point case were the independents made defendants. In other essential respects the basing-point complaint differed greatly from the suit. It was brought under statutes that had not been enacted until several years after the suit was begun.[1] The Pittsburgh-Plus practice, ignored in the dissolution suit, was now made the sole object of attack, whereas monopoly (or restraint of trade), the only offense alleged before, is in the Pittsburgh-Plus complaint not even hinted at. In all its stormy career of litigation, from its formation in 1901 to 1924, the Corporation succeeded in keeping these two issues from ever being seen together in public, whereas in very truth they are identical

---

[1] This "new legislation" was referred to by Judges Buffington, 223 Fed. Rep. 161, and Woolley, 223 Fed. Rep. 178, as affording a means of relief for any barely possible, though to them hardly conceivable, abuses that might appear in the future conduct of the Corporation.

twins, but two aspects of the same offense. "East is East and West is West, and never these twain shall meet"—such was the policy of the Corporation before the courts, regarding these two offenses, and it strove to surpass even Robert Louis Stevenson's imagination by being a Mr. Hyde all the time in its relation to the anti-trust laws, while showing always the benevolent countenance of Mr. Jekyll. However, it could, no more than did Stevenson's shady hero, succeed indefinitely in this difficult undertaking, and the real identity of monopoly with this apparently innocent price practice, of which glimpses had been caught from time, began to be more and more clearly revealed in the later stages of the Pittsburgh-Plus complaint. This was an all-sufficient reason, if it was not the only reason, why the Corporation chose not to rouse a sleeping dog by appearing again, so soon, before the door of the Supreme Court.

CHASING A GREASED PIG

The position taken by the Steel Corporation in its all-but-last defense of the Pittsburgh-Plus practice will repay examination, not because of the merits of the argument "in and of itself," but for the help it may give toward the better understanding of the larger question of basing points and delivered prices, of which Pittsburgh-Plus is only a part. It would be difficult for any one lacking acquaintance with the records in this case to believe how elusive throughout the hearings was the position and behavior of the Corporation in meeting the rather simple and direct issues presented by the complaint. The distinguished lawyers of the Steel Corporation and ornaments of the American Bar interposed four successive lines of argument, each charmingly inconsistent with all the others: (1) they denied the existence of any such practice; (2) they admitted the existence of the practice as a mere form of quotation, but denied that prices followed the quotation; (3) they admitted that prices followed the quotations, and claimed as an especial evidence of fairness toward its customers that the actual prices of its subsidiaries followed invariably the published Pittsburgh-Plus prices; (4) they argued that the complete and general use of the plan both of quotation and prices was perfectly in accord with the ideal competition (supply and demand) which is the aim of the law. Now, what could be a more complete answer than that?

It may be hard to imagine what purpose the Corporation could have hoped to accomplish by such a frivolous and self-destructive line of argument. But it served the practical purpose of evading the issue. It distracted and frustrated a large share of the attention and energies of the prosecution, compelling it to engage in the undignified chase after a greased pig instead of straightforwardly following the real issues of the case.

NOW YOU SEE IT

We have learned above just when and how Pittsburgh-Plus had its origin. The practice prevailed with brief interruptions and was commonly understood in the trade for at least fifteen years before the suit was begun. The Corporation in these proceedings claimed for it an immemorial origin. Mr. Gary testified in 1913 [2] that the Steel Corporation did not usually sell from any of its mills at prices which varied from those quoted in *The Iron Age*. He and others repeatedly declared, yea boasted, that it did not have two prices, one open and one secret. He also, in the preliminary conferences with complainants before the Pittsburgh-Plus suit was begun,[3] frankly admitted that steel was generally sold (not merely quoted) on the Pittsburgh-Plus plan. He claimed that it was necessary for the orderly conduct of the business, and also "for the benefit of the purchaser," to have "*one basing price . . .* something that was well understood so that every user of steel all over the country bought and used his steel on a certain basis, knowing in advance that every one else who bought steel had to pay exactly as he did" (that is, the same Pittsburgh-Plus identical delivered prices, which are exactly the same real steel prices for hardly any two buyers).[4]

The Corporation's amended answer, after a general denial, had admitted that

---

[2] In the Steel dissolution suit; see Commission brief in the Pittsburgh-Plus complaint, p. 55.

[3] See brief by Attorney for the Commission, p. 58, and brief for Associated States, p. 15.

[4] See Associated States brief, p. 15.

with certain exceptions mentioned in the complaint said subsidiaries usually quote their products on what is commonly called the Pittsburgh Basis, which represents their prices for such products in Pittsburgh plus the freight to the point of sale and delivery. This is the practice among steel manufacturers generally.

Mr. Gary testified somewhat confusedly, as follows, in the hearings on this case:

I will state that generally, since the incorporation of the United States Steel Company, we have quoted prices on a Pittsburgh base *and sold them on that base* but when business is dull we have absorbed a part of the freight.[5]

In other connections Counsel for the Corporation declared: "What Judge Gary himself said is of course competent and binding upon the corporation."[6] Many consumer witnesses testified that for years they paid invariably the Pittsburgh-Plus quotation of the date of sale, or in a few cases nearly that price within the small range of 5 to 10 cents a hundred pounds.[7] These statements applied almost as fully to the independents' prices as to those of the Corporation.

AND NOW YOU DON'T SEE IT

Concurrently with these plain admissions, the very existence and reality of the practice was again and again denied by the Corporation's counsel throughout the progress of the suit. This is involved in the general denial of "each and every allegation, inference and argument" in those paragraphs describing the method of quoting and selling steel manufactured outside of the city of Pittsburgh.[8] For nearly three years counsel wrangled over the reality of the practice. What a ridiculous situation is created by this plea! At every mention of the Pittsburgh-Plus policy, hundreds of times during the taking of testimony, counsel for respondents challenged the assumption that it existed. This became a part of the legalistic ritual of the case, distracting, time-consum-

---

[5] F.T.C. docket 760, pp. 10771-4. (Italics ours.)
[6] Respondent's brief, p. 41.
[7] Associated States Brief, p. 12.
[8] In paragraph VII (b) and (c) of answer, to paragraph V (b) and (c) of the amended complaint.

ing, truth-defeating, and involving the waste of thousands of dollars of the Corporation's and of the public's money.[9]

To this contradiction of admission and denial the answer then adds a false justification for a general use of the basing-point plan on these grounds:

The practice of quoting a base price is largely for the convenience of customers and is not confined to the steel industry nor to this country but exists throughout the world, and is followed by many, if not most, of the most important lines of production and sale.

Then comes historical misinformation to this effect:

In the steel industry it has obtained from the beginning and became a settled custom long before the United States Steel Corporation was formed. Pittsburgh was made the basing point in the early days because at that time nearly all steel was manufactured in the Pittsburgh district. It has remained the basing point simply because, notwithstanding the construction of steel manufacturing plants in other localities, the country outside of Pittsburgh is still under normal conditions dependent upon the Pittsburgh district for the major part of its requirements for steel excepting rails.[10]

Here is an extraordinary mélange of garbled facts and fantastic theory. The Pittsburgh-Plus method of pricing and sale was not only admitted to exist, but was declared to have existed from time immemorial in the steel industry, the Steel Corporation having had nothing to do with its origin and having no part in its operation except to follow a long-established business custom, in conformity with "economic law," and followed also in the "other more important lines" of industry. Those particular lines were not further specified, but if they had been, the curious fact would have emerged that they too are, and long have been, smirched by suspicion of monopoly and restraint of trade.

[9] A few among many examples of such interruptions and objections from the record of evidence taken the last week of the hearings are cited in the Appendix A to Ch. XII.

[10] Respondent's amended answer, Section VII, paragraph b.

BIG TENT AND SIDESHOW

The rule of Pittsburgh-Plus was admirable for the purposes of the Corporation, enabling it to name for each class of steel products a single base price at Pittsburgh, by which instantly the delivered price to be charged by all other mills (provided they played the game) was fixed, and enabling the Corporation to tell instantly whether any single independent anywhere was not faithfully conforming. But in attempting to justify, in reason, in theory, and in law, this simple working rule for·agreement among conspirators in restraint of trade, the Corporation found itself compelled to develop a rather complicated argument, having two contradictory branches, united only by the common feature that both were given the appearance of the operation of the "law of supply and demand." Coached well, no doubt by economic experts, the legal lights, Mr. Elbert Gary (no poor lawyer himself), Judge Lindabury, and their aides, learned for their purposes to parrot the phrases and ape the manners of true theory. The whole procedure may be likened to a circus; in the big tent was shown the proof that as a general formula to be used and conformed with by every mill in every part of the land, Pittsburgh-Plus was but the perfect result and expression of free competition. But such complete unity of mind and action by producers everywhere that they all sold at exactly the same delivered prices at each separate location in the United States was too perfect an exhibition. The simplest mind must suspect a trick. So it is necessary to take the audience into the small tent, where supply and demand appears in its other rôle of making prices vary from the formula—not much or always (for in large part the formula was unquestionably adhered to), but just a little, now and then, enough at least to suggest independence of action by each producer and the freedom of each customer to buy at "competitive" prices in his home town! The whole circus, main tent and sideshow together, was a fake worthy of the talents of Phineas T. Barnum, but hardly worthy of these eminent jurists and sworn officers of the courts.

SCHOOLBOY LOGIC

An unspoiled mind might be tempted to believe that if prices were quoted on a basing point for the information and convenience of customers, only adherence to the quotations would attain that object. But no, "they are seldom adhered to strictly." Again, one might reasonably suppose that if it be a special continuing virtue of the Pittsburgh-Plus formula that it is in accord with the infallible law of supply and demand, then the more closely it was adhered to, the more strongly its use would prove competition and the greater would be its legal merit. But no, the mysterious virtue of Pittsburgh-Plus, as expounded by the Corporation, seems to be precisely this, that it is *not* adhered to. The Corporation's Counsel were true disciples of that schoolboy who so logically declared that "pins has saved thousands of lives by folks' not swallerin' 'em." The solemn proposition is that the rule of Pittsburgh-Plus, sanctioned alike by time and by some mystic law of political economy, is to be honored in the breach rather than in the observance. So this is Messrs. Gary, Lindabury and Company's economic curiosity: the Pittsburgh-Plus price system is strictly in accord with the operation of the law of supply and demand, but non-adherence to it proves that competition as to prices is vigorous and unrestrained and that the price of "every article of production" in the steel industry in every locality is "determined by the law of supply and demand." Can you beat it? Like the old darky's wonderful trap, "it cotches 'em a-comin' and a-gwyin'."

The question of fact, it would seem, should be answerable by the evidence of actual contracts, and most painstaking studies of this kind have shown about 90 per cent of close agreement to the formula. Such discrepancies as occurred may mostly be explained because of differences between contract and delivery dates, temporary failure of the conspiracy, and various other details.[11] The testimony of customers that prices "varied" undoubtedly refer in most cases either to the brief transitional periods or to the periods of breakdown of the system.[12]

THE GENEROUS LEMON VENDER

A special word should be said of the discrepancies from the established Pittsburgh basing point in an upward direction. These premium prices were pointed to by the Corporation as if they

---

[11] Some of these cases are further discussed in Appendix B to Ch. XII.
[12] See above, Ch. X.

proved the non-existence of the system as fully as lower prices might. But they are of entirely different nature. Such premium prices occurred always, it is safe to say, in boom times, when the Corporation mills were booked up to capacity and could not give early delivery. The smaller independents are rarely, if ever, booked up as near to capacity as are the Corporation and larger independent mills. The reasons are readily understood, inasmuch as small mills are prevented by the Pittsburgh-Plus plan normally from making any concession in prices even in their own peculiar territory that would make up for a certain limitation otherwise in their facilities and service. In boom times, therefore, "the little fellows" are able to get, and often do get, a so-called "premium" for early delivery above the official Pittsburgh base. But the Corporation takes no offense at this; this is not shading the announced price or breaking the rule. Having nothing more to sell itself, the Corporation makes a virtue of keeping its old price posted for the public to gaze at. Many folks, fooled by this, have highly praised the Corporation for its generosity. It explains modestly that it is doing all it can to prevent a runaway market, to "stabilize" prices, etc. A quoted price is not really a price at all, it is merely a quotation, unless and until the trader stands ready to make delivery. The situation recalls a conversation at a fruit stand regarding the price of lemons:

"How much?"

"Thirty cent a dozen."

"But the stand around the corner sells them for twenty cents."

"Why you then no buy dem dere?"

"They haven't any this morning."

"Ah, if I no hava de lemon I sella dem at twenty cent too." [13]

OCCASIONAL COMPETITION

Premiums (necessarily rare and brief) may be taken by the independents with impunity and the system of price maintenance remain intact, but let any makers of steel in normal or in slack times cut the established prices except accidentally or for more than a brief moment, and it is *lèse-majesté*, the system is imperiled, and a war of prices may be on to bring the offenders to their senses.

[13] See testimony of Prof. W. Z. Ripley in the Pittsburgh-Plus hearings.

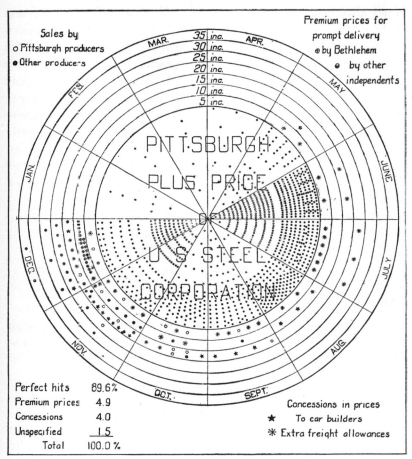

Sales by
o Pittsburgh producers
● Other producers

Premium prices for
prompt delivery
⊕ by Bethlehem
◑ by other
independents

MAR. 35 inc. APR.
30 inc.
25 inc.
20 inc.
15 inc.
10 inc.
5 inc.

FEB. JAN. DEC. NOV. OCT. SEPT. AUG. JULY JUNE MAY

PITTSBURGH
PLUS PRICE

U S STEEL
CORPORATION

Perfect hits   89.6%
Premium prices   4.9
Concessions   4.0
Unspecified   _1.5_
      Total   100.0 %

Concessions in prices
★   To car builders
✳ Extra freight allowances

FIG. 10. THE PITTSBURGH-PLUS TARGET. THIS REMARKABLE
CHARTING OF ALL OBTAINABLE SALES IN A CERTAIN PERIOD IS FROM
F.C.T. DOCKET 962 (BETHLEHEM-LACKAWANNA MERGER) AS AN-
ALYZED BY H. E. WHITE. DOTS WITHIN THE FIRST INNER CIRCLE
ACCORD EXACTLY WITH THE AGREED FORMULA; ALL OTHERS ARE
PROBABLY PERMISSIBLE PREMIUMS OR GENERALLY AUTHORIZED
CONCESSIONS ON SPECIALTIES. PERFECT MARKSMANSHIP IS INDI-
CATED, WHICH MEANS THAT THE ILLEGAL AGREEMENT WAS NEVER
VIOLATED IN LONG PERIODS OF NORMAL BUSINESS CONDITIONS

Here, also, in these occasional periods of the complete breakdown of the system, occur most of the cases often cited by steel producers and accepted by customers as evidence of the persistence of a state of genuine competition in the steel industry.

Again as in 1921, now in 1930, Mr. Schwab before a great gathering of the steel industry is deploring the fact that "several months ago price instability was permitted to come into our commercial structure." And Mr. Farrell "criticized unfair competition," declared "we have got to be honest," and denounced "price cutting" as "the main trouble with the steel industry." He declared that price cutting "killed business," a doctrine at variance with the usual view of the effect of lower prices in increasing sales.[14] In December 1930, as its generous contribution to the cause of relieving the depression, the steel industry, under the lead of the Corporation, raised steel prices generally.

In its answer to the Pittsburgh-Plus complaint, the Corporation referred specifically to such an exceptional period when, as it says,

market prices are frequently materially lower than the prevailing Pittsburgh price plus the freight rate from Pittsburgh to point of destination, particularly when the supply from the territory outside of Pittsburgh equals or exceeds the demand in such territory.

This statement is partially true, but garbles the facts and misrepresents their real nature. For these departures (called frequent, but in truth rare) from the Pittsburgh-Plus prices are of a totally different nature from those mere nibblings at the official prices which the Corporation tried to prove were daily occurring. In these exceptional periods, as even the Corporation in its ingenious version of theory admitted, "the supply outside of Pittsburgh exceeds the demand." But those are times when the whole system of official Pittsburgh-Plus breaks down (no longer is "prevailing"), and invariably at such times the smaller companies return more or less fully to the plan of mill-base prices.

Under critical examination, the evidence adduced to show that,

[14] The New York *Times,* October 25, 1930, reporting the meeting of the Steel Institute.

as a system of pricing, the Pittsburgh-Plus system had no existence, melts away like fog before the sun. That it prevailed most of the time as a system of quotations was undisputed; whenever it did so, it prevailed as a system of prices, adhered to by Corporation and independents alike with an exactness that is astonishing. But what if all the flimsy claims of non-adherence had been true, would they have proven the non-existence of Pittsburgh-Plus? Certainly not; merely that the adherence was in practice not 100 per cent perfect. It is not proof that a girl has no chin, to show that she has a dimple in it.

MR. GARY ENJOYS A LINCOLN STORY

In his testimony before the Stanley Committee in June 1911, Mr. Gary inadvertently confessed the truth that the live-and-let-live market-leadership policy of basing-point prices involved the same result as an explicit agreement. But when that keen lawyer, Mr. Martin Littleton (then a Representative and member of the Committee), restated the proposition in a way implying that it might fit the practices of the Steel Corporation, Mr. Gary drew back in alarm, as near to confusion as he ever was in his long career of elusive testimony. Here is the conversation:

Mr. Gary. Of course if you and I, knowing exactly what the other is doing from time to time, continue to do that same thing, then the result is the same as if you and I agree to do that.

Mr. Littleton. You will recall—I do not recall it exactly—one of Mr. Lincoln's favorite illustrations that if four men in four counties each whittled on a piece of wood for four or five days and met at the county seat and put their pieces of wood on a table and they all fitted with each other that he would ask nobody to furnish him with any evidence of the fact that they had had an agreement in advance that they would all whittle in a certain direction and that they would meet there, and he thought that was the highest authority.

Mr. Gary. I am not familiar with that. I am certain in our case the sticks do not fit. They never have fitted; they have never been like anything else.

Mr. Littleton. Although there has been a good deal of whittling?

Mr. Gary. Although there has been a good deal of whittling, but that is the trouble, they have been whittling at random more or less by trying to keep posted with one another's whittling. That is a very apt illustration and I am very glad it has been suggested.[15]

GREAT MARKSMANSHIP

It surely was an apt illustration, but was Mr. Gary really "very glad it had been suggested"? In any event, while his Corporation continued industriously to whittle on a pattern of prices that fitted almost exactly with that of all other steel producers, he and his legal staff performed an equal marvel during the next nine years of litigation in keeping the significance of this pattern from the knowledge of the courts.

Pricing by the various mills under the Pittsburgh-Plus plan may be likened to shooting at a target, namely, the formula of "the Pittsburgh-Plus equivalent." It was real sharpshooting, for the misses were mostly only apparent, not real, being shots intentionally a little higher (premiums), or not aimed at the target visible to the onlooker but at another target (as just when the base price has been shifted, or for extras not exactly comparable, etc.). Diagrams prepared according to this analogy show how nearly all the shots hit the bull's-eye, a most remarkable example of concerted action and of discipline strictly maintained among great numbers of rival enterprises, thus united in one grand conspiracy in restraint of trade. Now and then in bad times the temptation would become too great for the little fellows, and some would begin shooting at a different target, each at his own mill-base price. Then the Corporation would threaten to do some real shooting that would fill the hides of its small competitors with buckshot and leave them with large hospital bills and chastened spirits.[16]

---

[15] Stanley Committee Hearings, pp. 280-281.
[16] See Mr. Gary's remarks quoted above, Ch. IX.

CHAPTER XIII

TEACH A PARROT

A MIRACLE OF CHANCE

IT WAS probably Thomas Carlyle's none too gentle pen that first wrote: Teach a parrot to say supply and demand, and you have made a political economist. Any suspicion that Carlyle may have meant to refer to the spokesmen of the United States Steel Corporation is of course dispelled when one recalls that these words were penned some three quarters of a century before they began to display their fondness for the mystic phrase. But once they discovered its efficacy as a narcotic they used it in liberal doses —in Mr. Gary's public addresses, in statements before Congressional committees, in the dissolution suit, and in *crescendo* throughout the hearings on Pittsburgh-Plus. Never has greater faith been professed by able men in a mere jingle of words, in its power to accomplish nothing short of a mathematical miracle, unfailingly, bringing about a result which according to the theory of chances could not happen once in a million times. For this wonderful application of theory had two parts which were declared to fit into each other with the exactness of a piston in a polished auto-cylinder. First, "the law of supply and demand" was declared to determine in each of the different consuming localities so-called "market prices" (meaning delivered prices), varying according to the particular conditions of competition existing at each such place of delivery. But here is the miracle; the complete record and table of such delivered prices, said to be determined independently by local competition and the operation of the law of supply and demand, is found to be just that which must result if the Corporation and the independents alike, acting in perfect agreement, were using the Pittsburgh-Plus formula all over the country.[1] This system of delivered prices is exactly that which would result if all the steel produced in this country were made at Pittsburgh by one company and sold at the announced mill-base price, to which was added the freight from Pittsburgh to destination. The most miraculous aspect of this miracle is that this identity of delivered prices necessarily involves, and can only result from, the widest diversity of net mill prices charged to their various customers by each and every mill not located at Pittsburgh. For the moment that any mill began to treat its various customers alike at its own doors, the Pittsburgh-Plus pattern in that region would be erased, prices would be reduced to many customers, and shipments from Pittsburgh mills to that territory would be excluded. The significance of this will be further indicated below.

THE "MARGINAL THEORY" TO THE RESCUE

Now let us take a look at another way in which the "supply and demand" theory was applied to explaining and justifying, economically, the whole system of Pittsburgh-Plus prices. Reduced to its simplest terms, the main contention of the Corporation throughout all the proceedings and in its final brief was this: the "demand" for the various products in western territory had been and still was, they maintained, greater than the producing capacity (this being assumed to be the supply) of the Corporation and its competitors combined in western territory; this constant deficit called, they said, for the constant shipment of steel from Pittsburgh to Chicago, and as this, of course, when delivered in Chicago or its neighborhood from Pittsburgh mills, cost the buyer the Pittsburgh price plus the freight, these delivered prices necessarily registered, or determined, the regular market prices in Chicago for all steel, whether brought into Chicago or produced there. This argument was repeated in detail with reference to each of various kinds of steel products and in relation to what was called western territory.[2] There was here presented a version of a marginal supply theory—crudely and bunglingly applied, indeed, but

---

[1] With some arbitrary exceptions, such as the Birmingham differential, and with comparatively slight deviations in some cases, as discussed above.

[2] Specifically, in Respondents' brief: steel and wire, pp. 103, 122; sheet and tin plate, pp. 109-111, 124-128; and bars, plates, and shapes, pp. 117-121.

having a certain relative validity—as against the crude cost-of-production theory which more or less plainly at first [3] was made by complainants the ground of a plea for a separate base price at Chicago as low as that at Pittsburgh.[4] If, when true competitive conditions prevailed, a deficit of production at Chicago existed, a "demand and supply" price would for the time be justified in economic theory and by existing law, no matter how much above the estimated cost. Mr. Gary and others frequently admitted that such a situation was necessarily somewhat temporary, and that sooner or later "the law of supply and demand will eventually take care of the whole question" in some other way, apparently by bringing costs and prices together.[5] But before turning to that question, let us not fail to observe some other very significant features of the Corporation's supply and demand theory.

SAUCE FOR THE GANDER

This deficit argument, observe, was developed only in relation to "western territory," which was treated almost entirely as if it were limited to the Chicago district (within a few miles of the city) with occasional references to a similar situation, with a similar justification of Pittsburgh-Plus, at Duluth, St. Louis, and Birmingham. Most of the complainants (buyers of steel) were in territory neighboring to Chicago, with some from Duluth and from the south. Moreover, the complaint as finally issued was drawn only against the Corporation (to simplify the proceedings, it was said) and not against the independents, although they were just as fully participating in the maintenance and operation of the system as was the Corporation itself. Manifestly, this explanation and justification of the nation-wide system of Pittsburgh-Plus logically calls for the demonstration of a similar absolute deficit of products in the district contiguous to each mill in the country, at Pueblo,

---

[3] See brief, Associated States, p. 100.

[4] In unguarded moments, as in his Duluth speech in 1918, Mr. Gary had publicly implied that unit costs at the wonderful new Gary plants were less than those at Pittsburgh, as indeed seemed almost self-evident. The cost ratios were Pittsburgh 100, Duluth 113, Birmingham 101, and Gary only 82. No anti-trust statute authorized the fixing of prices in relation to cost of production, and if one had, the difficulties of ascertaining costs would have been insuperable. What would be the fate of such a definite price-fixing plea before the Supreme Court can easily be imagined.

[5] Record of Pittsburgh-Plus Hearings, p. 10832.

Duluth, Cleveland, Buffalo, Bethlehem, Philadelphia, Baltimore, and elsewhere, each of which regions near the mills must be shown to require constantly and regularly (except at the rare periods of breakdown of the system) to be supplied with a portion of each kind of products from the never-failing central reservoir of surplus production at Pittsburgh. The argument implies that not one of these mills, excepting rarely, had sufficient product to supply all the demand at its own doors! It would seem that if at any time steel moved from any of these outlying mills toward Pittsburgh—still more strikingly, if it moved actually into Pittsburgh, or through it and beyond—that the ingenious supply and demand theory would then show that said mill should not base its prices on Pittsburgh but become its own basing point. Why not become the basing point also for Pittsburgh? The rule should work both ways. This very movement into and past the Pittsburgh district occurred constantly while the system was operating most perfectly. There is a flaw somewhere. But slow—we shall come to this in due order.

PUBLIC MEDDLING AND MUDDLING

What, used accurately, does "the law of supply and demand" signify as a matter of theory? Just this: that if competition in a market is free and effective, on the part both of buyers and of sellers, a price will result which permits the maximum number of trades possible, leaving no motive to trade on the part of any one in the market. Such a price may be said to equilibrate demand (number of units taken at the price) with supply (the number that freely competing sellers are ready to sell at that price). Applied in practice, this "law" becomes a maxim of worldly wisdom, warning against artificial meddling with the automatic process of price adjustment in free markets. Such meddling is principally undertaken by two agencies: (1) governments endeavoring to fix or manipulate prices in the interests of certain favored classes; and (2) private and corporate industries, usually acting through combinations and by conspiracies in restraint of trade. Supported by history and example, this "law" teaches that even when undertaken with the best of motives, governmental price meddling to thwart (not, be it noted, to facilitate and insure) the truly competitive market price that results from the interplay of bids by buyers and sellers is usually futile or harmful. If prices are thus raised (as often they may be for a time) above what they would have been, the demand at the higher price is reduced (substitute goods are encouraged; diversion of trade occurs), whereas the supply is increased by the attraction of increased profits, and in the long run the plight of the industry and the producers is made worse. *Vice versa*, if prices are thus artificially reduced for the purpose of favoring certain consumers, the supply at the lower price falls off (so-called marginal producers and marginal units of product are cut off), and the demand at the lower price increases, but cannot be satisfied at that price. Either artificial increase or decrease of price results thus in destroying the equilibrium of demand (number of goods bought) and supply (number of goods offered) and actually reduces the quantity of such goods enjoyed by the members of the community. If they are wholesome, innocent, really useful goods, this presumably is injurious to the community's welfare.

MONOPOLISTIC MEDDLING

It is surely not necessary to parallel this explanation of the uneconomic nature of the usual type of government price meddling with a similar explanation in respect to private monopolistic restraint of trade. The same explanation very evidently applies in almost every detail, with additional aggravation of the offense against the public welfare. For higher prices resulting from manipulation by a private selling monopoly (the case of a buying monopoly is rare) not only injure the consumers by decreasing the amount of available goods, but they likewise limit the opportunities of other producers to engage with equal freedom in the industry (however, this fact may be obscured, since open price wars for the destruction of competitors have been avoided). Moreover, these private invasions of the rights of others have not the safeguards and legal justification of those undertaken by a duly authorized public agency for an avowedly public purpose. They are violations of the spirit and letter of the law, confessedly done with the motive of private profit— although, as in the case of the Steel Corporation, it is true that this action may be accompanied by generous professions of a desire to "stabilize" the industry while thwarting "the workings" of the law of supply and demand.

All this is written large in the history of Anglo-Saxon institutions and law since long before the Case of Monopolies in 1603. The thought of the essential virtue and validity of "the law of supply and demand," properly interpreted as a maxim of practical wisdom, underlies our whole public policy toward private monopoly. The anomalous case of the acceptance of private monopoly in the great public utilities and their regulation by Commissions should not confuse any one—although it often does—for in such a case monopoly has not been accepted as an alternative of free competition, but only because experience had abundantly proved that under the actual conditions competition had become ineffective or non-existent. And it is not to be overlooked that whenever private monopoly in any industry has been thus "accepted" it has, so far as price goes, been shorn of its private character and has been made subject to *public* price fixing. Intermediate between a condition where prices are without any public regulation, and are truly determined by the law of supply and demand and the condition of accepted monopoly with public price fixing there comes, however, a broad field of industrial action where governmental regulation of prices has to perform the most valuable function of strengthening the too feeble forces of competition and of protecting them against the anti-social attacks of private monopoly. It is in this ill-surveyed field that those problems of industrial price regulation lie, with which our whole study is peculiarly concerned.

IF SELLERS' COMPETITION FAILS

The truth of these ideas on supply and demand is so fully implied in economics and the law that their restatement may seem to be a work of supererogation. But the greatest fallacies are merely distorted versions of simple truths. The omission or alteration of any one of several conditions assumed may quite falsify any conclusions to be drawn in applying this so-called law to practical cases. Let us, therefore, examine in some detail the appeal of the Steel Corporation to the authority of supply and demand in sup-

part of the use, by itself and its competitors, of the Pittsburgh basing point for delivered prices on steel not made or shipped from Pittsburgh. We shall find that it leaves unperpetrated no possible error and avoids no possible fallacy.

A most elementary error is in forgetting that the truth of the "law" of "supply and demand" assumes full, two-sided competition, the two being linked as coördinate. It is a law of competitive price and does not apply in full, if at all, where competition is restrained. If producers, whether or not by formal agreement, in fact refrain from acting independently in their bidding, while buyers continue to compete actively, the resulting price might perhaps be said to be determined by a "law of demand," but not by a law of demand *and* supply. This is so obvious that even Mr. Gary in his testimony declared that if for any reason either buyer or seller "is compelled to act and is not left free, then to a corresponding extent the law of supply and demand is temporarily suspended or modified," but he denied often and emphatically that any "artificial arrangement for creating supply and demand," or "any arrangement contrary to law," had been made.[6]

The origin, the history, and the nature of the Pittsburgh-Plus practice were such as to refute such a claim of innocence. The plan and practice lacks every essential mark that characterizes a real market and real market prices. For note that the truth of the law of supply and demand assumes the existence of a market place (at least a meeting of minds and of bids through some means of communicating ideas). If buyers are not permitted to come together when they so desire, and buy where the sellers are dealing at the same time with other buyers, access to the market is denied, and this defeats the action of the law of supply and demand. In such cases both supply and demand are artificially limited and controlled.

MARKETS CREATED BY LEGAL FICTION

This is what is done by compulsory delivered prices which are a necessary condition to the successful operation of any basing-point system. Their indefensible character is revealed by the mendacious

[6] Hearings, pp. 10802-10816, and *passim* elsewhere. Likewise this is interwoven into the Brief as an essential contention of the Corporation.

explanation that always prefaces the apology for them: that they are quoted merely for the convenience of the customer! The description given and the defense relate merely to an *optional* delivered price, such as is a mill-base price (open to all comers) plus the actual freight from mill to destination. The fact is concealed that the buyer never is allowed to have this option. Instead he is told by Corporation counsel, with their tongues in their cheeks, that each locality where a single customer intends to have goods delivered *is* a separate market place, and that the identical artificial compulsory delivered prices which all mills, wherever located, quote to him *is* a true market price! The legal fiction that was strenuously defended by the Corporation's lawyers is that by the delivered price contract to which the buyer is a party, the place of delivery is the place of sale. The doctrine halts at no extreme of absurdity—thereby each distant country station. even though but one buyer be there, becomes a real market.[7]

INSULT ADDED TO INJURY

Can legal sophistry go further? Yes, it can add insult to injury. At one time, while they were opposing any effective Commission control, contemptuous railway officials were wont to declare that their discriminatory rates were really competitive because, if the passenger didn't care to pay the fare, he could get out of the train and walk, and if the shipper didn't like the rate, he could use a wheelbarrow. Just so, the usually cautious Mr. Gary offered this cold comfort to the hard-beset victims of the practice of compulsory delivered prices, who were pleading for the simple right to buy in Chicago steel produced at Chicago at the same net price as other buyers.

When the Pittsburgh basing system is in operation, the Chicago fabricator can get his steel at less than the Pittsburgh base price plus the freight by saying to the producer, "I don't propose to pay the Pittsburgh base price with the freight added to Chicago. I will wait. I will discontinue business." If the majority of the buyers feel that way,

---

[7] This was one of the favorite contentions of Mr. Cordenio A. Severance, special counsel in this case for the Steel Corporation. For one example among many interruptions of witnesses to enforce this ingenious assumption so essential to his contention, see Hearings, p. 18027.

they will bring about a reduction and the freight rate will be eliminated.[8]

So Mr. Gary's cheerful advice to the buyers to whom he denied free access to, and equal treatment in, a real market at Chicago, was that they should all commit industrial suicide, whereupon Mr. Gary and his fellow conspirators, having killed off all their local customers, would have to restore a mill base in order to re-create a body of buyers. And this is what some folks call industrial statesmanship.

NATURAL VS. ARTIFICIAL PRICES

The words "demand" and "supply" have no definite meaning except in connection with the idea of a definite price, either as a potential demand in connection with some price that may be, or of an actual demand in connection with an actual price at the moment. Such expressions as "demand exceeds supply" (or *vice versa*), so frequently heard, are loose and meaningless when used apart from a specific price to which the demand (or supply respectively) relates. In a truly competitive market where the constant adjustment of price to changing conditions of demand and supply is serving each moment to equilibrate them, there cannot, except in these fleeting moments of maladjustment, be such a thing as an excess of demand over supply (and *vice versa*). This expression, as frequently used, is nonsensical. However, in cases of continuing lack of balance between demand and supply resulting from price-fixing by a governmental agency, supply may somewhat more truly be said to be greater (or less) than demand as this manifests itself in the form of unsold stocks when price has been fixed too high, or *vice versa*, in that of waiting lines of buyers or of "rationing" scanty supplies of goods when price has been fixed too low. The same phenomenon of lack of balance between demand and supply appears under conditions of private restraint of commerce. The chief cause of the breakdown of many pools and other artificial agreements has been the strong temptation presented to each member of the combine or conspiracy to sell stock that accumulates; or again, to make use of unused capacity

[8] Pittsburgh-Plus, F.T.C. Record, pp. 11753, November 16, 1922.

when even a lower price would make its use profitable. Here supply and demand may for a considerable time be artificially equilibrated, but the supply is not the resultant of the choices of freely competing individual sellers. Clearly in such cases the artificial price is not a true "market" price in the sense of the law of supply and demand.

So, when Mr. Gary, justifying the maintenance of Pittsburgh-Plus prices at Chicago in 1914 at a time when most of the Chicago mills were shut down, stubbornly insisted "that the law of supply and demand was operating because the goods were sold at what the seller was willing to take and what the purchaser was willing to pay, and that makes the law of supply and demand," he was just talking nonsense.[9] Such facts do not "make the law" or prove that it is operative, for it is equally true that whatever be the price that the most effective monopoly may be able to maintain, the goods are sold only to such purchasers as are "willing" to pay, and by such sellers as are "willing" to take, that price. The buyers, however, represent at that time an *oppressed* demand, and the sellers a *suppressed* supply, and this is not the workings of "the law of supply and demand," for it can truly operate only in a free market.

PRICE RESULTING FROM COMPETITION

Price, demand, and supply may be suggestively described as having a functional relationship, a mathematical analogy with those numbers which vary in certain relationships with each other. But the analogy becomes misleading if competitive price is assumed to be equal and coördinate with demand and supply, as a causal factor in "the law of supply and demand." Rather supply and demand, taken together, each expressing and resulting from the willingness of traders, without conspiring, to trade on one or the other side of the market, under the existing conditions, are the only truly causal or active factors. Competitive price is the result of the interplay of supply and demand. Once under way, the market is a going concern, and comes to have a "going price," or rather a continuous series of going prices, spaced by brief intervals between transactions, much as are the separate pictures on a movie film, but

[9] Hearings, pp. 10798-10801.

which in like manner leave a continuous impression on the eye. All that any one buyer or seller (if not a monopolist) does or can do when acting independently is to decide whether himself to buy or to sell (respectively) at the going price; or if he is not quite willing to do so, he may announce by bid or offer how near to it he is willing to trade. While thus each trader viewed separately may be said to have his demand (or supply, respectively), i.e. his contribution to either, according to his valuation, yet, in the broader view, the collective demand and supply may truly be said to determine the going market price; whereas market price can never truly be said to determine demand and supply, taken collectively, in a competitive market.

The case, however, is otherwise where the conditions are not really competitive. Conspirators in restraint of trade usually reverse the order of events, begin by fixing some price other than that prevailing, and then later undertake to make such necessary adjustments of supply, by withholding or increasing goods, as will suffice to maintain the artificial price. Just here comes the acid test of the effectiveness of any conspiracy in restraint of trade, and many of them (especially the looser forms) fail to meet it fully or for long.

A SYSTEM OF LOCAL DISCRIMINATIONS

And just here, in the simple and effective method which the basing-point plan provides for limiting the amount which each conspirator shall add to the supply, lies much of its ingeniousness. The basing-point method of restricting supply is not by crudely fixing an absolute maximum for each mill, but by requiring and permitting any surplus to be "dumped" at lower *realized* prices in other territory. This involves, and results in, an elaborate scheme of discriminatory prices for steel charged to the various customers of each mill. The temptation of the mill to increase its sales (supply) in its best-paying sales-territory near it (and thus to reduce its prices, through the workings of the law of supply and demand) is not stopped with a jolt by an inflexible price (net receipt) but is allowed to be indulged, so to speak, on a downward sliding scale of net price realized, graduated according to the distance the product (steel) is shipped to the customer's destination in the direction of the basing point, and freight "absorbed."

The invention of this ingenious device (around the '80's) and its perfection by Messrs. Carnegie, Schwab, *et al.* after many experiments in illegal restraint, opened up after 1901 a new era of monopolistic practices and monopolistic profits in the United States, while the public, the government, and the courts looked on uncomprehendingly. An independent mill, at any location outside of Pittsburgh, selling for delivery at and near its mill at the full plus, without absorbing any freight, is making a highly profitable sale.[10] The fly in the ointment for the independents is that by the system, the Pittsburgh mills and mills everywhere else in the country are able to deliver in that same territory at exactly the same price (steel plus freight), and no mill dares, on penalty of breaking down the plan, to shade its prices to any one in its most profitable territory. This inability of the independents to make any price inducement gives to the great Corporation, with its great resources and ability to shift orders, some great advantages over the smaller independents, as evidenced by the regularly higher percentage of the Corporation's bookings to its capacity, a fact which, because of the well-known effect of overhead costs, signifies that the Corporation has here a great and regular cause of extra profits.

TWO PRICES IN ONE QUOTATION

The key to the riddle of this sort of discrimination is simple. A delivered price is not really a steel price at all, but is the sum of two prices, the price of the steel and the price of transporting the steel to the customer. In nearly every case the freight (price of transportation) is actually paid to a common* carrier, and when the mill is said "to absorb the freight" what it is doing is in fact

---

[10] E.g., when the Pittsburgh base is $30 and the freight $6.80, the mill in Chicago gets net $36.80. If $30 to Pittsburgh mills affords a unit profit of 10 per cent on sales, evidently $36.80 to Chicago mills (if their costs per ton are not higher) affords a unit profit about 36 per cent and the same on all sales directly westward, away from Pittsburgh.

The freight per ton of steel from Pittsburgh to Chicago at various dates was as follows: in 1901 it was $3.00; it was raised successively February 21, 1905, to $3.60; July 1, 1906, to $3.78; September 20, 1917, to $4.30; June 25, 1918, to $5.40; September 1, 1920, to $7.60; and was then reduced July 1, 1922, to $6.80. The evidence in Docket 760 (the Pittsburgh-Plus complaint) was all taken while either the $7.60 or the $6.80 rate was in force.

to reduce by that amount its net receipt for the steel, the only thing it is really selling. If, however, the steel mills owned the common carriers, the price theory would not be altered in any essential way. As common carriers with rates subject to regulation, they clearly would be discriminating either in their steel prices or in their freight charges when selling on a Pittsburgh base and "absorbing freight." If they are not common carriers but delivering by truck, just as clearly they are engaging in the transportation industry in addition to running steel mills. In giving to some customers of steel any costly incidental services, or services in varying amounts, a mill is in effect discriminating in its steel prices. Steel is steel, and freight is freight, and a so-called "delivered price" for steel is not either alone, but the sum of both. This conclusion is inescapable.

Dumping—this is the name for this process of selling goods at a distance at a lower net price than on sales nearer the mill. This important subject calls for a fuller discussion, which is reserved for a later chapter (Ch. XXI).

MAXIMIZING MONOPOLY BASE PRICES

An interesting question in regard to the Pittsburgh-Plus system of pricing is how the Corporation fixes upon the particular base price for each kind of products, whose weekly proclamation, like a command to a well-disciplined army, is sufficient to bend every will and to make every foot in the great ranks of steel move in unison. After the warning trust-busting decisions of 1911 the Corporation abandoned the clumsy, incriminating devices of central price committees and of Gary dinners, and adopted the simpler and more effective device of having the basic price itself named without consultation outside its own organization by the one dominating market leader. By this easy change it succeeded beyond all earlier hopes in "getting by" the public guardians of the law. An incidental but not unimportant feature in the operating of this new plan was no doubt the more enlightened self-interest with which such a single small executive body, as compared with the older type of representative committee, would perform the delicate task of selecting a base quotation for each standard type of steel products, a quotation that had the marvelous power of determining the delivered price of steel at every little remotest cross road and in every hamlet between the two oceans. It was a task calling for a broad view by the committee of the self-interest and profits of the steel industry as a whole, so largely coincident with their own. Undoubtedly such men will naturally strive more for stable prices and stable profits and be longer-sighted in their pursuit of profit than were the earlier cruder combinations. None could perform this task so well for their purposes as could the past-masters in the art of monopoly, the inventors of this very ingenious system. None knew better than they that the power which they exercised of a dictatorship over prices was tempered by the dangers of rebellion. None better than they knew, from long experience, how to foresee and to measure the forces of latent competition. They knew well that these forces, and the temptations to break away from the agreed system, grew greatly as the price rose (relative to costs) and also as mill capacity remained unutilized. To the constant temptation of each independent to poach a little upon the areas of relatively high local prices (involved in the scheme of discriminations), they dared not add too great an additional temptation of a too high base price which lifts the whole level of delivered prices at every location in the land. Occasionally, with all their astuteness, they overestimated the strength of discipline in the ranks and the tremendous force of the temptation in slack times to independents facing bankruptcy and booked up far less nearly to capacity than was the Corporation. But generally, the skill with which this fixing of the base price was performed by "the market leader" in steel is evidenced by its remarkable success in keeping the system of Pittsburgh-Plus in operation for a quarter of a century without the use of the older, cruder devices. This skill cannot but call forth admiration from all those who think that sort of thing is admirable.

TEACH A MONOPOLIST

Surely, though, no one of any intelligence could, at this stage of our study, believe that such a shrewdly calculated base price, though undoubtedly "limited" and "affected" by competition and by the fear of competition, is a price fixed by the law of supply and demand. It is no doubt "all the traffic will bear," not perhaps with reference to the moment and in particular localities, but so far as these most skillful price-fixers are able to determine, it is "all the traffic will bear" in the long run and with a view to stable conditions. Indeed such basing-point prices and the whole system of artificially related local discriminations are monopoly prices, altogether the most striking and stupendous example of them in this nation's industrial history. In the interests of truth, therefore, Carlyle's epigram must be amended. Neither a parrot nor a trust magnate, by merely repeating the phrase "the law of supply and demand," becomes truly a political economist. The one is still just a parrot; the other is a great captain of industry parroting phrases to befool the public and the guardians of the law in the interest of his corporation's treasury.

Many competent political economists have always admitted, certainly today admit, the essential justice of Carlyle's bitter epigram. Indeed, Carlyle's resentment was mostly directed not against the views of academic and scientific students but against the misuse by British business men in his day, for their private profit, of the phrase "supply and demand" without even an attempt to understand it. Used understandingly, it has always expressed and still expresses a truth; but carelessly used, it is meaningless—or worse. It is an edged tool, dangerous in the hands of law-breakers.

CHAPTER XIV

CLOSE HARMONY IN THE BRASS

MR. RYAN WISHES TO BE HEARD

IN THE midst of the hearings on trust legislation held by the Committee of the House preliminary to the passage of the Clayton Act, Mr. John D. Ryan, not unknown to financial fame and hailing from Butte, Montana, was introduced February 9, 1914, as one wishing "to be heard on pending anti-trust legislation." [1] The Amalgamated Copper Company, of which Mr. Ryan was the head, produced then in this country about one-fifth of the copper, while four other companies produced another two-fifths. The witness began by expressing general approval of the provisions of the bill relating to discrimination "as far as they apply to domestic trade," declaring them to be "in the interests of the whole country and in the interests of the large and small manufacturers, miners, and producers." But he quickly proceeded to alter this opinion into strenuous opposition. He suggested that the anti-discriminatory provisions, "in effect, that the price of any commodity shall be the same, taking rates of transportation into consideration, for every section and community, is an unworkable provision, especially if it relates to foreign business." But upon being assured by the Committee that "it is not intended to relate to foreign business," Mr. Ryan emphatically opposed the provision forbidding such discrimination in domestic prices.

MR. RYAN BEGS FOR FREEDOM TO COMPETE

He then proceeded, somewhat indirectly, to explain and justify the basing-point system of selling copper then and still in operation

[1] Clayton Committee Hearings, pp. 433-435, February 9, 1914.

in the copper industry. In answer to the question, "How would you criticism apply if the bill is simply to relate to the United States?" he said:

> We are refining and making copper ready for the market in Montana and we are making it in New Jersey. Frequently, when we make a sale of an amount, large or small, to a domestic manufacturer we do not know where we are going to deliver that copper from, whether it is to come from the Montana works or from the New Jersey works, because it all depends upon how business is in the West, whether the Montana plant is overloaded or how business is in the East, . . . we must meet the competition of the Michigan copper mines. We sell copper 1,500 miles from our own refineries and 500 miles from the Michigan refineries . . . On copper shipped from Montana we could not make a rate that would comply with this provision [forbidding discrimination] and at the same time meet competition in other sections. We would have to surrender the intermediate field to another producer who was nearer that district, because it would be absolutely impossible for us to compete with him. However, when we get farther East he is on the same footing, practically, that we are.[2]

WEEPING FOR HIS VICTIMS

Mr. Ryan then made an appeal "to take off all restraint and absolutely all the ties, bonds, and fetters from American producers and manufacturers in their foreign trade." Apparently he wanted legal sanction for American copper producers to combine *ad libitum* in the sale abroad of their product, an object pretty nearly achieved later by the Copper Exporters' Association under the Webb-Pomerene Act. In pursuing this argument the witness was treading on dangerous ground, and although he picked his steps with great care, he confessed at times that "You gentlemen are confusing me a little; you are getting me a little tied up" with questions about the control of the copper industry in the United States. But on the whole he succeeded in throwing his questioners off the main trail, which would have led them straight to the evidence of the discrimination practiced by American copper producers in their sale to American consumers. He strangely complained that "over

---

[2] *Idem,* p. 434. The unsound economics of this plea that Montana refineries must be allowed to undersell those of Michigan at their very doors, while keeping up their prices elsewhere, is shown in Chs. XIX-XXII.

a period of 12 or 13 years" American copper had been sold to
American manufacturers, on the average a half cent a pound higher
than to foreign manufacturers, placing upon them a burden of
"at least $10,000,000 a year on account of their inability to buy
as well as the European manufacturers." Here the argument became more confused, as Mr. Ryan declared himself to be, while he
deplored the sad plight of his fellow countrymen, forced by competition to pay him and his fellow copper producers higher prices
than foreign fabricators paid him for the same copper. He declared that this was not "dumping," for it was his novel idea that
dumping was the sale abroad, more cheaply, of a tariff-protected
product, whereas he stated copper had not "had any protection
for 16 or 17 years." He repeatedly expressed regret that the law
forbade American consumers of copper to combine, seemingly so
that they could force him to sell copper to them as cheaply as he
did to foreign buyers. When

trade was dull the European buyers combined and forced the unloading
of large quantities of copper [i.e. at the lower prices], and the domestic manufacturers were not able to combine; they had to trade in competition with those foreign manufacturers who were able to combine . . .[3]

—here shifting the thought from competition at home in the sale
of refined copper to the quite different competition abroad in the
sale of fabricated copper products. Again the same need of combination among American consumers of copper, as buyers, is suggested by him in his explanation of the success of copper-fabricat-
ing industries abroad:

the manufacturers of the world are able to combine and have understandings and agreements and do all the things that domestic manufacturers are not permitted to do, they are able to buy this material to
better advantage.[4]

He declared that among other reasons why so much copper was
fabricated abroad

the foreigner can buy it better . . . we penalize the domestic manufacturer by permitting the foreign manufacturers to combine and buy the
raw product to better advantage than he can buy it.[5]

[3] *Idem,* p. 435.   [4] *Idem,* p. 436.   [5] *Idem,* p. 436.

So the fault lies in our laws, not in Mr. Ryan and his friends, that American copper is sold at dumping prices in Europe.

AMERICAN CONSUMERS FORCED TO PAY

It is a strange notion that the American people "permit" foreigners to combine. Of course the Anti-Trust Act cannot apply to European territory. It does apply, though, to the territory of the United States and, if properly enforced, should have prevented the extortion which Mr. Ryan proceeds to confess in these words:

> When we sell that copper in Europe—to Germany, England, and France—we have to sell it to combined buyers. Repeatedly and regularly the dealers or consumers of Europe have combined to force American manufacturers of copper to unload, especially at times when business conditions were not good and when a surplus was accumulating. At those times they have almost named their own price . . . in 14 years, from 1901 to 1913, [raw copper was sold in] foreign countries, mostly in Europe, at a sacrifice of half cent a pound as against the price secured in the sale of the product to domestic manufacturers. I am speaking now of our own business.[6]

By what mysterious power were the American buyers of copper prevented from buying at these lower prices? If this was not dumping American copper abroad, there is no such thing as dumping. Further to the same effect Mr. Ryan said:

> When the concerns here had large quantities of copper to sell and the trade was dull the European buyers combined and forced the unloading of large quantities of copper, and the domestic manufacturers were not able to combine . . . they paid a half a cent a pound more for their copper and started with a handicap . . . of at least $10,000,-000 a year on account of their inability to buy as well as the European manufacturers.[7]

Here again spoke the sympathetic heart.

It is hard to believe that Mr. Ryan really meant to confess, as he did, that American copper producers had been collecting since 1901 a tax of $10,000,000 a year from American customers in excess of that charged to foreigners. In the desire to emphasize his particular point, he may have exaggerated. In any case, this same

[6] *Idem,* p. 435. [7] *Idem,* p. 435.

system of selling to the domestic trade has been in operation ever since that time, and still is.

A curious expression this—the American producers were "forced" to unload; it sounds as if they were held up by highwaymen. If what really happened is duress or coercion, then every seller of "surplus" stock at a time of a business slump is "forced" to sell when he accepts a price which, under the circumstances, he is glad to get! In truth, it was the American consumers who were "forced" to pay more for American copper than the producers were getting for it abroad.

Moreover, there is no truth in the impression which Mr. Ryan's words convey, that European buyers of various countries combined in a single buying corporation. At most, the German buyers, or some of them, may have had a buying cartel for themselves—but that the buyers of all Europe combined, sinking national differences, is simply a fantastic notion. The United Kingdom and Germany (of recent years) each has taken about 10 per cent; France, Holland, Belgium, and Italy, nearer 6 per cent each; and Sweden about 3 per cent of American copper.

DUMPING STILL REMUNERATIVE

What really distressed Mr. Ryan was that despite the very large measure of control of the sources of supply by his company and a few others, they still found, when it came to selling their "surplus" abroad, that the European markets were in pretty large measure open, and copper from mines throughout the world could be freely sold there in competition with American copper. And what he was yearning for—as for the flesh-pots of Egypt—was for compliant legislation not to enable the American manufacturers and their customers, the American people, to escape from his control and to pay less to him for copper in this country, but to enable him and his associates to deprive the European buyers also of the semblance of real copper markets.

Not that the prices received in Europe were unremunerative. For in answer to the question, "Do the copper operators sell all of their material abroad at a loss? Do they not make a profit out of it?" Mr. Ryan promptly replied, "Certainly they do." What he really was seeking was not to reduce prices to American copper consumers, but to raise European prices still higher, to a level with those paid by Americans. Thus, generously, he would have given to his fellow citizens prices not lower *absolutely* than they had been, but lower only *relatively* to the increased prices which he proposed to exact from European users of copper. Hunger for higher profits is revealed through his phrases of generosity.

COPPER MONOPOLY'S DREAM COME TRUE

Mr. Ryan's dream of linking up his already very effective domestic monopoly of copper with a world conspiracy in restraint of trade was pretty fully realized in 1926 in the formation of the Copper Institute, supplemental to and coördinate with Copper Exporters, Inc. Every large producer in the United States (except the comparatively small Miami Copper Company) joined both organizations, and the Copper Exporters included also as foreign associates nearly every large foreign producer in the world, all of whom, except the Société de Haut Katanga, in joining, specifically agreed to limit their production when called on so to do by Copper Exporters, Inc. These two organizations really began to function early in 1927, and much of the history of copper prices in the United States for the next three years is but the story of the activities of these organizations. The domestic price in 1927 averaged 13.17 cents, in January 1928 averaged 14.09 cents; it was 16 cents in October 1928 and rose steadily and rapidly to 24 cents, March 22, 1929. From January to March 1929 there was "a runaway market." On April 15 the price was "pegged" at 18 cents, and for a whole year, until April 15, 1930, through boom times and the stock market smash of October 1929, the copper price was held unchanged. In that time when industrial activities were declining, and for months after the October collapse in Wall Street, the copper monopoly gave one of the most marvelous exhibitions of artificial control of prices of a staple product that the world has seen. At the same time, needless to say, the great resulting "additions to dividends" to the copper companies (estimated as well over $60,000,000) gave the basis for enormous increase of stock-exchange capital values mounting into the billions, contributing very considerably to the orgy of speculation leading up to the smash of that year. By a miracle of discipline the pegged price of

copper was maintained for nearly six months in the face of col-
lapsing demand, but the inevitable break came, and copper prices
after April 15, 1930, declined until in October the price had
fallen to 9½ cents, a level not previously touched since 1895.
The significance of this situation was recognized by everybody but
the Department of Justice. Said one trade bulletin:

It must be remembered that a handful of men, controlling 75 per
cent of the production of copper in the United States, sit around a table
and decide what price copper should sell at and any prognostication
as to the future price of copper is in reality only a conjecture as to
what is in the minds of those gentlemen.[8]

In view of the news of agreements being entered into between
foreign and American copper producers at this writing (December
1930), it would seem to be a good time to administer Mr. Ryan's
own prescription, expressed in these words:

if domestic manufacturers combine with foreign manufacturers to fix
up trade so that there can be no reduction in prices to American consumers they ought to be put in jail.[9]

This would make a large and distinguished addition to our already
crowded prison population of bootleggers.

THE TRAIL OF THE SERPENT

To our subject and for American readers, the more important
(though unintended) revelation of Mr. Ryan's testimony on that
day relates not to European but to American conditions in the
sale of copper. For what he there describes and seeks to justify,
as the fair and competitive mode of selling copper in the United
States, is the basing-point method, still in vogue, by which discriminatory treatment of buyers of copper is universal throughout
the country. He neglected to mention the fact that New York
City is the basing point used, with some modifications, for a curiously complex system of local prices. Copper, no matter where it
is produced in this country, whether in Arizona, Montana, Michigan, New Mexico, California, or Tennessee (mentioned in the

---

[8] *Commodity Review,* by J. S. Bache and Company (42 Broadway, New
York City), November 21, 1929.
[9] Hearings, *op. cit.,* p. 437.

order of their smelter production of recent years), is sold from New York over a large area much as if it were mined out of the rocks underlying the skyscrapers of our financial metropolis. Thus Manhattan Island is poetically assumed to be the location of the chief copper mines and refineries on the continent. When Mr. Ryan speaks of his Montana producers "meeting competition" of Michigan and other producers, he really means that each is alike quoting (modified) New York basing-point delivered prices everywhere, and therefore they are truly "meeting" competition with each other nowhere. Neither all the profit from this device nor all the odium of its creation belongs to Mr. Ryan and the Anaconda Copper Company. The origin of the practice has, no doubt purposely, been kept in obscurity. But one thing is certain: it is not an immemorial business custom, the result of a "natural" economic evolution.

NOW SOME FACTS

The essential facts were set forth in a statement submitted to the Ways and Means Committee of the House in 1913 during the hearings on the then pending tariff legislation. The writers were men of the greatest experience and competence in the history and sale of these metals, being members of the "Committee appointed at conferences of American Manufacturers of Metal Products, held at New York City, November and December, 1912, relative to the Tariff on Lead and its products." We freely epitomize their statements, adding a few data taken from authoritative sources. The metal named throughout is lead, but the statements of facts, so far as they have to do with the adoption of the basing-point system, apply in large measure also to copper, zinc, and other non-ferrous metals.

MERGER STIFLES FREE MARKETS

Until the end of the nineteenth century the smelting industry in the United States was conducted by various independent smelting and refining companies located in the various states and territories. Some of the most prominent of these smelting companies were located at San Francisco, Pueblo, Omaha, Kansas City, St. Louis, Pittsburgh, etc. They were all competitors in the markets of the western mining states for the product of the mines of those states, and it was under such free competition that the great western mines were opened up and produced and made the fortunes of their owners, and that the smelting companies had become markedly successful. Any one could purchase lead from those independent smelters f.o.b. their works, Omaha, Pueblo, Aurora, Ill., St. Louis, Kansas City, Pittsburgh, etc., and could exercise the right to do with it whatsoever he wished—use it himself to manufacture anything anywhere, or sell it and ship it to any one anywhere who wished to buy it. In those days delivery could be taken by the buyer at any point in the United States to which he desired the metal transported, and it would cost him the purchase price (that is, the current uniform mill-base price) plus the actual freight.

April 4, 1899, the American Smelting and Refining Company was formed by the Guggenheim interests, and within a year had acquired thirteen important corporations, and soon owned and operated under leases many other mines. It was announced as having "a capacity to smelt and refine the entire product of all the mines east of the Rocky Mountains producing smelting ores." Three weeks later, April 27, 1899, was incorporated by Daly-Rogers-William Rockefeller interests the Amalgamated Company (a holding company) which at once purchased controlling interests in many important companies, the chief of which was the Anaconda Copper Mining Company (Mr. Ryan's) which had been incorporated in 1895. Together these two great mergers boasted a capitalization at that time of $140,000,000.[10]

MORE AND MORE MERGERS

Important as concentrating control of the whole lead industry of the country in the hands of one group were successive mergers: in 1891, the National Lead Company, uniting 16 independent manufacturers of lead products; in 1903, the United Lead Company, organized by the A. S. & R. Company, by absorption of 17—nearly all—of the remaining independent manufacturers of lead products; in 1905, merger of the United Lead into the National Lead, which thus became far the largest buyer and user of pig lead in the United States, with four members of the Board of Directors of the A. S. & R. Company on its Board. Thus the dominant group of smelters and the important fabricators of lead be-

[10] *Moody's Manual*, 1900, pp. 695-698, source of these figures.

came *de facto* the one medium through which most of the lead of the country passed from its primary production to the consuming public. Following the revelations in the tariff hearings of 1908, the A. S. & R. Company directors soon after disappeared from the Board of the National Lead Company, but who is so foolish as to think that this made any practical change in the situation?

It may be observed in this connection that a similar movement in the vertical merger under the proprietorship of a few closely affiliated great corporations of the metal-producing and of numerous fabricating plants has been steadily in progress since 1920 in the copper industry. As a result there is little in the form of copper or brass products that any one can buy that does not pass through the hands of this same group.

CURIOSITIES IN FREE CONTRACTS

To return to the story of the basing point in the sale of lead.

Shortly after the mergers occurred around 1899, the system of selling non-ferrous metals on a refinery base, generally prevailing up to that time, was abruptly abolished, and sales began to be made on a price plan which provided for the prepayment of freight by the smelting companies, the price being invariably a delivered one. Dealers (brokers and jobbers) were no longer permitted to purchase at a refinery for delivery to any place that they chose, but only at the points where they had their offices or warehouses and then only in such quantity as the producers prescribed. This prescription of quantity was made also a feature of the plan for ultimately controlling the manufactured products, for very shortly the consumer was wont to be told that he could have but a part of the quantity which he wished to buy.

Presently, buyers were permitted to buy only under a new form of contract in which the price was not mentioned. Nobody had ever heard of anything quite like this before. A contract had always been deemed to be the reduction to writing of certain specific details as to material, quantity, time, point of delivery, and price theretofore agreed upon by a buyer and a seller. As to delivery the new form of contract was less favorable to the buyer and more favorable to the seller in that the latter was no longer obligated to a specific time of delivery, but only "for shipment within 30 days or as soon thereafter as possible"; as to price, the strange thing is that this contract omits mention of any specific sum whatever, but reads only: "the price to be that of the American Smelting and Refining Company, on date of shipment," or in some cases, "on date of delivery."

TEETH PAINLESSLY EXTRACTED

The exceeding value of this delicate mode of expressing the amount to be paid for the metal by the immediate buyer (and ultimately, by the American people) is apparent when viewed in connection with the fact that any real open markets for these products in the United States had suddenly ceased to exist and that prices now were fixed privately somehow, at such time, and at such level as some shadowy committee of the management of this great corporation might determine. To particularize. If, any day, when "the price" of lead is 4 cents per pound, this committee of sellers, unknown to the public, meet and determine the price of lead to be 4½ cents, this price is announced to the public and simultaneously a hundred million or more people commence buying and using lead on that basis.

The miners of lead ore (many of them with small, independent mines), sell their ore under what is called their smelting contract. Who writes it? The smelters. What is the price named in the contract for the lead content of the ore? Mere vulgar figures are omitted, and the price is to be that for New York delivery (that is, New York lead price less freight to New York) at the time when the ore, bullion, etc., is delivered at the smelting works or refinery. It is easy to see that, under such conditions, the influence making the price of lead to the public is whether the ore people are, on their elastic contracts, shipping larger quantities to the smelters than the latter on their elastic contracts are selling to the public. Suppose that for two weeks the New York lead price has been 4 cents per pound; that, less freight to New York, is what the lead ore producer gets for all his lead delivered during the period. Then the mysterious committee advances the New York price to 4½ cents per pound, and the public pays that price. Who benefits by the operation? Not the lead miner. What power lies in human hands to manipulate supply, and market conditions, and prices, both those paid to miners of ore and those exacted from buyers and the consuming public!

BY MEANS OF LAUGHING GAS

The efficient device by which the non-ferrous metals monopoly puts its power into play is the basing-point practice. Thereby it is able to assume the function of the common carriers and can deny to buyers of its metals free access to markets. It is able constantly to do that which if done by a railroad would be a violation of the long- and short-haul clause. In further restraint of commerce, it can refuse to sell to those who persist in reselling to certain competitors of its allied producing corporations. It can misuse the right to choose its own customers—a doctrine born among competitive conditions as a safeguard to individuals, but now converted into a weapon of injustice in the hands of monopoly. The year 1899 witnessed a veritable revolution in the system of pricing the metals. Uniform treatment of customers at the mills was ended, while millions of imaginary freight began to be deducted from the prices paid by the great combination to scattered independent miners of ore, and other millions were added to the prices paid for these metals by helpless disunited consumers.[11]

BROTHERS UNDER THE SKIN

It was by no mere chance that the regular use of the basing-point plan began almost simultaneously about 1899 in the non-ferrous metals and in the steel trades, after it had for some years been tested out experimentally, through the use of pools and agreements, by Mr. Schwab and his associates. In manifold ways the commercial fortunes of these various metals were interlocked, through directors, corporation plants (the U.S. Steel always has been in a minor way a non-ferrous metal producer), and possible substitution in uses. When the basing-point plan proved its superlative merits as a means of destroying real markets in the sale of steel, it was at once adopted by the chief producers of the other metals, and no doubt greatly hastened and strengthened their monopolistic control. Of Messrs. Schwab, Morgan, Guggenheim, and Ryan, it might be said that in their adoption of the basing-point policy they were "all souls with but one single thought, all hearts that beat as one." For thirty years, while the Steel Corporation was twice legally arraigned, once in the Federal Courts on the charge of monopoly and once before the Federal Trade Commission on the charge of discrimination by the use of the basing-point system, the non-ferrous metal producers all but escaped the attention of the legal departments of the Government and never were

---

[11] Some of the puzzling details of the basing-point plans in the non-ferrous metal trade are given in the Appendix to Ch. XIV.

called before our highest Court. Doubtless, if so accused, they would, taking their cue from the Steel Corporation, have argued that the basing-point system was the result of natural economic evolution, a business custom extending back beyond the memory of living man. They would have sought to prove that, during these three decades, interstate commerce in these metals had been unrestrained, and the prices simply those arrived at in the normal way in the open markets according to "the law of supply and demand." If ever these practices in the kingdoms of Guggenheim and Ryan are challenged by the drowsy guardians of our public welfare, so long asleep at their posts, it will be interesting to see whether such arguments will still impress judicial minds. The Steel Corporation had the temerity to point to the pricing system in the sale of non-ferrous metals as a proof that the basing-point practice was the normal method of business competition and was in accord with the law of "demand and supply." The old adage of the pot calling the kettle black was inverted. The black iron pot pointed to the corroded copper kettle and exclaimed, "I am just as fair as it is!"

A POT FULL OF GOLD

The enormous profitableness to a few men of this system of restraint of free domestic commerce in these metals is patent to the eye. In the one direction the small producing mines find themselves in the grip of a buying monopoly; in the other direction the consuming public is exploited by the same monopolists turned sellers. Copper, lead, zinc (not to discuss aluminum), are *directly* a part of the daily purchases of every humble citizen for his private use, and *indirectly* through their extensive use by public utilities, whose legalized rates to the public for all future time are increased by every dollar of additional present costs of construction and maintenance. Even though the base price breaks now and then, through monopoly's overreaching itself, its gains in the meantime are great. At all times, the local price relationships are artificially distorted, and the free flow of interstate commerce is impeded. The beneficiaries of these practices are flouting the very spirit as well as the letter of our laws and the essential conditions of private property and of private enterprise. At this moment the daily journals abound in news items telling of the arrival of foreign copper producers to arrange a world-wide restriction of production, evidencing the combination of American producers under the Webb-Pomerene Act with foreign competitors. The papers are telling too of the refusal of domestic producers to sell to any one at the current price more than the amount of his current needs. Such inquisitorial methods reveal the lack of any free market in domestic copper. Every man in the street knows that this is the case, and that the law is openly defied. One law for the rich and another for the poor is a dangerous situation in a democracy. Not more laws, but the simple enforcement of the existing laws, is the need. Such practices, continued thirty years unchallenged by the executive guardians of the public rights, mean the breakdown of the system of economic liberty in domestic commerce.

PART IV

"NEW COMPETITION" AND OLD TRICKS

<hr>

CHAPTER XV

THE WHITE ROBE OF STATISTICS

OPEN PRICE ASSOCIATIONS

THE fortunes of the basing-point method became in 1920 strangely intertwined with the judicial adventures of a new and rising form of business organization called "the open price association." Regarding this there was, for five years, waged in the Federal courts a very interesting conflict of legal opinions, brought to a provisional close by two notable decisions of the Supreme Court in 1925. The name and in large part the idea of the "open-price association" seem to have been the invention of Arthur Jerome Eddy. A successful lawyer, he was well versed in corporation law, and was author of a treatise on *The Law of Combinations*.[1] A man of wide reading and cultural interests and of attractive and persuasive personality, he for years preached by word and pen and with kindling enthusiasm his doctrine of "the new competition." His book under that title[2] became the Bible of a new dispensation in wide circles of industry, and until his death in July 1920 the talented author was busy organizing, advising, and counseling numerous associations formed on the model he had invented.

The Eddy plan no doubt was in some respects in harmony both with the lessons of the history of markets and with contemporary needs for re-creating effectual competitive conditions. The territorial decentralization of large units of industry with accompanying changes had long since sadly shattered the local market situation of handicraft days.[3] "Access to the market," an adequate measure of "common knowledge" of conditions, including that of prices in actual sales in the same market, and other conditions in

---

[1] In two volumes, 1901.   [2] Published 1912.   [3] See below, Ch. XVIII.

which real (truly uniform) market prices emerge, had all become weakened or almost destroyed. Certain features of the Eddy open-price plan were shrewdly calculated to remedy some evils of the new situation and partially to restore something much more nearly fulfilling the old ideal of true market conditions. But its author's cast of thought was, probably in a far greater degree than he was aware of, molded by his long service as private counselor to industrial corporations whose insistent problem is to secure higher prices and larger profits. His conception, as well of the existing evils in modern sales methods as of the benefits to be expected through his "Plan," was thus colored repeatedly and unconsciously by an advocate's bias. He saw vividly the evils to the sellers in some contemporary selling practices; to the very existence of other evils to the buyers and to the public he had closed his eyes.

AN ENEMY OF COMPETITION

This habit of a lifetime explains also his two-faced attitude toward competition. Much of the time he professed a purpose of making competition finer and better to perform worthily its great function; he seemed to condemn only "cutthroat" competition and "brutal" competition. But again he denounced competition in general as "war, and war is hell." He condemned as "unhuman" the survival of the fittest in industry, and advocated a thoroughgoing displacement of competition by coöperation. Said he: "Rightfully viewed, there is not a single good result accomplished by man in . . . economics . . . that should not be attained by intelligent and far-sighted coöperation." [4]

His cure for the trust evil he compressed into a half-jocular and paradoxical phrase: "Compel them to make money." [5] This spoke his belief in the new policy of live-and-let-live, whereby the smaller independents would all be allowed to make "fair" profits, while the greater combinations naturally would obtain still larger profits. Through the simple expedient of keeping all prices high and all profits ample, all the sellers would be happy, but the unfortunate consumers had no place in this picture of industrial bliss.

Such was the man and such the book that awakened something of the spirit of a crusade among the leaders in many industries

[4] *The New Competition*, p. 26.   [5] *Idem*, p. 257.

where a medley of fair and unfair competition was always disturbing the peace and depressing the hope of secure and generous gains. Loud were the praises of "coöperation" heard on every hand, and a spirit of universal brotherhood (limited) reigned whenever big business gathered at the banquet board. Open-price associations began to be organized around 1911; then the movement was halted cautiously—"by advice of counsel"—through fear of further arousing public resentment against trusts in the campaign year of 1912 and in 1913 while new legislation was under discussion. Then the movement gained momentum as numerous new associations were organized and attained their greatest activity after the close of the war in 1919 and 1920. What would be the verdict of the Federal courts as to the legality of this form of agreement among producers? The five-year period from 1920 to 1925 gave the answer in a peculiar series of four cases which reached the United States Supreme Court on appeal from as many district decisions.

THE COURT CONDEMNS

The Supreme Court began (1921) by condemning the Hardwood Lumber Association but did so by a divided vote of 6-3. It followed this in June 1923 by a surprising unanimous condemnation of the Linseed Oil Association, flatly reversing thus a district judge in Illinois, who made an unlucky guess six weeks before the higher Court's Hardwood decision. It was then, when all doubt seemed removed as to the mind of our final repository of judicial truth, that in two Federal districts, New York and Michigan, two associations of this kind were unhesitatingly condemned. It must have seemed to the judges as easy as using a rubber stamp. But this was not the end of this winding judicial lane, and somewhat less than two years later, June 1, 1925, the Supreme Court reversed the District Courts and vindicated the open-price plan in principle and in practice, this time again by a divided vote of 6-3.[6]

[6] Assuming (as many do, but others doubt) that essentially the same major issue was passed upon in all four cases, and counting all the votes, it appears that in the four cases the Association plan was condemned by 24 votes and approved by 16. In the Supreme Court itself, the total votes in the four cases were 21-15 against the Association plan, 12 different justices voting at some time against and 7 for the Association plan; 6 voted on both sides, so that 6 justices were consistently against, and 1 (Stone) consistently for the plan.

In the Hardwood Lumber case was for the first time presented to the Supreme Court the question of the legality of the "Open Competition Plan" and of the "open price associations." [7] As the Court said, there was "very little dispute as to the facts," so that the legal issue was presented as simply as possible. Yet the majority and minority opinions could hardly be more directly conflicting both as to the legal and economic significance to be attached to those facts and as to the appropriate verdict. The majority believed that

Such close coöperation . . . as is provided for in this "Plan" is plainly in theory, as it proved to be in fact, inconsistent with that free and un-restricted trade which the statute contemplates. . . . To call the ac-tivities of the defendants, as they are proved in this record, an "Open Competition Plan" of action is plainly a misleading misnomer. . . . This is not the conduct of competitors but . . . clearly that of men united in an agreement, express or implied, to act together and pursue a common purpose under a common guide. . . . The "Plan" is, es-sentially, simply an expansion of the gentlemen's agreement of former days, skillfully devised to evade the law . . . the fundamental purpose of the "Plan" was to procure "harmonious" individual action . . . concerted action . . . tacit understanding. . . . In the presence of this record it is futile to argue that the purpose of the "Plan" was sim-ply to furnish those engaged in this industry, with widely scattered units, the equivalent of such information as is contained in the news-paper and government publications with respect to the market for commodities sold on boards of trade or stock exchanges . . . these re-ports go to the seller only; and [there are other differences]. . . . Convinced, as we are, that the purpose and effect of the activities of the "Open Competitive Plan" . . . were to restrict competition and thereby restrain interstate commerce . . . we agree with the District Court that it constituted a combination and conspiracy in restraint of interstate commerce. . . . [8]

The majority thus believed that despite all professions of mere desire to make knowledge of market conditions open and public, the true purpose and the effect of the plan and activities were plainly bad. Thus thought and spoke Justice Clark, with whom

[7] See statement of counsel for government, 257 U.S. 385-386, and Justice Clark, *idem,* p. 392.
[8] *Idem,* pp. 409-412.

concurred five of his colleagues (Chief Justice Taft, who was the most recent appointee to the Court, and Justices Day, McReynolds, Pitney, and Van Devanter).

THE PLAN FINDS FRIENDS AT COURT

But what is all so plain to the majority cannot be seen at all by the minority, Justices Holmes, Brandeis, and McKenna—strange judicial bedfellows. They, on the contrary, felt that the majority decision was plainly erroneous and involved great evil consequences. Justice Holmes, in one of his delicious epigrammatic and ironical dissenting opinions (with which no one else expressed concurrence, although he concurred with "the more elaborate discussion by brother Brandeis"), was all for freedom of speech and freedom of action and for the public distribution of information which he believed had been fully realized under the "Plan." He believed these liberties would be invaded by the majority verdict, and the noble old Roman, here as always, was strong for the under dog—or the cur he thought was under. He declared that even the fact, if it be assumed, that the acts have been done with a sinister purpose, does not justify "excluding mills in the backwoods from information." He plainly voices his belief that the Association did not "attempt to override normal market conditions" but merely "to conform to them . . . the most reasonable thing in the world." This was the crux of his opinion, most plainly implying that he would have gladly joined in condemning the Association if he had been convinced that it did more than merely "to equalize" prices (seeming to mean preventing violent "temporary" fluctuations resulting from ignorance of market conditions) or that it really raised prices so as "to override" normal conditions.[9]

Justice Brandeis in his much longer dissenting opinion (and Justice McKenna concurring with him), in failing to express concurrence with Justice Holmes' statements, possibly indicated unwillingness even to imagine that the Association might have acted "for a sinister purpose." Justice Brandeis entertains not a doubt regarding the blameless record of the accused. To him

[9] *Idem*, pp. 412-418.

the Plan is not inherently a restraint of trade, and the record is barren
of evidence to support a finding that it has been used, or was intended
to be used, as an instrument to restrain trade. . . . The coöperation
which is incident to this Plan does not suppress competition. On the
contrary it tends to promote all in competition which is desirable. . . .
The evidence in this case, far from establishing an illegal restraint of
trade, presents, in my opinion, an instance of commendable effort by
concerns engaged in a chaotic industry to make possible its intelligent
conduct under competitive conditions.

There is much more of fact, legal citation, and reasoning in the
opinions, but these laudatory passages contain the essential conclusions. Many have seen here a violent head-on collision in matter
of principle; others see in it, however, merely a difference in
interpretation of the facts. It is the story of the six blind men of
Hindustan, reporting their ideas of an elephant after a groping
examination; one thinks it all trunk, another tusk, and so on to the
tail.

MORE EMPHATIC CONDEMNATION

Barely a year and a half later, June 4, 1923, a decision was
rendered by the same court on the Linseed Oil Association. The
defendants were really twelve corporations with places of business
in six States, engaged in the industry of crushing and selling linseed
oil and by-products. The Association came into the Supreme Court
with an almost fulsome certificate of good character from Judge
Carpenter of the Illinois District Court. But now a completely
unified Supreme Court reversed his charitable decision with a bang
that echoed throughout the legal world. The opinion, delivered by
Justice McReynolds, consists mainly of a detailed account of the
rules and activities of the Association, concluding with a summary
condemnation of the Eddy Plan and "the new competition."

The obvious policy, indeed the declared purpose, of the arrangement
was to submerge the competition theretofore existing among the sub-
scribers and substitute "intelligent competition," or "open competition"; to eliminate "unintelligent selfishness" and establish "100 per
cent confidence"—all to the end that the members might "stand out
from the crowd as substantial co-workers under modern coöperative
business methods" . . . Certain it is that the defendants are associated
in a new form of combination and are resorting to methods which are

not normal . . . In the absence of a purpose to monopolize or the compulsion that results from contract or agreement, the individual certainly may exercise great freedom; but concerted action through combination presents a wholly different problem and is forbidden . . . the ordinary practice of reporting statistics to collectors stops far short of the practice which defendants adopted. Their manifest purpose was to defeat the Sherman Act without subjecting themselves to its penalties. The challenged plan is unlawful . . .[10]

Thus the opinion concludes with the united bench against this thoroughly typical open-price association, and naturally this was taken by the public to mean a condemnation of the trade-association plan in principle. The leading precedent on which this decision was based was the Hardwood Lumber case of two years before. Although three new justices, Sutherland, Butler, and Sanford, had meantime replaced Clark, Day, and Pitney of the former majority, this was no factor in the decision, as the newcomers united in this similar verdict. It has, however, occasioned surprise that the trio formerly supporting the association plan and principle, Justices Holmes, Brandeis, and McKenna, now united with the former majority in condemnation. Either to their eyes some special circumstances (which we cannot detect) differentiated the Linseed Oil case from the Hardwood case; or they believed further dissent on this subject to be futile in view of the fixed position of the majority.

If ever an issue of economic policy appeared to be finally adjudicated, this was one. Two judges of the Federal district courts thought so, and four and five months later in their courts they in quick succession turned thumbs down unhesitatingly on associations in two other leading industries, Cement and Maple Flooring. Then no doubt they awaited with perfect confidence the day when the Supreme Court would approve their judgments. But with another boom, both opinions were blown sky high on the same day, when the open-price associations were triumphantly vindicated.

AGAIN THE COURT DIVIDES

Justice Stone, who had just replaced Justice McKenna in the Court, delivered the prevailing opinion in both cases (reading

10 262 U.S. 379: 388-390.

first that on Maple Flooring). Concurring with him were five of his colleagues, Holmes, Brandeis, Van Devanter, Butler, and Sutherland, all five of whom had recently joined (however gingerly the first two) in the condemnation of the Linseed Oil Association. Now all united in vindicating two other Associations, certainly of the same kind. Justice Van Devanter, who twice before had condemned such associations, now voted in their favor. The three now composing the dissenting minority were Taft, McReynolds, and Sanford, the first two consistently through all four cases outlawing the new type of association, and Justice Sanford also in the three decisions in which he voted.

Mr. Chief Justice Taft and Mr. Justice Sanford dissent from the opinions of the majority of the Court in these two cases on the ground that in their judgment the evidence in each case brings it substantially within the rule stated in the *American Column Co.* and the *American Linseed Oil Co. Cases*, the authority of which, as they understand, is not questioned in the opinions of the majority of the Court.[11]

In a separate and longer opinion Justice McReynolds fully agreed with this view and, moved by righteous indignation, spoke words of a severity rarely heard in judicial halls. Asserting his belief that the principles laid down in the opinion delivered by himself two years before applied fully in the circumstances of these cases, he said:

United States v. American Linseed Oil Company; 262 U.S. 371, states the doctrine which I think should be rigorously applied. Pious protestations and smug preambles but intensify distrust when men are found busy with schemes to enrich themselves through circumventions. And the Government ought not to be required supinely to await the final destruction of competitive conditions before demanding relief through the courts. The statute supplies means for prevention. Artful gestures should not hinder their application. I think the courts below reached right conclusions and their decrees should be affirmed.[12]

The Supreme Court in these twin decisions reversed the lower courts with respect to the particular open-price associations at the bar, and the interpretation put upon the decisions in legal and business circles was that the Court had reversed itself. This was

[11] 268 U.S. 586 (June 1, 1925).　　　[12] *Idem,* p. 587.

flatly asserted by the three dissenting justices. Justice Stone, however, in his Maple Flooring opinion, attempts to distinguish the
decisions in the Hardwood and Linseed Oil cases from those in
the two cases at the bar. In so doing he repeats essentially the same
arguments vainly offered four years before by Justices Holmes and
Brandeis, who now join him in reaffirming and vindicating their
earlier judgment. He recites the evidence as to rules and acts in
the earlier cases in such a way as to imply merely that they were
different from the cases at the bar.[13] In the Cement opinion, of
which the greater part consists of a mere description of the Association, no differentiation whatever is attempted. But twice, briefly,
near the end of the Cement opinion, reference is made to the
Maple Flooring opinion "for reasons stated more at length" for
holding such activities not to be in themselves unlawful.[14]

The decisive feature in the Hardwood case pointed to by Justice
Stone was that the record there

disclosed a systematic effort . . . to cut down production and increase
prices. . . . The opinion of the court in that case rests squarely on
the ground that there was a combination on the part of the members
to secure concerted action in curtailment of production and increase of
price, which actually resulted in a restraint of commerce, producing
increase of price.[15]

Here Justice Stone is seeing things through the eyes of the
majority in the Hardwood case; but Justices Holmes and Brandeis,
now agreeing with Justice Stone, had protested at the time that
they saw no evidence whatever of such effects, on which ground
the majority opinion squarely rested. And Justice McReynolds,
who did see such effects in the Hardwood case, is equally sure
that he now sees those same effects in the cases at the bar: "men
busy with schemes to enrich themselves."

Justice Stone declares the decisive feature in the Linseed Oil
decision to have been the belief of the Court that activities of that
Association "could necessarily have only one purpose and effect,
namely to restrain competition among sellers." [16] He cautiously
declares that "each case arising under the Sherman Act must be

13 *Idem*, pp. 580-586.   15 *Idem*, p. 580.
14 *Idem*, pp. 604, 606.   13 *Idem*, p. 582.

determined upon the particular facts disclosed by the record," [17] but he points to no "particular facts" that are specifically different in the two sets of cases. Instead of indicating them, Justice Stone turns directly to declare as not "open to question" the desirability and benefits of the very activities generally understood to be condemned by the earlier decisions. [18]

These "reasons," which Justice Stone fixes upon as differentiating the later cases from the earlier, lie not so much in the objective facts but in the subjective condition of the judicial minds and the inferences drawn by them from the same essential facts as to the objects and results of trade-association activities. From the same type of factual evidence a majority of the Court now draws a different inference as to the probable results. Yet, as will be shown later, certain facts should have suggested illegality more plainly in the last two cases than in the first two.

VIEWS IN THE CABINET

Going with a high reputation from a distinguished academic position to the rescue of a sadly embarrassed administration after his predecessor had been driven from office, Justice Stone had served a scant eleven months, from April 4, 1924, to March 2, 1925, as Attorney General before taking his place on the Supreme bench. [19]

A remarkable division of sentiment and policies existed in the Harding-Coolidge Cabinets in respect to this discordant question of open-price associations. This had become something of a political sensation. While the Department of Justice under Mr. Harry Daugherty was for a time making a show of vigorously prosecuting them, though really accomplishing nothing, the Department of Commerce under Secretary Hoover was championing their cause and coöperating with them.

In his report under the date of September 20, 1922 (after the Hardwood decision), Secretary Hoover had made an extended

---

[17] *Idem,* p. 579.
[18] *Idem,* p. 582.
[19] The Maple Flooring case was argued December 1 and 2, 1924, and reargued March 3, 1925; the Cement case was argued March 3 and 5, 1925. Justice Stone was sworn into office March 2, 1925. Therefore he had been on the bench one day when the final oral argument of the two cases began.

plea [20] for a modification of "the restraint of trade acts," the working results of which, under the interpretation given by the courts, "in some directions are out of tune with our economic development." His well-poised argument, recognizing, but distinguishing, the possibilities of abuse from the numerous coöperative activities which "are in the interest of . . . the community at large," may well have served as the subconscious basis for Justice Stone's reasoning three years later.

JUDICIAL OPINION TRANSFORMED

But this voice from the outer world had not penetrated into the judicial chambers when, in June 1923, the Supreme Court unanimously condemned the Linseed Oil Association without distinguishing between the good and the bad in its activities. So again Secretary Hoover, under date of November 1, 1924, returns to the charge; but this time, apparently hopeless of aid from the courts, he pleads for a new "legislative definition" of these matters.[21] While still incidentally recognizing (without specifying) that "a small minority of these associations have been in the past used as cloaks for restraint of trade," he describes in more detail at least ten of the twenty-odd functions of coöperative action which, as before, he declared were praiseworthy.

As Secretary Hoover was writing these words, Attorney General Stone was sitting with him as a colleague in the Cabinet, and seven months later the sentiments and words of the Secretary's argument seemed to find an echo in the opinions delivered by Justice Stone (though somewhat less cautiously, as to the danger of abuse). Mr. Stone had gone from his distinguished deanship of law to Washington, no doubt, with pretty definite convictions regarding certain economic and social issues in the law. As has since been shown in numerous dissenting opinions, his thought was in large degree in harmony with that of Justices Brandeis and Holmes. His scholarly views had been further shaped, no doubt, by his brief public administrative career. His appearance as a member of the Court effected a transformation of judicial opinion and a judge-

[20] Report of the Secretary of Commerce, pp. 29-31.
[21] Report 1924, pp. 22-24.

made revolution in this feature of the law without the long delay usually attending legislative changes.

TWO ASPECTS OF THE TRUTH

We have not at this point meant to raise the question whether the later decisions were right or wrong as matter of law or of economics, so far as they relate strictly to the truth-divulging, publicity aspects of the open-price associations. There were, to be sure, sound economic grounds on which to base the major part of the decision thus carefully limited and safeguarded in scope and meaning. In the interest of truth and sound practice it was bound to come. What we would emphasize is this: that these cases involved not one but two major issues, the one the reasonableness of the coöperation practiced in collecting and publishing data on past and present prices and on production, and the other the legality of the entangling alliance of this (in itself, as was said repeatedly) innocent sort of coöperative activities, with some other activities in restraint of trade and in manipulation of prices, not so "open" to the light of day but practiced in a dim twilight.

If this is so, then the remarkable schism within the Court may be more easily explained. From the first some members of the Court, taking (shall we say) a more abstract and doctrinaire view of the merely informational work of the Associations, saw in them no evil. The other members of the Court, viewing the Associations more realistically, shrewdly sensed the presence of illegal purposes and behavior, the evidence of which had never been lucidly presented to the Court. Each group within the Court saw an aspect of the truth, but neither saw at once both phases: coöperative exchange of price data and the basing-point method, used in combination to thwart effectively a genuine competition in prices.

CHAPTER XVI

TRADE ASSOCIATIONS BECOME SUSPECT

GROUNDS OF THE HARDWOOD DECISION

THAT obscurer influence which some members of the Supreme Court sensed as affecting prices in the open-price association cases was in fact the basing-point device. While the counterfeit publicity given to price data no doubt had other incidental advantages for the sellers, its greatest advantage for the manipulation of prices was as an auxiliary of the basing-point system of identical pricing.

In the first of the four Association cases [1] not a word was said about the basing-point method by counsel on either side or in the judicial opinions. So far from its being a part of the Government's complaint that "the defendants conspired to fix uniform prices" (either mill-base or delivered), the prosecutor's brief expressly disavows any such charge and asserts on the contrary that prices were not uniform and that *therefore* there could have been no agreement in fixing them.

The Government's evidence showed at the outset that disparity of prices existed among the defendants . . . The complaint was that the defendants conspired to *maintain and enhance* prices by suppressing competition and substituting in its place coöperation and agreements having the *purpose and effect* of maintaining and enhancing prices. . . . When different prices are being charged there are obviously no agreements *fixing* prices, but there may well be agreements having the purpose and effect of *enhancing* prices, such as the agreements among the defendants in the present case to carry on the coöperative activities under consideration.[2]

[1] Hardwood Lumber case, 257 U.S. 377, December 1921.
[2] Brief for the U.S., pp. 67-68. Italics in original.

The case was argued and won by the prosecution on this ground. It is true that there was no "uniformity" of prices as in real markets, but there was an *identity* of delivered prices—that is, fixed somehow at each destination—possible only through agreement (explicit or tacit), to which the prosecution was quite blind. The majority opinion appeared to be a clean-cut condemnation of the "open-price," reporting, statistical, publicity aspects of the Association's activities, as having some such purpose and effect. Justice Brandeis thought they did not have such purpose or effect, and based his dissent (with which Justices Holmes and McKenna concurred) very directly on the mistaken assumptions that "no . . . monopoly was sought or created"; "no . . . division of territory was planned or secured"; "no . . . uniform prices were established or desired," and "it was neither the aim of the Plan, nor the practice under it, to regulate competition in any way."

HARDWOOD BASING POINTS

And yet—believe it or not—if the reader's curiosity leads him to examine the Record he can there find,[3] buried in a mass of facsimile documents and tables, a perfect description of a basing-point price system, never given a moment's attention in the briefs or by either the majority or the minority of the Court. There it is, with many details, a system of delivered prices, with not one basing point but two (called, with unconscious humor, "natural" gateways), one at Cincinnati for the Eastern Territory, and one at Cairo, Illinois, for what is called the Southern Territory. The line dividing the two territories (unseen by the usually keen eyes of Justice Brandeis) was boldly drawn from Chicago to New Orleans. The differential allowed between the Cincinnati and Cairo basing-point prices ranged between $3 and $10 a thousand feet of lumber, varying according to kinds and grades; and some special basing rates (not specifically described) were evidently allowed in all the region south of Memphis (analogous to the Birmingham differential in the steel industry). Lumber cut in northern Ohio and shipped direct to Boston or Philadelphia, and lumber cut in West Virginia and shipped directly east to Baltimore

---

[3] Transcript of Record, No. 369, October term, 1920; renumbered 71, October term, 1921, pp. 41-223, original paging.

and Washington, was *supposed* to pass through the "natural gateway" at Cincinnati, this to the substantial advantage of the seller's pocketbook. Of course none of the so-called "prices" thus printed were the actual prices realized by the sellers of lumber. The "uniformity" sought and in large degree attained was that of

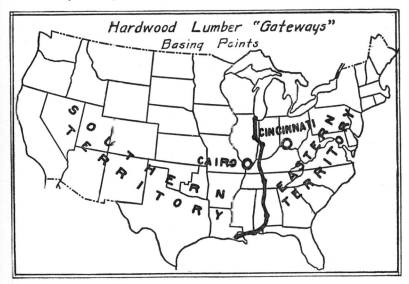

FIG. 11. BASING POINTS FOR DELIVERED PRICES OF HARDWOODS

basing-point delivered prices, while the net realized prices of each dealer to his own customers showed the greatest diversity.

MORE SHARPSHOOTING

It is a very charming play of imagination by which discriminatory prices were called uniform; and though this case has long passed into history and on to the junk heap, its reperusal still has much of interest to the student of economics and of judicial processes. As a guide and ever-pricking conscience there was sent to each member a weekly report of actual sales ("sent only to members") in which the actual delivered price of each sale was "audited" back to the basing point by deducting the official rail-tariff between the destination and the fictitious gateway. The arithmetical result (which is absurdly called "average price to destination") stands alongside another figure in a parallel column called "average price gateway." By a miracle of mathematics (one chance in billions), this "average price," presented by the facile manager of statistics as based on "actual transactions," was always in even dollars, a fact which should have been sufficient warning that it was just a fake figure. It probably was the amount set in the Memphis office as the official basing-point price to which members were to conform by an agreement plainly implied.

And in view of the variations in quality and of the lack of perfect standardization of grades (greater at that time than more recently after the valuable work of Herbert Hoover as Secretary of Commerce), the measure of agreement attained was remarkable enough. In this game (as in Pittsburgh-Plus), anything above the official "gateway" price is a perfect hit, the very best of bull's-eyes, since the agreement relates only to a minimum base price. Here, for example, in a list of 11 sales, sellers ring the bell 9 times, and the misses in the other two sales amount to only three-tenths of 1 per cent of a total perfect score.

What a sense of injustice these 333 producers and sellers of hardwood lumber (and their lawyers) must have felt when, four years after they had been enjoined as illegally "coöperating," two other Associations, essentially identical in character, marched triumphantly out of court. Had the Hardwood conspirators not been equally innocent and praiseworthy? Yet they got a kick instead of a compliment. Their chagrin must have been aggravated by the thought that they had lost despite their skillful concealment of the basing-point device, whereas the Associations in the later cases had won despite the glaring presence of that device of agreement.

LINSEED OIL EMULATES STEEL

Next comes the Linseed Oil case in 1923,[4] in which the Supreme Court unanimously overruled the District Judge and declared the Association of 12 corporations, called "crushers" of oil, to be a combination in violation of the Sherman Act. In this case, in contrast with the Hardwood case, the presence of a basing-point system was plainly apparent. It was thus described by Justice McReynolds:

[4] 262 U.S. 371, June 1923.

The United States were divided into eight zones for price quoting; and it was stipulated that each member should quote a basic price for zone number one and should add thereto one, two, four, six, seven, eight and eleven cents, respectively, for the others.[5]

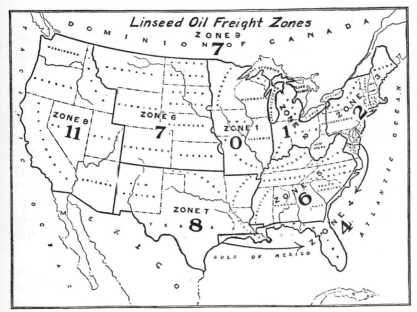

FIG. 12. LINSEED OIL BASING POINT, MINNEAPOLIS

Beyond this mere mention of "a basic price," nothing in the opinion suggests that the Court gave any special weight to it as a proof of combination, or that the decision would have been any different if no such feature had appeared in the Association plan, and the Court evidently did not comprehend its real character and effect. Yet here for the first time the basing-point system had not only been mentioned before the Supreme Court, but (in the words

[5] *Idem.* It should be understood that in essence this was not a multiple system of basing points, but that Minneapolis in Zone One was the basing point for the whole country. The amount added for each zone was the badly estimated *average* freight rate per gallon of oil from Minneapolis to that zone, and being added to the base price it gave a complete set of *delivered* prices to every point in the United States. The fallacy of these average rates and their statistical inaccuracy is discussed further in Appendix to Ch. XVI.

of the defendants' brief) the prosecution "laid great stress on the matter, and endeavored to portray the use of such zones as a plan or scheme by which the crushers were enabled to fix prices and control production."

GLIMPSES OF DISCRIMINATION

Indeed the brief on behalf of the United States in this case, filed in October term, 1922, evinced a more nearly correct understanding of the real part played by the basing-point device than is to be found anywhere before or since in anti-trust pleadings. Doubtless this reflects the influence of the Pittsburgh-Plus complaint which had then been in progress for two years, attracting much attention in Washington legal circles. The astute Mr. James M. Beck, who as Solicitor General represented the Government, broke a record in that he saw that the sale over in Ohio (Zone Two) of oil manufactured at Buffalo and New York (in Zone Three) at one cent a gallon less, although the freight was the same or even more, was a "discrimination." He justly declared that "no one attempts to give any reason for this," and "there can be no excuse whatever" for it. In broad terms he maintained that

The adoption of this zoning system was, in itself, an unlawful agreement in restraint of trade, because, while it did not fix the base price to be charged by each of the manufacturers, yet it did obligate them to observe these fixed differentials, and prevented them from meeting special competition that might exist in other zones.[6]

The Government's brief concedes the defendants' assertion that this zoning system is used in a number of other industries, but declares the method to be wrong wherever used. "The real purpose of its adoption is the same in every instance." Then, showing further that this makes the execution of an agreement regarding prices as simple as "a child's problem in arithmetic," the argument concludes:

Thus by agreement, of which a record was made, the defendants have departed from the custom of adding to the price at the point of manufacture the actual freight to the point of delivery, and have adopted arbitrary rates applicable to all of them.[7]

[6] Government's brief in Linseed Oil case, 262 U.S. 371, p. 33.
[7] *Idem*, p. 35.

Though this does not demonstrate a perfect insight into the differences between uniform mill-base and delivered prices, nor complete the analysis, it was the highest point of understanding yet reached in a court proceeding. Yet this part of the prosecution's argument was imperfectly developed and presented, and stood somewhat apart from the main contention of illegal combination which the Court took as the basis for its unanimous decision, and apparently it was not given the slightest attention by the Court.

A BEWILDERED JUDGE

The defendants, too, evidently expected (or feared) that considerable weight might be given to this aspect of the case, and their briefs marshaled all the familiar arguments in its defense: false history, confused explanation, and erroneous inferences. It was repeatedly asserted in the briefs and by witnesses that the zoning system as actually used made prices no different from what they would have been without it, presumably under a normal mill-base price system.[8] Here is involved the not uncommon illusion that when widely different figures are statistically averaged, the differences vanish for practical purposes. Further, zoned freight rates from an actual mill base are confused with zoned rates from an artificial basing point. The zoning of rates over such enormous territories must materially change the delivered cost to multitudes of buyers (as compared with actual freights) even with prices quoted on a mill base, but the difference it makes to the public in that case is small compared with that when the zones are related to an artificial basing point. The latter practice often quite reverses real geographical relationships, making the freight higher for the shorter distance (or the net price of the goods—take your choice). Judge Carpenter in the District Court was completely taken in by these fallacies, and though the Supreme Court in its decision on the Linseed case implied its rejection of Judge Carpenter's views, Justice Stone, in the Maple Flooring case, really adopted them fully in respect to the intelligence and fairness of averaged or zoning rates when related to a basing point. It seems worth while,

---

[8] For example, Walsh brief, p. 46; and citing the District Judge's opinion, p. 15; Matthews brief, p. 9, et passim.

therefore, to analyze this confusion with care in the Appendix to Ch. XVI.

LO, THE POOR FARMER!

Briefly summarized, the differentials above the basic Zone One were 20 to 30 per cent less than real average freight rates for the second and third zones, but for the other five zones were in excess from 12 to 133 per cent. The amounts charged for delivery were relatively higher to the agricultural sections than to the industrial sections of the country (and thus discriminatory), instead of being a fair average, according to the professed purpose of the plan. And the more distinctively agricultural the zone, the greater was this discrimination against it, when the farmers bought back the linseed oil made from the flaxseed they had grown. Whereas the marked industrial sections of the country were taxed less than real average freight, the southeastern Atlantic coast region was taxed 12 per cent more than the real freight, the southeastern largely agricultural States 50 per cent more, the Pacific and mountain States 66 per cent more, the great Southwest from Louisiana to New Mexico 80 per cent more, and the region of the great plains and eastern slope of the Rockies from Kansas to Montana 133 per cent more. Where the farmers raised the flaxseed and sold it to the linseed oil crushers on the open market, there, when they came to buy back the oil to paint their tools, furniture, houses, and barns, they paid two and a third times the actual average freight to get it delivered to them. Page Senators Norris, Borah, Brookhart, and other tribunes of the people. But the average results were mere child's play compared with some of the extremer cases of discrimination within these grotesquely exaggerated "zones." Here was Topeka, Kansas, the real freight rate on oil to which (from Minneapolis) was equivalent to only six-tenths of a cent a gallon more than the average freight in the Minneapolis zone; yet the proverbially patient Kansan was made to pay 7 cents imaginary freight added to the wholesale price for every gallon of oil he bought to paint his house and barn with the proceeds of his farm crops sold on the world's open markets. A mere disparity of 1000 per cent in this zone freight schedule which a judge on the bench charitably declared to be so intelligent and so fair! But enough

of these harrowing details. More might start a new political
revolution when next the western Senatorial champions gather in
Washington with the worthy purpose of redressing the wrongs
of the agricultural sections of the land.

THE CUSTOMER'S FICTITIOUS OPTION

The defense repeatedly asserted that "each buyer is at liberty
to pay his own freight and buy at the lower price." These and
similar expressions [9] give the impression that the basing-point
system had no real existence or distinctive character, or at least
that it existed only at the option of the customer in each case;
and that the difference between it and a mill-base system of prices
was so slight as to be negligible to the buyer. We have met this
hoax before. Judge Carpenter was completely misled, as is shown
by his confident declaration that "every buyer had the option of
purchasing f.o.b. point of manufacture or f.o.b. point of delivery,
and I must assume that the buyer would choose that f.o.b. point
which seemed most to his advantage." [10] He impatiently sweeps
the whole problem aside as a case of *de minimis non curat lex.*
A careful examination of all the statements in the Record carrying this suggestion of the buyer's option shows that they always
mean something else than Judge Carpenter takes them to mean.[11]
No one with an understanding of the true nature of a basing-point
system of prices can find in any of the testimony the slightest
ground for believing that the buyer was ever permitted to reduce
the delivered cost to himself by choosing to buy at a real mill-
base price. What the witnesses are describing is a merely imaginary
shift in accountancy practice; the buyer might have the bill submitted in two items instead of one; but the sum of the two items
would be exactly the same as the amount of the one; namely, the
basing-point delivered price. The "f.o.b. mill" would not be a
real mill-base price determined first, and uniform to all similar
buyers, but would be a special discriminatory price on each sale,
calculated by subtracting actual freight from the delivered price
deduced from the formula, which is an artificial base plus imag-

---

9 E.g., Walsh brief, 44, 46, 47, 48; Matthews brief, 9.
10 275 Fed. Rep., 945.
11 For examples see Record, p. 96, quoted in Walsh brief, pp. 42-44; Record,
p. 117, quoted *idem,* p. 48; Record, p. 109, quoted *idem,* p. 47.

inary freight. The basing-point delivered price is the primary and decisive figure; the figuring of a so-called "f.o.b. mill price" would be merely primary-school arithmetic. It is all transparent.

THE UNWRITTEN CHAPTER OF LINSEED

All this ingenuity (to call it by no harsher name) was wasted, and the case after all was decided in the Supreme Court adversely to the Association, in disregard of this issue. Dissolved as illegal in 1923 in obedience to the Court's injunction, the linseed oil group has not publicly reveled in the liberty granted by the subsequent decisions in 1925 in respect to price-rigging activities. It has made at least an outward show of living soberly and modestly, shunning the rude gaze of men. Linseed oil nowhere appears among the so-called open-price commodities in the list published by the Federal Trade Commission in 1929. He would be a rash man, however, who would conclude that linseed oil has since been, and is today, sold on a normal mill-base plan, rather than by zones, or basing points, or some other artificial device.

CHAPTER XVII

THE INVISIBLE ACCOMPLICE OF "OPEN PRICES"

ONCE MORE INTO THE BREACH

THE Maple Flooring and the Cement Protective Association cases were so alike in the main issues presented that the Court heard them and decided them much as though they were one. They were alike too in that both were plainly marked by the basing-point feature. Counsel for the defense evidently expected and feared that the basing-point issue might loom large. In the short year and a half between the adverse decision of these cases in the District Courts (late autumn 1923) and their oral argument in the Supreme Court (March 1925), while the briefs were in preparation, the Pittsburgh-Plus practice had been discountenanced (July 1924) by the Federal Trade Commission, and the Steel Corporation had unexpectedly bowed to this decision without appeal to the Courts. These circumstances, together with the adverse position taken by the Supreme Court in 1923 toward the open-price practice, spurred the distinguished counsel of the defendants, led by Mr. John W. Davis, to a final desperate effort to win a favorable verdict. They enlisted the aid of academic advisers from noted universities to analyze the economic materials, to prepare propagandist literature, to go upon the witness stand, or to shape the arguments of the briefs on points of an economic nature.

Government counsel, on the contrary, either heedless or too confident in the authority of the Hardwood and Linseed Oil decisions, and over-confident from their easy successes in the preliminary skirmishes in the two District Courts, appear to have enlisted no expert economic counsel to offset the special efforts which they knew the defense was making, and the decision, so far as it might have depended on the treatment of the economic issues, went by default. The voluminous record presented to the Supreme Court by Government counsel seems ill arranged and confusing.

THE MAPLE FLOORING BASING POINT

The basing-point device was a part of the open-price plan of both the Maple Flooring and the Cement Associations. All but

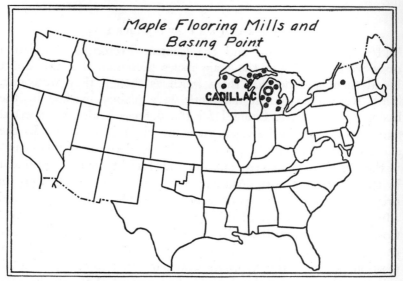

FIG. 13. BASING POINT, CADILLAC, FOR MAPLE FLOORING

three of the plants of the defendants in the Maple Flooring case were located in Michigan and Wisconsin, in which States they represented nearly 90 per cent of the total production, and nearly nine-tenths of this was produced in Michigan. In essentials, the basing-point features in selling maple flooring were like those in the Hardwood case, except that but one common basing point, Cadillac, Michigan, was used for the whole country. Prices were always "delivered," and a freight book was issued showing freight rates from Cadillac to between five and eight thousand points in the United States.[1]

[1] 268 U.S. Record, Vol. 1, p. 112.

These books formerly showed also what was called "delivered cost" (as in the Hardwood case), but after the suit was started, that was omitted, the only change being that the Association member now had to "make his own addition"—a very simple task. Defendants' answer admits [2] that this compilation was for their "convenience . . . to enable them . . . to quote delivered prices," but says that they are not under "any constraint, duty or obligation" to use it; and it denies that there is "any understanding or agreement . . . to be guided or controlled by the said list." There is no denial that the list did serve as a guide; the denial is only as to "constraint" or "obligation." Of course there could be no legal obligation, as any "agreement" or "understanding" would be illegal. Ah, there is a poser. No "understanding" about it? If its meaning was misunderstood, was unintelligible to those to whom and for whose use it was intended, then why was it issued? But this doubt does not trouble the Court.

AGAIN THE FALLACY OF AVERAGES

The defense explained that the Cadillac rate represented the "average" freight rate from all the mills, and the delivered prices seem to have been the sum of "*average* costs" and "*average* freight rates," not, except rarely by mathematical chance, *actual* individual costs or *actual* freight rates.[3] Here again we see the Court under the simple illusion that *averaging* differing sums in some magical way puts an end to the differences. Friends of ours, professors of statistics and of history, respectively, went out duck-hunting, and the statistician reported the results as follows:

Every time a duck flew by I shot six feet in front of it, and the historian, being more interested in the past, shot six feet back of it, so on the average we killed every duck. Statistically it was a great success, but historically it was a failure.

Here is the very similar statement of Justice Stone, seeming to echo the previously neglected reasoning of Judge Carpenter:

the freight-rate book served a useful and legitimate purpose in enabling members to quote promptly a delivered price on their product by

[2] *Idem*, p. 39.   [3] *Idem*, Vol. 1, p. 112.

adding to their mill price a previously calculated freight rate which approximated closely to the actual rate from their own mill towns.[4]

The second half of the statement contains two factual errors; first, the freight rate was not added "to their mill price" or to any real mill-base price, but to a so-called "average cost," which was not the actual cost of any one of the mills; and secondly, this so-called "calculated" freight rate was in many cases far from a close approximation to the *average*, and much less to the *actual* freight rates from the particular mills to many destinations. The actual conditions were grotesquely different from what the Court understood them to be. A few specific examples are given in the Appendix to Ch. XVII.

THE LEGALISTIC SHELL RACKET

It is an odd "approximation to the actual rate" that compels the Minnesota public to pay to the lumber mills 130 per cent more for freight than the amount which the common carrier may legally charge. We trust there is no impropriety in gently calling this situation to the attention of that distinguished citizen of Minnesota, the Hon. William Mitchell, Attorney General of the United States.

Of course the overburdened Supreme Court justices could not take the time to make these calculations. This was a neglected duty of Government counsel. With the proper analysis of these figures before him, Justice Stone surely would have had misgivings about the purpose being merely to promptly quote delivered prices, and even about such "delivered prices" being "legitimate" at all. Justice Stone and the majority of the Court in this case were the victims of a sort of legalistic shell racket, for while their eyes were focused upon the innocent gathering of statistical information, they missed seeing the basing-point device which was securing that "concerted action with respect to prices" which the Court, in concluding, declared would have put the whole case in a very different light. Recognition of the common action in devising, maintaining, and administering this price-fixing plan, surely would have re-

[4] 268 U.S. 571, June 1925.

sulted in a verdict of illegality for the Association and its activities. This issue was not touched by the decision, which in the final paragraph is cautiously limited to a vindication of the open and fair dissemination of information, "without reaching or attempting to reach any agreement or concerted action with respect to prices," though tacit agreement and *de facto* concerted action were plainly present.

MULTIPLE BASING POINTS FOR CEMENT

In the Cement Manufacturers' Protective Association case, the use of the basing-point device was somewhat more plainly set forth in evidence and briefs, but the majority of the Court quite failed to see its significance as an instrument for price control. The Cement Association has a membership of manufacturers in the States of New York, New Jersey, Pennsylvania, Maryland, and Virginia. It appears to be one of some ten or more similar cement associations which among them cover the whole territory of the United States. It is probable that in each of these territorial divisions a system of basing points and of delivered prices has for years been in force, in all essentials like the Pittsburgh-Plus scheme for steel.

This multiplication and greater decentralization of basing points for cement compared with the plan in selling steel no doubt is due mainly to the greater weight of cement in proportion to its value. Moreover, the materials and necessary conditions for its manufacture are more widely distributed than are those for steel. Cement, therefore, far more even than steel, is "a zone business," as the cost of freight soon becomes a large fraction of the mill price. Indeed the use of a single basing point within the combined area of five States must lead to as great discrimination among buyers of cement as does a single basing point for the whole continent in the case of the steel industry. Therefore, while the Atlas Mill at Northampton, Pennsylvania, was the main basing point, several other basing points at Hudson and Alsen, New York, Fordwick, Virginia, and (in sales to the west) Universal, Pennsylvania, were used by the mills in the territory of the five States covered by the Association. A similar plan appears to be in operation now in all other parts of the country; for example, California, being a very large State, is divided into two districts by the cement companies. In the southern part, the California Portland Cement Company at Colton (Riverside or Crestmore) is the basing point, and in the north the Davenport mill at San Juan. Every buyer, public or private, receives identical bids for cement delivered.[5]

The more general use of basing points for cement was not referred to in the case now considered, but the use of basing-point delivered prices in the five States was virtually conceded by all parties

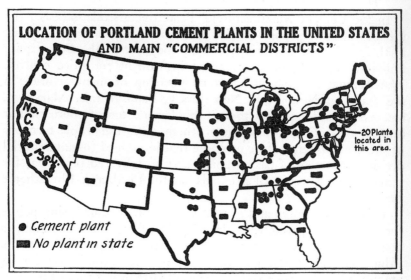

FIG. 14. MULTIPLE BASING-POINT SYSTEM FOR CEMENT

to the suit. It was a part of the "substantial uniformity of trade practices in the cement trade," which had prevailed, as the Court said, "before the organization of the present association," that is, before January 1916. These conditions included:

The selling of cement f.o.b. delivery. Using freight basing points in the quotation of prices. Including in all quotations for sale of cement, a freight rate from a basing point to the place of delivery.[6]

[5] See Reporters' Transcript of testimony in the matter of the investigation by a Special Committee of the Senate concerning the existence of a reported cement trust in California, January to March, 1929. See especially pp. 64, 66, 133, 693, 735.

[6] 268 U.S. 593, June 1925.

GARBLING THE FACTS AND ISSUES

The complaint against the Cement Association was not directed against the use of basing-point practice or any other specific price-regulating device, and the defense skillfully handled this issue so as to reduce to nearly nothing its importance in the eyes of the Court. The Court felt justified in saying:

here the Government does not rely upon agreement or understanding, and this record wholly fails to establish, either directly or by inference, any concerted action other than that involved in the gathering and dissemination of pertinent information with respect to the sale and distribution of cement.[7]

Reduce the issue to that form and the decision follows almost automatically. But how had it been possible for the Court to avoid seeing in the basing-point device itself the *direct*, not merely inferential, evidence of that concerted action whose presence, the Court indicates, would have set the case in an entirely different light? The main facts accounting for this judicial blindness seem to be the following:

In the garbled version of the facts as understood by the Court [8] "the custom," as the Court calls it,

in the cement trade of selling cement at a delivered price which includes the mill price, the price of the bags and freight charges, was an established trade practice before the organization of the defendant association.

This misunderstanding was strengthened by other evidence assumed to show that

similar lists of freight rates . . . were . . . used by individual manufacturers before the organization of the defendant association; [and] the basing points from which the freight rates were calculated were not selected by the Association, but were the same as those . . . [used by individuals before the formation of the Association].

Justice Stone took these ideas and expressions almost literally from the defendants' brief; [9] and he also fully accepted certain other

[7] 268 U.S. p. 606.
[8] *Idem*, p. 597.

[9] *Op. cit.*, pp. 18-19.

misleading assertions and contentions· of the defendants' brief in
the same connection that "there is here no arbitrarily established
basing point and all rates furnished are the actual rates between
actual points of shipment and delivery." Did the astute lawyers
not know perfectly well that the purpose of the freight books of
rates from arbitrary basing points was to name identical delivered
prices for the mills *not* actually shipping from those points or
paying those actual rates?

AN ARTIFICIAL DEVICE

Here and repeatedly in the opinion, the basing-point policy is
viewed as a truly competitive "custom" and not an artificial device
brought about originally by agreement. It is represented as being
essentially the same as the mill's *own* base price; being "established," the practice continued automatically and naturally, without any aid or connivance through the activities of the Association
(engaged solely in the innocent pursuit of statistical information!)
It followed, therefore, in judicial reasoning, that the condemnation
and dissolution of the Association would be a futile and irrelevant
act.

The Court overlooked the illuminating "History" set forth
in the Government's brief [10] "of events leading up to the organization of the defendant Cement Manufacturers' Protective Association." Various earlier organizations in the cement industry had
been abandoned because of fears of investigation or of prosecution.
Their illegal nature is really not open to question. Bald agreements
as to prices were entered into. Justice Stone incautiously assumes
that the basing-point practice grew up innocently and naturally
while these illegal organizations were functioning. After their
abandonment, the Association, constituted of the same men and
the same corporations, was formed for the same general purpose.
The Court was in a very trustful mood that day when it pronounced its judgment.

CEMENT TAUGHT BY STEEL

The assertion that the use of basing-point prices has long been
an established business custom in the particular industry is itself an

[10] *Op. cit.,* pp. 11-44.

established custom, a part of the approved technique of hokum, in the defense of anti-trust cases. In fact, the general use of basing points dates (after brief periods of experimentation) from the period of giant trust formation. As Pittsburgh-Plus (and a similar practice in the non-ferrous metal industry) became well established about the years 1898 to 1900, so the closely related building material, cement, first began in those years to be sold by the dubious practice of delivered prices. It is more than a mere coincidence that the U.S. Steel Corporation at its formation in 1901 acquired with the Illinois Steel Company two cement plants. In 1906 the Universal Portland Cement Company was incorporated as a subsidiary of the U.S. Steel, taking over all its cement plants and building others, one in the Pittsburgh district at a railroad station named Universal, which then became an important basing point for cement. The recent acquisition by U.S. Steel, in December 1929, of the entire business and numerous plants of the Atlas Portland Cement Company is but another step in the same policy of merging the domination of the cement and the steel industries. From the first, in adopting the newly invented "custom" of using basing-point prices, the cement industry had the guidance of the master hand of the inventor of that custom.

A MUSHROOM "CUSTOM"

The truth as to the date when the cement industry adopted the basing-point practice was revealed in an unguarded moment by one who should know. In an article printed the very week that Justice Stone ascended the Supreme bench and the oral argument of the Cement case began, occurs this statement: [11] "Twenty-six years ago cement manufactured in the Lehigh Valley almost invariably was sold on a mill price." That fixes the date of the general use as not earlier than 1899. Between 1900 and 1912 virtual agreement and suppression of competition in the cement industry were in considerable measure attained by bogus patent claims and finally in 1909 by an Association of Licensed Cement Manufacturers making and enforcing license agreements. The

[11] By the President of the Alpha Portland Cement Company, in *American Economic Review*, March 1925; a letter republished by the Cement Information Service under the title "Why Portland Cement is Sold at Delivered Prices."

patent which was used as the weapon to enforce compliance with this comprehensive scheme was disallowed in successive decisions in the District and Circuit Courts (1910-1912), and the Association was dissolved. As was said in the Government's brief in the Cement Protective case: "It is perfectly manifest that the Hurry and Seaman patent was used as a mere cloak to conceal the real purpose and intent of the parties." [12] A most essential part of that purpose and plan was the operation and enforcement of a basing-point system of prices in cement. Then, between 1899 and 1911, and not in the immemorial past, the basing-point practice was made a so-called "custom" of the industry, by means of artificial and illegal devices.

ESCAPED IN PETTICOATS

An economist testifying as an expert in price theory in the Cement case had maintained (on the alleged authority of numerous economic texts) that the basing-point identical delivered prices in the sale of cement exemplified that "uniformity of price" which "will inevitably result from active, free and unrestrained competition." [13] The learned Justice, usually clear in his economic views, was unfortunately misled by this testimony into a confusion of identical basing-point prices with uniform market or mill-base prices. It seems best to postpone the further discussion of this false identification to a later chapter.[14]

Springing from this confusion is another error accepted by the Court, that the use of a basing point is "the natural result of the development of the business within certain defined geographical areas," indeed, that competing mills "must" use the rate from a given basing point "in order to compete with the mills located in the vicinity of [a] chief point of production." [15] Here is judicially sanctioned the popular notion that, in order to be really competing with each other, each of two geographically distant mills must be selling everywhere in the other's natural sales territory, with all

[12] Government's brief in the Supreme Court, p. 16. The text of this license agreement is pretty fully set forth in the Government's brief in the District Court, pp. 13-29.
[13] Justice Stone's words, 268 U.S. 605.
[14] See Chs. XX-XXII.
[15] 268 U.S. 598-599.

that this entails as to wasteful cross freights, discriminatory treatment of customers, and sales unprofitable to the mills, a sum total of social waste and injustice. This problem, too, will be fundamentally treated later.

Justice Stone's two now famous majority opinions on open-price trade associations concluded for the time this comedy of errors, in four acts and eight scenes. A blunder four times repeated was made by the Department of Justice in founding the complaints against the open-price plan upon the merely superficial activity, in itself harmless, of collecting statistics. Twice, to be sure, the Supreme Court, guided by sound intuitions rather than by direct proof of other incriminating acts, upheld the defective complaints; but when skillful defense counsel, favored by a change in the personnel of the Court, succeeded in other cases in reducing the issue to the bare fact of statistical inquiry, the weakness in the whole theory of the prosecution bore its inevitable penalty. A simple stool pigeon was indicted as the principal in these offenses, while the guilty accomplice, delivered prices, always inconspicuous if not invisible to the Court, though really the chief offender, escaped scot free, concealed under the skirts of its paramour.

THE MILLS OF THE GODS

The Court's main conclusion was:

We decide only that trade associations . . . which openly and fairly gather and disseminate information . . . as did these defendants . . . without, however, reaching or attempting to reach any agreement or concerted action with respect to prices . . . do not thereby engage in unlawful restraint of commerce.[16]

The clause beginning "without" qualified very essentially the Court's sanction of the open-price associations; it still left them (as their attorneys ruefully discovered) subject to the full penalties of the law if, and when, any collusive price activities were to be disclosed. More than a thousand important open-price trade associations, including nearly all leading industries in interstate commerce, are in full swing in this country.[17] In itself, gathering sta-

[16] 268 U.S. 563, 586.
[17] See Report of the Federal Trade Commission on *Open Price Associations*, Senate Document 226, 70th Congress, 2d session, 1929. The report covers

tistics is as harmless as a game of ping-pong. The one really mischievous feature of this decision lay in the Court's assumption that basing-point prices were merely uniform market prices, the outcome and the evidence of perfect competition. That the basing-point practice will be found in most, if not all, of the thousand or more industries organized in open-price associations is a probability. Besides the industries mentioned elsewhere in this book, the basing-point plan appears to have been used in the asphalt shingle and roofing industry, industrial alcohol, fertilizers, sewer pipe, range boilers, hollow building tile, expanded metal lath, bolts, nuts and rivets, sugar, various other branches of the lumber industry, and others. One who has widely observed the price practices of many of the most important industries declares that "it is decidedly the exception rather than the rule to find one in which there is that freedom of market competition which the law contemplates." How much longer can the Courts ignore the economic truth that basing-point prices evidence "concerted action with respect to prices," and therefore are in illegal restraint of trade?

1,103 associations, of which 975 are interstate and 128 intrastate (pp. 30-31). "There are probably a number of trade associations not reached at all in the canvass" (p. 27).

PART V

THAT ELUSIVE IDEAL—FREE MARKETS

═══════════

MARKETS WANE AS FACTORIES WAX

S E E K I N G   F I R M   F O U N D A T I O N S

OUR main theme is the basing-point plan of delivered prices. This is "the masquerader" who has led a charmed life amid many vicissitudes, and who still is at large, flouting the law. But the story of the basing-point policy is interwoven since 1900 with that of other phases of monopoly and restraint of trade in interstate commerce, and with that of the largely futile efforts to enforce the anti-trust statutes meant to maintain or to restore conditions of competition.

Our survey thus far of the problems of price arising in the sale of industrial products, though limited to the state of facts presented by but a few leading cases in the courts, has taken a wide range. We have now before us a formidable mass of evidence and judicial opinions bearing upon almost every essential phase of our subject, and although we might easily amass many other similar data from the volumes of reported cases, we should thus but multiply instances of practices abundantly illustrated already. What is needed now is not more heaping up of repetitious facts but the clarification and more systematic interpretation of the facts at hand.

We have approached our subject in its more concrete setting, as the practices and problems of prices have actually appeared in judicial proceedings. In the reported cases and transcripts of records are preserved the richest existing stores of testimony and of arguments on this large subject. We have sought to analyze and criticize the evidence and opinions step by step as they have occurred in actual cases. While our references to economic history and our use of economic principles have, we trust, served to throw some light upon many obscurer issues, the order of our theoretical criticism has necessarily been somewhat unsystematic and opportunistic. We shall attempt now in these concluding chapters to give the whole subject a more systematic setting, to view it first against a larger historical background, and then to outline and lay down the firm theoretical foundations upon which alone consistent judicial opinions and sound public policy can be erected.

COMPETITION LINKED WITH THE MARKETS

Anglo-American law, as shaped by Parliament, by Congress, and by the courts, became increasingly, from the fifteenth until the nineteenth century, pervaded with the idea that competition in business is in the main a good thing for the public, and that its converse, whether this be called merely restraint of trade or private monopoly, is a bad thing, to be either destroyed or publicly controlled. But what is meant by competition? What is its nature; by what signs can it be recognized; under what conditions can it be maintained?

Instead of trying to answer these questions at once with abstract definitions, let us turn first to a historical survey of markets, for this will give us a picture of economic competition in action. Actually, economic competition appears at the point in place and time when goods come to be sold and bought; that is, when goods of any kind, services, or wealth, become articles of commerce. Just then is when the competitive comparison is made as to service, quality, and price, although the efforts of men, it is true, have been earlier stimulated by the anticipation of having to meet this competition on the market. This is likewise the point at which almost all the legal questions arise in regard to competition, so that there is hardly a legal or economic phase of competition that does not involve the consideration of the nature of markets, market conditions, and prices in markets. Economic competition began with markets, and grew as markets grew with the increasing use of money and of better means of transportation. Therefore (not strangely) the existence and vitality of competition in trade is essentially bound up with the existence and reality of markets. It seems well, therefore, to take a look at the more concrete visible facts of markets and their history, before involving ourselves more deeply in the more abstract definitions and concepts of competition and monopoly.

WHAT IS HAPPENING TO THEM

The aim of the law and of the courts for centuries has been to preserve in business in a real way the conditions making competition possible. This has never been an easy task. Competition, we find, far from being a natural thing (as is so often assumed), automatically brought about whenever private citizens are left to do as they please, seems rather to have been constantly destroyed by the self-interest and efforts of individuals and to have been maintained as an artificial condition only by the efforts of public authorities (if, indeed, they were not themselves hampering such competitive action as there was). This, we may see, was true even in the rural and manorial social organization of the Middle Ages, when conditions were much simpler in many ways than they are today. The peculiar difficulties of those times in the way of competition, some created by public charters and some by custom—gild privileges, special grants, franchises, etc.—have largely disappeared, but in the three-quarters of a century since 1850 the swift growth of industry and transportation has made possible new business practices and created new problems and difficulties in the way of true competition. These changes have shifted and greatly modified the meanings that can be and must be attached to the words competition, restraint of trade, and monopoly, as used in economics and in the law. As a result, popular opinion, the law, and the courts, find themselves in a maze from which only sound theory based on a study of the new facts can extricate them.

EARLY ENGLISH MARKETS; MARKET TOWNS

Markets had their origin in antiquity as meeting-places on the borders between tribes or villages, where traders met to exchange goods. The Latin name *mercatus* thus came, in the Germanic languages, to have the meaning of boundary (*mark*). Market meant first the place where the traders met, but it came to mean in the legal sense also the franchise or liberty of holding a market. This right to hold a market or fair was the result of a grant from the king (or of a prescriptive right presumed to have originated in a grant) to a neighboring nobleman or to a religious house such as an abbey or to the town authorities. There were two types of early periodical markets: town markets and regional fairs. Some regular markets existed in England in Saxon times as early, possibly, as the year 700. Their number slowly increased, and many others were founded soon after the Norman Conquest in 1066.

In several hundred good-sized villages and small towns, called market towns, in medieval England, town markets were held once or twice a week or oftener. To these central points of the neighborhoods the products both of town and of country were brought for sale. The owner of the market right (whether the town corporation or some other corporation, religious or educational, or some individual) had the duty of maintaining the market places and the right to collect moderate fees, or tolls, from the traders.

FAIRS AS MARKETS

Regional fairs were held in many places, usually just outside the limits of some important town, once or twice or four times a year and in rare cases oftener. The franchise was held by some abbey, bishop, nobleman, or private person, never by the near-by town authorities—an interesting detail, seemingly designed to insure fuller competition. Thus the fairs must have exercised a steady competitive restraining influence upon the prices in the market and in the gild-merchant towns. Several hundred such fairs were chartered in England in the Middle Ages. Most of them were of merely local importance, little greater than town markets; but some of them attracted producers, merchants, and buyers not only from all parts of Britain but from distant lands. Certain of these fairs came to be the chief national market places for special products, very like to certain great grain, cattle, cotton, wool, fur, and other produce markets of the present day.

In these fairs and in the local markets, after they were opened and the moderate prescriptive tolls were paid, exchange took place with a remarkable degree of effective competition. It is evident that when population was sparse, when roads were poor and travel usually very difficult, when few could read or write and there were no newspapers or other means of transmitting exact

information as to business conditions, these gatherings at markets
and at fairs were remarkably well designed to bring together the
largest possible number of traders from a trading area, and to
give them, before they began to trade, the largest possible commonly shared knowledge of conditions of "demand and supply,"
to use a more modern phrase.

OPENING OF A FAIR

A picture of a great English fair, sometime perhaps in the
fourteenth century, may serve best to make this clear (and the
local markets had within their several spheres essentially the same
effects). The hour for the opening of the fair arrives. From many
parts of England have come stewards of great estates, bringing
for sale such products as wool, leather, hides, salt, dried fish, and
metals. Artisans with their handiwork and shopkeepers with their
wares are there from far and near. Merchants are there not only
from the great towns of England but from those of the Continent,
bringing the luxuries of Flanders, of the Baltic Hanseatic towns,
of Italy, and of the Orient, all eager to sell their wares and
in turn to buy the crude products and the rougher textiles of
England. On long tables and in rows of booths, the goods are
laid out for inspection and for sale. Every one has been keenly
watching these preparations, and soon both buyers and sellers
know pretty well the quality of the goods and the amount of
the stocks compared with the number and probable needs of those
who have come to buy.

MARKET COMPULSION UPON THE TRADER

But as yet not a sale has been made or could lawfully be made.
Buying outside the actual market bounds within several miles of
any fair or market was a crime; it was "forestalling" or "engrossing," crimes long illegal by the common law and later repeatedly
forbidden by parliamentary statute.[1] One of the evils of forestalling was the creation of a temporary local monopoly in a commodity

---

[1] Forestalling was prohibited by English statutes as early as 1285, in the reign
of Edward I; see W. Cunningham, *Growth of English Industry and Commerce*,
Vol. I, p. 243, and W. Ashley, *English Economic History*, Vol. I, pp. 182-183.
Most noted are the laws of 5 and 6 Edward VI, c. 14, and 5 Elizabeth, c. 12,
which were repealed by 7 and 8 Victoria, c. 24.

by the large merchant buyer—"cornering the market," in modern phrase. Hence the offense of forestalling was closely connected with the other offenses of engrossing (buying large amounts of goods) and regrating (re-selling goods in the same market). These were the chief devices by which a limited monopoly power in those days could be obtained temporarily without a royal grant. These laws were, to be sure, designed in part to prevent the evasion of tolls to the injury of the owner of the market franchise; but undoubtedly, under the conditions of those times, they served also the larger public purpose of creating real markets and the possibility of real market prices. In markets or fairs the great merchant buyers of native products had to buy openly in the presence of the whole group of sellers assembled from far and wide and were subject to the competing bids of other buying merchants, instead of being able to take each small seller into a corner and deal with him separately. Likewise merchants coming from many lands and climes competed openly in the sale of their wares. Under conditions of that time, when the small traders would otherwise be isolated and in ignorance of the general situation, a real market could be created and maintained only as a somewhat artificial institution, a place to which the traders were, as a condition of trading at all, legally compelled to come together to trade at one time and place.

LAW OF THE MARKET

From the moment that a fair was formally proclaimed, trade was suspended in the neighboring towns and it was illegal for the town merchants to buy or sell outside the boundaries of the fair. The lord of the fair took over the functions of the town authorities, and a merchants' court was in continuous session to settle summarily all disputes according to the "law merchant," a special code of business laws and customs (in some respects the prototype of our Federal Trade Commission). Money-changers were present, and official measurers, weighers, and other public officials. For a day in a local market, and for one or two weeks or longer at fairs, buying and selling went on freely and openly. Every person could judge at each moment the state of the market as to amounts of goods remaining, number of buyers, and the prices at which goods were being sold. At the legally fixed hour for closing, sales had to stop and the booths had to be cleared of all goods and to be shut.[2] This must have meant usually the "clearing of the market," that is, the sale, at whatever price it would bring, of everything brought for sale (excepting such rarer and more precious wares of light weight as merchants could more profitably carry away).

OASES OF FAIR PRICES

In the midst of the conditions of feudal caste and status on the land and of the rigid organizations of merchant gilds and of craft gilds with their various artificial restraints in the towns, such markets with their open and active buying and selling must often have appeared like competitive oases in the midst of deserts of more or less monopolistic privileges and prices. Often, undoubtedly the various gilds of merchants and of craftsmen, with their jealously guarded group privileges within the towns, looked with hostile eyes upon these sanctuaries of free trade created by royal grants outside their own little realms, as they were forced to moderate their own restrictive policies because of this periodic open market competition. As late as the fourteenth century, but in slowly decreasing measure thereafter, fairs were "the seats of most of the inland trade of the kingdom,"[3] that is, of the larger inter-municipal and foreign trade; while the local markets were the seats of nearly all neighborhood barter and sale. Such markets, even with their slight tolls and taxes, fostered a relatively free competition and "fair" prices in trade far beyond their borders in the larger areas from which traders came. A growing freedom of commerce within and among the towns between 1300 and 1500, going along with the increasing use of money and greater division of labor, favored the growth of a freer social organization, helped powerfully to break down feudalism, caste, and status, on the land, and eventually also, after 1500, with the strengthening of national power under the Tudors, to break down many of the selfish privileges of the merchant and artisan classes in the towns them-

---

[2] To prevent the abuse of continuing the market a special statute was passed in 1328, 2 Edward III, c. 15.

[3] Macpherson, *History of Commerce*, quoted by C. Walford, *Fairs Past and Present*, p. 34.

selves. Thenceforth, for three centuries, freedom of trade steadily widened within the national boundaries.

GILD-MERCHANT TOWNS

Along with the regional fairs and town markets created by special grants of the king as just described—both of them periodic markets—there existed in England from the time of the Conquest (if not before) some towns where groups of buyers and sellers could meet at all times under conditions of competition somewhat resembling those of the markets and the fairs. Two types of these can be pretty clearly distinguished. Of the first type were the gild-merchant towns, usually of medium size, larger than the typical market towns, but not so large as the great towns of the kingdom. Here ideal market conditions and competition were imperfectly realized. In each such town a gild of merchants had (also by grant) a "group monopoly" of trading, not to be condemned outright by us today as without some real reason of public weal and necessity in the conditions of that day. However, trade by outsiders was subject to severe restriction in the gild-merchant towns, and the policy of the merchant gilds was often so selfish that, especially after the fifteenth century, it drove trade away and caused the decay of once flourishing centers of trade.[4]

PERPETUAL MARKET TOWNS

Trading centers of another type were the so-called "free trade" towns, which included from the earliest times London, and later Birmingham, Manchester, and Leeds. They had no merchant gilds, but were "perpetual markets," having the legal character of markets "overt." The conditions in the "perpetual" market towns gradually came to be those of all larger English towns between the sixteenth and the middle of the nineteenth centuries. Here production was in numerous small shops with hand tools rather than by the mass production of the later nineteenth and early twentieth centuries. This size of the shop unit is a matter of great significance in our present subject. Even in medieval times in the larger towns, it was customary for all or nearly all the shops of the same craft to be grouped on certain streets. There, all customers wishing to buy goods of that sort could come, and there,

---

[4] See Gross, *The Gild Merchant*, pp. 51-52.

even outside of fair times, they had great opportunity to pick and choose from well-stocked shops, or to give special orders, according to materials, patterns, workmanship, and prices. The privileges conferred by craft-gild membership related to learning and practicing the craft and did not extend to the right to combine in price fixing. Although there were doubtless often tacit illegal restraints of competition among craftsmen, there were on the whole in the larger towns, and in a less degree elsewhere, the main conditions of perpetual markets in each kind of goods. The growth of town population, of handicrafts, and of transportation, gradually made these conditions normal throughout the greater part of England by 1800 (and usually in the colonies and in the United States before 1865) and led to the almost complete decay of the old markets and fairs—though some of them still survived with merely trivial importance.

SOURCE OF MODERN COMPETITIVE IDEAL

The conditions and method of buying and selling in the medieval markets is undoubtedly the main original source of the ideas of modern law, as well as of economics, regarding the nature of markets and the effects of competition. The price fixed in the earlier medieval markets gave a standard for the "just price" at other times and places, a standard highly prized by the medieval mind. The conditions of the medieval markets, somewhat idealized, and later those of the perpetual market towns with their numerous small shops, became the norm tacitly used by moralists, by jurists, and by the new science of political economy in the eighteenth century, in judging of the existence of markets and competition. About 1750, the eve of the mechanical industrial revolution, the grouping of independent small artisans and merchants in towns had become the regular situation. Adam Smith in 1776 and the contemporary French Physiocratic economists alike advocated the abolishment of the medieval hang-over of special gild privileges of the artisan and commercial classes. In their thought, the ideal conditions for efficiency and justice in commerce were those of the independently competing merchants and handicraft shopkeepers of the larger towns. The reality was undoubtedly approaching this ideal in England for generations before the date when the railroad became a success, about 1830, and in some aspects continued to do so until about 1850. In the century between 1750 and 1850, both in England and in America, a condition of local perpetual markets, of small independent shops, and of truly competing handicraft producers was probably more nearly realized than ever before or since. As a result of this, and without much special intervention and control by public authorities, free market conditions then generally prevailed and competitive prices were the rule.

EARLY NINETEENTH CENTURY COMPETITION

Each New England village had its "green" around which were the stores and the craft shops, serving as late as 1860 as a real market center for all the countryside within driving distance. As settlement moved westward after the Revolution, each new county west of the Alleghenies had its "county seat," with a "market square," which was the main market place of the region for miles around. Before 1860 it was still the rule that several local shops and local mills for grinding grain, sawing logs, weaving cloth, making wagons and carpets, furniture, shoes, and iron tools, were found in any town of considerable size in the United States, and they sold their products (or services) to every buyer coming to their doors. Blacksmith shops, the originals from which developed all factories fabricating iron and steel, were at every important crossroads so that two or more of them were within a day's driving distance of nearly every farm. Little local iron blast furnaces and forges by the hundred dotted the countryside in many regions. Almost universally under these conditions, the buyers of goods came in person to the mills, shops, and stores, and carried away the goods in their pack saddles or their wagons. The shop or the mill was the place of sale, and there was a well-understood prevailing price in market towns, and at each mill usually a price posted on the door, the same to all customers. Many buyers had access to two or more buying centers where were groups of independent artisans, mills, and shops, to which also many other buyers came. Each somewhat isolated mill, shop, or store, in order to attract buyers, had, in fixing the price at its doors, to reckon on interregional competition with other mills, shops, or stores not far away. Even when the goods were shipped by common carrier, either in freight wagons using the public roads or on sailboats or steamers on sea, lake, or river, it was always the buyer who either himself transported the goods or hired the transportation. Moreover, the conditions were largely those either of true competition or of uniform rates in transportation. The old law of common carriers always sought to compel equal treatment of shippers and localities on the public highways in a way preventing the exercise of monopoly power in freight charges.

A THING OF THE PAST

These were the conditions, present in larger measure in the first half of the nineteenth century than ever before or since, of that effective competition resulting from the freedom of the individual to trade honestly where, when, and how he pleased, which even from the days of medieval privileges and customs had been the subject of an almost sentimental solicitude on the part of the law. It is of trade in these circumstances (not of much trade today) that it might truly be said that "freedom of contract" is "the essence of freedom from undue restraint on the right of contract." [5] It was this state of affairs that the economists of the epoch of Ricardo and J. S. Mill (from 1815 to about 1860) had before their eyes when they assumed that free competition among numerous independent producers was both the normal and the desirable condition of business. The corporate form or organization was still infrequent in manufacturing, and outside of a few lines (textiles and iron) shops were still small and numerous. It was this state of affairs which, too, the courts of that period had in mind as, in many decisions, they wrote ever more deeply into the law the doctrine of freedom of competition as the rule of equity between individuals and as the palladium of the social good. It is this state of affairs, we are sadly forced to think, that many lawyers and judges, more learned in legal precedent than in the understanding of current economic events and changes, have assumed still to prevail as they reasoned high on competition, freedom of contract, and restraint of trade. How swiftly the stream of economic change (not always moving toward greater justice

[5] The words of Chief Justice White, 221 U.S. 62, October 1910.

between man and man) carried commerce away from this organization, still largely prevailing in America before 1860, and brought it into the very different régime that began to show more clearly its ominous outlines by the decade of the '80's in the nineteenth century!

LAW LOSES CONTACT WITH REALITY

After the middle of the nineteenth century, events fast crowding upon each other began to destroy piecemeal the real competitive conditions of true markets in many lines of industry. This was even more the case in America than in England. The courts and the economists alike began to lose their bearings and, in the actual conditions, were left without a compass of normality as to price such as that found in the old ideal of the typical market. It is this ideal or some new one to replace it that society is groping to attain under the complex and difficult conditions of modern industry.

The economic evolution of the United States since 1865 has been so swift as to be catastrophic, whereas legal evolution has been so slow as to be calamitous. Great economic changes have been wrought since the Civil War by growing forces which had begun to operate one, two, or three generations earlier. These changes have been manifest in every direction and in every part of our industrial life, but nowhere more than in the conditions affecting commerce, markets. competition, and industrial prices.

REVOLUTIONARY CHANGES IN COMMERCE

As we survey these events, seeking for some explanation of causes, we undoubtedly find it first in the rapid spread of the great mechanical technical inventions in transportation and manufacture. The new labor-saving machinery was brought together with many workers to produce in one factory an output equaling that of many formerly competing little shops. Before 1800 the turnpikes and canals, by 1807, steamboats, and by 1830, railroads, were assured successes, though their economic effects were not to become very clearly manifest for a generation or two later in each case. Factory machinery and railroads, as they were improved and extended, combined to make production on a progressively larger scale possible and inevitable. This meant larger units of production, fewer of a kind in any one locality, and the shipment of goods farther and farther from the shops and mills. Many local markets became less producing centers and more mere retail distributing centers. The wide adoption of improved machinery and of better means of transport are but two phases of one great movement. They made possible greater mass in production, which means ever larger and ever fewer physical plants or establishments, separated, often isolated, by great distances, and shipping their products farther and farther from the points of physical production and economic origin. The greater the efficiency and cheapness of production on a large scale compared with that on a smaller scale, the greater are the distances that the goods can be transported even with the old carrying agents and still undersell the local stores. The market area of each factory becomes greater. Likewise, the more efficient the means of transportation become, the wider the area over which goods can be distributed from larger factories, and this offers an inducement to invent and adopt more specialized and better factory equipment and to enlarge the unit of production further until again the limit of advantage is attained as to size of factory and breadth of market area.

It is only after these technical, mechanical agents have resulted in larger production that there appears another agency of a very different nature, not to be confounded with the others; that is, financial combination or merger of physically separate and geographically distributed plants. The motive leading to financial merger appears to have arisen after large production and distance carriage had broken down the old ideas and practices of local markets and of competition.

RAILROAD MONOPOLY APPEARS

The confusion and evils as to rate or price policies, connected with this rapid growth of market areas, appeared first most distinctly in the practices of the railroads, suddenly beginning after 1830 the mass production of transportation, replacing competing freight wagons and stage coaches. Factories still for a time continued to be mostly small and local. It was in transportation that the breakdown of the old rules of competition, even supported as they were in some degree by the old law of common carriers, became first glaringly manifest. Public opinion was unenlightened and did not see, as a few minds of clearer vision saw almost from the first, that a railroad is necessarily a monopoly, or it may be better to say, has a considerable measure of locally limited monopolistic power. The transportation services, which are the railroads' products, are sold to locally separated shippers whose alternative mode of shipment (e.g., pack mules, wagons, etc.) is usually not to be compared with the railroad in technical efficiency. In most cases, therefore, there was at any one point but one seller of efficient transportation, and though the buyers might be several, they were a small, unorganized group. Thus at most stations there was no true market for transportation services, and no true market price for rail transportation could become established by competition. In that case each rate for a particular kind of goods, to particular shippers, at particular points of shipment, is the price of an isolated sale and not a real market price. The monopolistic power of the railroad extends to much of the traffic it carries, to most shippers, and to all those stations along its lines that are not served directly by any other railroad.

REGULATION OF RAILROAD COMPETITION

It was four-fifths of a century after the beginning of railroad history in the United States in 1830 that the amendment in 1906 of the Interstate Commerce Act of 1887 began an effective regulation of railroad rates by Commission control and curbed railroad monopoly. In this period the public had been slow to learn, but it at last had learned some lessons. Stubbornly it had persisted in putting faith in unregulated "competition" between railroads—a misnomer for unregulated monopoly power. It hoped to get real and effective competition by the building of more and more trackage, always ahead of the population and traffic needs, by the paralleling of lines between the great terminal markets, and by the construction of new roads radiating from the few large manufacturing and commercial centers. For nearly a half century, until the decade of the '70's, although popular discontent against the frightful inequalities of rates was steadily growing, the railroads were actually left to do pretty much in the matter as they pleased, or as the men in control chose to do in the conditions. They were forced (at least it seemed so to them), at points of intersection with other roads, to carry goods at rates so low that it would be ruinous to apply them to all the traffic. They were pleased at other points to charge every cent that the shipper could be made to pay rather than use a cart instead of the cars. Competition? Yes, a doubtful yes, at competing points and on some kinds of goods, but competition unregulated, excessive, destructive, not only to the industries and localities at every other place excepting these competing points, but to the railroads themselves. Yes; a few students of the subject early saw, though the public did not, that in respect to most shippers and shipments the conditions of "a market for transportation" were non-existent, and that each railroad inevitably had a large measure of monopoly power. Important lessons surely may be drawn from this experience with railroad monopoly that are helpful in solving the problem of local monopoly in industries.

A NEW BREED — INDUSTRIAL TRUSTS

Between 1850 and the end of the century there occurred, at first slowly, then with accelerating speed, a veritable revolution in market conditions, more remarkable in America than anywhere else. This involved increased size of industry, mass of production, extent of market area or tributary territory, and average length of haul of many commodities, all being but different aspects of one great movement. The changes in these respects in these fifty years were greater than those of the preceding millennium. While the industrial world was undergoing these rapid physical changes, the very nature of the economic, legal, and social problems associated with markets, competition, monopoly, and prices was also being transformed. First this became apparent in respect to the railroads, and already in the last quarter of the nineteenth century their local monopolistic character was recognized and active steps were taken to bring their prices under public control. More slowly, lagging by a full generation, began to appear evidences of the local monopolistic power of many industrial enterprises. The transformation was much more rapid and far-reaching in the United States than in England or in continental Europe. Alfred Marshall, a keen observer of economic conditions on both sides of the Atlantic, truly remarked as early as 1890 that "since distances in America are large, many local monopolies are possible [there] which are not possible in England; in fact the area of local monopoly there is often greater than that of the whole of England." [6] It was in the last decades of the century that the American "trusts" burst into bloom like dandelions in the green fields of competition. The early trusts utilized railroads as tools of local monopoly by obtaining rebates and discriminatory rates, while at the same time employing such crude devices as pools and various agreements openly in restraint of trade. But these methods became increasingly difficult to apply as public disapproval grew. Already, as early as 1898, after various experiments "to get the knack of the thing," began the widespread use of basing-point delivered prices, the newly discovered device by which industrial enterprises were enabled without suspicion of illegality to take advantage of these conditions of local monopoly. Before we examine in more detail that system of industrial prices, let us prepare the way by a careful examination of the essential nature of competition and of monopoly.

[6] See this and further comment in *Memorials of Alfred Marshall*, p. 267.

CHAPTER XIX

MARKETS AND COMPETITIVE PRICES

MARKETS ESSENTIALLY LOCAL

EVERY real market is a concrete thing, an actual place where traders gather, to which actual goods or certificates of ownership are brought for sale and delivery, where special facilities for trade exist, where buyers and sellers alike have an opportunity to learn and know the amounts and qualities of goods present and the probable intentions of other traders, where traders are forbidden to get apart and trade outside, and where they act independently, without collusion with each other, and without discrimination against any traders on the other side. If we imagine all these conditions to be completely attained we get an idealized picture of a market, and in the degree that these conditions are imperfectly realized, any particular market falls short of the ideal.

Against one alteration in this ideal picture of markets a warning is especially needed. A market must not be thought of either as the various places or as the whole area to which the goods are taken or delivered after sale. It is, therefore, an error to say that when goods are shipped from one market to another, the two markets constitute a single market. Thus Liverpool is often carelessly said to be "the world market" for wheat, and (as if it meant the same thing, which evidently it does not) therefore the whole world is said to constitute a single market for wheat. Such a use of language utterly confuses the sound proposition that in one market at one time the prices are uniform. The prices in any two places differ usually, though not always, by about the amount of the freight and other charges. For example, Chicago being in a surplus area and Liverpool in a deficit area, the movement of wheat is pretty steadily from Chicago toward Liverpool, but there is always the Chicago market and market price, as distinct from the Liverpool market and market price. By a sort of arbitrage process and by adjusted shipments the price•in Chicago is kept from ever falling for long below that of Liverpool by more than the total transportation costs. But there are always the two market prices. In principle they are primarily different, and only secondarily are they kept approximately related by the differential of place costs. A simple proof of this is that whenever in the surplus market the price fails to fall below that in the deficit market by quite as much as the full exchange costs, the two markets may continue indefinitely to be independent of each other, no shipments being made from one to the other.[1]

ESSENTIAL CONDITIONS OF TRUE MARKETS

What are the essential conditions of a true market? First, *freedom of access*. A market is a meeting-place where two groups of persons come together for the purpose of trade, some bringing sale-goods, things they would like to sell, and others bringing price-goods, which may be money or other goods with purchasing-power. Anything that keeps any trader from coming, if he would, to the place where others are trading, there to trade under the same conditions possible to others, is an interference with freedom of access to the market and to that extent limits or destroys a true market. *For example, the recent business "custom," or tacit conspiracy, by which producers refuse to sell except at delivered prices, results in the destruction of markets.*

Common knowledge is a condition of a true market. This means the publicity of transactions and prices. Competition implies a general understanding on the part of all the traders, both as to

---

[1] Here doubtless is one key to the confused thinking regarding the market for steel extending over the whole country, that repeatedly appeared in the Steel dissolution suit. (See above, Ch. VIII.) This notion of a nation-wide or even a world-wide market appears again and again in the attempt to justify the basing-point practice. To point to a uniform price for goods at one market as justification for a complex system of identical delivered prices, over a wide territory, for products never really at that market, sold there, or shipped therefrom—all this under the pretense that this exemplifies the working of "the law of supply and demand" in a market—is to attain the peak of absurdity in economic theory. Recall the argument of Mr. Gary. See further below in connection with the economic law of market areas, Ch. XX.

kinds and as to quantities of goods offered for sale and as to the number and needs of the persons wishing to buy. This condition was in large measure insured by the old market rules requiring that buyers and sellers assemble at a common meeting-place, that the goods be brought in and displayed in the booths, and that no trading be permitted until the moment when the market, or fair, was officially opened. In the one aspect of publicity (when genuine and not limited to the sellers) the later trade association decisions are undoubtedly sound in economic principle.

In a true market there must be the condition of *freedom of competition* in trading. This is a continuation of that freedom that gives access to the market. Any influence or pressure from others, compelling a trader to act or restraining him from acting, otherwise than as he would like to act if left to the guidance of his own interests, is an interference with freedom of competition and makes the market imperfect. The particular means of interference with competition are numberless, but most of those that concern the public are of three sorts: first, those imposed by legalized favoritism; second, self-imposed by traders conspiring in their own interest in the hope of larger gains; third, imposed by other traders upon some of their competitors. The chief motives limiting freedom will be discussed more fully below.

In a true market competition must be *two-sided*. If the sale-goods are all held by one seller (or controlled within certain limits by a combination of sellers), then the competition is one-sided on the buyers' side only. Conversely, if there are numerous sellers and but one buyer (or one united group of buyers), there is one-sided competition on the sellers' side only.

Finally, in order that there shall be a true market there must also be the *capability* of competition; that is, the capacity of economic subjects to perform the services or produce the goods, in order that there shall be effective competition. This important condition is further discussed below, in this chapter.

Free access, common knowledge, two-sidedness of competition, capacity—these are the essential conditions of a true market in which there can be *effective* competition. When all these conditions are present the law of supply and demand fully operates and uniform market prices result. Observe how remarkably these conditions of a true market were attained through legal requirements in the public medieval markets and fairs, and how they developed rather simply in the perpetual market towns of England. After the systematic favors to gilds and trading companies had pretty well broken down, these conditions prevailed increasingly in the towns of Europe and America up to about 1850. They were found wherever several independent shops and mills were within driving distance of a group of buyers or of sellers of farm produce.[2]

COMPETITION IN MOST GENERAL SENSE

The idea of a market is so interwoven with that of competition that markets and market competition are but different aspects of the same thing. But competition in its broadest sense goes much beyond market problems and includes every form of rivalry, of struggle, and of effort, to attain an object upon which others are also bent. In love, in sport, in war, in law, in science, in the arts, in business activity of every kind—agriculture, mining, manufacturing, finance, and commerce—competition is a word fraught with suggestions of good and of evil, of life and of death, of success and of failure, of progress and of destruction. Through competition individuals prosper or fail, civilizations advance or decay, kingdoms rise or fall.

Competition in trade is a feature of the relations of buyers and of sellers respectively. It is primarily an economic fact, although it has many legal aspects. Competition in trade is in legal phrase

the struggle between rivals for the same trade at the same time; the act of seeking or endeavoring to gain what another is endeavoring to gain at the time; that series of acts or course of conduct which is the result of the free choice of the individual and not of any legal or moral obligation or duty.[3]

In economic phraseology, competition in trade is the attempt of two or more persons by means of their bids or offers of goods to buy or to sell the same thing in trade, each being guided by his own valuation and not restrained by any outside force or any agreement to abstain from bidding.

[2] The effect of competition on the neutral zone of transportation costs in the areas between markets is discussed below in Ch. XX.

[3] As cited from various cases in *Corpus Juris,* article "Competition."

MARKET-COMPETITION SPECIFICALLY

Yet these definitions and descriptions need some further qualification to delimit accurately what has been the ideal of our Anglo-
American law and of economics in its analysis of the competitive
process of arriving at market prices. The broad definition of competition is wide enough to include a physical fight to the death and
the use of any and every form of weapon of fraud, deceit, and
destruction. We must recognize the distinctions between fair and
unfair, legal and illegal, social and anti-social competition. Otherwise the admirer and the critic of competition must talk forever at
cross-purposes, the one seeing in it a blessing and the other a
curse to mankind. The legal, economic, and social ideal of competition is essentially the ideal of *market-competition*, not just of
any and every kind and mode of competition. The ideal market-
competition is synonymous with fair and effective competition.
Market-competition is a peaceful and constructive process of rivalry
in efficient production and service; it is neither an immense legalized gamble for capital prizes for the strong and successful few, nor
a duel to the death for the unsuccessful many. Rather it is ideally
a process of trial, stimulation, and selection by which each finds
a fit place. Competitors unable to hold their own in one market
may easily continue to sell in another, while others will find their
greater gain by shifting to another occupation.[4]

NOT AUTOMATICALLY "NATURAL"

Such a condition is not a simple "natural" state that comes about
automatically unless violently opposed and that reëstablishes itself
easily and quickly if temporarily interrupted. The notion that it is
so is an erroneous heritage of the eighteenth century nature-
philosophy which constitutes today a grave obstacle in the way of
the right development of legal principles and practice in this
field. True it is that acquisitive motives are ever latent and ready
to impel men, under favoring conditions, to compete in the market-
place. But those same acquisitive motives under other conditions
frequently impel men to evade and refrain from competing, and
rather to agree and conspire with their former or usual competitors

---

[4] Recall the discussion in Ch. II.

to reap larger prices and profits. The ideal state of competition often assumed alike by law and by economics to spring so spontaneously into being, or to be so easily achieved, is rather, like liberty, a rare and precious possession, to be won anew by the community through new struggles in each generation.

RARITY OF PERFECT COMPETITION

Truly it has been said that though "the opinion is often expressed that the so-called laws of competition have existed since time out of mind, are a part of the order of nature," such "a view is contrary to fact." Our present "competitive system grew out of previous monopolistic conditions" and "it was welcomed because it was thought a vast improvement upon the old system and in the interest of the public." [5] The period of pretty effective competitive industrial conditions in England and America from 1750 to 1850, instead of being a normal historical condition of trade, was rather a mere passing episode between the earlier stage of feudal custom, status, and monopolistic privileges (mitigated by royal decrees and by markets and fairs) and the newer industrial feudalism of the last half-century (mitigated as yet by rather futile attempts to prevent restraint of commerce). The glib phrases of the older law have come to mean little in these new conditions, and novel phrases such as "the rule of reason" are slight aids to wisdom when used by judges still thinking in the terms of an outmoded economic world.

An enlightened system of competition must be an essential component of a defensible régime of private property. It is not merely a multitude of physical agencies—markets, exchanges, stores, means of transportation and communication. It is not merely a code of statute laws supplemented by judicial opinions. It is a cultural institution, the product of a long process of social experience. It must become incorporated in the habits, practices, consciences, and ideals of the people, as well as be expressed in statute law and in intelligent judicial opinions, before it can function effectively.

[5] H. B. Reed, *The Morals of Monopoly and Competition* (1916), p. 93.

ASPECTS OF EFFECTIVE COMPETITION

Market-competition when it actually occurs and exists (and only then) is *effective* competition. To this is necessary not only freedom of competition but capability of competition. Usually capability is merely assumed to be present, while freedom is the more discussed. But these two ideas must be clearly distinguished. Freedom is primarily a political fact, and capability primarily an economic one. An economic subject is *free* to compete when he may act independently as a member of the body politic, in choosing an occupation and in selling his goods and services in the full measure that any one else may. An economic subject is *capable* of competing when he is able (that is, technologically, not politically, able) to perform certain services and to produce certain goods. Thus, without freedom, the subject is unable to demonstrate his capability to compete by engaging in certain work; and without capability he is unable effectively to make use of his freedom to compete.

Either there must be implied as a part of capability, or there must be recognized as a third and separate condition to effective competition, a psychological element. That is, the economic subject, if free and capable, must also be willing, desire, and choose to compete in any specified occupation or industry. For "capability" is a relative, not an absolute, quality, and it appears that a person's capability to engage in any particular trade may be great absolutely, or relatively to that of other men, and yet be too small relatively to his own capability for something else, to give him an advantage, profit, motive, to engage in that trade. This very versatility may prevent his competing in one or more of the occupations. To choose the less skilled job would be to abandon the more skilled. The economic student will recognize here the reflected outlines of the doctrine of comparative advantage in foreign trade. Thus these three qualities or conditions must all be present to realize competition, to make it effective: freedom, capability, comparative advantage; these are, respectively, political, technological, and psychological in nature.

It needs no argument to prove that the competition which it is the ideal and policy of the law to encourage and to rely upon to secure the welfare of the community is effective competition (or, at times, what we may call latent effective competition, i.e. the motive of a very real expectation of its prompt appearance causing traders to act as if it were actually present). In the attempt, however, to maintain effective competition, the law and the courts are rightly concerned almost entirely to detect and punish the limitation of freedom, that being the political (legal) aspect of the subject. We shall analyze this more fully below.

LIMITATIONS OF FREEDOM: SUBJECTIVE

An enumeration and description of individual instances of the various ways in which freedom of competition may be limited would fill many volumes, but all essential types can perhaps be put into two main classes, which we may designate as objective vs. subjective interferences. Under each of these species may be distinguished several important varieties, which blend into each other at some times and places with hardly perceptible differences. Moreover, these varieties are often but positive and negative aspects of the same forces, external influences which favor one competitor being so fully and unquestioningly accepted by others and determining their mental attitude that they, as well as others, look upon their choice as voluntary. However, we are not called upon to debate the philosophic question of the freedom of the will.

The principal varieties of subjective limitations of freedom of competition are:

1. Sympathy: personal affection, patriotism, and other altruistic motives.

2. Ignorance: lack of knowledge of market conditions and opportunities.

3. Conformity with custom and social opinion: social standards implicitly accepted as part of the individual's own habitual code of conduct.

4. Desire, stimulated by objective rewards: governmental legal favors in subsidies, bounties, tariffs; payments (often illegal) by competitors to induce others to refrain from competition entirely or to carry it on under various agreements affecting output, prices, etc. Under the latter group comes the great mass of cases of contracts and conspiracies in restraint of trade where the parties enter "cheerfully" and willingly into the arrangement, though the mo-

tives may be strangely mingled with its opposite—fear—of what might happen if they did otherwise.[6]

LIMITATIONS OF FREEDOM: OBJECTIVE

The principal varieties of external interferences with freedom of competition may be distinguished as:

1. Legal interference: restrictive tariffs and other taxation for restrictive rather than revenue purposes; rewards by patents, monopolistic franchises, bounties, subsidies, and tariffs, to favored industries.

2. Social compulsion (and fear): force of custom, social prejudice, or ostracism, in religious, social, political, business, neighborhood, or other groups.

3. Physical violence (and fear of it): war, brigandage, various crimes against persons, and threats of any of these.

4. Crimes against property and the laws of trade: various forms of fraud, dishonesty, bribery of employees, unfair competition, conspiracy to destroy competition.

5. Financial compulsion (and fear): threats of withdrawal of credit, fear of local price cutting or of various other discriminatory price practices.

6. Merger: complete unity of ownership and control of all sellers (or buyers) within a certain sales area.

Complete competition does not exist if any of these limitations are present. Public policy, legislation, and efforts at administration and control have virtually nothing to do directly with the subjective limitations, but do affect them indirectly, especially the desires of individuals, through efforts to modify every one of the objective limitations. Through legal limitations upon competition the public is interfering in multitudes of cases, no doubt in large part unwisely and unfairly, between individual citizens and classes, in ways designed to enhance the prices and incomes of some and reduce those of others. The benefit is seen, the injury unseen. These instances form a gigantic aggregate system of exceptions to the general rule and professed ideal of the present régime of private property and individual freedom of contract, and, usually, are the work of the selfish, dishonest, and politically

---

[6] See Chs. III-IV and IX-X.

corrupt and corrupting efforts of the beneficiaries. The irony in the situation is that the very men and powerful classes who quietly scheme and publicly clamor for these special favors proclaim most loudly the sanctity of the doctrine of individual freedom of contract and of freedom of trade as against any measures designed to favor and protect other members and classes of society. It is true, however, that many well-meant, altruistic, measures are ill-advised. In large measure, too, this double moral standard is countenanced by the courts.

COMPETITION, LEGAL AND ILLEGAL

The question as to the economic or political soundness of the various duly legalized limitations of competition lies outside our present field of inquiry. Likewise does that subtler social compulsion of an extra-legal sort, so long as it is a matter of individual action that does not take the form of acts that are specifically illegal. We may deplore certain forms and certain cases of intolerance and prejudice, but it is usually at least expedient for the state not to attempt to invade the field of merely individual conscience, feeling, and judgment. The use of physical violence to prevent freedom of commerce is a crude offense against political rights that may be left outside our present inquiry, although racketeering has of late become a great factor in restraint of trade—a new and ominous social phenomenon. What we have left, then, as constituting the great bulk of the questions regarding limitations of the freedom of competition which concern us in studying the operation and judicial interpretation of the anti-trust laws, relate to the last three headings only in the foregoing list. These may all eventually be narrowed down to one question: What actions shall be included within the crimes against the laws of trade?

THE PRINCIPLE OF INDIFFERENCE

Assuming the presence of truly competitive conditions (that is, the absence of any limitations), let us see what principles would determine the behavior of the prices of some standard commodity. We limit our question to a certain time and place, not inquiring about long-time movements or the ultimate underlying forces which may lead to different situations in later periods. The first and most general proposition is that in such a market "the principle of indifference" would be effective. This is merely the mathematical axiom that things that are equal to the same thing are equal to each other, when applied to human choice of goods either for use or for sale. When all the preceding conditions are realized and all the units of a class of commodities are physically alike in kind, they will be alike in value to each trader actually in the market, though the valuations of the several traders approaching the market had differed widely. Each buyer will be indifferent as to which unit he gets, or from which seller he gets it; each seller will be indifferent as to which purchasing power (money or other goods) he receives (provided it be of equal amount) or from which buyer he receives it. It might seem needless to formulate as a principle a truth that seems so self-evident, but it is very essential to clear thinking in the complexities of the actual markets in which frictions and obstructions to freedom of choice occur in so many and in such subtle ways.

THE VALID MARGINAL PRINCIPLE

In such a market *the marginal principle* would hold; indeed this phrase is but another term for the same thing as the principle of indifference, looked at from a little different angle, that of the comparative strength of the desires traders have for different uses of goods. Each trader's valuation of the least urgent use to which goods may be put—the choice on the margin of use—sets a limit to his valuation of all the other like units. This is the marginal principle. The principle of indifference in *actual* valuation prevails over the merely *latent* differences in the valuation of uses that may be presented at different times and under different conditions. The valuation of the least urgent use, that on the margin of use, sets the outside valuation of all other uses of the same goods, at one time and place.[7]

---

[7] The word "marginal" describes the valuation of buyer and seller, respectively, at which the market price settles, far better than do such words as "average," "mean," or "medium," etc., of the various reserve valuations on the curve. The reserve valuations of the different individuals cannot be averaged, either logically or to any practical purpose. The price (marginal valuation) at the moment may remain the same though various changes have occurred in the intra-marginal reserve valuations.

The principles of indifference and of marginality are inseparably linked with the presence of effective competition. If the principle of indifference is not operative, then there is not truly one market but two or more. Somehow common knowledge is lacking, or some one has failed to get free access, or some one is buying or selling from motives other than the valuations put upon the commodities impersonally. It is through the working of the principle of indifference that one uniform price for a certain kind of goods can come to prevail in a market of many traders. It is often declared: "There can be but one price in a market," or "In the ideal market the prices in all sales at any one time are uniform," thus making uniformity of price at once the definition and test of a true market. This test is of significance when we wish to consider the essential nature of discrimination.

ENTER SUPPLY AND DEMAND [8]

It is only in a market fulfilling these conditions that the much-proclaimed "law of supply and demand" can be said to operate fully, if at all. Supply is the number of units of a standardized commodity offered for sale at a specified bid, and demand is the number of units of the same commodity taken, or on the point of being taken, at a specified offer. The bids (of the various buyers) and offers (of the sellers) are the expressions, respectively, of their monetary valuations. It is well to contrast actual supply as the amount which really is sold, or on the point of being sold at a specific price, with merely latent, potential, or conditional supply, as the amount which would be offered if the price were different —and likewise as to demand, *mutatis mutandis*. At any moment in a market there is but one actual supply and but one actual demand, and these two are just the same in amount and consist of the same goods at the point of equilibrium of a theoretically correct market price. At other prices demand and supply may be unequal at the moment. A table of the amounts of goods that would be offered at various prices constitutes a supply schedule, and a graph of these amounts at various other conceivable prices is called a supply-curve; so likewise of demand schedule and curve.

A demand schedule is a composite of the various valuations of

[8] Recall here the discussion of Mr. Gary's economic theory in Ch. XIII.

individual buyers and would-be buyers, arranged from left to right in the order in which they will begin to buy if prices fall, or inversely as they will drop out as prices rise. These may be called the hypothetical valuations or the reserve valuations of the traders; that is, the highest price at which each trader would become a buyer, and the lowest price at which each trader, respectively, would become a seller. Each trader may be assumed to enter the market with some such reserve valuation, and despite hesitation, sales talk, market news, and various influences impinging upon him in the market, he has in fact such a reserve valuation at which he drops out or comes into the trading at any moment. It is not essential to the real theoretical and practical usefulness of the hypothetical curve as a logical device that its shape should be known outside of a narrow zone on either side of the usual range of actual prices. In that zone most problems of price lie. In various ways, however, experience and experiments reveal in each business more or less the probable outlines of these hypothetical curves for some distance on either side of actual prices.

SUPPLY, DEMAND, AND PRICE AS FUNCTIONS

It must not be forgotten that these schedules and curves express not a set of contemporaneous, actual prices, supplies, and demands, but a relationship shown by experience to exist under varying conditions and at different times. To each price corresponds conceivably some demand and some supply, as quantities of goods. In a mathematical sense there is a functional relationship among the three quantities, price, demand, and supply, on a graph of prices. However, in a *competitive* market the vital, dynamic forces that initiate all changes in price act first upon or through demand or supply, expressing shifts in human desires and choices of buyers or of sellers, whereas price change is merely a passive result.

In the case, however, of monopolistic control, price may in point of time be first artificially changed, supply and demand being left to adjust themselves in accord with latent schedules. A monopolistic price is artificial and thus different from that brought about under free competition; it is not fixed by the free play of supply and demand. A selling monopoly, therefore, has always to reckon upon some curtailment of demand as the result of artificially setting a higher price and must be prepared to restrict supply if it is to maintain a monopolistic price. Logically, in all cases of competition, changes in demand or in supply are seen to cause changes in price (and not the reverse). The conception of hypothetical demand and supply schedules is helpful in the understanding of what occurs in many monopolistic cases of great practical importance where price is artificially fixed first.

A MARKET AS A SYSTEM OF AUCTIONS

A true market may be thought of as a double system of simultaneous auctions: [9] one in which every would-be buyer seeking to buy as cheaply as possible, begins by bidding low and gradually raises his bid, toward the limits of his reserve valuations, until he gets some one to sell to him; and at the same time, one in which every would-be seller, starting with high offers, gradually lowers them until he gets some one to buy from him. The purpose of any preliminary bids and offers at which no sales occur is to "feel out" the situation. Such bids and offers result in the discovery of the one price at which the number of supply and demand units respectively will be just equal. At this price no buyer with a higher valuation and no seller with a lower valuation than this price will be left outside the trading. When the number of units to be sold and bought has thus by competition been brought into agreement, it follows, according to the principle of indifference, that every buyer, even one having originally a higher reserve valuation, is able to buy at this "marginal" price and need not pay more; and every seller, even one beginning with a lower reserve valuation, is able to sell at this price and need not take less. In other words, at a true equilibrium market-price the valuation of the marginal traders in the market becomes the actual "market valuation" of all traders who remain included in the market. The reserve valuations are merely latent.

GRAPHIC EXAMPLES OF PRICE ADJUSTMENT

Suppose that there are at a time and place, and for sale within a certain period, ten units of a commodity, the highest reserve

[9] The reader, if not already familiar with the usual treatment of price, may be referred to any standard economics textbook for other details. See the author's text, *Economic Principles*, The Century Company, 1915, pp. 61-85.

valuation of any unit being 5, and that 15 units would be bought if the last units could be had at a valuation not to exceed 6 units. This may be illustrated by the simple graph below (Fig. 15).

All of the 10 units can be sold, because there are 10 buyers willing to pay more than the reserve valuation of the least urgent seller. This is what is often called "a sellers' market," because the sellers can sit back and let the buyers "fight it out," and yet every seller can get more than the least he would be willing to take if he were forced to it. The price in the example would be just high

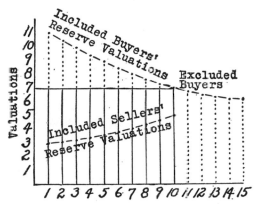

FIG. 15. "A SELLERS' MARKET" WHERE BUYERS "FIGHT IT OUT" AND BID UP THE PRICE

enough to exclude the eleventh buyer; this would be 7 if bids varied only by full units of price.

Imagine, now, that the conditions are reversed and that there are, let us say, 10 buyers, the least urgent of whom has a reserve valuation of 7; whereas there are as many as 15 sellers or units to be sold, the minimum valuation of the fifteenth unit being 7. This would present the picture shown in Fig. 16.

It is equally clear that this is distinctly "a buyers' market," because the sellers have the motive for active competition to lower the price. All of the sellers with maximum valuations above 5 must be excluded, and at that price even the least urgent of the 10 buyers

will, by the principle of indifference, be able to buy at the price
of 5 though his reserve valuation is 7.

Now doubtless the more usual case in real life is that of the
gradual tapering off rather than of the abrupt cessation of the
reserve valuation on either side of the market, presenting some
such picture as that in Fig. 17.

Here, as the result of competition among the buyers and sellers
nearest the marginal valuation point, demand and supply coincide
at 13 units; the equilibrium price would be 6. In this example,

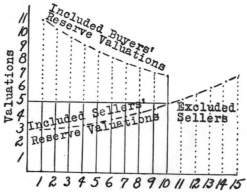

FIG. 16. "A BUYERS' MARKET" WHERE
EAGER SELLERS OUTNUMBER BUYERS AND
BID DOWN THE PRICE

as no doubt usually in such a situation in real life, the price is a
medium between the two extremes and more goods change hands
than in either of the other cases.

Changes in the conditions, physical, social, psychological, lying
back of the traders' reserve valuations, may raise or lower either
the buyers' or the sellers' schedules, with resulting shifts in the
price-point of equilibrium and in number of sales.

ᒍHOW MONOPOLY REPLACES COMPETITION

This is only a brief outline, not a complete treatment, of the
logic of competitive price, but perhaps it is enough for our immediate purpose. We have just seen (in simple abstract terms)

how seemingly small changes in the number, or in the state of mind, of competitors may greatly affect the outcome in price, to the benefit of one group of traders—buyers or sellers, respectively. A few buyers cropping out here, a falling off in demand, or a few new producers coming in there, may greatly drop the price, to the gain of the buyers and the corresponding loss of the sellers. And *vice versa*, prices may be considerably raised by comparatively slight changes in the reserve valuations of marginal traders on one side or on both.

In this effect, often comparatively large, that the withdrawal

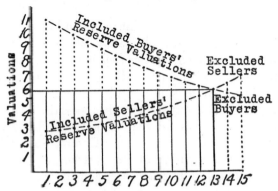

FIG. 17. MORE NORMAL TWO-SIDED MAR-
GINAL BIDDING WHERE BUYERS' AND SELLERS'
MARGINAL VALUATIONS COINCIDE

of a part of the supply may have in raising the price of the remainder, are both the motive and the means for restraint of trade and monopoly. Especially in locally limited monopoly, zone businesses, under modern conditions of mass production, if only a few competitors can be coerced or bribed into limiting production or limiting their bids, the price may be raised more than the output is reduced, so that the "restraint" is highly profitable. It seems needless or inadvisable to go further here into the details of the theory of monopoly pricing. Suffice it to add that monopoly usually is one-sided competition and is the situation where competition is active among the divided buyers but is restrained, repressed, among the sellers. It is well illustrated in the various legal cases before discussed.

CHAPTER XX

THE ECONOMIC LAW OF MARKET AREAS [1]

THE legal character of basing-point prices and of any other forms of local discrimination must ultimately be determined by their economic character. The enterprises that have followed the basing-point practice have, whenever challenged, defended it as fully exemplifying "the law of supply and demand." In the one case in which the Supreme Court consciously touched this issue, though in a very minor way, it somewhat casually approved this view.[2] On the other hand the Federal Trade Commission in its notable opinion ordering the cessation of the Pittsburgh-Plus practice in 1924 held an entirely different conception of the practice. They declared it to be a violation of the Clayton Act, Section 2, forbidding unlawful discrimination, and a negation of competition and of "the law of supply and demand." As the defendant ostensibly accepted this decision, the case was not taken into the Supreme Court. If ever such a case should be taken there, by what criteria can the economic and thus the legal character of the practice be tested?

The answer is not hard to give, and the test should not be hard to make. Consider what is the main effect of the basing-point practice: it is to determine a certain relationship of prices territorially

---

[1] A brief essay with this title was published by the author in the *Quarterly Journal of Economics*, May 1924. The reader unfamiliar with economic theory may find this the most difficult chapter in the book, but the problem has been discussed in a concrete setting quite fully in the chapters dealing with Pittsburgh-Plus. Here is the generalized statement applying to all cases of local price differences. It throws a clear light on many problems of local price discrimination, including that of basing points.

[2] In 1925. See above, Ch. XVII.

between two markets and among the purchasers in each particular market. Therefore in order to test basing-point prices we have but to set up the norm of a competitive price system, to see, first, how prices behave under conditions of competition in real markets, and how, secondly, these prices in various markets are related. If, then, basing-point prices in particular markets behave otherwise and present a different picture of territorial relationships, we must conclude that they are not competitive, that they are in restraint of commerce.

The foundation for such a test has been laid in the foregoing theory of markets and competition. We may now consider the logical and necessary price relationships between these locally separated markets and in the areas lying between them. We seek the economic law of market areas.

TYPES OF MARKETS

In every market there is both buying and selling, but in relation to scattered buyers and consumers the market from which they buy presents the aspect of selling; and to scattered small producers the market to which they ship their produce presents the aspect of buying. In the case of the one, the movement of the goods is centrifugal, away from a market; in the other case it is centripetal, toward a market. Manufacturing centers where goods are produced in great quantities and shipped outward to consumers may be said to be primarily selling markets; produce exchanges, to which move the products of scattered farms, to be primarily buying markets. To be clearly distinguished from the marketplaces themselves are the regions from which the goods are brought for sale, or to which they will be shipped after sale. Such a region may be called the market tributary area, or for short the market area, or simply the area. Each market may, at times, through the efforts to enlarge or to retain certain tributary territory, exert a real competitive influence upon other neighboring markets. Actually, the choice of buyers (or sellers) between two markets may turn upon a fraction of a cent and may alternate as a result of slight changes in the relationship of the two market prices. We may confine our attention to the problem presented in the sale of standardized commodities, as commodities differing widely in variety and in quality, being really different commodities, present complications that do not concern us here, such as the economic and social stratification of groups of purchasers, who may be widely scattered over non-contiguous territories, rather than geographically grouped as in the case of buyers of standardized commodities.

GOODS PRICE PLUS FREIGHT PRICE

If there were but one place of production and competitive sale, then the cost to the buyer of the goods delivered at each of the various points on the radii of that market would be the uniform price at the market plus the freight to destination. This may be graphically shown as a cross section on one diameter in the following figure:

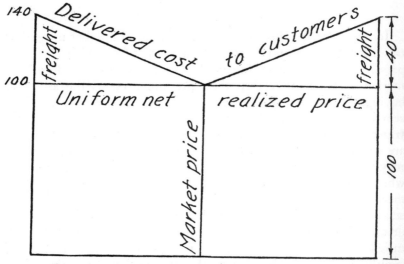

FIG. 18. UNIFORM MARKET PRICES IN A SINGLE MARKET, PLUS FREIGHT RESULTING IN DIFFERING DELIVERED COSTS

It is evident that the delivered cost to the buyer is made up of two prices, one price for the commodity in the market, and another price for the transportation service for carrying it away from the market. This fact is most clearly apparent when the freighting is done by a common carrier, but may be obscured in case the seller delivers the goods with his own equipment, thus engaging in two different productive activities.

WHEN INTER-MARKET SHIPMENTS ARE POSSIBLE

If, now, two producing, selling markets, which we may call A and B, are geographically so situated that there is a physical possibility of shipping goods from one to the other, obviously the prices in the two markets cannot (except accidentally and temporarily) differ by more than the amount of the freight (and incidental expenses) between the two points. If the difference exceeded that sum, the competition of the one market would destroy the industry in the other.

For example, as shown in Figure 19, if freight per unit between the two places is 40, then when the base price in B is 100, that in A may be at the utmost 140; for if it were higher the competition of B would wipe A off the map. Or, if the base price of A should be reduced below 60, it would sooner or later wipe B off the map, unless B in turn reduced its base price below 100.

Both markets can exist so long as the price difference of the two markets is less than the freight difference. To the amount of the difference of net delivered costs to the buyer each producing center has in respect to sales in its immediate neighborhood an advantage over outside markets the same in its effect as a protective (restrictive) tariff on goods coming to its very doors. Conceivably, also, at a time when the two net delivered costs from the two markets were to the buyer, just equal, some portions of the purchases in the market with the higher commodity price might be bought from either producing center, and the very slightest differences in quality, or in styles of goods, or in the personal tastes of buyers, would suffice to give motives for buyers' dividing their purchases between the two markets.

POINTS DIRECTLY INTERMEDIATE

What now as to the effect that price differences in the two markets have upon the sales to buyers at points between the two markets? Let us assume that a single railroad line connects the two and that a simple distance tariff of freight rates is in force.

Assume further that the buyers may travel in either direction to make their purchases freely at the uniform market price in either market and ship them to destination by the railroad. A graph of such a situation shows a profile view of price plus freight taken along one line. The distance from which each market can attract buyers from points along the intermediate line is determined by the comparative delivered costs, which are the sums of base prices and freights. If freight for the whole distance between A and B is 40, then when A's price is 120 and B's is 100, A can sell only

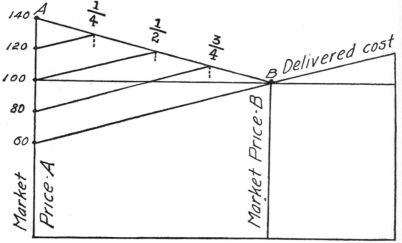

FIG. 19. DELIVERED COSTS FROM COMPETING MARKETS AT VARIOUS
MILL PRICES

¼ of the way; at 100, A can sell ½ the way (both base prices being 100); at 80, A can sell ¾ of the way; and as before noted, at 60 or less A could sell right into the B market. In strict theory (if freights varied for every mile) there would be no neutral zone, but merely a point of indifference, the watershed, so to speak, at which the two streams of demand would begin to flow in either direction.

THE CURVE OF COST INDIFFERENCE

Thus far we have considered only a one-dimensional division of the tributary area between the two markets, that occurring at a point on a single connecting line of transportation. Let us now consider the problem more generally, to determine the nature of the curve dividing two market areas on a two-dimensional surface map, that is, as seen in a bird's-eye view. Railroad freights are paid to overcome distance, and (despite much corruption and many blunders and historical accidents still persisting in the rate structures) rates vary more or less proportionally with distance. Just as a *point* of indifference in delivered costs to buyers between two markets is determined by the combination of base prices and freight rates, so likewise a line or *curve* of indifference is determined by the succession of points at which the sums of base prices and freights in respect to two markets are exactly equal. On either side of the points on this curve the delivered cost from one market is greater or less than that from the other. The difference of base prices in the two markets is at a certain time the same for all buyers, no matter where they live; whereas the relative freight costs from the two markets respectively differ according to the distances. The curve of indifference in advantage to the buyers is traced through the points where the difference in freight rates exactly equals (offsets) the price difference. These conditions fulfill exactly the definition of a hyperbolic curve. A hyperbole is a curve composed of a succession of points the difference of whose distances from two fixed foci is always the same. In this case the difference at every point on the curve is that in the freight rates from the two foci, or markets, respectively.

STATEMENT OF THE LAW

We thus get the following formulation of the general law of market areas, in sales at uniform prices from competitive markets

The boundary line between the territories tributary to two geographically competing real markets for like goods is a hyperbolic curve. At each point on this line the difference between freights from the two markets is just equal to the difference between the prevailing market prices, whereas on either side of this line the freight difference and the price difference are unequal. The relation of prices in the two markets determines the location of the boundary line: the lower the price in a market relative to that of a neighboring market, the larger the tributary territory.

In Figure 20 A is supposed to be the market whose price is taken as 100 per unit. The freight on that unit to B, the other market, is 10. The curves connect all points of equal differences of freight, by differences of one unit from plus 10 to minus 10. If in each of these markets the conditions are competitive, and consequently the rule holds of "one price in a market," a supply and demand

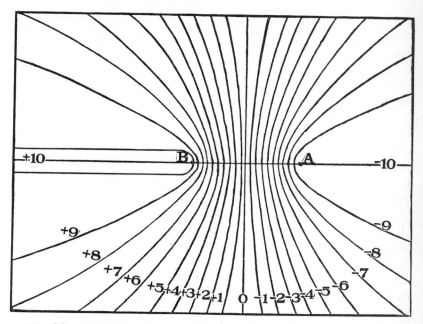

FIG 20. MARKET AREAS DETERMINED BY COMPETITIVE PRICE DIFFERENTIALS AT B (PLUS OR MINUS), SHOWING ALSO THE POTENTIAL MONOPOLY "PLUS" WITH A BASING-POINT SYSTEM

price of 110 (the full "plus" freight from A to B) could prevail only while the supply in B is insufficient for, or barely sufficient for, demand in the narrow strip of territory along the line marked B to plus 10. With a differential price of the full "plus," all the area north and south of the line B to plus 10 should be supplied by A. If the price in any of this area is less than 110, then, on the marginal principle, the f.o.b. market price at B should be the same for sales to all the area to the left of the curve touched by such

lower price. If the output exceeds the amount demanded at price
110 by enough to supply the needs of the area delimited by the
line plus 9, the "supply and demand" price must fall to 109, and
so successively as supply increases at B. The larger demand is
partly called forth by the lower price in the area already tributary,
and partly is captured from the area formerly supplied by A.

The irregular black areas on the map of Figure 6 correspond
theoretically to the maximum + 10 area in Figure 20; the curious
shape of this full Chicago plus area betrays certain accidental and
unfair elements in the structure of freight rates. (Compare Figures
21, 30, and 35.)

SOME CHARACTERISTICS OF AREA BOUNDARIES

Size of market territories thus may be said to be a function of
the differential of market base prices, the freight tariff remaining
constant; that is, the higher the price in any market, relative to
that of its geographical competitors, the narrower the territory
that economically is tributary to it. Conversely, size of market
territories is a function of the freight differential, base prices remaining constant. Market territories vary inversely with increase
either of base price or of freight rates relative to geographical
competitors.

In the case of buying (centripetal) markets, to which products
are sent for sale from numerous decentralized producing points,
the foregoing principles hold, *mutatis mutandis*. The boundary
curve will change in location and in shape with changes in prices,
but will be curved around the market of lower price, thus embracing a smaller area, and will curve away from the market of
higher price and include a larger area. The higher the relative
buying market price the larger the area from which sellers are
attracted.

The assumptions made and the abstract nature of the formula
must not be forgotten or misunderstood. It is in the nature of a
first approximation to the solution of the various practical problems that may arise. If freight rates are not plain mileage rates,
but are tapering by any fixed rule, the limiting curves between
markets may still be symmetrical, though differing somewhat in
location from those resulting from rates on the mileage principle.

Inasmuch as the actual structure of freight rates departs from the principle of strict proportionality to distance, the boundary lines will be shifted; likewise, according to other irregularities in freight, whatever be the cause, such as water transportation with lower rates or topographical obstacles making longer routes and higher rates necessary. In peculiar cases of freakish freight differentials relative to distances, geographical relations may be quite inverted. Thus the ground plan of hyperbolic curves corresponding to different base prices must then be more or less obscured on the map, appearing as contour lines traced on slopes at various elevations, marked by the freight differences between the two markets; but despite great irregularities at many points the underlying pattern of the hyperbolic curves must be revealed on almost every portion of the map. This fundamental feature of constant difference having the mathematical basis of a hyperbolic curve may be said to continue still as measured by freights, but to be distorted graphically by the lack of correspondence of freights to distance. A chart so drawn as to show each place of delivery located with reference to dollars in freight instead of at its actual location on the map, shows the exact hyperbolic curves; a chart drawn on the actual map reveals the irregularities in freight. The law of market areas, in its general theoretical form, might be deemed to be merely a corollary of the general law of demand and supply. It is, to be sure, derived deductively from this, taken in connection with the assumption that transportation costs vary with distance.

MARKETS COMPETE ON THE AREA MARGIN

The law of market areas sheds light upon various of the problems both of competitive and of monopoly price. It makes clearer how the prices in two or more producing centers, while still distinct and different, come to have a certain relationship through geographically marginal competition. This might in rare cases occur through mutual shipments between competing markets, but in the case of really standardized goods this is "carrying coals to Newcastle." The only normal thing in such a case is competition along the geographical margins of the market areas lying between the markets. If both markets are truly competitive, there will be not only intra-market competition of the sellers in each mar-

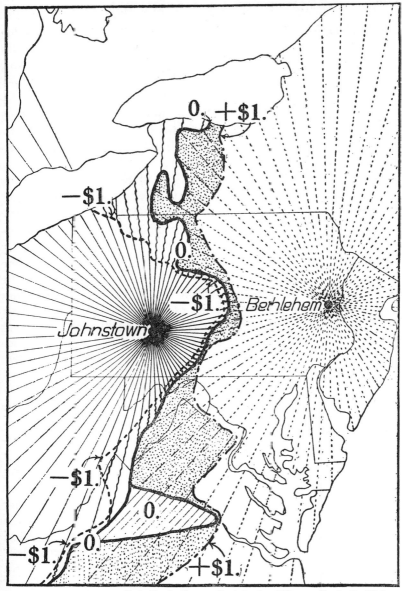

Fed. Trade Comm. Docket 962, Witness, Hugh E. White

FIG. 21. BETHLEHEM'S FREIGHT ADVANTAGE (+ OR —) AT DIF-
FERENT LOCATIONS, DETERMINING MARKET AREAS UNDER COM-
PETITION, AND MONOPOLY "PLUS" POSSIBLE WITH BASING-POINT
PRICES. COMPARE WITH FIGURES 20, 30 AND 35

ket, but inter-market competition as the sellers in each market seek to increase or maintain their sales by attracting the geographically marginal buyers against the pull of the rival market. The outcome of inter-market competition is determined by buyers' choice on the geographical margins of the two market areas. Under the principle of indifference any inducements thus offered to attract marginal buyers operate through uniform prices to benefit all the buyers within the market area. Here is a fact of tremendous practical importance to the buying public.

It is evident, too, that even if at one of the producing centers (say at A) a powerful monopoly were effected, either by merger or by conspiracy, its monopoly power would be limited on the geographic marginal of the neighboring market area B, if competition among independents were still active there. The monopoly (limited) might be said to exist in the market A and for some distance beyond, but to be moderated by competition toward the outer limits of the territory which would be tributary to that market under competitive conditions. For the slightest increase in a uniform monopoly price (at A) would enable the competing market B to annex a certain zone of customers and thus to reduce further the monopoly's sales.

LOCAL MONOPOLIES COMPETE—OR MERGE

This inter-market competition would still operate, though less strongly, in case both of the markets became monopolized, provided these two combinations did not further merge into a super-combination whereby all the tributary territories became subject to one monopoly. The reader may recognize here a picture of that situation brought about by the United States Steel Combination in 1901 and may see here the motive that has impelled many other industries in recent years to greater and greater mergers under the myopic vision of our public guardians, deceived by the reputed economies of so-called "integration" and of large "production." Of this, more later.

LOCAL PRICE CUTTING

It is doubtless true that in a real case where a monopoly in a market A found itself subjected to geographically marginal competition, whether that came from one of its peers, a monopoly in another market, or from some pestiferous little independent or some group of independents in a competitive market B, the challenged monopoly would probably not resort to the weapon of a reduction of its prices uniformly to all customers in all tributary territory. Being a monopoly, it is not confined to this crude method as is a really competitive seller. Even a restricted monopoly can use another weapon, cheaper, for it, yet more deadly, in price rivalry. It would rather seek to make some agreement, pool, or merger with the competitors, and either as a means to force compliance or as an alternative if it failed, it would discriminate by lowering its "delivered" price to buyers in the marginal territory while maintaining its prices higher elsewhere. That is when the practice of uniform treatment of customers at the market and the mill begins to break down, and soon the very idea of it may be lost. If this discrimination is done brazenly and brutally for the evident purpose of killing off competitors or forcing them into a combination, and these results are actually attained, the public is angered and the courts sternly condemn.[3] Local discrimination more moderately and more shrewdly exercised, that excludes competitors from territory and trade which under a régime of competing markets and uniform prices they should enjoy, that merely keeps them "in their place" or lets them die slowly of sales-starvation, is blindly looked upon as normal legitimate competition. The "local price cutting" is then said to be done "in good faith to meet competition." This apologetic phrase was written into some statutes, and judges began to condemn as unconstitutional any forbidding of discrimination without this limiting phrase, because it deprived the individual (that is, the powerful corporation) of freedom to compete. Limiting the freedom of whose competition? That of a corporate monopoly, exploiting its local monopolistic power! Freedom to compete how? In a manner that would be impossible if the conditions of a true market and of market competition existed.

[3] See Chs. I–IV.

COMPLEX AREAS MUTUALLY EXCLUSIVE

The theory of the division of areas between two markets can easily be extended to explain the complex situation presented by the inter-marginal competition of several markets. In the accompanying figures three markets are shown, each with a different uniform market price, and at various distances apart, freight-wise.

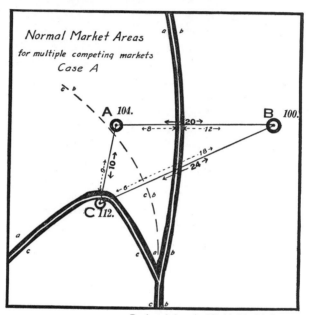

Designed by Archibald M. McIsaac

FIG. 22. CASE A, MUTUAL EXCLUSION OF THREE
COMPETING MARKETS

Each competing market has an area tributary to it, mathematically fixed by the relationship of prices and of freights. These territories, in strict theory, do not overlap at all. Every business is, in some degree, "a zone business" limited in its sales territory, relative to any particular relationship of market prices and freights, under truly competitive conditions, though of course in the case of unstandardized, very light-weight, and valuable goods the influence of freights may become well-nigh negligible over considerable areas. Moreover, price discrimination serves partially to blur the line of demarcation. The popular vague notion that each market, or that even each producer, must sell or be able to sell

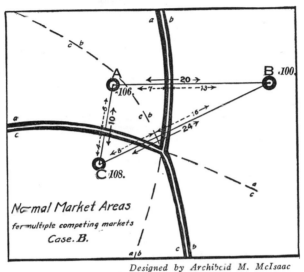

Designed by *Archibald M. McIsaac*

FIG. 23. CASE B, SHOWING EFFECT OF RAISING A'S
AND LOWERING C'S PRICE

everywhere in the normal sales territories of competitors in order that effective competition shall exist has not a vestige of truth in it (as applied to strictly standardized commodities sold under competitive conditions and with rational freight rates). Numerous partial and apparent exceptions to this statement are partly cases where the commodities differ in quality, or where habit, custom, established trade relations, etc., make a difference in valuations. In larger part, however, these exceptions in the past thirty years are plain cases of monopoly and discrimination by the basing-point practice.

APPLICATION OF THE ECONOMIC LAW

The law of market areas brings order out of chaos in the understanding of many of the aspects of geographical price relations, in-

cluding those of our special subject, basing-point delivered prices.
An interesting inductive study made recently by a firm of advertising experts for one of their wholesaler clients, reached a result
essentially in accord with our theoretical statement, though mis-
taking the curve for an ellipse instead of a hyperbole, a mistake
well-nigh unavoidable in a purely empirical study, because of the
resemblance in appearance between the portion of an elliptical
curve around one focus and that of a hyperbolic curve around the
market focus with higher prices. The problem these experts were
investigating was that of a wholesaler at St. Louis reselling goods
which had been shipped from the east. The investigation showed
that in such a case the logical, that is, the profitable, sales territory
was to the west in (what looked like) an elliptical area; that sales
outside of this area were more costly to make, involved waste in
cross hauls and freights and in loss of net profits (principally
through rising selling costs per unit). The fuller description of the
case is so enlightening that it is given in the Appendix to Ch. XX.

This study by an advertising firm for a private client has ex-
posed the wastefulness even in terms of private profit of a widespread practice of "hard-headed business men" supposed to be
infallible judges of their own business. We have shown more
fundamentally why such a practice by a seller is not normal behavior under competitive conditions. We shall later show more
fully why the practice of pricing on a basing point so that shipments of identical goods are overlapping from different markets
is conclusive proof of monopolistic restraint of trade, involving
discrimination, social waste, and social injustice. The interest of
truly competitive sellers when properly advised is in almost complete accord with the public interest and against such a practice;
the self-interest of a local monopoly is often, perhaps always, out
of accord with the public interest and is favored by violating "the
economic law of market areas."

WHEAT: AN OBJECT LESSON IN COMPETITION

We may supplement our theoretical formula of market areas
by two object lessons. The first, in a field where there can be no
question that the conditions are those of effective competition, that
is, the average farm prices of wheat throughout the United States,

will conclude this chapter. The other, that of the Pittsburgh-Plus system of prices, in which the effective reality of competition is lacking, is already familiar to the reader and will be discussed further below. The contrast between the geographical price structures in the two cases and a comparison of each with the theoretical law of market areas may do much to banish any lingering doubt as to the monopolistic character of the basing-point practice.

In Fig. 24 on p. 295 is a map showing the average geographic differences in the local prices of wheat in the United States.[4] No doubt some wheat is consumed in every county in the United States, and in a large majority of the counties some wheat is produced, the main exceptions being some unirrigated arid regions in the west and in the half dozen States lying south of the thirty-fifth degree of latitude. In almost every neighborhood, therefore, every year between harvests a balance is to be struck between production and consumption, between local demand and supply, with a resulting surplus or deficiency as the case may be.

The conditions of a real local market are favored further by the very general grinding of wheat for use as food in each neighborhood. At the time to which this map of wheat prices relates[5] there were still nearly 7000 wheat flouring mills in the United States, of which nearly 5000 (almost 2 per county) were mills producing each less than 5000 barrels of flour, and some wheat was ground in every State but Louisiana and Florida.

DEFICIT AND SURPLUS AREAS

The deficits and surpluses, whether regularly recurring or accidental, due to fluctuations in weather, crops, etc., have, of course, to be adjusted by sales for outward shipment or by purchases and inward shipments. Every one of the thousands of such neighborhoods in the United States may be said in the economic sense either to export or to import wheat (though not in the sense of crossing the political boundaries of a foreign country). If in any year there is a surplus in neighborhood A, some wheat is shipped outward and the price at A must be less than at the destination

---

[4] The sources of the data, and the method used in preparing the map, are given in Appendix B to Ch. XX.
[5] As shown in *Census of Manufactures* for 1914.

(which may be called B) by approximately the cost of shipment. If on the contrary there is by chance a deficit at A, wheat must be purchased elsewhere and shipped inward, making the cost at A higher than at the place of purchase by about the cost of shipment. Suppose the shipment cost to be 10 cents per bushel from the nearest market A to B, and balanced demand-and-supply price at A to be usually 100. Then when there is an excess of products at A the price would fall, and when it came to 90 wheat could be shipped to B or anywhere else where the price was 100, and this would put a lower limit to the fall of prices at A. If on the contrary there is a chance deficit at A, the demand-and-supply price would rise, and when it reached 110, wheat could be shipped from B or any place where the price was not over 100, and this would put a limit to the rise of price at A in case of abnormal shortage.[6] Observe that in either case the marginal principle is operative, and that if any wheat whatever is "exported" (shipped outward), the price of all wheat at A must be less by the cost of shipment than the market price at destination, and if any wheat whatever is "imported" the price of all wheat (of the same grade) at A must be more by the cost of inward shipment. In strict theory, if the local usual demand-and-supply price is 100, then a surplus of even a few per cent might reduce the price to 90, and a deficit of like amount raise the price to 110. If the shipping costs to or from the nearest other market were 10 cents, and the price there were 100, a range of 20 per cent in price might result from a fluctuation of a few per cent in the balance of supply and demand (the demand for wheat being unusually inelastic). In practice such abrupt fluctuations are modified by some slighter adjustments along border zones where the shipping costs are less.

GREATER SURPLUS AREAS

By this process of sale and shipment, a large part of the wheat surpluses in the United States go to supply the deficits in other parts of the country, moving southwesterly, southerly, and southeasterly. There are two great surplus wheat areas in the United

---

[6] On condition, of course, that at the same time there is not an abnormal shortage at all the neighboring sources of supply, in which case the level of prices would rise in all that larger region.

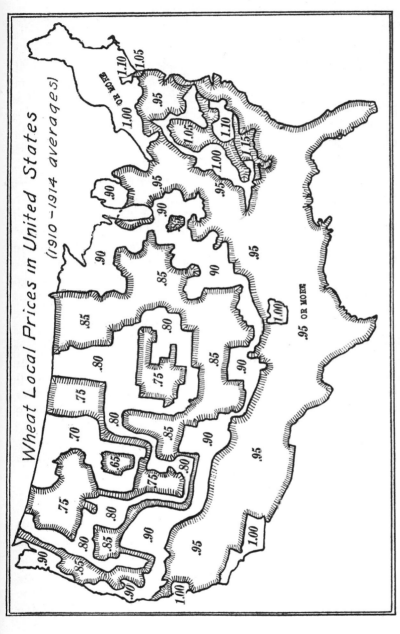

FIG. 24. SHOWING CONCENTRIC RINGS OF COMPETITIVE PRICES AROUND SURPLUS AREAS OF WHEAT PRODUCTION, AND OUTER RINGS IN DEFICIT AREAS

States which touch at their borders, the one in the far northwest, mostly on the western slope of the Rockies (Washington, Oregon, Idaho, Utah), and the other on the eastern slope and eastward to the Mississippi River (including the very great surplus States of Montana, the Dakotas, Nebraska, and Kansas, and other smaller surpluses as far as Indiana). The price zones lying between the two centers of surplus production and of lower prices (65 cents) in eastern Idaho and in western Nebraska (75 cents) conform very well with the theoretical picture of market areas, due account being taken of the great obstacles of mountains and deserts with lack of transportation agencies over large territories. Both centers sell outward in every direction, and the wheat moves toward whatever place will yield the largest price (net at point of shipment) or until the prices netted by sales to various destinations come to equilibrium. Evidently, under these conditions there can normally be no cross shipments at the same time, as constantly occurs by the basing-point practice in other industries.

LOCAL PRICES AND LIVERPOOL

It is often said that the price of wheat at Liverpool sets the price everywhere in the world, but this is inaccurate. The local prices in some of the deficit regions of the United States are even higher than those at Liverpool, and the prices in some small surplus regions supplying those deficit regions must usually be more (sometimes very much more) than the Liverpool price minus the freight. Many local wheat prices in this country are not directly geared with Liverpool prices at all. But those zones from which the actual movement of wheat is pretty steadily outward along the great transportation routes by rail and by water for export bear a pretty regular and constant relationship to Liverpool prices. For, after the inequalities in domestic supplies and demands in a multitude of localities in the United States have been smoothed out (or as they are being smoothed out) after algebraically canceling pluses and minuses, there still remained (at the period of this map) a net surplus for the country as a whole of about one-fourth the total production (a surplus of about 2.2 bushels per capita of the whole population). This national surplus of wheat, about 200,-

000,000 bushels, moves from those surplus regions that are best situated in respect to connected lines of shipment.

Toward some thirty principal (so-called "primary") markets throughout the country the larger surpluses move, much being retained for local consumption at these great urban centers (Chicago, New York, Seattle, etc.), much being distributed to near-by domestic deficit areas, and the rest going abroad, largely to Europe,

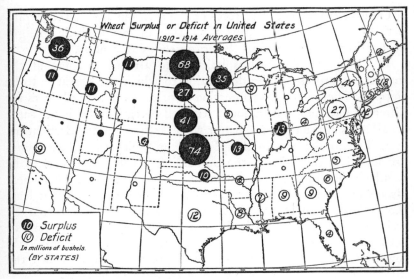

FIG. 25. TO COMPARE WITH FIG. 24

and in some cases to Asiatic or to South American destinations. The local prices not only at the American markets of Portland, Oregon, Galveston, St. Louis, Chicago, and New York, but those of Argentina and Australia, which ship to England, do form a system of local prices for these regions exporting to a common destination. All are competitively contributing to the supply in Liverpool, and the several local prices are constantly adjusted into accord with the Liverpool price figured back (minus the freight, etc.) to the various regional markets and places of shipment. From Blackfoot, Idaho, in the 65-cent wheat zone, the combined cost of rail and ocean freight was almost exactly the same (45 cents a bushel) to Liverpool via either Puget Sound or New York harbor. In a very true sense there is a local balance of demand and supply and a local price in each of the many local markets, an important part of the demand, however, being in many parts of the country (not all parts) that of those buying for export to some distant market.

ESSENTIALS OF FREE SURPLUS MARKETS

Observe two essential features of the prices in any of these competitive markets with surpluses, whether in the producing neighborhood or in the principal American shipping centers.

1. The price of wheat is uniform to all buyers there at the market, regardless of the destination to which the wheat is to be shipped. There is no discrimination in prices as between buyers for different localities. The amount received by each seller is the same on all sales at the time, no matter what be the intended destination.

2. The local prices in the places from which the wheat comes are less than the price in the purchasing market, and tend to be regularly less by the cost of shipment to that market. The wheat always moves toward places where the prices are more, by at least the freight, than at the shipping market. Therefore, except by accident or blunder, cross shipments do not and cannot occur as between two truly competitive markets, for each can sell only toward the other to a certain neutral point or line at which the difference in local prices is just offset by the freight costs.

NO BASING POINT FOR TRUE MARKETS

These simple facts and principles present an enlightening comparison between a system of truly competitive local prices and a system of basing-point prices. What would be the effect of making Kansas City, or Minneapolis, or Chicago, any one of the primary markets nearest to the great surplus wheat areas, the basing point for wheat prices everywhere in the country? It would force a revolution in the geographical price relations of the various markets. It could be accomplished only by the tacit conspiracy of all sellers of wheat. The delivered cost (or local price) to buyers even in surplus areas shipping outward at much lower net realized prices, would always be (approximately) the agreed base price plus the freight (often merely imaginary freight) to destination. This would involve the waste of cross freights and a gigantic system of discriminatory prices to consumers. Repeatedly the defenders of the Pittsburgh-Plus plan declared that it was merely a "mode of quotation" and made no difference whatever in the actual structure and relationship of local prices, being itself a perfect exemplification of the operation of supply and demand. Is it? Does the use of a basing point "make no difference"? We now have a theoretical standard, in the economic law of market areas, and a practical object lesson in the local variation of wheat prices in the United States. By these norms the basing-point plan may be tested, and it is found wanting. It is not a mode of competition but a device of monopoly.

CHAPTER XXI

DUMPING AND THE GENTLE ART OF SLOW MURDER

INDUSTRIAL PRICE UNIFORMITY WANES

A "UNIFORM PRICE" is a conception originating in the market place. It is the same price paid by all buyers and received by all sellers at a certain time in a market. Where price is uniform, it means that any buyer, if buying from more than one seller at that time, pays the same to each, and any seller, if selling to more than one buyer, receives the same (net) price from each. The opposite or negative of a uniform price is a set or system of discriminatory prices. We already have observed them in practice, and we have now to examine more theoretically their nature and effects in various aspects of price problems.[1]

Except when discrimination referred to some political act, as that between taxpayers or on account of color under the Fourteenth Amendment, etc., the word seems to have been used in law until after 1900 only in connection with freight rates, not with industrial prices. Professor A. T. Hadley (later President of Yale University) recognized that the practice of discrimination might appear also in the sale of manufactured goods, though he explained why, as it seemed to him, it was of greater importance in respect to railroad rates.[2] He recognized clearly, too, that "discriminations" of all kinds arise out of monopoly and are closely correlated with it.

---

[1] The derivation, and earlier legal definitions, of discrimination are discussed in Appendix A to Ch. XXI.

[2] Hadley used the word "industrial" in a broad sense, as applicable both to railroads and to manufactures, and not in the latter more specific sense that is now usual: "Wherever there is industrial monopoly of any kind there is a liability to discriminations. They have become most prominent in the case of railroads because the monopoly of railroads has been in some respects most

RAILROAD DISCRIMINATION: AS TO GOODS

Inasmuch as the problem of discrimination arose earlier in the field of railroad rates, was earlier studied there, and has found there a more nearly satisfactory solution in public control, it is instructive first to glance at that phase of our economic history. As the American railroads were rapidly extended between 1830 and 1860, revolutionizing the conditions of transportation,[3] the absence of market competition in the fixing of general, uniform rates became quickly manifest. The sale of transportation was broken up into a multitude of separate transactions along the line of each railroad, the result being a variety of discriminatory prices instead of uniform prices for like services. These discriminations were of three main types: as to goods, as to individuals or shippers, and as to localities. Discrimination between classes of goods (when not merely a camouflage of other forms, personal or local, as it often was, and if applied honestly, moderately, and equally to all localities and shippers to increase the railroad revenues) has always been more defensible than the other two kinds and need not long detain us. Particularly since the belated acceptance of the principle that as a general policy the total revenues of railroads and public utilities should be high enough to afford adequate service and "reasonable" returns, the charging of higher rates (relative to weight) for carrying more compact and valuable goods has been increasingly regularized and legalized in "classifications." Yet it is well to observe that even at its best, this kind of discrimination exercised by a common carrier approximates, if it is not essentially, the exercise of the public power of taxation, and is now pretty fully under public control through the "strong" railway commissions.

PERSONAL DISCRIMINATION

The conditions often have been such as to lead railroad officials, in order to secure the traffic, to make special rates (or rebates) to some individual shippers, usually not the weaker shippers, but the more powerful bargainers having some alternative means of ship-

---

complete, their activity most extensive, and the investigation of their doings most searching; in short, because the railroad has attained a fuller development than other forms of industrial monopoly." (*Transportation,* p. 124.)

[3] See above, Ch. XVIII.

ment, etc. The reports of the numerous public investigations made after 1870 are filled with flagrant examples.[4] The practice here was ostensibly in the interest of the road, but the temptation was strong for the railroad officials to grant favors also to friends and to industries in which they themselves had financial interests, thus betraying the stockholders as well as other shippers deprived of their common-law rights to equal treatment. The result was a welter of irrationality in which both common honesty and common sense were lost. As late as the first decade of the twentieth century, after years of reforming efforts through State and Federal legislation and regulation, and after general conditions had been no doubt greatly improved, the public was shocked at the exposure that such practices were still continued by some officials of the "standard" railroad of America. The verdict of time and experience is that personal discrimination in rates is most unqualifiedly to be condemned. Any rate should be open to all shippers alike under like conditions if freedom of commerce is to be maintained.

LOCAL DISCRIMINATION

The third type of discrimination, that between localities, is the most suggestive in our study of industrial price policies. It alone exhibits the peculiar aspects of local monopoly. Where there is no competing road (about nine-tenths of all stations) the railroad is a monopoly within certain local limits in its dealings with every shipper and in respect to every class of goods. The upper limits of rates are those above which the goods either will not be shipped at all or will go by an alternative means of shipment. Because of the great technical superiority of the railroad over most other means of transport by land, this upper limit of rates is usually very high. (The autotruck has now, to be sure, greatly altered this situation.) The individuals shipping from or to most local points have thus no access to a "market" for transportation, and there is no effective competition among sellers of transportation services. The exercise of this monopolistic power over rates at non-competitive localities was carried early in the history of railroads to absurd extremes, by

---

[4] A typical case related in 1887 by a Union Pacific official regarding rebates granted for years to the Standard Oil Company may be found in the Trust Investigation of the 50th Congress, 1st session, p. 717.

charging not merely more in proportion to the distance that goods were carried, but by inverting geographical relations and charging more for a shorter than for a longer distance on the same line and in the same direction. Goods were carried right through towns and cities and hundreds of miles beyond for less than would be charged if they were unloaded on the way. The railroad officials came to look upon this as a natural and just practice, especially in view of the desperate financial straits to which many of the roads had been brought by the early and reckless overbuilding of railroads. The resulting structure of freight rates in their geographical aspects was fearful and wonderful, ranging from one extreme where fierce competition for traffic to and from the junction points cut revenues to an amount that would hardly pay for axle grease, to the other extreme where the monopolistic charge at competitive stations made the survival of industries there impossible. This was not truly a *system* of freight rates; rather it was a *chaos* of freight rates.

THE BLIGHT TO EFFICIENCY

The total volume of traffic being usually insufficient at first to utilize nearly all the carrying capacity of even a one-track railroad, the traffic agents threw aside all thought of making each shipment contribute a proportionate share toward net revenues. They plunged into the dubious practice of "charging what the traffic will bear," seeking not a "fair" price or a uniform price on all like shipments, but rather the highest price obtainable under monopolistic conditions on each shipment and from each shipper (excepting personal favorites), hoping that the surplus above the average on some would offset the deficiency on others. Thus blunderingly they killed off thousands of technically efficient small factories well located otherwise, but where freights were discriminatorily high, thereby forcing or attracting industries to other places which contributed least proportionately to railroad revenues. Thus did short-sighted business selfishness kill the goose that laid the golden egg. The countrysides were strewn with the bleaching bones of industrial enterprises slain by this policy of economic waste and social injustice.

VESTED RIGHTS IN DISCRIMINATIONS

An unhealthy stimulus was thus given to the growth of large cities and to the uneconomic development of large industry at some locations without naturally superior advantages. The chaos of freight rates resulted in a chaos of industrial prices. The apparently greater efficiency of larger factories located wide apart at competitive stations was in great measure (no doubt entirely, in many cases) artificial and unreal. It was due to the discriminatory freight rates they enjoyed both on the assembled materials and on their products shipped to customers, rather than to real superiority either in the technical features of location and operation or in managerial efficiency. Today, after more than a half century of efforts at regulation of railroad rates by Federal and State laws and commissions, many marks of these accidental, irrational, economically unwarranted freight charges, some too high, some too low, are still visible in the distribution of population and industry in every part of the land. To some regions they are a perpetual injustice; to others they are a kind of vested right, stubbornly defended by powerful private interests and blindly protected by custom, the courts, and the inertia of the public. (See Figure 21 and its cross references.)

GROPING TOWARD EQUITABLE RAILROAD RATES

At first, for a brief period, faith was put in a sort of stage-coach competition. The naïve notion was held that cars and engines would be owned and operated independently by various common carriers paying toll for the use of the railroad tracks, after the manner of freight wagons on the turnpikes. Then, for nearly two-thirds of a century, faith was placed in another sort of competition to be secured through the rapid construction of parallel roads reaching to all parts of the land. This faith in competition was engendered by the sight of the fierce cutting of rates that occurred at the comparatively few stations (about one-tenth of all) where railroads met or crossed. Finally, tardily and reluctantly, the public recognized that the railroad was in its very nature a local, limited monopoly, and came to the policy of commission control.

In the I. C. C. Act of 1887, the famous long- and short-haul clause (the fourth section) made the practice of local discrimination unlawful "under substantially similar circumstances," but the Commission was authorized to grant exemption in special cases. However, the whole long- and short-haul clause and the Commission's power to administer it were nullified by judicial interpretation until the further amendment in 1910.[5] Soon thereafter the Commission "declared that the intent of the amended law was to make the prohibition of the higher rate for the shorter haul a rule of well-nigh universal application, from which deviation should be permitted only in special cases in order to meet transportation conditions that were beyond the carriers' control"—that is, not of just one carrier, but of all subject to the Commission's jurisdiction. "In general it may be said that it has been the effort of the Commission to construct a harmonious and properly graded rate structure, freed from the anomalies of the earlier situation."[6] Slowly, thus, not always consistently or with clear vision of the ideal, the movement has been toward a system of railroad rates in more rational relationship and proportion to distances and transportation costs and freed from local discrimination.

REVOLUTION IN INDUSTRIAL SALES METHODS

Neither the public nor the courts quickly saw, or yet has clearly seen, the application of these lessons of the local monopoly power of railroads to the problem of industrial monopoly. Certain it is, however, that step by step with the spread of the railroads in America, accompanied by these discriminatory practices, went a change, silent and hardly noticed but in some respects revolutionary, in methods of sales and marketing of manufactured goods and in price policies in many lines of manufacturing. This change began much earlier and proceeded more rapidly in some businesses than in others, and in a few, even yet, has been scarcely manifest at all.[7] This change seems to have occurred mostly after 1865 and increased noticeably after 1880. As the groups of small local shops and mills were gradually displaced by larger factory units and the

---

[5] An illuminating account of this phase of railroad history is given by Frank H. Dixon in *Railroads and Government* (Scribner, 1922), pp. 28-42.

[6] The two quotations are from Dixon, *op. cit.,* pp. 33 and 35.

[7] Its main features have been sketched above in our brief historical survey of markets, Ch. XVIII.

area of distribution of the products expanded, customers came less and less to the factory door; instead, salesmen ("drummers," commercial travelers) went out from the factories to the far corners of the land, carrying samples, catalogues, and descriptive price lists to sell to separate, isolated customers at the places where the goods were to be delivered.

DELIVERED PRICE POLICY ENTERS

As this came to be more the rule in some industries, the thought of a uniform market price at any one place where there were groups of buyers and sellers gradually faded and became overcast with the notion of numerous distinct "delivered prices" to different customers. These might or might not be expressed as including freight or as price of product and freight separately specified; this is merely a matter of words. The really essential point is that the net amount realized for the goods, figured at the mill after deducting freight, began increasingly to be varied from customer to customer at various points of delivery as had not been before customary. Buyers lost the habit of buying at the mill at a price uniform to all, and sellers began to refuse to quote any mill-base price and would sell only at delivered prices. In a number of different industries this gave the final blow to the ideal and the reality of a real market and real market prices in such cases. It destroyed the competition at uniform mill-base prices even on the local margin in the area between mills and markets. Buyers in many lines, being unable to secure the equal treatment at a market that was the rule a generation earlier, ceased even to expect it. It was a momentous change, for virtually the mill was refusing to sell its products except to those who would buy transportation services from it also. The monopolistic sellers were thrusting themselves between the buyers of their products and the common carriers. The buyer of steel, or oil, or cement, or brick, or what not, was forced to buy transportation through the manufacturer.

MONOPOLY VIA FREIGHT RATES

Now in thus changing from mill-base prices to delivered prices the manufacturer became possessed of, and could exercise, that same power of local discrimination in the sale of his own goods which the railroad as a local monopoly had possessed and exercised before it was stopped by statute and by Commission control under the long- and short-haul clause. The illegal and prohibited power of the railroad to discriminate was grasped and used by industrial monopoly. It is the game of "button, button, who's got the button?" The button is monopoly. The public did not see when it passed into other hands, and kept looking in the wrong direction. With the old practice of selling at uniform prices at places where others were actively competing, local discrimination in the prices of products was impossible. The factory had a fixed habitat, and though in a competitive market its prices might vary from time to time, they did not and could not vary according to place, that is, according to the varying distances the several buyers came to the market. But, in sales at delivered prices, very unequal net receipts at the mill could be and were mixed up and confused with the freight charges. Freight charges, even if not made discriminatory by the railroads, became so by the manufacturer's acting as a middleman and charging more or less than the rates received by the carrier, a practice known as "absorbing the freight." In reality the discriminations in freights were shifted to the prices of the products realized by the manufacturer at his mill.

How this practice cuts down the "net realized steel prices," making them grossly discriminatory though the "delivered prices" of all mills are identical (miscalled "uniform") is shown in Figure 26 (based on data from the Pittsburgh-Plus complaint). Each mill outside of Pittsburgh secures the full freight "plus" when selling in its immediate neighborhood (and directly away from Pittsburgh), but cuts more and more into its real steel prices as it "absorbs freight" on shipments toward Pittsburgh. The effects are shown for Duluth, Chicago, Lackawanna (Buffalo), and Bethlehem, in the order of their maximal pluses. The Pittsburgh mills always net the same. It is far from unusual, as is shown in Figures 27 and 29, for outside mills to sell actually into Pittsburgh and beyond, in which cases the real steel prices become much less than the Pittsburgh base. But this loss to the mill is not a penny's gain to the consumers, for it all goes uneconomically to pay useless freight. If the consumers were well advised and would righteously conspire, they might break the back of this unrighteous conspiracy

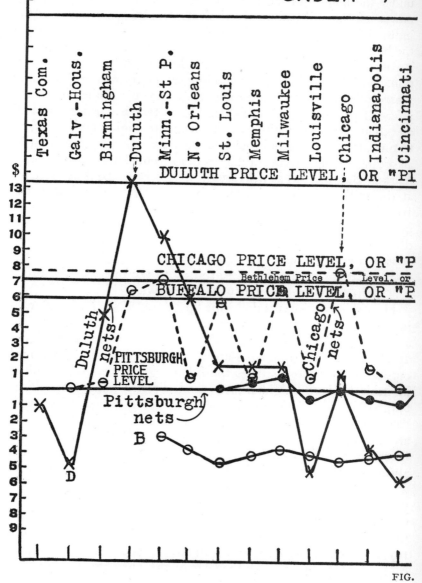

FIG.

STEEL PRICES
-P PLAN

Detroit Cleveland Pittsburgh Erie Buffalo Rochester Baltimore Philadelphia Bethlehem Boston Richmond New York

TTS. PLUS" $13.20 PER TON

Price netted more
than "Pitts. Base"

ITTS. PLUS" $7.60 PER TON

"Pitts Plus" $7.00 per ton

ITTS. PLUS" $5.90 PER TON

Buffalo nets→

Bethlehem nets↗

"PITTSBURGH BASE"

Price netted less
than "Pitts. Base"

$
13
12
11
10
9
8
7
6
5
4
3
2
1
1
2
3
4
5
6
7
8
9

B

D

e

of the producers in any basing-point system, by placing all of their orders with the most distant mills, which make such sales only at a loss. As yet, however, the consumers have not got together on such a policy of defense and retribution, but they may some day do so if the courts do not grant relief.

DOMESTIC DUMPING

This modern practice of local discrimination in the sale of industrial products, so closely connected with the development of the railroad, has a remarkable family resemblance to an old practice of dumping goods in foreign commerce, begun and continued in some industries (especially by monopolistic trading companies) long before the railroad was dreamed of. Dumping has been defined as unloading upon a foreign market goods for which there is little or no demand at home, or, somewhat more mildly, as selling goods abroad below the ordinary trade rates. But these otherwise good definitions connect the essential economic fact of local discrimination called dumping with the often rather accidental historical and political fact that the goods happen to cross a political boundary. In its economic nature local discrimination by lower prices for use at a distance from the market of sale is simply domestic dumping.[8]

Of the many forms and varieties of domestic dumping, the more important, if not all, may be reduced to three. Two of the three might be called lone-hand dumping, of which one is moderate, to make a profit immediately, and the other is extreme, to kill off competitors (and thus to make greater profits ultimately). The third sort might be called coöperative or play-the-game dumping, that which is done systematically and by agreement among otherwise independent sellers. The most important species of this last genus is the now familiar case where basing-point prices are charged. We shall consider these in this order: 1. Cutthroat competition to kill off competitors. 2. Lone-hand, unsystematic local price cutting in competitors' "natural territory." 3. Systematic local discrimination by agreement, usually in a basing-point system.

[8] See Appendix B to Ch. XXI, on dumping and monopoly.

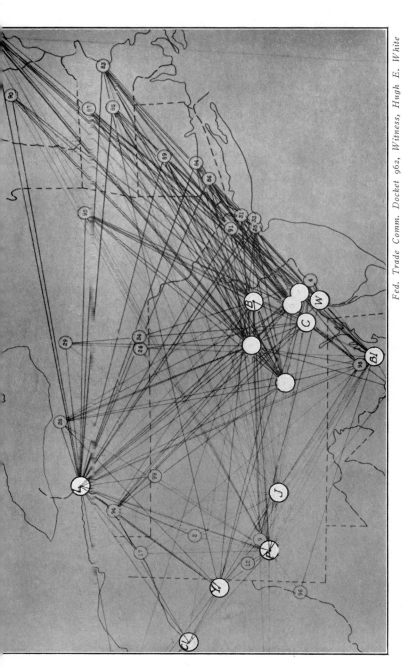

Fed. Trade Comm. Docket 962, Witness, Hugh E. White

FIG. 27. STEEL MILLS AND DUMPING FROM CLEVELAND, YOUNGSTOWN, PITTSBURGH, JOHNSTOWN, LACK-
AWANNA, BALTIMORE, COATESVILLE, WILMINGTON, AND **BETHLEHEM** (INITIALED) AND OTHER MILLS.
SMALLER CIRCLES LOCATE NON-PRODUCING DESTINATIONS

HUNTING A DANGEROUS CRIMINAL

Cutthroat competition, though not the first phase of local industrial price discrimination, is the one whose uneconomic character was first clearly recognized and condemned by the law.[9] It is difficult now to realize how recently, that is, up to 1911 in the oil case, its beneficiaries unblushingly defended this form of discrimination before our highest Court, as a normal form of competition essential to private enterprise. Yet before that time, for at least fifteen years, even prior to the creation of the Industrial Commission in 1898, public attention and reform efforts had been directed almost exclusively toward remedying this one evil. It was assumed to be not only the chief, but practically the sole, weapon or agency by which monopolies were brought about. Between 1905 and 1913 nineteen States had adopted statutes aimed to prevent unfair discrimination in price, probably all containing some clause limiting the prohibition in some way to discrimination "for the purpose of creating a monopoly" or to that "not in good faith to meet competition," etc.[10]

This aim was reflected in the original draft of the Clayton Act, which made it a misdemeanor "to discriminate in price . . . with the purpose or intent to thereby destroy or wrongfully injure the business of a competitor." The Committee Reports [11] declare that Section 2 of the bill

is expressly designed with the view of correcting and forbidding a common and widespread unfair trade practice whereby certain great corporations and also certain smaller concerns which seek to secure a monopoly in trade and commerce by aping the methods of the great corporations, have heretofore endeavored to destroy competition and render unprofitable the business of competitors by selling their goods,

---

[9] "Cutthroat competition" is a phrase used loosely. Sometimes it means (1) selling at a price that yields less than a "fair" profit; or again (2) selling still lower, actually below the cost of production (erroneously assumed to be a very easy matter to be ascertained); or it means (3) cutting prices for the express purpose of killing off a competitor, and therefore utterly regardless of any profit on the particular sales—though the ultimate intention is to recover the lost profits by raising prices. The first two cases are not really distinguishable from any ordinary case of discrimination; we limit our use of the term to the third case.

[10] See list in H.R. Report 627, 63rd Congress, 2d session, reprinted in Senate Reports 698.

[11] House Report, H.R. 627, p. 1, repeated by the Senate Committee.

wares, and merchandise at a less price in the particular communities where their rivals are engaged in business than at other places throughout the country.[12]

FALSE IDEALS OF COMPETITIVE CONDITIONS

The ideas of that period regarding the nature and methods of competition (without restraint of trade and resulting in real market prices) were far from clear. It was generally assumed that local discrimination to invade and capture as much as possible of a competitor's territory was a normal and commendable form of competition, without which, indeed, no competition whatever would be possible between geographically separated sellers. Some examples of this view, strongly and repeatedly urged at that time and still today, are given in Appendix C to Ch. XXI.

When, therefore, the Clayton Act was under debate, in the summer of 1914, Congress, especially the Senate, was very much at sea as to what to do about prohibiting discrimination outright. They started boldly, then lost courage, then did what they dared. The Senate first struck Section 2, prohibiting discrimination, from the bill,[13] but in conference with the House, restored it, somewhat modified, to the present form. The Senate Committee explained that "the enlargement" (by permitting discrimination "in good faith to meet competition," etc.) "will tend to foster wholesome competition." There was little dissent in the Senate from the bewilderment expressed by Senator Cummins, as follows:

If the section (2) were to stop there [with the first clause making it unlawful to discriminate] it would have teeth but it would operate upon many transactions which we do not desire to prohibit. . . . There would be no difficulty at all in applying it . . . to prove that a seller had discriminated in price between different localities or different buyers in the same locality *but competition cannot be preserved unless there is some discrimination.* (Our italics.) [14]

And then after enumerating the successive provisions and exceptions by which (as also in the final draft) all significance was pur-

---

[12] *Idem,* pp. 2-3. This and similar expressions in Congressional reports and debates were the grounds upon which the Mennen decision was based—later overruled.   See below, Ch. XXVI.
[13] *Cong. Record,* August 26, 1914.
[14] *Cong. Record,* August 26, 1914, p. 14250.

posely whittled away from the prohibition of discrimination,
Senator Cummins declared:

> We might just as well have said . . . that the seller can do any-
> thing he desires or pleases to meet competition that is not in violation
> of the anti-trust law.

"REASONABLE" MEANS "OUTRAGEOUS"!

Senator Cummins, at least, among the Senators, honestly wished
to prevent "cutthroat competition," but despaired of finding a way
to do it without destroying legitimate competition. Was there one?
Surely, for the difficulty lay simply in the erroneous popular theory
of price which he held. It is not true, as he believed, that discrimination is an essential condition to real competition. What if he and
his colleagues had recognized the plain economic truth that local
discrimination is itself a violation of the uniformity which is essential to a real market price, that it is the exercise of a certain graduated monopolistic power whether or not it is being used in the
particular case to destroy competitors? What if they had understood that normal markets, with uniform market prices, are mutually limited through geographically marginal competition? Would
they then have so easily consented to filling Section 2 with as many
jack rabbits as a magician's hat? Senator Cummins, as well as
others, saw the difficulty, and he exclaimed:

> Made in good faith to meet competition. Imagine the government
> endeavoring to prove that a particular instance of price cutting was not
> made in good faith to meet competition.[15]

Oh, my prophetic soul! Then Senator Reed of Missouri calmly
interrupted:

> I do not think there is the slightest difficulty about the proposition
> the Senator is discussing. . . . If an independent company . . .
> should drop the price of gasoline at a given place and the Standard Oil
> Co. should meet it, that would be an act in good faith to meet com-
> petition. If, however, the Standard Oil Co. were to drop the price
> . . . so that it drove the independent concern out of business, there
> would not be any difficulty at all in a jury finding that they did not do

[15] *Cong. Record*, August 25, 1914, p. 14228.

it in good faith. I will undertake, in any reasonable case, any outrageous case, to get a verdict every time under that section.[16]

TENDERNESS TO SINNERS

There speaks the lawyer, apparently interested not in preventing
economic murder, but only in convicting (or defending) the mur-
derer after the victim is dead—interested not at all in mere economic assault and battery, but only in holding a judicial post-mor-
tem on the corpse—interested not, as a legislator, in encouraging the
competition of small, efficient enterprisers (who incidentally are
demonstrating that a lower price is high enough to afford an adequate profit) to force large corporations with all advantages of mass
production to moderate generally their prices to the public—only
interested, shortsightedly, to preserve to large monopolistic sellers
the malignant privilege of exploiting the public in their own non-
competitive territory, while cutting prices locally in other territory,
to the discouragement and possibly to the destruction of smaller
independent undertakings.

Senator Cummins, public-spirited and well-meaning, but men-
tally entangled in the belief that discrimination was somehow
essential to competition, could only reply frankly but feebly to this
legal sophistry:

I think the Senator probably could get a verdict from a jury in an outrageous case, but we are not making this law to arrest the progress of
monopoly in outrageous cases only. We are making it to preserve competition.

IS IT A GOLD BRICK?

The experience since the enactment of the Clayton Act has in
large part verified the gloomy contemporary prophecies of the
futility of the second section with its numerous jokers.[17] Except
that its administration was entrusted to the Federal Trade Commission, that section seems to have given no protection against local
price cutting that was not already possible under the Anti-Trust
Act of 1890, if the Supreme Court could have interpreted it in the
light of sound economic principles. Until the Pittsburgh-Plus complaint, no important case was brought before the Commission

---

[16] *Idem.*
[17] These are discussed in detail below in Ch. XXVI.

under this section; it remained practically a dead letter. Recent surprising Supreme Court decisions seem, however, to have opened up new possibilities in its application. The courts have not recognized any more clearly than had Congress that even a comparatively small isolated plant may have within the surrounding territory a certain degree of monopolistic power over prices which it can exercise through discrimination; that a local discriminatory price, therefore, is an exhibition of monopoly rather than an evidence of competition; and that excusing, in any class of cases, local discrimination under the mistaken belief that it is a necessity to competition "in good faith" is but preserving in bad faith and in all cases the evil powers of monopoly.

CHAPTER XXII

DISCRIMINATION, FINE AND SUPERFINE

LONE-HAND PRICE CUTTING

IN LOCAL price cutting of the more moderate sort, the price-cutter is presumably acting quite independently and to his own interest. His policy is live-and-let-live, mere limitation, not annihilation of any locally restricted competitor. Instances are undoubtedly numerous where this is the policy of nationally advertised specialties, particularly those of light-weight, cheaply transported goods, in the production and sale of which some one company holds a dominating position. To take a typical example, the able head of such a business says frankly that it is not altruism but self-interest that has led his company after long experience to adopt a restrictive rather than a destructive policy. When one factory produces from 50 to 75 per cent of the national product it finds that to get a larger share reduces profits. The costs of selling over a larger area increase; the purchase of competitors' inefficient plants is expensive, and if this is done other plants will be started for the purpose of cutting prices until they take on a nuisance value and are bought out to get rid of them. The leading company, with its fuller lines, better advertised and more skillfully sold, may succeed in pretty regularly getting prices about 20 per cent higher than its competitors. Goods are sold mostly f.o.b. the factory in New England, but if at certain points, as at Albany, New York, or Chicago, or St. Louis, *bona fide* competitors on certain kinds of goods spring up, a cut is made in delivered prices at and near these places. Our business man, exceptionally intelligent and public-spirited though he be, frankly admits that it is "all opportunistic," no principle except "to meet competition" by a local cut price, where and when it arises, and to keep incipient competition in its place, to keep it from growing bigger and more dangerous. What he is doing is not by agreement or conspiracy, or in any way underhand, and he would righteously resent your calling it by its true name "discrimination," for it has come to seem to him natural and good, since it is good for his own business. And he does not see that he is exercising and maintaining, by means of discrimination, a limited monopoly.

THE EVILS TO THE PUBLIC

Look, however, at the effects upon the public interest. This policy, repeated in a thousand lines of products, becomes a veritable blight to enterprise. "Competition is the life of trade," "competition reduces prices"—good old maxims, made in the days of real markets. But such local price cutting as this introduces a great hazard and discouragement into the starting of any new business in a neighborhood where the regular delivered prices (mill-base plus freight) of the dominant concern are high. If the promoters of new enterprises were sure that prices would not be cut in that one locality without a reduction of the competitors' uniform mill-base price, small industries would be greatly stimulated. True, the uniform mill-base prices of the distant factory might be reduced, but if so, the reduction would not be abrupt or so great as a merely local cut, but the benefit would inure to buyers in every other part of the land. The very fear of local price cutting must prevent the birth of industries even where a dominant concern holds prices far above a reasonable remunerative level, and the first actual local price cuts may easily stifle an infant industry in the cradle. Merely opportunist, no rational principle; who can know, but who can doubt, that such a method of starving young and struggling local enterprises has killed its thousands? And when they die, back go the prices of the market leader to the old level in that locality. Yet this is not the "outrageous" case of cutthroat competition, nor, being the action of one dominant seller only, is it conspiracy in restraint of trade, and could easily be proved not to be such, by brilliant jury lawyers such as Senator Reed of Missouri.

THE FAIRMONT CREAMERY CASE; THE FACTS

This sort of lone-hand moderate local price cutting, though frequent, is mostly carried on quietly and inconspicuously, by concerns whose total product does not bulk large in the national economy. One case presenting such a state of facts has, however, come before the Supreme Court, and that recently.[1] This case involved discrimination under a Minnesota statute forbidding creameries to purchase cream at higher prices (net at the creamery) in one locality than in other localities, a law passed, no doubt, to prevent large central creameries from crippling the local coöperatives. Of slight importance in its immediate practical bearings, this inconspicuous case is highly significant because of the astonishing legal and economic doctrine sanctioning local discrimination, set forth by Justice McReynolds and concurred in by five of his colleagues (Taft, Van Devanter, Sanford, Sutherland, and Butler). Three members of the Court (Holmes, Brandeis, and Stone) dissented but unfortunately filed no opinion.

The essential facts were not in dispute. A centralized creamery located at Sioux City, Iowa, bought at various villages in Minnesota and shipped to Sioux City milk, cream, and butter fat, and was accustomed to pay a higher price at some stations farther away where there were local creameries (coöperatives) than at other stations nearer where there was no such competition to meet, all shipments being over the same railroad going in the same direction. The complaint was based on particular transactions of a typical character, June 11, 1923. Whatever of monopoly and discrimination is here involved is of the buying sort, but the legal and economic problem presented is essentially the same as if it concerned discrimination in selling.

THE LEGAL ISSUES

Minnesota had in 1909 enacted a statute prohibiting such local discrimination when "done with the intent of creating a monopoly or destroying the business of a competitor." Statutes of this sort making discrimination an offense when "intent" or "purpose" was "an ingredient thereof, have been uniformly sustained."[2] Other

---

[1] Fairmont Creamery Company v. State of Minnesota, 274 U.S. 1. (April 1927).
[2] Brief for the State of Minnesota, p. 6, citing State of Iowa v. Fairmont

cases upholding laws against discrimination with intent to destroy competition are cited in Appendix A to Ch. XXII.

In 1923 the Minnesota legislature amended the law of 1909 by striking therefrom the ingredient of intent or motive. The legal issue presented for decision by the U.S. Supreme Court was as definitely agreed and uncomplicated as was the statement of facts; it was simply this: whether this change in the statute in 1923, so that it prohibited local price cutting "irrespective of motive" to create a monopoly or to destroy a competitor, made the statute unconstitutional as impairing the private right of freedom of contract guaranteed by the Fourteenth Amendment (as now construed by the courts).

THE COURT'S REASONING

The answer of Justice McReynolds and the majority was an unqualified yes. Their reasoning runs thus (the essential phrases are gathered from the opinion). *Major premise:* The Fourteenth Amendment guarantees the liberty to make normal contracts and to carry on business in a manner "essential to the freedom of trade and commerce and beneficial to the public." *Minor premise:* Where, as in this case, intent to create a monopoly is not an ingredient of the statute, local discrimination by a large factory, buying over a wide territory, is the exercise of "liberty to enter into normal contracts." Such discrimination is a mode of "carrying on business in the usual way heretofore regarded as both moral and beneficial to the public." *Conclusion,* very simple: the statute is therefore unconstitutional under the Fourteenth Amendment.

Here, as usual, when a conclusion is wrong the error is not in the logical form of the syllogism, but in a false premise. Here the minor premise baldly begs the question. Discriminatory prices are called "normal contracts," "long regarded as essential; . . . and as moral and beneficial," "the usual way" of "carrying on business." How long so regarded, and by whom? Our review of the history of markets and of the elementary principles of market price has shown how recently this sort of local price discrimination became a business practice where competition became weakened, and how

Creamery Company, 153 Ia. 702, a State case upholding an Iowa statute of the same sort against the same company.

different from that normal bidding in a market that is the safeguard of the public and the means to just and uniform prices.

IMAGINARY MARKETS

Justice McReynolds and five of his colleagues were innocently sanctioning the economic and legal revolution that was, and still is, in progress, the change from common central markets where until little more than thirty years ago all buyers enjoyed the advantages of uniform competitive mill-base prices, to the practice of selling (or buying) at delivered prices, without uniformity. In their mental picture, Sioux City is not a real buying center to which, as of old, each seller is free to resort or to ship his cream. They see each little village as a "competitive market" (whether there was another buyer there or not) "and the payment [by the one company] of different prices at different places is the ordinary consequent" of this counterfeit freedom of trade in which the customer has no part. There is here not a glimmering of the economic law of market areas whereby, in competitive trading, buying markets attract sellers from a certain area through uniform market prices. The central creamery has no uniform price whatever determined by the totality of competitive conditions within the area from which it draws its supplies, but it has merely a multitude of logically unrelated prices, each supposed to be fixed separately at the various collecting stations with "regard to ordinary trade conditions" in each restricted locality. In this separatist, isolating treatment of prices there is lost all sense of an interplay of demand and supply having some organic unity within a large buying market area.

REGULATION IS NOT PRICE FIXING

The climax of this reasoning is reached when Justice McReynolds declares that

Enforcement of the statute would amount to fixing the price at which the central creamery may buy, since one purchase would establish this for all points without regard to ordinary trade conditions." [3]

Here are two errors in the economic thought. For, first, the State does not *fix* the price when it merely regulates the *relative* prices

---

[3] Fairmont Creamery Case, 274 U.S. 1.

by prohibiting local discrimination. The trader is left free to fix and announce whatever uniform price he wishes in the light of all the market conditions. The Supreme Court itself condemns local discrimination if done with intent to destroy a competitor; therefore, by Justice McReynolds' reasoning, it sanctions price fixing by public authority in such cases. But this is a *reductio ad absurdum*. The truth is that the distinction between *price fixing* and the *regulation* by public authority of *relative* prices, the prevention of discrimination, is a fundamental one, not lightly to be thrown aside.

A further economic error is the statement that if local discrimination is prohibited "one purchase would establish" a fixed price at which the central plant "may buy for all points without regard to ordinary trade conditions." This simply reverses cause and effect; it is the ordinary trade conditions that determine the price the buyer chooses to establish. Equally bad is the phrase, "a uniform price fixed by a single transaction," for a single transaction would no more fix the price than the tail wags the dog. Rather it is the *sum total of trade conditions* within the market area in which the enterprise is operating that should, and does, in a free market, establish the price in the "one purchase," that is, in each and every purchase at a given time. And, recalling the first error, observe that in any case it is the seller and not a public official who would determine for himself what his uniform bid price should be.

A striking feature of this opinion is the unhesitating admission by the majority that the kind of discrimination which the statute sought to prohibit "may tend to monopoly," though in *this* case "not shown to be accompanied by evil results as ordinary incidents." The majority thus, admitting the danger of abuse, throws the burden of proof in every specific case upon the injured party or upon the public to prove the "purpose to monopolize or destroy competition," and there is no way in which this can be done except that once cheerfully suggested by Senator Reed, of holding a coroner's inquest over the body of the "late lamented." [4]

[4] The writer journeyed by auto from Sioux City to St. Paul in 1929 through the villages along the railway, but found no evidence that either before or since the change in the law any independent creamery actually had been put out of business (though apparently discrimination is still practiced to some degree). Inasmuch as public sentiment in Minnesota was strong enough to secure the amendment of the law in 1923, it is probable that the motive of

PRICE ANARCHY AND INSTABILITY

The Fairmont Creamery decision was of small importance in its immediate practical application, but the principles that it sanctioned are calamitous if applied generally to the problem of local discrimination. Once the mill-base price policy is abandoned, there is no certainty that the prices of products to buyers at different distances from the shipping point will vary by any rule whatever. Without some sort of special agreement among the sellers, their net product prices, like unregulated freight rates, are likely to vary merely according to the pseudo-rule of "charging what the traffic will bear," which, at those places where competition is lacking, means exaction by monopoly, and elsewhere means cut prices in little or no relation to costs or reasonable profits. Just as the traffic agent went out to sell transportation for whatever he could get for it at any point along the road and created a chaos of rates, so the sales department of a large factory may go out to get an increasing volume of orders at whatever cut price will make the sale in each case. This ordinarily means that the nearer the buyer is to the mill, the higher the net price realized by the mill, for there its local monopoly power over price is greater. The farther away the buyer, the lower the net price realized by the mill, for its freight advantage declines, or is restricted, as it extends its sales toward other mills. This sort of competition comes to mean going after business in the other man's usual territory and meeting his price there, or underselling him on that one sale or at that one point; it does not mean making a lower general mill price as it would in a real market. But two can play at that game, and in turn the territory near the first mill can be invaded by a distant competitor using the same tactics, so that there is no longer any territory that can be safely counted upon as belonging to any one mill that adheres to a uniform price. Temporary local conditions or the desire to keep his

the amendment was to put an end to the unsettling and demoralizing effects upon the coöperative membership that may be wrought by local price cuts made by central creameries in towns where farmers' coöperative creameries are operating. However, the motives attracting and holding the coöperative membership are complex and go beyond the mere "cash nexus." In general the more prosperous thrifty farmers with larger production belong to the coöperatives, which usually pay a few weeks later as dividends somewhat more than the private companies pay spot cash.

factory going may lead a producer suddenly to cut prices very deeply in some localities, absorbing freight close up to the competitor's doors. Thus, much greater uncertainty and instability are introduced into all business by the destruction of uniform market and mill-base prices.

FROM MONOPOLY TO MORE MONOPOLY

The larger the factory unit of production and the greater the distance that separates it from its competitors in any direction, the greater the margin of monopolistic profit it can reap from its near-by sales and (usually) the more able it is financially to cut prices for delivery into its competitor's natural sales territory. But each competitor finds it more dificult and costly to absorb the freight and invade its rival's most profitable territory. Thus, each mill is always (barring most exceptional conditions) realizing a greater net price (and adding more to total net profits) through near-by sales than by distant sales. There is presented here an example of a series of graduated monopoly advantages greatest near the mill and shading off to zero at the outer zone of delivery points.

Factories are led to quit "going it alone" in discrimination when two or more independent companies located some distance apart have been selling toward each other similar or identical goods, each endeavoring by "absorbing freight" to annex and retain as much sales territory as it can. Under such conditions the usual result must be either the disappearance of one of the two (either by bankruptcy or by merger), or coöperation in some sort of basing-point practice. This always involves an agreement, expressed or implied, by which separate discriminatory acts are organized into a system of discriminatory prices.

POLICY OF THE C.F. AND I.

We may take as a recent example of complicated discriminatory practice the case of the Colorado Fuel and Iron Works, located at Minnequa, a few miles from Pueblo, Colorado. The company has throughout a wide territory very substantial freight advantages over its distant eastern competitors, whether their products have to come by all-rail or by water-rail via the Texas ports or the Canal.

The freight advantage at Pueblo over Chicago amounts in Utah to 84 cents a hundred pounds on steel ($16.80 a ton). Before the modification of Pittsburgh-Plus in 1924, the Colorado Company, in common with the other independents, probably adhered faithfully to the practice. In 1924 it began to follow a modified basing-point plan adjusted to the new Chicago and Birmingham differen-

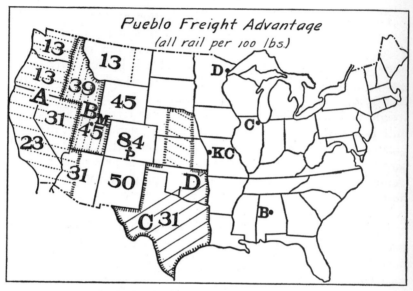

FIG. 28. AMOUNT BY WHICH THE FREIGHT TO VARIOUS STATES IS LESS FROM PUEBLO (P) THAN THAT FROM NEAREST EASTERN MILL. PANAMA CANAL RATES REDUCE THE ADVANTAGE IN THE A AREA, UTAH MILL COMPETITION IN THE (LARGE) B AREA, GULF WATER AND RAIL RATES IN C, AND LOCAL COMPETITION IN D

tial bases, absorbing freight toward Pacific coast and Texas territory. Two small western independents are little more than six hundred miles away by rail, the Midvale Company at Salt Lake City, which has been manufacturing only bars, and the Sheffield Steel Company at Kansas City, which manufactures not only structural steel and bars but wire and nails. Of course, each of the three companies enjoys a freight advantage in its own neighborhood, relative not only to each other but to eastern mills. Midvale (at

Salt Lake) shuts out the Colorado Company (at Pueblo) from Utah and Idaho in the sale of bars, and the Sheffield (at Kansas City) makes local cuts of prices below Chicago and Birmingham base-plus prices in a large part of Texas, Oklahoma, Kansas, and Nebraska. These cuts are met or possibly slightly undercut by the Colorado Company in the two more northerly States by absorbing freight. The practice is no doubt tantamount to a multiple basing-point agreement, each mill matching but usually not undercutting the delivered prices of the others. Considerable selling areas thus overlap with much resulting cross freighting, and widely varying net prices are realized from different sales. The policy of discrimination here again is purely opportunistic, without consistent principle except to get as much business as possible, at any price "within reason"—whatever that may seem to be. The Colorado Company makes no pretense of establishing a base price open impartially and uniformly to all customers at the mill. It discriminates and dumps by a multiple basing-point plan and in turn is "dumped upon" in its normal sales area.

SELF-INTEREST V. GENERAL INTEREST

Viewing the matter from the standpoint solely of his own self-interest, each producer deems it out of the question for all mills to sell on a mill-base instead of by this complication of tacit agreements and sporadic local price cutting. As the Colorado Company no doubt sees it, such a change would cause the loss of the monopolistic profit that comes from the higher prices it now gets near the mill, and its sales territory would be cut off on all sides by the local discrimination of near-by competitors. But, of course, this quite overlooks the fact that if the mill-base plan were legally enforced as a general policy, all competitors would have to stop local price cutting and would be unable to pilfer away "normal" territory from each other by that method. Price changes would be uniform at the base for all customers. Clearly there would be a gain under the mill-base plan for all customers near the mill if (as is always, and with good reason, assumed) the new base is somewhat below the present net prices realized on near-by sales. Also there would be to every mill a uniform unit profit on every sale to the very limit of its sales territory, not as now under local discrimination, a profit fading away to nothing or even changing to a substantial loss. The policy of mill bases would put an end to the economic waste of cross hauls which, as we shall soon see, result on an enormous scale from the practice of absorbing freight. The great saving in this respect must be an advantage to some one, either to producers or to consumers, and probably shared by both in some measure. No comprehensive view of the public problem of industrial prices—nay, not even of producers' interests alone—is to be had by squinting through the knot hole of profits to a single enterprise.

The Colorado Fuel and Iron Company is not held up as a particularly flagrant discriminator or as one reaping large profits from this policy. Situated as it is, in a region of sparse population and limited demand for steel, and laboring under certain technical disadvantages in the situation, as is well known, it has merely taken advantage of whatever price-exacting power it found it had. Its price practices have not been conspicuously "unfair" or exceptionally in violation of the anti-trust statutes—although it is our firm belief that all such practices are in violation of the statutes. It is just a fairly typical example of a numerous class of enterprises which honestly find themselves in some such price situation and wallow in a welter of local discrimination, powerless, by separate action, to get out even if they would.

STOP THROWING STONES

The uncertainty, waste, and loss of profit that results from local price discrimination by the method of freight absorption mingles the bitter with the sweet to the local price cutters. Striking evidence of this was given when a poll and inquiry of "thousands of American manufacturers" was made public in 1927. We have before us the answers in their particular bearing upon the rock products industry (including cement), where in large measure the ingenious device of multiple basing points, the cult of coöperation, and the cant of the Golden Rule in business, had been widely and hopefully adopted to create a new industrial heaven upon earth.[5] It will be noted that in the case of the heavy and cheap raw materials, stone, sand, gravel, etc., the factor of freight has a relatively great

[5] *Rock Products,* June 25, 1927, p. 70.

influence upon monopolistic zones. In editorial comment we are told that each man answering is rationally recognized as an outstanding figure in his industry, but no names are given, as "most of them did not wish to be quoted." The views are varied, the extremes agreeing only in the thought that the price cutting by their neighbors is bad and ought to be stopped. One solemnly announces as his "personal opinion and conviction" the truth that "absorption of freight is price-cutting." Suggestions of treatment are mostly opportunistic and vague. The notion most frequently expressed is that absorption of freight should not exceed about 10 per cent, or better not over 5 per cent, of the standard selling price (a sort of ghostly mill-base), though it is pretty plainly implied that the cuts often far exceed this ratio if any plant happens to want the business. Some seem to take pride in the brilliant idea that freights may be absorbed "up to the point where a normal average selling price can be attained," but what is normal or what is the meaning of this normal average is left to the imagination, with such pretense of help as is found in the phrase, "enough to yield a satisfactory profit." But what is satisfactory? Evidently in this satisfactory average might be included numerous sales which yield an unsatisfactory unit profit or a substantial loss balanced by other sales yielding monopolistic prices—all is vague as to where to stop extorting or cutting in the case of a particular sale.

NO HALFWAY REMEDY

The groping for a remedy sometimes takes a half-enlightened, pseudo-scientific direction of trying to relate the discrimination somehow to cost of production. Some say the price (net at mill) should not be less than cost, others that it should always show some profit above cost (but how much?); and one ventures the judgment that no producer should sell "a considerable quota of his production at a net plant price less than the cost of production." And there we are, back just where we started. What all these gentlemen rather innocently mean is that their neighboring competitors should practice the Golden Rule, but that they themselves would rather like to be left free to serve the devil at convenient times.

Now and then, however, above this rather aimless chatter is

audible the more rational note that "the proper price for a manufactured commodity is the production cost plus a fair profit at its
point of manufacture or production." One, indeed, declares that
after an extensive experience in the gravel business he has "never
met any well-founded argument to the contrary." He has
"preached this theory for many years" but confesses that he has
found his competitors "taking the other side of the argument" and
following the plan of "getting all the traffic will bear." We welcome this clear-thinking practical man of wide experience as our
nameless ally, who, though now a voice crying in the wilderness,
will, we trust, yet live to see a truer theory and a sounder practice
come into its own in his industry and in all others.

MONOPOLY DEPLORES ITS OWN WASTEFULNESS

Even from the high priests of the steel industry, the founders,
so to speak, of the religious observance of the basing point, have
come, of late, criticisms of its uneconomic workings. Mr. Charles
M. Schwab,[6] whose Bethlehem Steel Company, because of its
almost complete control of the steel situation in the east, has probably profited more from close adherence to the Pittsburgh-Plus
practice than has any other so-called independent (or perhaps than
the U.S. Steel Corporation itself) finds that all is not well with
his world. The tacit agreement in restraint of trade involved in the
use, by competitors, of a common basing point, has the sad defect
that the practice is merely to sell at the same delivered prices and
does not forbid discrimination by absorption of freight. Indeed,
that is the very essence of this ingenious scheme. Mr. Schwab sees
here a loss of profits to the steel producers. Both his ideas and his
language suggest that he had been reading the economic testimony
in the Pittsburgh-Plus case, refuting the unyielding contention
first set up by him for the Steel Corporation, that the practice was
strictly competitive and involved no discrimination between buyers
of steel. The resulting wastes of cross hauling had been clearly
set forth in the professional economic testimony in the Pittsburgh-
Plus hearings. Mr. Schwab now declares, as if it were his discovery,
that "the methods of distribution in our industry" involve waste

[6] In his address as president of the American Iron and Steel Institute, in
New York, May 25, 1928; reported in the *Iron Trade Review*, May 31, 1928.

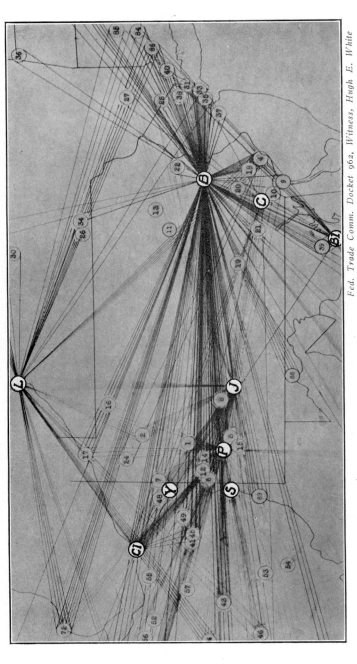

Fed. Trade Comm. Docket 962, Witness, Hugh E. White

FIG. 29. CROSS SHIPMENTS OF STEEL, RADIATING FROM PRODUCING CENTERS. ACTUAL SALES IN 1919, AT P-P PRICES. A CARNIVAL OF WASTE, BETHLEHEM LEADING. SEE ALSO FIG. 27. COMPARE WITH NORMAL ECONOMIC SALES AREAS NECESSARILY RESULTING FROM UNIFORM MILL-BASE PRICES, IN FIGS. 18-24, 30, AND 35

in the cross hauling of steel products. "It is manifestly uneconomic
for a steel manufacturer in Chicago to ship 100,000 tons of steel to
Pittsburgh when a Pittsburgh manufacturer is shipping a like quantity of like material from Pittsburgh to Chicago." Even he pro-
fesses to be shocked by this, although he had contentedly watched
and profited by this economic malpractice for a third of a century.
It certainly does make the captains of industry who invented the
basing-point practice look a bit silly. So he hastens to declare:

the example . . . is an extreme case which, in actual practice, probably seldom occurs, but is illustrative of cross hauling which does occur
in very large quantities from various districts. . . . It is obvious to
every one that there is an economic waste in permitting the cross
hauling to exist and it should be obvious that this waste is paid for
jointly, although perhaps indirectly, by the consumer as well as the
producer of steel products.[7]

WASTE AND WICKEDNESS

Economic waste obvious to every one! This in 1928 from him
who in 1901 declared that he saw no other way. An obvious waste,
yet defended for more than a third of a century by all spokesmen
of the steel industry as an ideal example of the operation of supply
and demand! That Mr. Schwab was not exaggerating but stating
mildly the wastes through cross hauling of which he had so recently become conscious is shown in the accompanying diagram of
actual cross shipments of steel as revealed by a Federal investigation. These spider webs graphically portray every producing center shipping right to the doors of its competitors and beyond, not
truly its competitors in giving a lower price to consumers, for both
are restrained by the mutual tacit agreement of identical delivered
prices—competitors only in wasteful shipments which benefit no
one in the end. This is the insane working of the beautiful basing-
point system which a generation ago the steel leaders adopted as
a mode of restraining trade, abandoning the good old uniform
mill-base market price and all pretense of equality in the treatment
of the buying public.

[7] *Idem.* Mr. Schwab's immediate concern, however, was merely to convert this
waste into corporation receipts, which, by the Bethlehem-Lackawanna merger,
doubtless has been done in large measure.

SHALL WE BE GOOD IF IT PAYS?

Six months later, before the same Institute, Mr. Schwab returned to this theme with some further thoughts on discrimination, gathered perhaps from further academic reading. He depicts as an ideal the one-price policy of a department store, where each is paying

the same price that any other purchaser on the same day will pay . . . We in the steel industry have been charging many prices, often quoting different customers different prices for the same products on the same day. Such a policy has resulted, and will inevitably result, in harming certain of our customers through price discrimination. . . . It is advantageous to consumers and economical to the industry that in the great majority of cases the product should be supplied at a fair price from the nearest available plant. . . . The adoption of the policy of open prices, open to all without preference or discrimination, would be of benefit alike to our industry and to our customers.[8]

It is a far cry from the masquerading monopoly of Pittsburgh-Plus from which, for a third of a century, Mr. Schwab had been profiting, to these frank confessions of the injustice and waste that the basing-point practice has caused. We should more heartily hail Mr. Schwab as a repentant sinner, meet for forgiveness, were it not for the lurking suspicion that he may be merely trying to eat his cake and have it too. Discrimination in prices in the steel industry cannot end until the basing-point practice is abandoned, and that practice has been and is a gold mine to the Bethlehem Steel Company, probably even greater since the merger completed in 1925 of all the great steel plants east of Pittsburgh.

NOT IN OUR LAWS BUT IN OURSELVES

To suspicion of Mr. Schwab's reforming zeal is added astonishment at his innocence, or his artistry, when in the next breath he charges that the anti-trust laws "force" this wasteful and unjust process to go on, and on that ground he pleads for their modification. Here are his words:

Many of us have for a long time been thinking along these lines and yet have felt powerless to remedy the situation. The steel industry is a

[8] See *The Iron Age,* November 1, 1928.

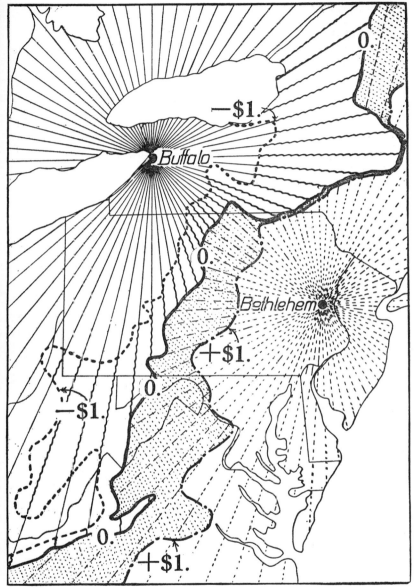

FIG. 30. BETHLEHEM FREIGHT ADVANTAGE OVER BUFFALO (PER TON, + OR —). WITH THE SAME MILL BASE PRICES, BETHLEHEM COULD SELL WESTWARD ONLY TO THE 0 LINE. TO SELL AS FAR AS THE —$1 LINE IT MUST REDUCE ITS BASE PRICE $1

law-abiding industry and the members of it are law-abiding citizens. But surely where laws force uneconomic conditions into existence one may well consider whether the laws should not be changed.[9]

So he announces his intention to move for "such modification of existing law as will enable the factors in the steel industry and possibly in other industries to achieve those economies which are so important"—the ones mentioned before having been cross hauling and discrimination among customers. To one of the great inventors of the basing-point practice, we bring the comfort of economic counsel that he is not required to continue the basing-point practice, indeed that it is in violation of economic as well as of statute law. The only way to be law-abiding is to abide by the law.

THE BASING POINT IN COURT

We ought not take leave here of the basing-point practice without glancing at the sophistical argument by which it has been twice defended before high public tribunals, and which unhappily has been honored by the approval of the Supreme Court. It is peculiarly pertinent to refer to this subject after listening to Mr. Schwab's acceptance of the truth (*et tu, Brute*) that basing-point prices are discriminatory. The Steel Corporation, when before the Federal Trade Commission in the hearings on the Pittsburgh-Plus complaint, stoutly maintained from first to last that these so-called "uniform" delivered prices fulfilled the condition of competitive prices. However, the Commission adopted a different view, presented by economists in last-day hearings (the view now accepted by Mr. Schwab above). Eight months later, however, the U.S. Supreme Court listened in another case to extended arguments on "uniformity" of prices and (by a majority vote) explicitly sanctioned the confusion of uniform mill prices with identical delivered prices.

Justice Stone, in one of several references to "uniformity," said in the majority opinion in the Cement case:

A great volume of testimony was also given by distinguished economists in support of the thesis that, in the case of a standardized product sold wholesale to fully informed professional buyers, as were the dealers

[9] *Idem.*

in cement, uniformity of prices will inevitably result from active, free and unrestrained competition; and the Government in its brief concedes that "undoubtedly the price of cement would approach uniformity in a normal market in the absence of all combinations between the manufacturers." [10]

VOICE OF A MIGHTY HOST—MISUNDERSTOOD

The Court here magnified one professor of Yale University into a mighty and distinguished host, for he is the only economist of any sort who testified on this particular phase of the subject in either the Cement or the Maple Flooring Case.[11] However, he gave impressive weight to his own words by erroneously invoking what he called the "practically unanimous" opinion of seventeen economic authorities, from the time of J. S. Mill to the present. The present writer was included among them—needless to say, much to his disgust when he discovered how his name had been used.

Sad to relate, the witness, expert in matters of taxation, had industriously collected quotations on price theory which he did not understand. His misinterpretation of the "distinguished" dead was enough to make them rise from their graves in protest. The "uniform prices" which the cited authorities agree will result if competition is effective, are market prices at the place of sale; whereas the witness and his lawyer colleagues are discussing and trying to justify *identical delivered prices*, the very antithesis of "uniform" market or mill-base prices. Basing-point delivered prices (as another witness innocently showed) work out as a great variety of discriminatory net prices at the mill. It has been abundantly shown how, under concrete conditions, this identity of delivered prices is proof that bidding has not been free, and that by agreement, express or tacit, sellers are selling on a formula, discriminating grossly among their own customers.[12]

[10] 268 U.S. 605-6.

[11] Professor T. S. Adams' testimony is epitomized in Transcript of Record, Vol. 1, pp. 294-308.

[12] See especially Chs. XII and XXI. Further comment on the uniformity fallacy is given in Appendix B to Ch. XXII.

A MIX-UP OF SIGNALS

In the Maple Flooring Case extensive statistical studies of price were made by a group of teachers in, and graduates of, the Harvard Graduate Business School. But these studies bear little relation to the proposition in question, excepting one elaborate compilation to prove that maple flooring prices were *not* uniform, plainly on the assumption that if they were uniform they were open to the charge of being not competitive but collusive. This All-New England team was confusing the signals, for the one argument heads toward the opposite goal from the other; Yale was trying to prove "uniformity" as a sign of innocence, and Harvard to disprove "uniformity," assuming that it was a sign of guilt. This mix-up on the field escaped the referee's eye. But the statistical witness, though strong on adding-machines, had the queer notion that uniformity of prices meant equality of average realized net prices at each of the 17 different mills, calculated by deducting actual freights from the delivered prices. Under the basing-point plan these net figures inevitably vary from mill to mill and from month to month according to the mere chance of destination of current sales. They are not true f.o.b. mill-base prices at all, as the witness assumes. The argument is a statistical calamity.[13]

Thus endeth, for the present, the lesson on discrimination in general, and on basing-point prices in particular. It is a sad conclusion, with the Supreme Court, misled in simple economic matters, declaring black to be white and white to be black. However, even the high authority of 6 to 3 cannot ultimately make such a muddle of economic thinking into sound law.

[13] See Vol. 2, Transcript of Record, esp. pp. 714-715, and Chart 28 in Vol. 5, p. 969.

———

MONOPOLY IN NAME AND IN FACT

MONOPOLY AS AN ENGLISH WORD

DISCRIMINATION, we have seen, occurs only in connection with monopoly. The special subject of our inquiry is the basing-point practice, and this, being discriminatory, is necessarily also always monopolistic in some measure. Therefore, clear notions of the nature of monopoly and its meaning in economics and in law are essential to sound conclusions on our main inquiry.

Monopoly in name has a history of five centuries in the English language, and defined in its original sense (recently again become usual), monopoly in fact has a history in Anglo-Saxon law of nearly another thousand years. The word monopoly comes from a Greek compound meaning sole-selling.[1] Its first discovered use in English occurred in the period of the renaissance of Greek learning, specifically in 1534, in More's *Treatise on the Passions*. It was used in the original Greek sense: the exclusive control of trade in some article or the exclusive exercise of some craft or business.[2] The word also occurs in the first English translation of Sir Thomas More's *Utopia*, 1551, the original of which had been printed in Latin in 1516. Book I, p. 43, of 1910 reprint: "Suffer not these riche men to bie up al, to ingrosse, and forstalle, and with their monopolie to kepe the market alone as please them."

Again, in 1576, an example occurs in the closely related, perhaps identical sense, of exclusive sale of a commodity by one person. In all the glimpses that we get of the use of the word in its first half century of English use, the word monopoly is applied to a condition originating in the efforts of private citizens and not from a

---

[1] See Appendix A to Ch. XXIII.   [2] See *The Oxford Dictionary*.

sovereign grant (except for the thought that the right to "the exclusive exercise of some craft" might have been derived from a sovereign grant, or from the civic authorities).

ROYAL PATENTS OF EXCLUSIVE SALE

By the mere chance of contemporary English politics, the word was, just before the end of the sixteenth century, to take on the peculiar meaning in Anglo-American law which it was to retain for three centuries, a meaning somewhat out of accord both with etymology and with more general non-legal usage. The English Crown had for centuries exercised the prerogative of issuing patents and franchises granting privileges of various kinds (e.g., charters, markets, etc.) or promising protection to individuals and certain classes, such as foreign artisans. This prerogative was generally used by the sovereigns rather to liberalize trade and to combat local exclusiveness than to create or confirm monopoly, and Elizabeth, following some Continental examples, began to use it ostensibly to encourage the introduction of new arts or their improvement. In the decade 1561-1570, called "the first ten years of the patent policy," grants of such trade privileges rapidly increased (but not yet called monopolies). Gross abuses soon appeared; the patents at first were for terms of ten years, but later were made for twenty or even thirty, often were reissued, and no longer were confined to new arts.[3]

Patents for making necessaries were granted to men not even claiming to be inventors. The fiscal advantages to the treasury were slight, though the Queen in some cases made use of her power quite scandalously to safeguard indirectly her own financial interests. "The frugal queen" bestowed valuable patents upon the servants of her household "in lieu of salaries."[4] It was the importunity of influential and unscrupulous suitors that led to the gravest abuses. The courtiers entered into a race for favors, not to improve the arts, but to secure lucrative exclusive privileges to carry on old industries such as salt, starch, etc. The favored grantees acted in a mercenary and extortionate manner. "In the hands of the corrupt courtiers," says Dr. Price, "the system of

[3] W. H. Price, *English Patents of Monopoly*, p. 8.
[4] *Idem*, pp. 15-16.

monopolies designed originally to foster new acts, became degraded into a system of plunder." [5]

PUBLIC PATENTS CALLED MONOPOLIES

When after thirty years the muttered resentment of the people broke out into open protests, the word "monopoly" began to be used popularly and in parliamentary debates, in 1594, if not earlier.[6] A bill was offered in Parliament in 1597 "touching sundry enormities growing by patents of privilege and monopolies," and the Crown then promised redress of the grievance. The promise was not kept, and a more violent protest by Parliament in 1601 led the Queen to issue a proclamation revoking the more obnoxious patents and leaving to the courts to decide what grants should be allowed to stand under the common law.[7]

The leading Case of Monopolies soon followed, and in 1603, just after the Queen's death, the Court announced its decision that a patent for the sole importing, making, and selling of playing-cards was a dangerous innovation, contrary to the common law. The Court declared that monopoly had three inseparable incidents: prices were raised, commodities deteriorated, and former artisans were impoverished. However, as James I continually neglected, evaded, and violated Elizabeth's proclamation and the decision in the Case of Monopolies, the Statute of Monopolies was enacted in 1624 after violent popular protests and much agitation. This Act reaffirmed the principles of the common law, but with certain inconsistent exceptions confirming numerous existing grants, including all those theretofore made by act of Parliament, and all charters to cities and towns and to trade corporations and craft guilds.[8] However, this act also was violated by the Crown in letter and in spirit. In the Long Parliament of 1640 monopolists were denounced as "a nest of wasps, a swarm of vermin, that have overspread the land. . . . These are the leeches that have sucked the commonwealth so hard that it is almost hectical." Parliament then canceled many patents of monopoly, and never since has this form of monopoly been a great grievance in England.

[5] *Idem*, p. 17.
[6] See examples, *idem*, p. 18.
[7] *Idem*, p. 20-22.
[8] Set forth in detail by Sir Edward Coke in *Institutes*, third part.

In this period from 1597 to 1640, through the leading case and the fundamental statute, a special limited meaning of monopoly became firmly fixed in legal usage. "Monopoly" in the law meant not, as elsewhere, any power or right to be the sole seller, but only such a power acquired by grant of the sovereign, of something formerly of common right. Monopoly in this legal sense was out of accord with the etymology of the word as well as with its general usage before and since outside of the law.

NARROW LEGAL SENSE OF MONOPOLY

A great mass of exclusive privileges and practices had survived from the Middle Ages, many acquired by prescription (use immemorial, later reduced to twenty-one years) and many others by royal and parliamentary grants: ferries, bridges, mills, bake-houses, all excepted from the Statute of Monopolies. All these would in common speech today be called monopolies. Not so in the law until hundreds of years later; there they were described otherwise, as grants, patents, franchises, prescriptive rights, etc. The special legal meaning of monopoly was all too narrow to include many powers of a monopolistic nature acquired by private citizens in various ways other than through grant from the Crown. Buying up and getting control of large quantities of "dead victuals" so as to raise the price was not in legal phrase monopoly but "engrossing." "Forestalling" was another method of attaining monopoly. Nor did the legal term monopoly apply to unified control over prices attained by private agreements, understandings, coöperation, and conspiracy among a number of individuals. Chief Justice White, with no hint of the simple historical explanation, expressed his surprise in 1911 that "It is remarkable that nowhere at common law can there be found a prohibition against the creation of monopoly by an individual." [9] But anything else would be remarkable, for in Hibernian phrase, a monopoly created by an individual was not a monopoly, but the same thing with another name. The inference which Chief Justice White draws from this fictitious marvel is a quite unwarranted glorification of the medieval mind. "This would seem to manifest . . . a profound conception as to the inevitable operation of economic forces," and more in

[9] 221 U.S. 55.

that vein. The simple fact, as shown above, is that the word "monopoly" did not come into use in English until the sixteenth century, and was then almost at once by political chance appropriated to a specialized meaning in English law, that of monopoly created by royal grant. That seems to be all there is to this "instinctive recognition" of economic and legal truths which the learned Chief Justice discovered in this absence from the common law of any prohibition of monopoly.

ABSOLUTE V. SPECIAL RESTRAINTS

And this was the situation (as to the legal usage of words) up to nearly the end of the nineteenth century. But it is erroneous to infer that "monopoly" in its original and broader sense, and as it is now defined even in the law, did not exist in fact and was not under other names prohibited by the law in the period between 1603 and 1890. Far from it. What happened in this regard in that period has been summarized in various fairly recent American decisions, among them the one by Chief Justice White himself in the case just cited. Partly, the words "forestalling" and "engrossing" were used to carry the meaning of the monopolistic power acquired by the efforts of private citizens. Chief Justice White cites a statute of the Province of Massachusetts, 1778-1779, "by which monopoly and forestalling were expressly treated as one and the same thing." [10]

More recently, however, it is the term "restraint of trade" which, first slightly altered from its earlier very different use, at last has been quickly transformed into an almost perfect synonym for monopoly. "At a very remote period the words 'contract in restraint of trade'" meant merely "some voluntary restraint put by contract by an individual on his right to carry on his trade or calling." [11] In the earliest reported case of such a contract the agreement by an artisan not to exercise his trade of dyer for six months in the same town with the plaintiff was declared void, and this was long the doctrine of the common law.[12] Centuries later a notable change came. In 1711 in the leading case of Mitchell v. Reynolds,

---

[10] *Idem*, p. 56; see also, on forestalling, etc., pp. 52-55.
[11] *Idem*, p. 51.
[12] The Dyer's Case, 2 Henry V, 1415.

the facts were that a baker had sold his rights in a bake-house and agreed not to exercise the trade of baker within the parish during five years.[13] The judge made a sharp distinction between "restraints general and restraints particular," the former being void, whereas the latter were permissible if made on proper consideration. In applying this distinction certain fixed rules thereafter "were followed by both English and American courts until within the past few years when a new view was introduced making the validity of the agreement dependent upon the reasonableness of the restraint." [14]

COLLUSIVE RESTRAINT OF "COMMERCE"

This doctrine of restraint for nearly five centuries was confined to cases where, for a consideration, one party in selling out his business agreed not to continue, or to resume, the practice of his own trade (in the sense of a handicraft), whereby he would compete with the buyer. This did not reduce the number of shops in the place, or seemingly in any way tend to restrict output or raise prices above what they were. Notice, too, that in the leading case of Mitchell v. Reynolds the judge concludes with the emphatic statement: "In all restraints of trade, where nothing more appears, the law presumes them bad." Rather suddenly in the nineteenth century, this doctrine of limited (or particular) restraint was extended to cases of agreements regarding prices, etc., between two competitors, both of whom continue in business. Thus "restraint of trade" takes on a new meaning really better expressed as "restraint of commerce," which is used synonymously. In various American State cases, beginning in 1847, the meaning of the term was thus extended and agreements as to prices were held to be general and void.[15] In the first case, of date 1847, the words "contract in restraint of trade" do not occur, but the conspiracy was said to be "injurious to trade or commerce." This seems to have been the entering wedge for the use of the expression "restraint of

---

[13] In Williams, *Cases in Chancery*, p. 181.

[14] *Cyclopedia of Law and Procedure*, Vol. 9, p. 525 (1903), citing cases of date 1892 on.

[15] Hooker v. Hardewater, 4 Denio (N. Y.) 349 (1847); Stanton v. Allen, 5 Denio 434 (1848); Morris Run Coal Company, etc., 68 Pa. 173 (1871); Craft v. McConoughy, 79 Ill. 349 (1875); Central Ohio Salt Company, etc., 35 Ohio 666 (1880).

trade" in the new sense of "restraint of *commerce*" by agreements among competitors affecting prices. This change is a much more important one, in the economic view, and in relation to monopoly, than the gradual widening of the distinction between general and particular restraint upon a man's own trade in which alone the courts seemed until very lately to be interested. That the phrase "restraint of trade" thus became ambiguous (trade *or* commerce) seems not to have attracted the attention of the courts. This movement to utilize the old prohibition of "restraint of trade" in its peculiar restricted sense, as a legal device against monopoly in commerce resulting from private agreements, strikingly coincides with the contemporary changes in economic conditions through the growth of canals, railroads, mass production, and local monopoly power, which became marked toward the middle of the nineteenth century, as described in Ch. XVIII. Thus to convert "restraint of trade" into restraint of commerce and this into monopoly was like improvising a jury mast and sail out of a fishing-pole and an old shirt, or like fashioning for fast-growing little Willie an overcoat out of Dad's one-piece bathing-suit.

MONOPOLY BY PRIVATE ACTS

How swiftly the last stage of this change was traversed would hardly be inferred from the language of the recent decisions, supported as they are by few specific citations. Chief Justice White, to be sure, declared that in the 1711 case "a classification is made of monopoly which brings it generally within the description of restraint of trade." [16]

But for nearly two centuries thereafter monopoly still continued to be formally defined in the law as a royal grant; and search has failed to discover any clean-cut example of the adoption before 1889 by the higher American State courts of what may fairly be called the economic definition, that is, monopoly as a degree of special non-competitive control over prices, whether resulting from a public franchise or from private efforts and agreements.

The word monopoly in its broad sense was then on every tongue in popular discussion. In the case of the North River Sugar Refin-

---

[16] 221 U.S. 54. Further comment on the language used in Mitchell v. Reynolds (1711) is given in Appendix B to Ch. XXIII.

ing Company a trust association formed for the purpose of controlling the whole industry, the New York Court said that:

The board under this executed deed . . . can come as near to creating an absolute monopoly as is possible under the social, political and economic conditions of today.

Speaking in a most enlightened and progressive spirit, the Court added:

Any combination, the tendency of which is to prevent competition in its broad and general sense and to control and thus at will enhance prices to the detriment of the public, is a legal monopoly.[17]

and commented further on "the unlawful purpose" of "every monopoly." Evidently "legal" here meant "in a legal sense," rather than either lawful or created by a legal grant.

The phrasing seems to suggest that, as under present political conditions, an absolute· monopoly in the old sense of a royal grant is quite impossible, here is something so near in its practical effects that it may now by "legal" definition be declared to be monopoly. In another State the same year the Court declared:

All combinations among persons or corporations for the purpose of raising or controlling the prices of merchandise . . . are monopolies, and intolerable, and ought to receive the condemnation of the Courts.[18]

WHAT DID THE 1890 STATUTE ADD?

Did the famous Anti-Trust Act, enacted the next year, go essentially beyond the judicial opinions of State courts just cited? It is often declared that the Anti-Trust Act, while reaffirming the common law against restraint of trade, went further in making such contracts explicitly unlawful, whereas by common law they were merely void and unenforceable in civil suits. No doubt this is true of restraints of trade in the original sense, involving mainly private interests. But is it true of restraints of commerce, where the rights affected are almost wholly those of third parties, those of the general public? Even in 1711 Judge Parker declared that "a monopoly . . . is a crime." Before 1890 at least two highest State

[17] 54 Hun (N.Y.) 354, 376, 377 (1889).
[18] Richardson v. Buhl, 77 Mich. 658 (1889).

courts had already redefined monopoly so as to include private control of prices, had stigmatized it as "unlawful," "intolerable," and a "detriment to the public," and had declared its condemnation to be the duty of the courts. If these propositions had been affirmed by the Federal Supreme Court, would not a new chapter in the American common law of monopoly and "restraint of trade" have been written? If Chief Justice White's assertion in the Standard Oil Case [19] is correct, that the Act contained "no direct prohibition of monopoly in the concrete," then in this one important respect the Act stopped short even of the prior judicial condemnation of monopoly.

Chief Justice White, with his dangerous gift of casuistry, inferred from the prohibition in the Act of all "unlawful contracts having a monopolistic tendency" that this "indicates a consciousness" [presumably in the mind of Congress] that the freedom of the individual right to contract, . . . was the most efficient means for the prevention of monopoly." Thus arguing from the fact that the Act prohibited the making of certain kinds of contracts, the subtle Chief Justice half circumnavigates the globe of reason and arrives at the opposite pole: that the purpose of Congress in prohibiting certain kinds of contracts was to preserve and enlarge "the freedom of the individual right to contract." Strange that the same ingenious mind was unable to detect a "prohibition against monopoly in the concrete" in Section 2, which makes it a misdemeanor either to "monopolize, or attempt to monopolize"; or even in Section 1, which declares "every contract . . . in restraint of trade . . . to be illegal"; for the Chief Justice had just finished saying [20] that the two terms, "restraint of trade" and "monopoly," were now properly used in the law as synonyms. Yet he says that the statute contains "no direct prohibition against monopoly in the concrete," whatever that may mean!

[19] 221 U.S 62.   [20] *Idem*, p. 57.

THE SUPREME COURT SEES PRIVATE MONOPOLY

In 1905 the Supreme Court said:

The idea of monopoly is not now confined to a grant of privilege. It is understood to include a condition produced by the acts of mere individuals.[21]

In the Standard Oil Case in 1911, Chief Justice White after a learned historical survey concluded by recognizing the identity of monopoly (in the newer legal sense) and restraint of trade (in the newer sense), two terms and ideas long kept punctiliously distinct by lawyers and judges.

Acts which although they did not constitute a monopoly were thought to produce some of its baneful effects, so also because of the impediment or burden to the due course of trade which they produced . . . came to be referred to as in restraint of trade.[22]

And again he said:

Monopoly and the acts which produce the same result as monopoly, that is, an undue restraint of the course of trade, all came to be spoken of as, and to be indeed synonymous with, restraint of trade.[23]

Thus by a long process of gradual adaptation, two English terms which, three and five centuries ago, respectively, began their legal history, with quite different meanings, came at last, rather swiftly, to be accepted as nearly or quite synonymous in American law. By this devious route the legal definition of monopoly was at last brought into accord both with its etymology and with its general use by the public and in economic discussion.

PRIVATE MONOPOLY ALWAYS RELATIVE

It all appeared simple at this point, but if this had been all there was to it, the judicial history of the efforts to control monopoly would have been very different from what it has been in the past forty years. The human mind, and preëminently the legal mind with its strongest habit the regard for precedent, finds it difficult,

---

[21] National Cotton Oil Company v. Texas, 197 U.S. 129. Justice McKenna did not give the source of his authority for this new definition.
[22] 221 U.S. 54.
[23] *Idem,* p. 61.

even after giving formal assent to new definitions, to quit thinking in terms of the old ones. The law books and libraries were bursting with cases of verbal usage shifting through the centuries, but those before the years 1850 to 1889 all conflicting with the recently authorized conceptions. When the eighteenth-century doctrine of limited restraint had become modified to that of reasonable restraint, and then in the nineteenth century the conception of restraint of trade was altered to that of restraint of commerce, and finally that was merged into the concept of monopoly, there was carried into the thought of monopoly with disastrous results the fuzzy notion that private, unregulated monopoly might be "reasonable," or vary in degrees of reasonableness. It was for the Court in its wisdom to decide, "in the light of reason."

Likewise the older legal conception of monopoly as a public franchise cast a baleful shadow over the newer economic conception of private monopoly. For it was the essence of the old political definition that the grant, and therefore the monopoly, was absolute and exclusive; whereas, private monopoly (i.e. monopoly attained by the action of private persons) is never either absolute or wholly exclusive.[24] While public and private monopolies are alike in the essential nature of their control over prices, they differ as to the source of their power and in the degree and extent of their control. The use of the two conceptions develops and requires different habits of thought. A political monopoly is *"a"* monopoly —it either is or it isn't—that is the main question it presents to a court. A private monopoly is never *"a"* monopoly, but merely a person, business, or corporation which through various means has come to have some degree of monopolistic power (or it is the limited power in the hands of such persons or corporations). The one concept of monopoly is absolute in degree even when limited in space; the other is relative in a variety of ways, grading down to the least appreciable amount.

[24] "Absolute" relates to the conditions in general connected with monopoly, such as entire national territory, unlimited duration of time, sale of all varieties and patterns of goods, etc., and "exclusive" relates to persons (the fact that no one else may engage in that trade). Exclusive, therefore, is but one aspect of absolute; and its opposite inclusive is but one aspect of limited.

EXCLUSIVE AS STATE OR AS ACTION

The legal mind was thoroughly habituated to the older view, and naturally this idea of exclusiveness (completeness) has continued since 1890 to intrude itself into many judicial cases as a quality of monopoly. But two meanings of exclusion (and exclusive) were confused. In the one, exclusion refers to merely *being* (the sole seller); in the other, to *action* or *behavior* (efforts to exclude others and thus become or remain the sole seller). In some legal cases the emphasis is clearly on the *being* exclusive, on the fact that the business in question *is* in a sole control.[25] This thought is slightly qualified to make exclusive (sole) control include cases where "practically" or "substantially," or "nearly" all of a trade or business is under one control.[26]

In other statements there is a shift of emphasis to the action of exclusion of others from a business, from which purpose or intent could be inferred as the means by which sole control is attained. Such a false definition is this: "It is the exclusion of others from the opportunity of doing business that is regarded as monopolizing."[27] The attitude of the Court has been thus paraphrased: "Absorbing every formidable competitor . . . could not show an intent to monopolize, unless such a policy were accompanied by practices designed to keep out new rivals."[28] Other cases are cited in Appendix C to Ch. XXIII.

Another phrasing of the definition brings exclusion in twice, in two different senses: the exclusive control of trade or business *plus* exclusion or attempts to exclude others.[29]

OIL CASE V. STEEL CASE "EXCLUSION"

The cases cited in the notes are but typical of many others to be found in the court reports. The Supreme Court in the Standard Oil case was unmistakably attaching importance to the idea of

[25] Examples are: C. & O. Fuel Company v. U.S., 115 Fed. 624 (1902); State v. Central Lumber Company, 24 S.D. 152 (1909).
[26] Harriman v. Menzies, 115 Cal. 20 (1896); Burrows v. I. M. Company, 156 Fed. 389 (1907); Pereles v. Weil, 157 Fed. 419 (1907).
[27] National Biscuit Case, 299 Fed. 738 (1924).
[28] *Mergers and the Law*, p. 64, commenting on U.S. v. Keystone Watch Company, 218 Fed. Rep. 502 (1915).
[29] *In re* Greene, 52 Fed. 104 (1892); Trans-Missouri Freight Case, 58 Fed. 58 (1893).

"exclusion" in both senses, but it seems to have given much less attention (and weight) to the established fact that the company controlled between 85 and 90 per cent of the refinery business (exclusive in the sense of nearly the sole ownership, the state, being, or condition) than it did to the "intent and purpose to exclude others which was frequently manifested by [its] acts and dealings" (i.e. behavior).[30] This was quite in accord with the trend of popular interest at that time, which was focused upon the practices then commonly used by dominant corporations to crush their competitors. Evidence of these practices were superabundant in the Oil case. But when this same criterion of exclusiveness was applied by the Court a few years later in the Steel suit, this choice foreordained a very different outcome. For here (as to behavior) the evidence pointed rather to the *inclusion* of competitors in a policy of live-and-let-live, which the court failed to recognize as *collusion* with them. As to state of ownership, the Steel Corporation had but 50 per cent of the national total productive capacity and, although it had grown greatly, its percentage of the total had not increased. The economic fallacies in the reasoning of the Court in this matter appear more clearly against the background of this understanding of the monopoly concept held by the Court.[31]

The Steel decision left upon the minds of the gild of corporation lawyers a strong impression that 50 per cent control was somehow the safe limit; they could "get by" with that much in the Supreme Court in merger projects; a weak idea as economics, but a very sensible working rule for the lawyers, no doubt, for the simple reason that it worked.

COMPETITION, MONOPOLY, AND NONSENSE

Whenever a word has come to have various shades of meaning in the law, it is certain that some judge will sometime go to the limit of verbalistic folly and propound a definition that is mere sound without sense. Circuit Judge H. E. Jackson made a bid for the prize when, in 1892,[32] amid confusing thoughts as to monopoly

[30] 221 U.S. 76.
[31] See above, Ch. VIII.
[32] *In re* Greene, 52 Fed. 104. Judge Jackson was commissioned as a Justice

and acts of exclusion, he declared: "All persons . . . carrying on business enterprises . . . will, in a popular sense, monopolize . . . just in proportion as the owner's business is increased, enlarged, and developed." We sincerely question whether this "popular sense" of the word was not a mere invention of the judge himself, for it is a slander on "common sense" which we have never been able to find outside of judicial opinions. The notion served Judge Jackson as a straw man to belabor, but it was to reappear more seriously in later opinions.

The doubtful honor of perpetrating the real *reductio ad absurdum* of this notion of exclusion as the distinctive mark of monopoly seems to belong to Judge Walter H. Sanborn of the Eighth Circuit, shared with his two colleagues concurring in a decision in 1903. It is incredible, but here it is:

> Every sale and every transportation of an article which is the subject of interstate commerce is a successful attempt to monopolize that part of this commerce which concerns that sale or transaction. An attempt by each competitor to monopolize a part of interstate commerce is the very root of all competition therein. Eradicate it, and competition necessarily ceases—dies. Every person engaged in interstate commerce necessarily attempts to draw to himself, and to exclude others from, a part of that trade; and, if he may not do this, he may not compete with his rivals, . . . [33]

By exclusion this judge plainly meant not the act of a person in excluding other persons from trade in a certain class of commodities, but rather that every seller, even in the most competitive market, excludes some one else from selling the unit that he himself sells, and *therefore* is a monopolist. Thus by this wordy legerdemain, every competitive sale becomes monopoly, and monopoly becomes indistinguishable from just plain competition. When white is called black and competition is called monopoly, then follows the sage conclusion that the eradication of monopoly necessarily ends competition. Observe that this is not now said to be the "popular sense" of the word, but is the sense or nonsense of

of the Supreme Court February 18, 1893, and served until his death, August 8, 1895.

[33] Whitwell v. Continental Tobacco Company, 125 Fed. 462 (1903).

three Circuit Judges. In such elementary errors as this germinated the "rule of reason."

A WISE JUDICIAL PROTEST

This case never reached the Supreme Court, but the inventor of this notion was so pleased with it that in the much more important Oil Case (which did come on appeal to the Supreme Court) he reiterated it in slightly different phraseology.

Undoubtedly every person engaged in interstate commerce necessarily attempts to draw to himself, to the exclusion of others, and thereby to monopolize, a part of that trade. Every sale and every transportation of an article which is the subject of interstate commerce evidences a successful attempt to monopolize that trade or commerce which concerns that sale or transportation. If the second section of the act prohibits every attempt to monopolize any part of interstate commerce, it forbids all competition therein, and defeats the only purpose of the law; for there can be no competition, unless each competitor is permitted to attempt to draw to himself, and thereby to monopolize, some part of the commerce.[34]

Two other judges concurred with Judge Sanborn without comment, but the third, Judge William C. Hook, to his credit filed this sane and sensible protest:

What is monopoly in contravention of the statute? I would not say that every person who strives to gain as much as he can of the commerce in a commodity is thereby attempting to monopolize that commerce, within the meaning of the term as it is employed in legislative acts and understood in the courts. . . . Success and magnitude in business, the rewards of fair and honorable endeavor, were not among the evils which threatened the public welfare and attracted the attention of Congress. But when they have been attained by wrongful or unlawful methods, and competition has been crippled or destroyed, the elements of monopoly are present.[35]

[34] 173 Fed. 291 (November 1909), decision in the Circuit Court in the Standard Oil Case. In the Tobacco Case, Judge Ward based his dissenting opinion in the Circuit Court on the same grotesque notion of competition: "As this section prohibits a monopoly of or an attempt to monopolize any part of such commerce, it cannot be literally construed. So applied, the act would prohibit commerce altogether." (164 Fed. 727.)

[35] *Idem.*, pp. 195-196.

Here again we breathe the air of clear thinking. So far from being the same, competition and monopoly are mutually exclusive: monopoly is not present unless competition is in some degree limited and to just that degree.[36]

THE COURTS ADRIFT

The Supreme Court, so far as we have found, has never in a clean-cut way consistently applied the new meaning of monopoly (sanctioned by the Court itself), and expressly abandoned the old idea of exclusiveness. The newer conception of monopoly is essentially economic; it is such a degree of control over supply that within limits (of various kinds, as to location, time, kinds of goods, etc.) prices can profitably be raised by the controlling group above the competitive market norm. The nearest to such a definition in a Supreme Court case seems to be "unified tactics with regard to prices." [37]

With a veritable glut of definitions of monopoly in the law, the courts have not yet come to complete agreement upon any one. Nor can they, until they recognize economic facts and economic opinion. Without a clear economic conception of monopoly and with no clear distinction between it and the older confused legal conceptions, the courts are impotent to detect and prevent the multitude of limited, territorial, as well as national and flagrant operations, of private monopoly in America.

[36] Justice Holmes' passing reference to the notion is given in Appendix D to Ch. XXIII.

[37] Quoted, without giving the source, in the National Cotton Oil Case, 197 U.S. 115, 129 (1905). Other cases in which this idea is expressed (besides the two of date 1889 cited above) are the following: American Tobacco, 164 Fed. 700, 721 (1908); Conley v. Daughters, etc. (Texas), 151 S.W. 877, 833 (1912); Commonwealth v. Dyer, 243 Mass. 472, 486 (1922).

PART VI

MARKETS——RESTRAINED AND LIBERATED

—————

CHAPTER XXIV

MERGERS MULTIPLY IN JUDICIAL SUNSHINE

WAYS TO MONOPOLY

PRIVATE monopoly power may be attained and exercised in one of four ways: by growth and extension of a single enterprise without resort either to the destruction or to the acquisition of competitors; by cutthroat competition; by collusion (agreements) with competitors; by consolidation of separate concerns either by merger or by acquisition. In all these cases patents and special public favors may, however, be contributory causes.

Monopoly attained by natural growth has been rare except in cases of specialized products with quite limited monopoly power, probably assisted and favored by other conditions. The methods of cutthroat competition are best illustrated in the records of the Standard Oil Case. In the period from 1870 to 1900 both cutthroat competition and collusion (through pools and agreements) were employed quite openly and successfully. The increasing force of public protests and fear of public prosecution led in the later '90's to the pretty general abandonment of cutthroat competition except in emergencies and as a threat.

Open agreements and illegal pools as tools of collusion were replaced by the subtler methods of basing-point pricing, abetted both by trade associations and by complete proprietary merger. To a further discussion of the latter mode of attaining monopoly we now turn.

LOCAL LIMITS TO MASS PRODUCTION

In discussing mergers, three terms and ideas need to be carefully distinguished: mass production, integration, and merger itself (consolidation). Mass production means the turning out of great quantities of goods of a certain kind under a single working organization connected with one establishment. It is almost wholly a technological fact (mechanical, chemical, etc., together with the technique of commercial—not financial—operations). The economies of large production embrace nearly all the advantages of "division of labor" and of "specialization" of occupations discussed at length in the economic texts ever since the days of Adam Smith. Mass production combines two ideas, one qualitative, the other quantitative: (1) specialization by plants, and (2) output of one sort of goods on a large scale.

The popular belief is that mass production in single plants has been steadily and on the whole enormously increasing ever since the days when the small handwork shop was the typical mechanical industry (say until 1850). This belief is not fully confirmed by the figures in more than a few industries. The statistics greatly moderate and qualify the popular view that there is a universal drift toward well-nigh unlimited mass production. The statistics indicate rather that relativity and the golden mean will determine the normal and final distribution of industrial plants over our vast national territory.[1]

PROGRESS AWAY FROM INTEGRATION

Integration is the grouping and uniting of successive processes in the production of goods from the raw materials to the finished products. This, too, is a relative term, including under various conditions few or many stages. Now there are two sorts of grouping and uniting that have been called integration; the one, true integration, is technological, within a factory—the completion of all the processes within a single plant (or localized group in physical connection), this being the opposite of plant specialization. This arrangement yields certain economies of a nature quite different from those due to division of labor between men, trades, and factories, its chief effect being through continuity of process, saving of fuel (as in metallurgy), etc. The other mode of uniting factories is proprietary, bringing under a single ownership several distinct plants (usually far apart) in successive stages in the production of

[1] See Appendix A to Ch. XXIV.

goods. This is also, and more properly, called vertical merger, and will be further discussed with mergers, below.

Technical integration might be greatly increased if (for example) a factory cut its own timber (as was done at one time), and began to make its own nails, screws, metal fittings, glue, paints, etc.; yet if the total final production of the factory is to be undiminished, the factory would have to be greatly enlarged, while the mass, or scale, on which each of these accessory materials was produced would be diminished. Those who assume that increasing technical integration is always in line with a natural evolutionary trend of industry toward greater efficiency are blind to the fact that progress in efficiency since the machine age began has been largely through plant specialization (up to the most economic point). This means less, not greater, technical integration. Wool was once cut from the sheep's back and made into clothing on the same farm. Each village smith integrated many stages of production and made final products which now are scattered among a thousand highly equipped factories. The modern steel blast furnaces or rolling mills are far less integrated industries than their predecessors of a century ago, as any one will realize who visits the old iron works of eastern Pennsylvania where guns were made for Washington's army. There, in a little space, was performed every stage in the process of iron manufacture from coal and iron ore to fabricated final product. "Progress" in economy and efficiency by mass production has been chiefly secured not by more technical integration of all the parts and accessories in the same plant but by less. In some industries this has come to the point where the factory for the final product is little more than an assembling plant, a thing inconceivable in colonial industry. Here and there, however, as certain factories reach great size, with enormous mass production, it may become advantageous even today to retrace this process and reintegrate some of the abandoned processes—but certainly not often.

THE STEEL CORPORATION'S FAIRY TALE

This confusion between technological integration and merger (that hypnotic illustration of the molten pig iron!) did much to win the dissolution suit for the Steel Corporation. Four members of the Court, convinced that thither led the path of economic progress, forbade that path to be blocked to the "evolution" of industry. Twenty-six years of experience have thrown much light upon this judicial illusion.

It thus appears that the formation of the United States Steel Corporation was not really responsible for the integration of the industry. . . . The formation of the Corporation involved rather a combination of integrations. . . . That economic integration was not greatly furthered by the consolidation of these groups of interests is manifest. They were geographically so far separated that neither in the transporting of ore, the transforming of raw materials into pig, the converting of pig into steel, nor in the manufacture of the steel into finished forms could any considerable further economies have been anticipated from joint ownership.[2]

The same holds true in respect to every considerable enlargement of plant ownership by the U.S. Steel Corporation since its formation. Some increase occurred by purchase, as the much-discussed Tennessee Coal and Iron case in 1907, and the most recent acquisition (effective February 1, 1930) of the Columbia Steel Corporation on the Pacific coast—itself a merger in 1922, increased by several subsequent acquisitions, so that it was already a formidable combination of coal, ore properties, blast furnaces, and fabricating mills. Again, in January 1930, the enormous cement properties of the Atlas Company were added to the already powerful group of cement mills within the Steel Corporation. Other stupendous additions were by new construction, as at Duluth and at Gary. But in these accretions, one and all, not technological integration and operating economics, but the duplication, in new territory, of the type of plants and processes already possessed elsewhere has been the outstanding purpose and result in the field of physical operations.

INFLATED CLAIMS FOR PSEUDO-INTEGRATION

Consider in this connection the contention of independent producers in the Steel suit that despite their small (financial) size as corporations they were fully integrated in their producing proc-

---

[2] Myron W. Watkins, in *Industrial Combinations and Public Policy* (1927), pp. 117 ff. The author appears to be using the term integration mainly in the technological sense; see his note, p. 118.

esses, and were as efficient (technologically) as the Corporation itself. The judicial conflicts of opinion involved in accepting both this (probably correct) testimony and the contradictory claim that the formation of the Corporation was a necessity (or at least a "facility") to technical progress may well be recalled at this point.[3]

In truth, "integration" as pictured by Mr. Schwab, which seems to have hypnotized both bankers and judges, was not integration at all, but extreme specialization, involving mass production at each mill, which would devote itself exclusively to one stage of process and one kind of product—all rails, all plates, all cars, etc. This would not involve necessarily any advance whatever in real integration—indeed, the very opposite is strongly suggested. According to this uneconomic conception of extreme mass production, one mill of each kind was to produce for a market area embracing the whole nation, in defiance of freights.[4] Though Mr. Schwab's proposal was merely a romance, it served its financial purpose, and twenty years later it still had plausibility enough to deceive four members of the Supreme Court.

An interesting comment on this idea has recently been made by a writer on practical business problems, one of whose claims to fame is that he is co-author with Henry Ford of *My Life and Work*. On the question of the advantages of integration he says:

The moment that we attained a practical interchangeability (of parts) the reason for the large factory vanished in all those industries where the finished product was only an assembly of parts, for then those parts could more cheaply be assembled at the point where the product was to be used than at the factory, for the parts did not take up as much shipping space as the finished products. . . .[5]

Thus fade most of the claims for the magic technical economies of integration in the single establishment. We shall consider later the reputed marvels of vertical merger.

---

[3] See Ch. VII.

[4] See above, Ch. VII. Compare Bureau of Corporations, 1911, cited by Watkins, *Industrial Combinations*, p. 118.

[5] Samuel Crowther, in *Annals of the American Academy*, May 1930, pp. 22-27, on "The Future of the Small Corporation."

TYPES OF MERGERS

Consolidation is a broad term which includes the proprietary union of formerly independent enterprises either by merger into a new corporation or by acquisition of smaller corporations by a larger one. Generally, consolidation and merger are used as synonymous, the difference in the methods of merger and of acquisition not being clearly made, or perhaps not significant to such an economic inquiry as our present one. Mergers are (1) horizontal, when uniting under one ownership like plants, with like products and processes, and (2) vertical ("proprietary"), when uniting under one ownership different stages of the productive process from the raw materials to the finished product. Of late, a third type, the "circular" merger, is recognized, which unites the production and sale of two or more products rather supplementing than directly competing with each other; e.g., a general foods company. We are concerned here only with mergers in the manufacturing and mining industries, and incidentally in merchandising, not with the merger of banks, railroads, and public utilities—equally important problems.

No doubt mergers in manufacturing began actively before 1865, and they increased rapidly thereafter. The purpose of the Sherman Anti-Trust Act in 1890 was surely to prevent this as well as other modes of attaining monopoly. Yet since that date most of the great combinations possessed of monopolistic power have been formed, and monopolistic practices favored by merger have been enormously extended.

PERIODS OF MERGERS

The forty years from 1890 to 1930 appear to fall into the following four periods, which may be briefly characterized as follows:

1. 1890 to 1894, moderate activity in the formation of "trusts."

2. 1895 to 1904, greatest epoch of merger formation to date: increasing, 1895-1898; enormous, 1899-1902; moderating, 1903-1904. The total capitalization of the corporations merged was approximately 5 billion dollars.

3. 1905 to 1918, merger movement quiescent. Increasing activity, however, 1915-1918.

4. 1919 to 1928 (limit of data). Second great period of merger formation. Renewed activity, rising steadily to great heights in the six years 1923-1928; a process of "mopping up" in which, in general, neither the constituent units nor the resulting consolidations were so large as in the movement terminating in 1904, but involving many other industries and combining important competitors of special products in large neighborhoods and sales areas.

The years of most active "trust" formation were 1895-1904

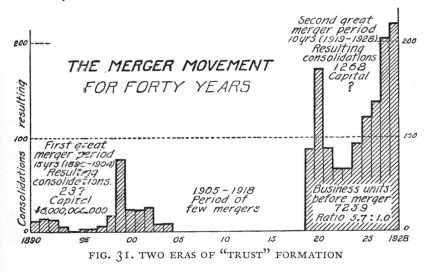

FIG. 31. TWO ERAS OF "TRUST" FORMATION

and 1919-1930, with a comparatively quiet interval in 1905-1918.

Certain data for the two chief merger periods are charted in the accompanying figures.[6] In the earlier period of fifteen years there were 237 resulting consolidations and in the later period of ten years 1268, an average of 16 a year in the earlier, and of 127 a year in the later, period. In the process many thousands of originally independent establishments disappeared, narrowing in all directions the field of competition and enlarging the domain of monopoly. In the earlier period the average capitalization involved was about $25,000,000. If in the last period it were only one-fifth

---

[6] Other data are not exactly comparable, as the number of original units are not at hand for the earlier period, or the capitalization for the latter. See Willard L. Thorp, in *Recent Economic Changes*, pp. 167-218, and M. W. Watkins, *Industrial Combinations*, Appendix, pp. 317-324.

as great (probably an underestimate), the total involved in the last period would exceed that in the earlier (about 6 billion dollars).

Throughout these forty years, merger activity, while correlated somewhat with business prosperity, was also in a large degree a reflection of the shifting attitude of the courts (or what the bar and business thought was their attitude) in the interpretation of the Anti-Trust Act, together with the efforts and success of the Department of Justice in enforcing it.

VACILLATION OF THE COURTS

The Knight decision in the Supreme Court,[7] foreshadowed by several adverse decisions (especially that on the whisky trust) paralyzed, in the Federal trial courts, the law as a check on consolidations, until 1904. The period 1896-1904 was an open season for mergers. Then in 1905 the Northern Securities decision,[8] adverse to a holding company as a device for consolidating railroads, put new life into the Act, and temporarily the fear of God and man into the monopolists. For if the Act were held to forbid mergers in transportation, *a fortiori*, it forbade them in industry.[9] The merger movement was halted, and apparently a more vigorous attempt was made by the Department of Justice to see whether those combinations formed before 1905 could be reached by the law and dissolved. Although the decisions in the Oil and Tobacco Cases in 1911 dissolved two of the greatest of existing combines, they gave no clear guidance for the future, but with their rule of reason left every one guessing. At the time this was generally taken to be a calming assurance to the jumpy nerves of "big business" that nothing rash would be done in unscrambling the other industrial omelettes.

A CALM BEFORE THE STORM

In 1914, Ex-President Taft, who had gone down in defeat in 1912 with a policy of the Sherman Act and nothing more, was probably almost alone in his still cheerful belief:

[7] 156 U.S. 1, January 21, 1895.
[8] 197 U.S. 244, March 6, 1905.
[9] The decisions in 1897 and 1898 in the Trans-Missouri Freight and Joint Traffic Association cases had no such effect, for although they were a well-meant attempt of the Court to undo in part the mischief of the Knight decision, these cases related only to agreements and not to property merger.

The terms of the statute have been given a scope which leaves little doubt that every other one of these octopuses, as its organization and methods are disclosed and analyzed, will be subjected to the heavy hand of the law.

The hand remained uplifted, but never fell again. However, Mr. Taft described the facts more accurately when he said:

The effect of this series of decisions to prevent new organizations of this kind is already manifest. New combinations of large capital are few in number, and when projected they are made with the greatest circumspection to avoid breach of the law.[10]

"Circumspection" was the right word. Stop, look and listen, but cross the track whenever there is no danger that the cowcatcher will catch you.

The same year a broadly experienced student of the subject disagreed with Mr. Taft's view that the old trusts would be broken up, but confirmed his opinion that the closed season for mergers had arrived.

Difficult as it may be to break up trusts already formed and firmly knit together, there seems no serious difficulty in preventing by law the formation of new trusts. Indeed, it is noteworthy that since the government began somewhat actively to bring proceedings under the Sherman anti-trust act, almost no trusts have been organized.[11]

This in 1914. Within a year the Circuit Court had given its vindication to the Steel Corporation.[12] Several other cases between 1912 and 1918 showed that to secure dissolution the prosecution would have to assume a practically impossible burden of proof. By its decision in the Steel Dissolution suit in 1920, the Supreme Court took off the lid, and out came pouring a swarm of mergers to settle upon the land. The Department of Justice had weakly permitted the Court to drift into opinions which left the legal arm of the government powerless, even if it wished, to prevent new mergers or to dissolve old ones.

[10] *The Anti-Trust Act and the Supreme Court,* by William Howard Taft, Kent Professor of Law, 1914, p. 130.

[11] *The Trust Problem,* by E. D. Durand, p. 39. Lectures originally printed in the *Quarterly Journal of Economics,* 1914. The author had been secretary of the National Industrial Commission, 1899-1901, and later deputy commissioner of the Bureau of Corporations.

[12] 223 Fed. 161, 1915.

SHAPING THE WEDGE TO SPLIT

The two trust dissolution suits of 1911 were so complicated with considerations of unfair practices and violent exclusion of competitors that they formed no precedent against merger in conditions lacking these peculiar elements in the same shocking degree. Then, too, the decision darkened the murky air with "the light of reason." The work of a Federal trial judge became an extra-hazardous occupation. No wonder that one of them lamented the next year in a consolidation case:

There is such a chaos of decisions in reference to the Sherman Anti-Trust Act, and such a chaos of understanding or misunderstanding with reference thereto, . . . that any conclusions a single judge may reach may prove of very little importance . . . The practical application of this branch of the law is very uncertain . . . The history of the law as shown . . . also in the Standard Oil case is in a continuous state of development, and will so remain for an indefinite period.[13]

The harassed Judge made a lucky guess, however, for the next year his decision in the Winslow Case was affirmed by a unanimous Supreme Court. The Winslow Case [14] seems to have been the thin edge of the wedge which, within a few years, was, in the judgment of many, to split the Anti-Trust statute in two. It was to continue to prohibit agreements among independents, while ceasing in fact to prevent attainment of monopoly by the merger of formerly competing independent units into a single corporation.

SEVERITY TOWARD INDEPENDENTS

Let us look at what happened between 1912 and 1927 (chiefly between 1915 and 1920) as seen through the eyes of several economic and legal students.[15] A survey of the cases shows that where

---

[13] Judge Putnam, in U.S. v. Winslow, 195 Fed. 578 (March 1912); affirmed in 227 U.S. 202 (February 1913).

[14] Involving some peculiar and interesting conditions, discussed further in Appendix B to Ch. XXIV.

[15] Pertinent references to cases and discussions will be found in the following: M. W. Watkins, *Industrial Combinations* (1927), esp. pp. 233-273; same, *Quarterly Journal Economics*, pp. 30 ff.; *Mergers and the Law* (1929), esp. pp. 40-43, 44, 82; Keezer and May, *The Public Control of Business* (1930), pp. 42-57; Prof. E. P. Schmidt, "The Changing Economics of the Supreme Court," in *Annals of the American Academy* (January 1930), pp. 61-66.

unity of action regarding price is attained by a price-fixing agreement among competitors (as in the Trenton Potteries Case, 1927), it "is not to be judged by the reasonableness of the terms agreed upon in view of the situation of the parties and of the effect upon the public, but is illegal as such." [16]

If a group of independent competitors admit having or are proved to have, engaged in any activity impairing full and free competition, the courts will not consider extenuating circumstances, or examine the actual effects of their coöperation. The courts here assume, by logical processes, that certain tendencies must invariably follow from the concerted action.[17]

Competing firms, however small, have been restrained from acting in concert to accomplish ends which are attained with perfect legality by large consolidations.[18]

LENIENCY TOWARD COMPLETE MERGER

We come here upon a fact curious as matter of law and grave in its economic implications. The reluctance of the Federal courts from the first to construe the prohibition of "every combination in restraint of trade or commerce" so as to prevent outright merger has resulted, as many now see it, in a policy of discriminating against independents merely acting somewhat in agreement.

The fact of merger, says one writer, though it is

technically and actually in restraint of trade is no longer sufficient to procure conviction under the Sherman Act. The allegations and proof must go farther, and demonstrate the ill effects upon the community or else upon potential competitors from the use, or abuse, of the power which control of the market gives without a nice regard for the interests of others.[19]

Again, he calls attention to the significant fact that

in recent years not a single adverse decision has been rendered requiring the dissolution of an actually functioning business merger.[20]

---

[16] Watkins, *Industrial Combinations*, p. 259.
[17] Watkins, in *Quarterly Journal of Economics, loc. cit.*, p. 38 (1928).
[18] Keezer and May, *op. cit.*, p. 50.
[19] Watkins, *Industrial Combinations*, p. 259.
[20] *Quarterly Journal of Economics*, p. 37 (1928).

Another, declaring the "established conception of the law reversed," adds:

The Court goes a long way toward the conception that even monopoly is no longer illegal . . . [In various cases] the Federal Supreme Court has departed a long way from its early conception of free competition under the Sherman Law. Instead of espousing economic individualism the Court now endorses large scale production, integration and the elimination of the competitive wastes.[21]

Two recent coworkers conclude:

Judicial interpretation of the anti-trust laws has had the effect of legalizing almost any degree of concentration of economic power if certain legal formalities are observed. The question may be raised as to whether this treatment of the laws has not robbed them of much of the effectiveness that Congress seemed to wish them to have . . . Through their interpretations of the anti-trust laws, the courts have more than established the legality of large consolidations; they have actually encouraged them.[22]

Another declares:

There are indications that those in authority are favorable to the merger movement as a general proposition.[23]

The Industrial Conference Board, looking benignly on this development, concludes:

The restrictions upon the merging of competing enterprises are not as drastic as those imposed upon interference with the business rights of others.[24]

The Board reasons from the fact that proceedings for relief against monopolization through merger have been few and decreasing (to wit, only 7 in the decade 1917-1927 against 31 between 1890-1917) to the illogical conclusion that "the occasions for legal attack upon business mergers are diminishing." The statistical evidence would indicate rather that the occasions for attack have increased by many thousands, while the instances of attack by

[21] Schmidt, *op. cit.,* pp. 63, 64, 66.
[22] Keezer and May, *op. cit.,* pp. 49, 50.
[23] Prof. A. L. Bishop, N.Y. *Times Annalist,* January 22, 1926, p. 151.
[24] *Mergers and the Law,* p. 151.

the executive branch of the government have reached the vanishing point.

Now last, listen to the words of a New York attorney, long active spokesman of a more liberal, even indulgent, attitude toward large corporate enterprises. Mr. Gilbert H. Montague declares with a certain pardonable spirit of jubilation, that [25]

> the time has gone by when the anti-trust laws can be blamed if business men do not consolidate. . . . Consolidations among manufacturers and distributers, under proper conditions, are not prevented by the present attitude of the courts and the Government, but are virtually invited . . . When companies which previously have been in competition are merged, care must be taken that the consolidations be accomplished by acquiring their assets and not their capital stock [probably referring to the Eastman Kodak decision] . . . We have now reached the time when it may truly be said that never in the history of the anti-trust laws has there been such complete sympathy between business, the Government and the courts as to the necessity of interpreting these laws in a way that will be compatible and consistent with the present and future needs of American business.

No such statement from an advocate of consolidation is complete without the inevitable hokum about the public interest—for this, they would have us believe, is the sole thing that determines the "need of American business"—not the power and the profits, business or speculative, of the promoters of the mergers! So here it is.

> They have come to appreciate, at last, the social benefits that arise from reduced manufacturing and distributing costs, higher standards of wages and the increased purchasing power of the entire nation.

Warming to his theme, the prophet of bigger and better mergers concludes:

> There will be more consolidations. The legal obstacles in their way have become secondary. . . . We are on the eve of what can almost be described as a commercial millennium.

The stock market "millennium" of the following year was the fulfillment of this prediction—a sad commercial millennium, much

[25] Interview in the New York *Times,* February 12, 1928.

of the doubtful credit for which great achievement no doubt must be awarded to the intoxicating mergers.

HOW GREAT THE MENACE OF MERGERS

As to the fact there can be no dispute. Mergers have been vastly multiplying. Against the formation of consolidations the Sherman Anti-Trust Act is of no practical effect, so friends and foes of effective control of monopoly seem to agree. In contrast, they agree that even since the Trade Association cases the Act still is pretty strictly applied against plain agreements as to prices between separate corporate entities.

Where does this leave the Sherman Act in respect to mergers? Has it, as many pessimistically believe, virtually been repealed, nullified by judicial decisions? And, since merger gives the most effective conceivable unified control over prices, more so than any mere agreement among competitors, is monopoly by mergers threatening to possess the whole industrial field? The answer must vary under several conditions, among which are these: (1) Are large mergers inherently, as a rule, more efficient economically than are large well-equipped unit establishments? If so, there would seem to be nothing either in law or in economics to oppose them. (2) Is the urge to attain greater technical efficiency by this means, or is it some other motive that has inspired the great merger movement? (3) Has the Court countenanced (appeared even to favor) mergers *as a form of monopoly* or merely been unable to detect the evidences of monopoly? (4) Is there no way still open to curb or end the use of merger as a legal device by which monopoly is attained and increased? Let us, in the next chapter, seek an answer to questions (1) and (2) above, and we shall find that we are then able to answer the final questions in a spirit of hopefulness for the future of American industrial policy.

CHAPTER XXV

THE DOUBTFUL VIRTUES OF MERGERS

WORDS OF WARNING

THE Court has accepted with slight hesitation the alleged economies and hence public benefits of mergers. Surely these notions
should have been strictly scrutinized before being used consciously
or unconsciously to effect a change resembling a *de facto* revolution
in public policy toward the organization of industrial enterprises.
Beginning with the report of the Industrial Commission in 1901,
special investigations, economic theory, and business experience
have pretty thoroughly "debunked" these inflated claims, and have
revealed evils invisible in the glowing picture of the merger
boosters.

In the years following the first great outburst of merger formation, many warnings against false claims and false hopes were
uttered by thoughtful men. Here is one who both as metallurgist
and public accountant had intimately known many industries, and
who early saw that business organization was getting on the wrong
trail. Declaring that though mergers had turned out fine business
machines they were lacking in the fire and force of individual enterprises, he further said:

> Knowledge and technical ability have given place to financial in-
> fluence. . . . We have learned that the limit of growth is soon
> reached at which a central control is effective. . . . The idea that
> centralization and combination always produce increased efficiency and
> profit is a bubble that has been pricked.[1]

---

[1] Ernest Salisbury Suffern of New York City in N.Y. *Times Annalist*, November 3, 1913, article on "The Apparent Failure of Industrial Eugenics."

A couple of years later, another, who among many business activities ranging from St. Louis to the east, served for years as chairman of the Committee on Statistics of the Chamber of Commerce of the United States, wrote of "The Handicaps of Bigness":

> Great consolidations are not the surest way to efficiency in production. . . . Mere size, especially if it be much extended, means vulnerability as well as strength. . . . The essential weakness of the large extended organization is the failure to achieve, save in part, the very thing for which it is principally created, namely, the economies supposed to be brought about by concentration. . . . The smaller unit has an incalculable advantage in the matter of overhead charges.[2]

The former of these observers was speaking in 1913, a quiescent period in trust formation, when men were mostly interested to determine what, after a decade under test, had happened to the mergers formed in the first great epoch before 1904. The latter was speaking when signs were already showing of a new merger movement, destined to have an enormous growth continuing until the year 1929.

LATER JUDGMENTS CONFIRM

Again, after some years, in 1926, another student of the merger movement summed up his main conclusion in these words:

> The acceptance of this idea [that the larger the business unit the more profitable the enterprise] as a basic principle in business expansion, at least in the field of industry, is unsafe.[3]

Another, after careful studies, declared at the very height of the last merger madness that the potential economies long claimed for combinations of large plants are more than offset by real losses in efficiency.[4]

A specialist in business management said in 1930:

> The horizontal merger has been held to offer marked advantages to production. . . . Results however, have been somewhat disappointing.[5]

---

[2] Archer Wall Douglass, in N.Y. *Times Annalist,* February 14, 1916.

[3] Prof. A. L. Bishop of Yale University in N.Y. *Times Annalist,* January 29, 1926, p. 182.

[4] W. Thorp, in *Recent Economic Changes,* p. 217 (1929).

[5] Erwin H. Schall, Professor of Business Management, in *Annals of the American Academy,* May 1930, p. 31.

In midsummer of 1930 the New York *Times* commented thus upon the effect of widespread mergers finally affecting almost every industry:

These mergers and expansion programs were expected to result in economies in operation and management, but in many instances the falling off in business showed a number of glaring inefficiencies.[6]

The head of a leading firm of accountants is quoted as saying:

A large organization has much the same susceptibility to defective operation as has the small business, and in addition has potential weaknesses peculiarly its own. . . . Properties may be added one after another too quickly . . . resulting in industrial indigestion.[7]

THE VERDICT OF HISTORY

The general results of merger history are in close accord with these observations. Most notable trusts have fallen behind the aggregate of the independents in rate of growth and proportion of the total national production (the fact that so impressed the Court in the Steel Case and betrayed it into false inferences). A study in 1921 of the most notable mergers formed before 1903 showed that in 23 of the 35 cases the earnings in the next ten years were less than before merger, and in half of these less by one-third to nine-tenths, and in the aggregate earnings of all 35 were nearly one-fifth less than those of the separate competing establishments prior to consolidation (this despite the inclusion in the later period of earnings on large additions to capital and plants of new financing which could not accurately be estimated).[8] Even the U.S. Steel Corporation—a surprising fact—earned only about 85 per cent as much in its first ten years as the previous earnings of its constituent companies.[9]

A more specific statistical comparison in 1930 showed that, in the

---

6 July 27, 1930.
7 Arthur Anderson, accountant, in the New York *Times*, August 24, 1930.
8 Dewing, *Quarterly Journal of Economics*, Vol. 36, pp. 84 ff. (November 1921).
9 If, despite this, the Steel Corporation must be deemed a great financial success, this outcome must be because of other reasons than those given by its "formers." It has failed to display the superior technical efficiency that was prophesied for it, but it has undoubtedly exercised a strong power to enhance prices (about which nothing was said). Perhaps its most marked success has

general fall of stock prices, ten large merger stocks, "well established concerns with strong banking sponsorship," had fared much
worse than the general list. The merger issues had fallen 60 per
cent, whereas general industrial average stock prices had fallen but
40 per cent.[10]

THAT DARK BROWN TASTE, NEXT MORNING

Wisely it was said of old, "It is better to be in the house of
mourning than in the house of feasting." Truth gets a better hearing. This is a good time in which to contemplate the besetting sins
of merger management. A year or two ago the business world was
too drunk with paper profits to listen to reason. Philip, drunk, got
many things confused; Philip, sober, is able to recognize his former
confusion. Why were the hopes and claims of great economies to
be gained by merger so exaggerated? Chiefly, it would seem, because they were thought to have all the combined virtues of mass
production and technical integration. It ought now, however, to be
clear that these are technical matters in a single establishment and
have nothing to do with merger, which is almost entirely a matter
of the proprietary (financial) unification of separate plants. Therewith have we blown away half of the fog that envelops this subject
in the public mind and in the courts. Large size of the single establishment, to be sure, is of itself not an economic evil or an offense
against the law (though it is possible for even moderate size to
occur under conditions such that it is used in a manner evil and
illegal).

A large part of the fog remaining may be dissipated by clearly
distinguishing between vertical and horizontal mergers, which are
alike only in being the proprietary unification of formerly separate
properties. They differ economically and should be differentiated
legally in respect to the anti-trust laws. A vertical merger in the

---

been not as a manufacturing enterprise but as a land investment, holding
enormous rich ore deposits for the rise of land values, which have gradually
grown up to the heavily watered capitalization with which it began business.
But such appreciation of mine valuations is not the result of superior management in production; it would have occurred in any case, though doubtless
somewhat enhanced by (partial) monopoly through ownership by the Corporation of ore lands in certain localities.

[10] The New York *Times*, August 24, 1930.

strictest sense links only plants that have been, and continue to be, engaged upon different stages of the process from raw materials to finished products, and that were thus, before merger, in the relationship of buyer and seller, not in that of competitors. Particular mergers, however, such as the U.S. Steel Corporation, not infrequently comprise both horizontal and vertical features.

Probably the popular belief in economies from mergers is greater in regard to the vertical than to the horizontal kind. Now we must keep our eye on the ball. Vertical merger of non-competing processes has been doubly confused, first with technical integration in a single plant, and secondly with horizontal merger of different plants. The substantial virtues of technical integration within a plant were transferred first to vertical financial merger of separate plants, and thence to the horizontal merger that forms the completest monopoly. This is known as a completed double pass— pretty work.

EXPERIENCE DISCREDITS THE VERTICAL TRUST

Without these skillful shifts of thought and cumulative exaggeration, horizontal merger would never have become endowed in popular thought with such magical potency. The claims for vertical merger are most plausible—indeed have been far too readily conceded.[11] The possibilities of operating a large combine as a vertical merger (each plant specializing on one process) are far more limited than is popularly supposed. This appears to have been the case with the International Harvester Company, a combination of five of the leading manufacturers of farm machinery in 1902.

Economic integration, therefore, was only of secondary importance. . . . In view of the size of the constituent concerns and the extent to which the industry is affected by transportation costs, which often determine the economical limits of large-scale production, there is no ground for thinking that combination would be attended by any economies of this sort. This inference is confirmed by the actual course of events. . . . [Here a note is added: If anything, the tendency has been away from rather than toward specialization of the use of plant equipment.] The elimination of competition in the marketing of the

11 But see below, Mr. Eddy's warning of the danger of concealed discrimination by a vertical merger in the competition by one of its subsidiaries with specialized fabricators.

products of the industry must have been the only anticipated source of substantial gains.[12]

The literary partner of Henry Ford expressed a like view:

> At first it was not grasped that this theory of assembling at the point of use was other than a way of saving freight. . . . It has been taken for granted that the great corporations of the future would all have to be vertical trusts because on a blackboard the vertical trust worked out beautifully. . . . It was all very pretty. But soon it appeared that the vertical trust was for one reason or another not quite what it had been cracked up to be . . . Lately it is becoming apparent that the theory of the vertical trust . . . does not comprehend the limits of human management. . . . In any complex assembly the making of each part is a business of itself. It has been discovered that a factory making exactly one part will, under independent management, in nine cases out of ten, produce that part at a profit to itself better and more cheaply than will a division of a great corporation.[13]

An expert on business management early in 1930 gave this balanced judgment:

> The vertical merger [is] an attempt to extend the general theory of serialization. We know that important gains have resulted to some concerns along these lines. On the other hand these linked processes demand the careful balancing which frequently has been found difficult. Furthermore, the management of widely dissimilar industries in the chain of production is difficult.[14]

THEORETICAL ANALYSIS DISCREDITS IT TOO

The imaginary source of the great economies from vertical merger is almost wholly the so-called "saving of profits" connected with those stages of production that are taken over. But is the merger to get no profits from those parts of its investment, labor, and enterprise that continue to be engaged in each stage of the production? It is only as technically that stage is conducted more efficiently under merger than under independent management that any economies of this kind could be attained, and this begs the question and

[12] Watkins, *Industrial Combinations,* pp. 120 ff., and note, p. 122.
[13] Samuel Crowther, *Annals of the American Academy,* May 1930, pp. 25-26.
[14] Erwin H. Schell, Professor of Business Management, in *Annals of the American Academy,* May 1930, p. 30.

flies in the face of the principle of specialization. It has been truly said by another after examining this argument: "In whatever way they are regarded these particular 'commercial economies' of integration evaporate under analysis." [15]

Efficient management! To that explanation of the chief cause of success in enterprise, in anything like a fair field with no favor, come at last all those who study the subject, whether they be statisticians and economists or impartial men of wide business experience. And scarcely a ray of evidence suggests that either vertical or horizontal consolidation (provided each unit plant is of size suitable to insure the full economies of integration and of large production within its market area) insures or increases managerial or technical efficiency. On the contrary, there is much evidence that the opposite is normally the case. Since the melancholy days of October 1929, false merger theory has been about as heavily deflated as have merger stocks; and the difficulties of central management of overgrown organizations is everywhere recognized as the fatal weakness.

ARE SELLING COSTS REDUCED?

No claim of virtue in mergers has been more readily accepted by the public than that of great economies in selling expenses, including advertising. Partly this is expected, and is said to come, from reducing the number of salesmen, avoiding useless duplication of effort in the same territory, and in the case of nationally advertised articles, in reducing the unit cost of advertising (the total cost being spread over a greater output). A certain validity in this claim in the case of some businesses cannot be doubted. Especially chain merchandising (far more than manufacturing) of standardized goods obviously has some technical features giving opportunity for noteworthy economies.[16] However, little if any specific proof of such actual results has been made public. Such savings seem *prima facie* probably in the case of horizontal industrial mergers, but a man-

---

[15] Watkins, *Industrial Combinations*, p. 118, note, refuting the "specious reasoning" which the Bureau of Corporations had countenanced.

[16] Observe, however, that in these cases the retail outlets have been at first absolutely non-competitive with each other—competing only with independent unit stores. When merger reaches the stage when one chain absorbs all the rival stores of a considerable retail area, there will be a different story to tell—especially regarding price control.

agement expert, quoted above, warns that "distribution costs may be found actually increased by a superimposed organization." The case seems to be no better (to our surprise, rather worse) with vertical mergers, for we are met by this report of the meeting of the American Management Association in Chicago, March 5 and 6, 1930:

> The general opinion was that the mergers have complicated sales and distribution of these products, particularly mergers of companies making dissimilar products with different price classifications.[17]

To like effect a well-known management engineer spoke of

business officials as having lost their effectiveness in the mesh of personnel attendant upon mergers, and asserted that mergers were detrimental to the effectiveness of important men in consolidated companies, and that drastic steps must be taken to overcome this disadvantage. There is no absolute guarantee that mergers will decrease selling costs. Wherever businesses in exactly the same field unite [horizontal mergers] it seems fairly logical to expect a saving through consolidation of sales effort, but . . . in such instances distribution costs may be found actually increased by a superimposed organization . . . The interests back of a merger may sincerely believe that its consummation will cut costs, but they are likely to overlook the sometimes dangerous element of human judgment, which, if in error, may easily defeat the objective of the whole proposition.[18]

THE VIRTUES OF PRIVATE ENTERPRISE

Undoubtedly these sobering statistics and opinions help to explain a lot of things. The disappointing technical success of mergers looks strikingly like the proverbial weakness of government business compared with the old-time efficiency of private ownership and management. The champions of "big business" are usually fanatical opponents of "government in business," and laud the virtues of private enterprise, which they assume are always exemplified by large corporations. In truth, as single factories grow larger and the founders pass off the scene, and separate concerns are merged into

---

[17] *The Iron Trade Review,* March 13, 1930.

[18] J. P. Jordan, of Stephens, Harrison and Jordan, management engineers, addressing the American Management Association, as reported in the New York *Times* of May 14, 1930, and in an interview, May 18.

great combinations, one master ceases to know all and one master's eye to see all, responsibility becomes subdivided, the motives of personal financial gain of the management are weakened, red tape multiplies, office overhead costs mount, and often nepotism and favoritism begin to honeycomb and undermine the morale of the whole organization. Such a big "private business" has in its internal operation ceased to be truly "private" (that is, "individual" in the old sense), has ceased to have the peculiar virtues reputed to be the mark of private enterprise. Then is when its management is tempted to misuse its greater financial powers to assert and maintain by restraint of commerce a domination in the industry to which its technical efficiency in no manner entitles it. The highly lauded "industrial statesmanship" of its president, for which, besides his salary, he receives in a single year a bonus of $1,600,000, consists in what? Not in making better steel to be sold cheaper to the public, but rather in acquiring one after another all of the company's competitors in a great industrial region, a process not justified by increasing technical efficiency, but only by the added control it gives over price policies, by the dominating power it gives to a single enterprise, and perhaps by the speculative gains it makes possible in the stock market.[19]

The traditional virtues of private property and management developed amid conditions of decentralized industry where the responsibility for each separate plant and its rewards were intimately linked. As establishments are merged into greater and greater proprietary unity, those traditional virtues are weakened through new strata of workers and in wider and wider circles. In various new ways, no doubt, such as professional education, better methods of organization, etc., they may be in part and for a time maintained, while the very real technical economies of larger units of production for a good while and to a certain point more than compensate for their partial loss. But mechanical improvements cannot indefinitely serve as substitutes for dynamic motives and human nature. Somewhere there must be a golden mean of adjustment between the meager mechanical, impersonal gains of the concentration movement and the very serious losses it entails in business fiber and motivation. There is grave reason to think that in many directions

[19] See map of the Bethlehem-Lackawanna merger, Figure 32, Ch. XXVI.

the movement toward financial size and plant combination has gone much too far even for technical efficiency; yet it is threatening to go much further.

MERGERS STILL FIND ONE DEFENDER

A recent report of the Industrial Conference Board [20] is in entire agreement with the foregoing facts and opinions in certain respects only; to wit, that "by and large, mergers have not provided a safe, easy, and sure way to business success." In other respects, however, the Board's report is out of harmony with all other serious investigations. For it concludes (forgetful of numerous cautions given throughout the book as to the reliability of the data, and "insofar as these conclusions are fair deductions") "that in a very practical and substantial way industrial consolidations have been an economic benefit to the community." [21]

The Board particularly urges the claim of superiority in scientific research on behalf of mergers, which, if a real merit, is a very recent one. However, as already indicated, research enterprise has not been confined to merged industries, and in most of them has been entirely lacking. [22]

MERGERS AND RESTRAINT OF TRADE

If these are the true facts and these judgments of the advantages of mergers are sound, why have mergers been so eagerly formed? They must be advantageous to some folks, and most obviously to those who form them. It should be observed that the outright failure, or the meager and disappointing success, of numerous mergers as corporations is no proof that they did not secure and exercise large monopolistic powers, and still less proof that some individuals did not profit by their formation. It indicates rather that this private gain at public expense was either offset by the wastes and inefficiencies inherent in artificially inflated organization or went to various individuals who were "in on the ground floor." The advantages from mergers appear to lie almost wholly in the field of

---

[20] *Mergers in Industry,* 1929, pp. 170-171.

[21] *Idem,* p. 174. Some reasons why this conclusion is unwarranted by the evidence on which it is based are given in the Appendix to Ch. XXV.

[22] See Appendix to Ch. XXV; also Watkins, *Industrial Combinations,* p. 138, and *Mergers in Industry,* pp. 109-119, 147.

proprietorship and of private profit, rather than in that of productive efficiency and public benefit. The chief source of expected increased operating profits from mergers is doubtless "control of the market"—monopolistic power.

What joint ownership did produce, and undoubtedly was expected to produce, was . . . advantages in the marketing of products as the result of diminished competition for each constituent within its particular area. In short, the corporation was designed not so much to reduce cost as to raise or maintain prices.[23]

On the anniversary of the stock break of October 1929, under the title of "merger season closed," the following skeptical comment was made in the financial columns of a great daily:

It was remarked in Wall Street yesterday that when times are good, when every one is making money and when stock prices are soaring, mergers of this and that company come thick and fast, all for the purpose of "more economical operation." Under more difficult conditions, however, when, presumably, operating economies would be welcome, these mergers fall off sharply in number. . . . The apparent anomaly is said to provide material for those who charge that mergers are frequently effected for reasons of other than economy.[24]

WALL STREET DANCES, MAIN STREET PAYS THE FIDDLER

Next to price control in strength, possibly even greater, as a motive for the formation of mergers, the evidence points to speculative profits. These gains come to various insiders in the shape of liberal legal and promotion fees, banking underwriters' commissions, inflated prices for constituent properties sometimes on the verge of bankruptcy, and enhanced prices for the securities of the newly formed merger immediately following the merger.[25] The securities of the larger consolidations have greater publicity and greater saleability and generally a market price higher than their earnings relative to the smaller companies. This at least appears to have been so in the highly speculative period between 1918 and

---

[23] Watkins, *Industrial Combinations*, p. 119.
[24] The New York *Times*, October 29, 1930.
[25] See Industrial Conference Board, *Mergers in Industry*, p. 81, for earlier favorable stock price results of mergers, and later less favorable.

1929 in the case of some industries (though not in iron and steel).[26] The optimism (real or pretended) of the promoters leads them to exaggerated estimates of future earnings. In the aggregate of 35 of the principal early mergers, the actual earnings of the first ten years were less than three-fifths of the "estimated" held out in alluring prospectuses to the investing public.[27]

In 1930 the disappointing results of recent mergers, in comparison with independents, were "regarded by bankers as an indication that last year investors formed an exaggerated idea of the value of mergers."[28] Observe the generosity with which "the bankers," who underwrote these mergers (frequently promoted their formation, it is said) and sold them to the trusting public, attribute the exaggeration to the investors instead of to themselves. But we are told further that during the bull markets

mergers were considered synonymous with prosperity. . . . The prospect of a merger added an element of mystery to a stock's value . . . which carried the issue to a higher peak than the general list of industrials, bankers say. . . . It is now generally agreed that the benefits of many mergers were exaggerated by the financial community. . . . Estimates of future earnings were frequently overoptimistic . . . expense contingent upon . . . financing was not fully appreciated. . . . That there are dangers inherent in certain types of mergers and in too rapid expansion through consolidations is now the general opinion in banking circles. . . . Many recent mergers have been based on financial considerations rather than on careful economic and industrial analyses.[29]

The public seems to have been as credulous as the Supreme Court regarding the statements of promoters. A confused "belief in the universal advantages of size and large-scale production is thus expressing itself in the value of corporation securities."[30] Many mergers have been essentially a gamble in Wall Street, linked arm in arm with a violation of the letter, spirit, and purpose of the Anti-Trust Act. Obviously, in the end, all these promotion

[26] *Recent Economic Changes*, pp. 196-200.
[27] About 58 per cent; and as noted above, were only 85 per cent of the previous earnings. Dewing, *op. cit.*, pp. 90-92.
[28] The New York *Times*, August 24, 1930.
[29] *Idem.*
[30] *Recent Economic Changes*, pp. 199-200.

and speculative profits are dug out of the pockets of the patient common man. It would take great "public benefits" from mergers, in no way proved, to offset these billions of evident losses to the public.

WANTED — PROOFS OF PUBLIC BENEFITS

No doubt the very success of the merger propaganda makes the public hesitate to accept any evidence to the contrary, even after Wall Street has awakened from its delusion. The public argues thus: there must be a deal of truth in these claims, else so many people would not have made them and we would not have believed them. That's the logic of Demos. "All I know is what I read in the papers."

What is meant by "benefits"? A merger of formerly *competing* plants is *prima facie* "a combination in restraint of trade." When the Supreme Court declared in the Steel dissolution suit that it deemed the combination was a necessity (or a facility) of technical efficiency and progress, it tacitly assumed perfect competition, and, therefore, that the greater efficiency and lower costs were passed on to the public in the form of lower prices, better service, and a more bountiful supply of goods. In this consists the "benefit," as the Court viewed it—a benefit to the public. It is hardly conceivable that the courts would pronounce the restraint involved in any merger contract "reasonable" if these savings were retained by the combination (or shared only with independents conspiring in the use of the basing-point plan) and not passed on in large part to the public. That much, at least, must be said for the good intentions of the courts in this matter—even though they may have contributed mainly to the paving of a certain broad road that leadeth to destruction of our anti-trust statutes.

Ought not the burden of proof to be on those forming a combination of formerly competing enterprises to show that such public benefits actually result? No amount of proof of the self-evident truth that merger may (under many circumstances) increase control over prices and thus raise private profits at the expense of the public, that it makes certain stocks sell relatively higher than they otherwise would and thus benefits some citizens at the expense of other citizens, serves to demonstrate public benefits—rather the contrary. These are gains to private pockets, mere illicit transfers of income, not additions to public wealth and welfare.

This being the situation, economic and legal, in regard to mergers, what, if anything, can be done to get back upon the right road? Many believe the outlook to be dark and the merger to be the greatest threat to our system of industrial liberty. The solution for the merger problem that is suggested in our concluding chapter gives a more hopeful prospect.

CHAPTER XXVI

THE MEANING OF THE CLAYTON ACT

ITS MAIN PURPOSE

THE two legislative instruments by which the nation has sought to enforce its will to maintain industrial liberty and the policy of free domestic markets are the Clayton Act and the Sherman Anti-Trust Act. This chapter will be given to an examination of the Clayton Act with the purpose of determining how it may be applied as a remedy for the prevailing evils of industrial price practices. The main purpose in the enactment of the Clayton Act was to put an end to discrimination of certain kinds in industrial prices. No doubt, adequately interpreted in the light of economics, the Sherman Act already forbade discrimination, but judicial doubts and decisions seemed to make necessary the new legislation of 1914. The most honest efforts to shape the Clayton Act to this purpose were hampered by confused notions of the real economic nature of discrimination. This confusion is betrayed in many details of the Act which have weakened and delayed its effective operation.[1]

In Federal anti-trust legislation the word discrimination first appears in Section 2 of the Clayton Act (1914). To put an end to the demonstrated abuses of cutthroat discrimination as a weapon in the hand of stronger competitors seeking monopoly (or to strengthen monopoly already partially realized) by the forceful exclusion and ruthless destruction of competitors, discrimination was to be prohibited under certain conditions and with certain provisos. This action came very belatedly, for cruder forms of cutthroat discrimination had already been replaced by the subtler method of collusion in restraint of commerce (inclusive rather

---

[1] On the debates in the Senate, see above, Ch. XXI.

than exclusive). The Act declared discrimination to be unlawful in two types of cases (or in one type, described in two ways), subject, however, to seven exceptions and provisos.

FURBELOWS ON THE STATUTE

Let us examine each of these nine features (more or less decorative elements) of Section 2. The prohibition of discrimination is limited to cases (1) where the effect of such discrimination may be to substantially lessen competition . . . in any line of commerce, and (2) or tend to create a monopoly in any line of commerce. These two phrases are probably but two ways of expressing the same thought. The word "substantially" reflects a vagueness of thought which passes the problem along for judicial interpretation, but it can hardly be intended to designate a really separate qualification of the prohibition. It seems to mean merely *de minimis non curat lex.*

These two clauses as applied to the discriminator invert cause and effect, for (as we now know) discrimination can occur only where full and free competition are already lessened. Discrimination is the actual exercise of a certain degree of monopoly power existing before the discrimination is practiced, rather than an act having a mere tendency to create a future monopoly. The phrasing reflects two erroneous ideas; one, that discrimination is a normal incident and evidence of true competition; the other, that the great evil of discrimination was its use by competitors to bring about "a" monopoly for themselves in the future.[2]

MERE TAUTOLOGIES

Five other provisos in the section are merely tautological. Difference in price on account of differences in (3) the grade, (4) quality, (5) quantity, (6) cost of selling, or (7) transportation are, by definition, not discrimination at all. Discrimination relates to the same class of commodities in the same market; not to make a difference in price where such "substantial" differences exist would be to discriminate.

---

[2] How a kindly Providence and the Supreme Court have recently transformed these two clauses into the most useful features in the whole statute will be discussed further below.

There was no need, therefore, to guard against the danger that the courts would treat as discrimination differences in prices under such "substantially" different conditions. Indeed, years before the passage of the Clayton Act this conception of discrimination had been adjudicated by the Supreme Court and declared to be a part of the law governing interstate commerce, when in respect to the charges of a telegraph company the Court explicitly (and unanimously) affirmed "the inherent justice of the rules laid down" by the lower court in these words, in part:

> In order to constitute an unjust discrimination, there must be a difference in rates under substantially similar conditions as to source. . . . It is not an undue preference to make one patron a less rate than another where exist differences in conditions affecting the expense or difficulty in performing the services which fairly justify the difference in rate.[3]

This surely met the need and gave scope for reasonable differential charges to the degree that the services or goods differed or involved different costs. The real difficulty against which Congress needed to guard was of just the opposite nature, that sellers would use the pretense of such differences as an excuse for discrimination. Against this, the complex qualifications of the section gave no protection, but only multiplied the difficulties in its enforcement to the desired purpose.

THE JOKER IN THE PACK

The eighth qualification of the section is that it does not apply to "discrimination in price in the same or different communities made in good faith to meet competition." This is by general consensus of opinion the biggest joker in the pack. The prosecution is required to produce evidence, not simply of behavior and of actual conditions, but of the secret motive of the discriminators—a task not for attorneys and commissioners, but for mind-readers, crystal-gazers, and clairvoyants. This clause has no patent purpose that is not already attained in the first two limitations discussed above, and, therefore, it is again merely tautology. If, however, it is something more, it means that the prosecutor must prove not only that the particular discrimination has the effect "to lessen competition"

[3] Western Union Telegraph Company v. Call Publishing Company, 181 U.S. 92, 97, 99, April 15, 1901.

and "to create a monopoly" but further that this lessening of competition and creation of a monopoly is not being done "in good faith to meet competition"—a grotesque contradiction.

For what would such proof require? What is the meaning of the vague phrase, "in good faith to meet competition"? Discrimination involves a relationship. It is any difference between two compared prices, one higher than the other, and at the same time, *vice versa*, one lower than the other. The higher and the lower prices as between buyers are both alike discriminatory. Any act of discrimination may logically be viewed from either standpoint, and the factor of "good faith" must be determined in each case by the relation of each price to the other.

"GOOD FAITH" IN LOWER PRICES?

Let us take first the case of the lower price. Evidently the purpose of every lower price is always to "meet" some sort of competition, somewhere. By what right and with what proof may any one else claim that in one case it is made "in good faith" and in another case in bad faith? A part of the purpose of Congress, at least, can be read in the circumstances of the time. It was to prevent the use of a lower discriminating price in a "war" of prices regardless of immediate consideration of costs and profits, with the purpose of destroying competitors or forcing them into a combine.

The main ultimate purpose of all anti-trust legislation is to safeguard the interests of the general public viewed as consumers, and the protection of the rights in commerce for the comparatively small class of producers in any industry, though incidentally not unimportant in itself, is chiefly a means to this larger good. But so important had it become in the eyes of the public to prevent the stronger producers from killing off the weaker, that the prohibition of discriminating lower prices to destroy competition, although against the immediate interests of all consumers, had, at the time, come to be thought of as the best means to insure their ultimate interest. The main significance of this feature of the statute at the time lay thus in this near paradox: to protect the whole public, lower prices, if discriminatory, must not be given to a part of the public. Viewed in this historical light, "good faith" in charging discriminatory lower prices was, it seems, intended by Congress to mean: with the direct object of making some profit on the particular sale; whereas the same lower price, if used as a means for the ultimate object of creating (or perhaps of further strengthening) a monopoly (for the discriminator) would be made "in bad faith."

This use of a discriminatory lower price as a fighting weapon has been frequently adjudicated, and it was condemned quite clearly in the very recent Porto Rico Case.[4] The Fairmont Creamery Case (an appeal from a decision not under the Clayton Act but under a Minnesota State Law), so unimportant in its own state of facts and in the financial interests at stake, was yet profoundly significant in its revelation of the belief of the majority of the Supreme Court that, without this qualification of "in good faith," any law, even a State law to prevent discrimination, must be unconstitutional as interfering with the normal freedom of contract.[5] The proof of bad faith in charging a lower price can be made only in such bald circumstances that the section has no practical application in the great mass of cases where such discrimination is practiced.

"GOOD FAITH" IN HIGHER PRICES?

In fifteen years, from 1914 to 1929, no attempt had been made, and it seems to have occurred to no one in the legal departments of the government to make the attempt, to apply this second section against discriminatory higher prices. Then a case in which this chanced to be a feature arose on appeal from an order of the Federal Trade Commission.[6] The principal question calling for answer was whether the section applied to lowering competition, etc., "not in the line of commerce wherein the discriminator is engaged, but in the line of commerce in which the vendee of the discriminator is engaged." To this the Court, in an opinion delivered by Justice

[4] Porto Rican American Tobacco Company v. American Tobacco Company, 30 Fed. Rep., Second Series 234. U.S. Circuit Court of Appeals, Second Circuit, January 1929.

[5] See Ch. XXII for reasons given. Observe that the defendant in that case was a buyer and the offense charged was that of paying a higher price.

[6] George Van Camp & Sons v. American Can Company and Van Camp Packing Company, 278 U.S. 245, January 2, 1929. The American Can Company had been selling cans to one packing company 20 per cent cheaper than to the other and discriminating against the complainant by higher charges in other respects. The Court without special discussion assumed that the effect of the discrimination was to "lower competition," etc.

Sutherland, gave a unanimous answer in the affirmative. The reasoning is refreshingly clean-cut and simple, being based upon a literal reading of the words, "in any line of commerce."

AN ANTI-TRUST LAW MEANS WHAT IT SAYS!

The Court flatly refused to seek the meaning of these words in "reports of Congressional committees and other familiar aids to statutory construction," which, as appellees claimed, showed "that the words must be confined to the particular line of commerce in which the discriminator is engaged," etc. The Court held that even proof of this fact would not and does not lead to the conclusion that the words "must be confined," etc., when the words plainly have a broader meaning. As the Court says:

The general rule that the province of construction lies wholly within the domain of ambiguity (Hamilton v. Rathbone, 175 U.S. 414, 419, 421) is too firmly established by the numerous decisions of the Court either to require or permit us to do so. The words being clear, they are decisive. There is nothing to construe.

This utterance is like a fresh breeze clearing away a fog. Alas, that this vitalizing principle of construction has not guided in some other applications of the anti-trust statutes! Beside the simple proposition that a law of Congress forbidding restraint of commerce and monopoly means simply what it says, the rule of reason glimmers like a sputtering candle in the noonday sun.

PREVIOUS DECISIONS GO OVERBOARD

This decision explicitly overrules the Mennen Case.[7] The Court says:

The decision in that case was based upon the premise that the statute was ambiguous and required the aid of committee reports, etc., to determine its meaning, a premise which we have rejected as unsound.

The Van Camp decision also overrules the National Biscuit Company decision (expressly following the Mennen decision) by which an order of the Federal Trade Commission under Section 2 of the Clayton Act was unanimously reversed by three judges in the Cir-

[7] 228 Fed. Rep. 774.

cuit Court of Appeals (the Supreme Court then declining to issue a writ of certiorari).[8] In the National Biscuit Case the Circuit Court, reiterating the doctrine of the Mennen Case, had refused to apply the section to discrimination that lessened competition between the different buyers of the goods (that being the only lessening of competition that was alleged and found by the Commission), and the Court therefore declared the order to have been "improvidently granted." The National Biscuit Case decision had been deplored by some as an almost complete nullification of the section prohibiting discrimination and had been heralded by others (hostile to all control of corporations) as a deserved reproof to the Federal Trade Commission for recklessly exceeding its powers. By the Van Camp decision, all this controversy seems to have been wiped off the slate.

Throughout the hearings of the Pittsburgh-Plus complaint, 1920-24, counsel for the Steel Corporation contended for the narrower construction of this section, maintaining that evidence tending to show lessening of competition under the basing-point policy among the customers of the Corporation (e.g., between Pittsburgh and Chicago fabricators) was "incompetent and irrelevant." They contended that the statute forbade only such discrimination as lessened competition between the discriminator and its competitors. The complainants feared (because of the Mennen decision) that if the order discontinuing the practice were appealed to the courts, the statute might be given this narrower interpretation. By the Van Camp decision this doubt has been cleared away.[9]

HIGHER DISCRIMINATORY PRICES NOW ILLEGAL

This same opinion means that Section 2 prohibits discrimination in the form of charging a higher price as well as that of charging

---

[8] 299 Fed. 733, May 5, 1924; 266 U.S. 613, October 20, 1924.

[9] The first American Can Case has been followed fully by the Circuit Court of Appeals in the 7th Circuit in a second case against the same company, the result being that treble damages were awarded for a similar discrimination against the Ladoga Canning Company (A. C. Company v. Ladoga C. Company, decided October 28, 1930). The Court held invalid the pleas (1) that, as the discriminator gave the rebates because of fear that the former customer would manufacture its own cans, the action was in good faith to meet competition, and (2) that the discrimination as a matter of law did not substantially lessen competition (i.e. the Court held that the statute applied to lessening competition among customers).

a lower one. This issue was not specifically raised, but the only prices questioned and declared to be illegal were higher prices. To some it had always seemed logical to argue (though others thought this to be a hair-splitting contention) that a discriminatory higher price could never be defended as "made in good faith" to *meet* competition, for to "meet" implies lowering prices. There were just grounds to fear, however, that the Court, resorting to the Congressional debates as an aid to construction (as in the Mennen Case), would rule that the statute was intended to prevent only lower cutthroat prices (aimed at the seller's competitors). The way now seems clear to attacking any and all discrimination in prices to customers who resell the goods either at wholesale or retail, whether unchanged (mere merchandising) or after further fabrication (manufacturing). Under recent conditions, in every case, the higher rather than the lower price should be the one attacked, as a matter of tactics. It would be difficult to find a case where a customer compelled to pay higher discriminatory prices is not put at a "substantial" disadvantage in interstate commerce in his competition with others in his industry in the same market, or market area, or in marginal competition between two market areas. The Clayton Act may now enter upon a new era, if a proper effort is made to enforce it.

SELECTING CUSTOMERS—WHEN A RIGHT?

The ninth and last of the qualifications of Section 2 is to safeguard the right to select one's own customers:

and provided further, that nothing herein contained shall prevent persons engaged in selling goods, wares, or merchandise in commerce from selecting their own customers in *bona fide* transactions and not in restraint of trade.

Interpreted in connection with the earlier clauses of the section, the main part of this proviso, too, is tautological, for as discrimination is prohibited only in cases when it lessens competition and tends to create a monopoly, therefore the prohibition does not apply "in *bona fide* transactions and not in restraint of trade." This sacred liberty of the individual trader would seem to be already fully safeguarded, as the courts had already gone to extremes in this matter. In the A. & P. v. Cream of Wheat Case, the Circuit Court of Appeals remarked sarcastically:

We had supposed that it was elementary law that a trader could buy from whom he pleased and sell to whom he pleased, and that his selection of a buyer or seller was wholly his own concern. "It is a part of a man's civil rights that he be at liberty to refuse business relations with any person whatsoever, whether the refusal rests upon reason, or is the result of whim, caprice, prejudice or malice." Cooley on Torts. . . . Before the Sherman Act it was the law that a trader might reject the offer of a proposing buyer, for any reason that appealed to him; it might be because he did not like the other's business methods, or because he had some personal difference with him, political, racial or social. That was purely his own affair, with which nobody else had any concern. Neither the Sherman Act, nor any decision of the Supreme Court construing the same, nor the Clayton Act, has changed the law in the particular. We have not yet reached the stage where the selection of a trader's customers is made for him by the government.[10]

WHEN IN RESTRAINT OF TRADE?

Such a broad doctrine of *laissez faire* may be sound as economics and social policy under conditions of real market competition where any would-be buyer, if rejected, has other opportunities to buy. But under modern conditions of local monopoly brought about by mergers, it may mean serfdom or industrial death to the smaller individual trader. Moreover, this doctrine of the right to choose one's customers is quite misused as a justification of discriminatory prices where, as in the National Biscuit Case,[11] discredited now on other grounds, the sellers are not refusing to sell to any one, are selling to all parties gladly, but are refusing to sell on as good terms to some as to others (under substantially similar circumstances). In that case, therefore, the Commission was not attempting to "select" the seller's customers, as the Court inaccurately declared, or ordering the seller to sell when he did not wish to, as opponents of the law have caustically affirmed.

Indeed, such an application of the doctrine ignores the conditions in the phrases "in *bona fide* transactions and not in restraint of trade," as interpreted in the broader spirit of the American Can

[10] 227 Fed. 46 (1915); same case in the District Court, 224 Fed. 566 (1915).
[11] 227 Fed. 610.

decision. For, if refusal to sell a particular customer lessens competition between him and others to whom goods are sold, then is such refusal in restraint of trade. The doctrine of the seller's right to select his own customers is, in free markets, sound as economics and, therefore, as law, but ceases to have validity in economics at that point where full competition ends and limited monopoly begins. There, refusal to sell may become far worse than discrimination merely in price. It might fairly be called the worst form of discrimination, depriving the customer of any possibility of buying goods he must have to survive. It may spell business excommunication and utter ruin. Yet monopolies today have been known to boast that they can legally blacklist a buyer for the reason that they do not like the color of his hair, or for any other reason, or for no reason whatever. And they cite legal opinions to support this assertion. Can such a manifest injustice be valid law?

TROUBLESOME QUALIFICATIONS

Thus surveying the useless and troublesome qualifications which clutter up the second section of the Clayton Act, they are seen to reflect the confused thought that discrimination is a normal condition of genuine market competition. The sincere reformers, torn with doubts and fears that they were rendering futile the whole legislative effort to prevent discrimination, voted with tears in their eyes for the measure as it now stands. Skillful lobbyists had done their work in loading the law with persiflage. It had been rendered not quite useless but far less useful for its well-intended social purpose. A simple proposition forbidding discrimination in prices in interstate commerce would, in the economic view, have been far better to accomplish the ends desired. The Court could be depended upon, either taking the word discrimination in its plainest meaning, or, be it by the "rule of reason," to interpret, or read into, the section, all these conditions that were needful or helpful. Against the possibility, however, that the Court, because of its economic views, would in the absence of these qualifications pronounce the whole act unconstitutional, it seems impossible to have insured.

ANOTHER CASUALTY TO THE CLAYTON ACT

We cannot leave the subject of the Clayton Act without regretful mention of the construction that was put by a bare majority in a 5 to 4 decision on Sections 7 and 11, which were intended to prevent merger by the acquiring of stock.[12] The clear dissenting opin-

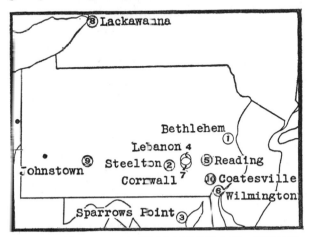

FIG. 32. BETHLEHEM-LACKAWANNA MERGER, COMPLETED 1923 BY ABSORPTION OF NOS. 6, 8, 9, 10, AND LAST REMAINING INDEPENDENTS IN A SALES AREA GREATER THAN THE GERMAN EMPIRE. DISSOLUTION SUIT UNDER THE CLAYTON ACT, DOCKET 962, WAS WRECKED BY EASTMAN KODAK DECISION IN 1927

ion of Justice Brandeis in 1926 (with which Chief Justice Taft and Justices Holmes and Stone concurred) and that of Justice Stone in 1927 (with which Justice Brandeis concurred) appear to an economist's eye to be utterly disarming to the majority's argument. The majority held that the Commission cannot order (physical) property and business, though obtained by means of "stock unlawfully held," to be devested, although the statute makes it the duty of the

---

[12] Originally in the Thatcher and Swift Cases, considered with the Western Meat Company Case (somewhat differently decided upon a different state of facts), and decided November 1926, in 272 U.S. 554; later followed closely in the Eastman Kodak Case, 274 U S. 619, May 1927, in a 7 to 2 decision.

Commission to act and grants it the power to do so if it "shall have reason to believe that any person is violating or has violated any of the provisions" of the earlier sections. The Court seems to suggest that if any relief from the unlawful situation is to be had, it can come only on the initiative of the Attorney General, acting under the Sherman Act. The Court's words are: "If the purchase of property has produced an unlawful status a remedy is provided through the courts." [13] How reassuring, in view of the Court's own attitude toward mergers! Thus is the public, in its efforts to check further mergers under existing laws, batted back and forth like a tennis ball, from one court to another.

THE OLD DOCTRINE OF PUBLIC CALLINGS

We conclude this chapter with a brief consideration of a fundamental question which may arise, and ultimately must be answered, in regard to any and every sort and instance of governmental control and regulation of industrial and commercial prices, as well under the Sherman Act as under the Clayton Act. That question is: On what grounds can the prices in any business in private ownership be subjected to price regulation in any degree whatever, other than that to which the great mass of private business, through ordinary civil law, is subjected?

Recent economic conditions, especially those brought about by unhindered concentration of ownership of industries, have reproduced in magnified form the situation in which the old doctrine of common employments arose and prevailed.[14] Those engaged in common trades—tailors, victualers, bakers, millers, and many others—had the duty to serve all comers. The reason for this doctrine lay in the need to protect the public against non-service and extortion at a time of sparse population and scanty industries. As conditions of real competition extended,[15] the doctrine of common employments was narrowed (continuing, however, to include common carriers) before its transplantation to America. Other economic changes forced a new growth of the doctrine in certain

---

[13] 272 U.S. 561 in the Thatcher Case.
[14] Bruce Wyman, *Public Service Corporations*, pp. 4-16 (1911); *Harvard Law Review*, Vol. 17, pp. 156, 217 (1903-1904); see also *Harvard Law Review*, Vol. 28, p. 135.
[15] See Ch. XVIII.

ways.[16] Again the courts faced the question: When and why does a particular business become "affected with a public interest"; in other words, when does it become a public calling? Such enterprises, when so designated, are subject to exceptional governmental regulation. Recent students of the court decisions have been impressed with the elusive nature of public callings and conclude that, in the light of the cases, "very little" can be said about the general characteristics of such enterprises. In their judgment, the grounds of the decisions have been so constantly shifted that the possibility of forecasting the future scope of the "public interest" classification has been entirely eliminated.[17]

MONOPOLY THE TEST OF PUBLIC INTEREST

It seems to us clear, however, that businesses recognized by the courts of old or of late as "affected with a public interest" in respect to prices and services are all in some degree characterized by monopoly. This is true of the three classes said by Chief Justice Taft to be clothed with a public interest and thus "justifying some public regulation": (1) those carried on under authority of a public grant of privileges (not open to every one); (2) certain exceptional trades and callings among which still are innkeeping, cab driving, and grist milling; and (3) certain businesses that "have come to hold such a 'peculiar' relation to the public" that they have been subjected "to some government regulation." [18] Monopoly is the common quality marking these three as of "special privilege," or as "exceptional" or as "peculiar" respectively.[19]

---

[16] Munn v. Illinois, 94 U.S. 113, 1876.
[17] Keezer and May, *The Public Control of Business,* 1930, p. 97 ff., especially p. 118.
[18] Wolff Packing Company v. Kansas Court of Industrial Relations, 262 U.S. 522 (1923).
[19] R. J. Swenson, in *The National Government and Business* (1924), pp. 133-140, after a survey of the rival theories of public business: monopoly, the doctrine of assumpsit (set forth by Blackstone) and the public character of all business by common law, and sovereign legislative will, concludes with the view above expressed, that "the monopoly and public interest theory is the most satisfactory." J. M. Clark, in *Social Control of Business,* pp. 300-301, although declaring that "the theory of monopoly (or virtual monopoly), is too narrow and will not account for all the cases," yet (following R. G. Tugwell, *The Economic Basis of Public Interest,* 1922) regards it as "the essential economic fact" in all cases "that the nature of the business is such that competition . . . does not afford protection to buyers and sellers," that it is not working freely, "the individual is not in a position to avail himself of the

RELATIVITY OF MONOPOLY AND PUBLIC INTEREST

As pointed out by J. M. Clark,

the traditional attitude of the courts prevents the conception of public interest from being applied to a large part of the cases in which a real public interest exists.[20]

The difficulty seems to be that the courts incline strongly toward an absolute conception of public interest (employments, or callings) rather than toward a relative concept; they declare a calling to be either fully affected with a public interest or not at all. This view is related to the absolute conception of monopoly to which the courts cling.[21] Grounds other than monopoly for the special regulation of some businesses are found in the police power to safeguard health, suppress nuisances, or prevent fraud in public fiduciary relations (banking, insurance, etc.); but none of these is price regulation. We submit that a relative concept of a public calling should correspond with a relative concept of monopoly, and accordingly, a particular business should not be classed as always and entirely either public or private. It is quasi-public or more or less private according to the absence or presence of competitive conditions.

Before indicating further the practical applications of the subject of this chapter to the solution of the monopoly problem, let us consider the attempts now being made to undermine the very theory of the Sherman Act and to repeal or to amend it in essential particulars.

options which competition offers." This is in essential accord with the view expressed above.

[20] In *Social Control of Business,* p. 200.
[21] See Ch. XXIII.

———

CHAPTER XXVII

IN DEFENSE OF THE SHERMAN ACT ?

THE AGITATION TO REPEAL

THE present is a fateful hour in the history of American, indeed of all, free social institutions throughout the world. For two generations our people and our governmental agencies have first resolved boldly to maintain the system of commercial liberty, then weakly doubted whether it could be done. Meantime the forces of self-interest and special privilege have never slept and never faltered. The battle is not yet decided; on some parts of the field the principles of industrial freedom seem to be fairly secure; elsewhere on the industrial field the forces of monopoly are confidently triumphant.

Popular faith in the older ideals has been undoubtedly much weakened in the last two decades by a well-organized propaganda constantly pounding in our ears the faults and failures of the Sherman Act and the necessity of a radical revision of its terms— if not of its complete repeal. We stand now at the parting of the ways and must choose, whether we will or not, the road to greater artificial control of prices by private privilege or the road that leads toward freer markets and personal freedom safeguarded by public agencies. After a period of comparative respite from these complaints, during the super-speculative period culminating in 1929, when the combinations and industrial conspiracies had everything that their hearts could desire, the agitation for trust law revision, as one journal puts it, "has taken on new vigor as a result of the difficult conditions created by the business depression."[1]

[1] The New York *Times*, November 16, 1930.

STARTING THE HUE AND CRY

Mr. Thomas W. Lamont, spokesman for the House of Morgan, has recently attracted wide attention by his declaration that

Our somewhat antiquated anti-trust laws have been in part responsible for encouraging excessive construction of plant and equipment in the industrial field. The present law constitutes almost a mandate to every wide-awake manufacturer to duplicate the facilities of his rival, and the result is bound to be a great economic waste. I am not assuming to suggest the sort of remedial legislation that should be had in order to avoid this obvious wastage of capital brought about through almost unbridled competition.[2]

Mr. Lamont's charge that the present laws compel "wide-awake manufacturers" to duplicate wastefully the facilities of their competitors has no rational basis of fact. The insinuation is that mergers are impossible under the present law (this in view of the recent history of unhindered mergers!). Yet we are told that manufacturers can never buy up their competitors' plants and therefore can compete only by uselessly duplicating plants! Nor has the Sherman Act compelled "unbridled" competition. Mr. Lamont places the blame for excess capacity upon the laws forbidding restraint and conspiracy, although this difficulty is most pronounced in those very industries in which the anti-trust laws have been most flouted. Let the apologist for monopoly laugh that off if he can. It is the violation (not the observance) of the law that has caused such wasteful duplication. Much of the recent outcry against the Sherman Act is like the cry of stop thief by the real criminals joining in the chase.

President Hoover in his message to Congress, December 2, 1930, recommended "an inquiry into some aspects of the economic working of" the anti-trust laws, especially "upon those enterprises closely related to the use of the natural resources of the country." Although he flatly declared, "I do not favor repeal of the Sherman Act," he inclined a sympathetic ear to those who charge it with "the wasteful and destructive use of our natural resources together with a destructive competition which impoverishes both operator and worker." How far he would go in amendment of the Act is

[2] In address reported in the New York *Times,* November 15, 1930.

not indicated. Mr. Samuel Untermyer, well known as counsel for mining and industrial corporations and the formation of mergers, added his voice to that of Mr. Lamont in denunciation of "our outworn, misfit anti-trust laws," "our archaic anti-trust laws." [3]

DEFEATIST ADVICE

By a persistent campaign in high places it is attempted to depict the Sherman Act as the cause of all the evils that have resulted from its partial nullification. In the same breath its blighting effects are deplored and it is declared to have been practically a "dead letter." Says Mr. Untermyer:

The laws to enforce competition were never given a fair trial by our administrative departments or by the courts. They were uniformly treated as a "stepchild"; fitfully, half-heartedly enforced, and were tolerated only to appease the public clamor of the day against the "trusts." . . . The laws were vastly more "honored in the breach than in the observance" until now they would be impossible of enforcement if we were so disposed. [4]

It is a disquieting picture of our democracy thus set before us, of Congressional laws flouted, and of the public humored and tricked like an unreasoning child by the superior wisdom of the lawbreakers. Much of this, indeed, is verified by the economic analysis of cases in the foregoing pages. But the betrayal of the Sherman Act by the "administrative departments" of the government seems ground for a change of administration rather than for the repudiation of the policy of the law.

SLANDERERS OF THE SHERMAN ACT

Most of the "wasteful duplication" and "destructive competition" attributed to that statute by its critics is truly the result of discrimination in prices. Our earlier analysis of the nature and effects of discrimination has shown that, to the economic eye, discrimination appears to be about as illegal under the terms of the law of 1890 (if soundly interpreted and enforced) as under the Clayton Act. The sort of talk that we have been listening to may

[3] Statement given by Mr. Untermyer to the press. The New York *Times*, November 17, 1930.
[4] *Idem.*

be labeled: slandering the Sherman Act. The campaign has been carried on for forty years, until, like persistent advertising, it is believed by multitudes just because they have seen it and heard it so often. Mr. Gary was an artful expounder of this doctrine, by hint and evasion. In 1911, antedating Mr. Lamont by twenty years, Mr. Gary declared it to be his "position that the Sherman anti-trust law recently interpreted by the Court nevertheless leaves an archaic law to deal with the modern situation." [5]

Returning to the same notion, Mr. Gary a few days later developed further his contention that the Sherman Law's provision "against restraint of trade" was antagonistic to its other provision "against monopoly," actually forcing competitors into price wars which resulted in a monopoly. He broadly claimed (in conditional phrases) that unless manufacturers were permitted "to enter into a combination or agreement, express or implied, to fix prices, to restrict output, to divide territory . . . except for such basis whereby destructive competition could be avoided . . . it would mean that a large percentage at least of the manufacturers of steel would be wrecked; and that would secure to the survivors, to a greater or less extent a monopoly." [6]

He was here justifying the Gary dinners, which, he said, had "prevented the destructive competition to which I have adverted" —though he plainly implies an admission that his action was in restraint of trade. He characterized his own remarks as a "frank and honest state of facts, whether they are justified or not." However, the claim, or even the insinuation, that the Sherman Act compels cutthroat discrimination, or any other kind, was neither frank nor honest.[7] Probably the last thing that Mr. Gary desired was the complete stopping of discrimination, for this would have put an end to the basing-point practice, so essential to the mode of price control adopted by his Corporation.

[5] These are the words of the question to which Mr. Gary answered, "It is." His further view that the Sherman Act practically orders a continuance of a "warfare of competition" was quoted above in Ch. IX. Testimony before the Stanley Committee, June 2, 1911, p. 79.

[6] Stanley Committee Hearings, June 7, 1911, p. 195.

[7] For Mr. Schwab's similar views, see Ch. IX.

THE WASTES OF MONOPOLY

The opponents of our anti-trust laws have surfeited us with complaints against the wastes of competition, but they are silent on the wastes of monopoly. Some wastes of competition there undoubtedly are, but we have abundantly proved, we believe, that most of the "competition" in which these wastes appear is pseudo-competition, neither economic nor legal. Now indeed, from many competent sources, we are beginning to hear a truer explanation of the wasteful surplus productive capacity which has appeared most strikingly in the industries where either private conspiracies or mischievous governmental favoritism have offended against economic and statute laws—either or both. Even Mr. Lamont, in the same address from which we have quoted his opposition to the Sherman Act, ascribed this world-wide depression also to another cause:

in part to the effort made in many parts of the world to hold up commodity prices artificially, whether in rubber, cotton, wheat, coffee, copper or what not. When prices for such commodities finally gave way, the severity of the business collapse was accentuated.[8]

Two weeks earlier, Dr. David Friday, a keen critic of current economic affairs, though not such an accredited spokesman of "big business," had indicated as one of the noteworthy causes of the present depression,

the stabilization pools in various products, formed to keep prices far above the cost of production. He cited the rubber pool in Great Britain which caused rubber to sell at $1 a pound in 1921, and pointed out that the price had dropped to 21 cents in 1929. . . . The same thing happened in Japan with silk, in Australia with wool, in Brazil with coffee, in America with copper, in Canada with wheat.[9]

A CAUSE OF BUSINESS INDIGESTION

A writer who knows how to combine a goodly measure of true economic insight with practical comments on business conditions had written to the same effect in an article entitled significantly, "The Drastic Cure for Business Indigestion." That painful ail-

[8] The New York *Times*, November 15, 1930.
[9] Report of an address in Chicago in the New York *Times*, November 3, 1930.

ment, said he, consists in the present supernormal productive capacity due to the all too rapid extension of mechanization. One of the causes of this is a growing group consciousness in industry, resulting in

a pronounced effort to keep all the members afloat . . . to hold prices at a level that will keep the marginal [inefficient] plants going . . . prices higher than the modernized plants require. . . . The degree to which obsolescent plants and processes hold on, even in America, is amazing. Sometimes they gnaw into capital for decades. . . . The most drastic and at the same time the most effective way of dealing with one phase of overproduction is to eradicate obsolescence—to arbitrarily write off and demolish such excess capacity that is not up to the standard of modern practice . . . leaving the field to the better plants. . . .

Group restriction . . . offers a temptation to raise prices even beyond the margin demands by the inefficient plants, thus making the industry liable to new plants or enlargement of the efficient ones. The solution of the problem is merely postponed. Business in general is now going through a restriction of production. . . . It is a healthy process, tending toward the survival of the fittest.[10]

PRIVATE AND PUBLIC PRICE RIGGING

There is a true picture of what has been going on in the past ten years and of the inevitable consequences. There is illegal restraint of commerce by secret or tacit agreements and a live-and-let-live policy within leading industries. With short-sighted greed for quick profits, prices are fixed and maintained so high that demand is curtailed, and at the same time inefficient producers are enabled to survive and even to increase their capacity. This adds powerfully to the unhealthy forces of inflation and speculation, only to make the general collapse more disastrous by the still greater collapse in these particular industries. Having brought upon themselves the righteous penalties for their sins against economics and the anti-trust laws, these industrial leaders have the temerity to launch a renewed attack upon the Sherman Act at this very time, denouncing it as the cause of all their troubles.

Most of the preceding quotations are so worded as to apply

---

[10] Theodore M. Knappen in *The Magazine of Wall Street,* October 18, 1930, pp. 919-920.

The Magazine of Wall Street, Oct. 18, 1930

FIG. 33. VICTIMS OF EXCESS PRODUCTIVE CAPACITY, INDUCED BY
ARTIFICIAL PRICE CONTROL, AS IN STEEL, COPPER, CEMENT, RUB-
BER, COFFEE, WHEAT, SUGAR, LUMBER, SILK, ETC. THE TRUTH NOW
SEEN IN WALL STREET

only to private price control, but they apply with equal truth to efforts at governmental price control (British rubber restrictions, Brazilian coffee valorization, Canadian wheat purchases, American Farm Board plans, etc.). Spokesmen of large banks, who are more closely linked in interest with manufacturing and mining than with agricultural investments, readily detect the mistake of the long-suffering agricultural producers in imitating, by aid of governments, the example of the big industries in artificial control of prices. The gratuitous financial advisers of the farmers expose the futility of attempting to solve the problem of farm surpluses by keeping prices up and thus stimulating greater surpluses. They see no hope of ultimate relief save in "the law of supply and demand," the elimination of the submarginal producers. "Why not allow the marginal lands and marginal farmers to drop out of production?" [11] But there is not a pin's difference in sound theory and healthy public policy between urban and rural, between industrial and agricultural, price control "in defiance of the law of supply and demand," as the phrase runs. A real difference is, however, that large private business (conspiring) is usually able to do it for a time more successfully and to the greater profit of a little group of insiders, than can any governmental board for the benefit of a multitude of competing citizens. Among several explanations of this difference, the greater ability of industrial enterprises to restrict production artificially is most important.

SWAPPING AFFLICTIONS

Many American business men have long looked enviously upon the German "cartels," which are legally tolerated pools and looser agreements as to output and prices among otherwise independent producers. The assumption that these cartels are unanimously favored in Germany is far from correct. A book entitled *The Fate of German Capitalism*, by Professor Moritz Bonn, which appeared in 1926, has attracted wide attention and has run into several large editions. Professor Bonn shows that the cartel plan has deep medieval roots in the feudal system of caste and special privilege in Germany, and is maintained at the expense of higher prices to the people. But even to the favored industries the final benefits

[11] *National City Bank Letter,* April 1930.

are doubtful. He finds in the legalized German cartels the same objections that we have just observed in respect to the illegal "cartels" (pools and agreements) in America. They load the back of industry with the weight of obsolescent plants, always to the injury of the public and ultimately to that of the industries themselves. Today there is a widespread doubt even in Germany, the home of legalized cartels, whether the stopping of orderly, legitimate competition has not caused more evil than good. As distant pastures always look green, some Germans (including Professor Bonn) even would prefer a real super-combination—an American "trust"—to their own self-defeating cartel system.

MONOPOLY OVERREACHES ITSELF

The topsy-turvy school of political economy whose method of preventing the creation of surplus capacity is to boost prices to the public and thus make the business profitable to the inefficient has no more typical exhibit than the copper industry. Its achievement in maintaining for a whole year a pegged price of 18 cents in the face of accumulating stocks and despite curtailment at the low-cost mines deserves the ignoble prize for Simple Simon economics.

Just before the break in copper in April 1930 this episode in artificial price fixing was discussed in one of the leading financial journals by a professional mining engineer, active for thirty years in the copper industry in various capacities.[12] He concluded from the statistical data that at the pegged price of 18 cents, stocks of copper must continue rapidly to accumulate despite large voluntary curtailment of output by the big producers who control 75 per cent of the plant capacity. Citing the figures of leading authorities, he showed that 93 per cent of the total world's copper is produced at an operating cost of less than 12 cents a pound, and concluded that a price not much above 12 cents is what is warranted by the "marginal principle," and the supply at that price should be sufficient to meet the needs of the world for possibly a half century to come. The whole burden of recent curtailment in the effort to maintain the excessive (and monopolistic) price of 18

[12] Percy E. Barbour in the New York *Times Annalist,* three articles on the price of copper, March 7, 14, 21, 1930.

cents fell upon the large producers (whose costs mostly range from 4 to 8 cents a pound).

In other words, the large producers are operating on a scale that would be stimulated by a price of less than 13 cent copper. The big producers . . . are maintaining 18 cent copper . . . at the expense of their balance sheets.

THE COPPER RACKET

There was thus presented the spectacle of the great copper junto levying from the world a sheer tribute of $100,000,000 a year (say 2 billion pounds of copper at 5 cents monopoly plus per pound), one half of which was paid by the people of the United States. Yet it begins to be questioned whether this in the long run resulted in much net benefit to the producing companies except those operating the inefficient mines that in sound economics would better not have been opened. It is incredible that the copper princes did not get something more out of it than this. The wiseacres shake their heads and say: stock speculation. The mining magnate's concern in maintaining metal prices is at critical times subsidiary to his interest in boosting stock prices. Greater fortunes may be dug out of Wall Street than out of Montana and Arizona—and more lost there. This is not the economics of public welfare, but rather the wastes of monopoly.

ALICE IN COPPERLAND [13]

When copper prices had hit the cellar below ten cents in 1930, another financial analyst showed that in the more normal year of 1928 about 88 per cent of the output of the leading American plants (far more than is needed for present consumption) was produced at an operating cost of less than 10 cents. He concluded that "low cost producers can," if they wish, "capture the market" by continuing to give the public low prices.[14] Instead, the financial journals began to teem with notices of visiting representatives of foreign copper interests and of agreements for world-wide restric-

[13] Some readers will recognize in this phrase the title of a series of witty Carrollesque bulletins on the copper price situation in 1929-30, written by a well-known non-ferrous metal broker in New York.

[14] William Knodel, in *The Magazine of Wall Street*, September 6, 1930.

tion in plain violation of the Sherman Act and of the Webb-Pomerene Act, which provides that domestic prices shall not be raised by agreements under it. Thus the wonderland political

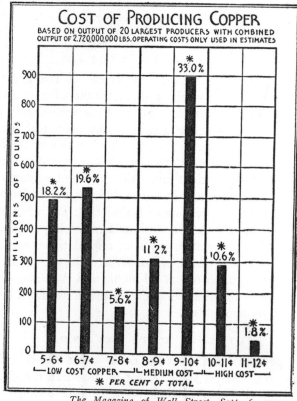

The Magazine of Wall Street, Sept. 6, 1930

FIG. 34. MONOPOLY FLOUTS ECONOMIC AND STATUTE LAWS IN FIXING ARTIFICIALLY THE PRICE OF NATURE'S GIFTS TO THE NATION

economy of the copper kings has made the richest copper deposits extra-marginal with restricted production, while wastefully keeping in operation the high-cost mines, which in a saner economic world would be left for use in the distant future when the better deposits were nearing exhaustion.

CLAD IN THE LION'S SKIN

Just now a plea for "conservation" is being used as a smoke screen under cover of which the general policy of our anti-trust laws is being assailed. The charge is made that the Sherman Act really compels the wasteful exploitation of our natural resources. Outright waste of resources such as opening up wells, only to let the oil run away to no purpose, should of course be prevented by whatever means will do it. But this is not to be confused with the other idea of conservation, that of the present generation's voluntarily abstaining from the liberal use of natural resources in order that future unborn generations may enjoy more of them or enjoy them longer. Regard for posterity is a not unworthy human and patriotic sentiment, shared in some degree by all good citizens. In practical expression that means that each of us in our generation must be willing to use less and pay more (much or little more) for each gallon of oil and of gasoline, each foot of lumber, each ton of coal, each pound of copper, etc., in order that our grandchildren (or somebody else's) shall pay less and use more of these good things a hundred years hence, let us say. Well and good—"We're game. What have you got up your sleeve?" Here come forward distinguished corporation lawyers with their plan, as follows. Permit agreements in restraint of trade among the present owners and corporate leaseholders of these natural resources, which will prevent the prices falling to the level fixed by the supply, as indicated at the marginal wells, mines, etc. That way you "rationalize" (stabilize!) the price at, say, 25 instead of 15 cents a gallon, which present conditions warrant, and thereby reduce the consumption by, say, one-third. This is all for the sake of our grandchildren, you understand. But wait! Who gets this extra 10 cents per gallon, amounting to hundreds of millions, yes, billions of dollars yearly? The owners of the land and the producers—and they capitalize it at once into more billions as the increased present worth of their private property.

But why should "we the people" take this way of raising the present price of oil, etc., voluntarily taxing ourselves and our children to make a few more lucky and greedy contemporaries billionaires? "In vain is the net spread in the sight of the bird."

Exactly the same result of raising prices could be attained and the profits would go to the public treasury if an output tax of, say, 10 cents a gallon were imposed on all oil produced. This would reduce consumption and make the sub-marginal oil lands unprofitable until prices rose much above present levels, and it would produce an enormous revenue for public purposes. The same sort of output tax could be applied to mines and forests. What? You object because that would be a great burden on industry? Oh, you philanthropists! Then it is not conservation for the benefit of posterity you really want; it is exploitation of your fellow citizens for the benefit of your own pocketbooks. The animal wears the lion's skin of conservation, but whence comes that bray?

BACK TO FUNDAMENTALS

No doubt there are real problems of conservation, such as the peculiar one of the wasteful duplication of wells in newly discovered pools of oil, which should be dealt with by changes in State and Federal land laws or in other ways. How about keeping in public hands, henceforth, all under-surface minerals on the national lands? Wouldn't that help? But listen to the protests of our counterfeit conservationists at any such suggestion.

The problem of bituminous coal mines is in some measure the fairly common case of an industry suddenly checked by the rapid growth of substitutes; largely, however, this industry, like others, is the victim of an unsound policy of railroad freight rates, the so-called equalization principle. With the erroneous idea that local monopoly must be the result if industries are permitted to enjoy the full advantage of their locations (without discrimination), rates have been and still are fixed so as to make market areas "common fighting grounds." Transportation costs are all but ignored in fixing rates that nullify distance to the shipper. Present resulting evils in the coal industry and others can only be cured by steady approach to the distance principle in railroad rates, with enforcement of uniform prices by each producer at his plant.

It is the same old story over and over: ignorance of simple economic principles causes a mistaken public policy to be adopted and seeks to correct the evils by another equally mistaken. The solution of the most complex problems of industrial price policy

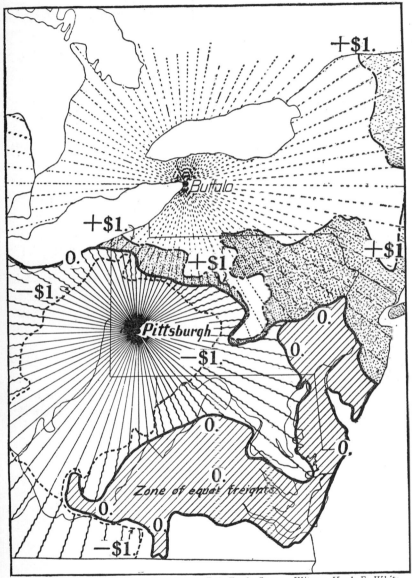

+$1.

+$1.

+$1.

0.

−$1.

+$1.

Buffalo

0.

0.

0.

Pittsburgh

−$1.

0.

0.

0.

0.

0.

Zone of equal freights

0.

−$1.

Data from Docket 962, Fed. Trade Comm., Witness Hugh E. White

FIG. 35. FREAKISH FREIGHT SCHEDULES. GOODS ARE CARRIED FROM BUFFALO HUNDREDS OF MILES BEYOND PITTSBURGH FOR $1 LESS. THE EQUALIZATION PRINCIPLE INVERTS NATURAL LOCATIONS

must be sought through the logical application of the elementary principles of prices and markets in each set of practical conditions.

COMPETITION, THE NORM OF REGULATION

It is often overlooked, in the attempt to belittle or discredit the place and function of competition in our industrial system, that the only norm or guide we have for fair and reasonable rates and prices, even for regulated monopolies, is the estimated (conditional) competitive price that *would* result in the long run under normal competitive conditions and yield the average rate of profits estimated to be sufficient (and no more) to attract and retain the private investment necessary for adequate service to the public. Monopoly affords no standard; its limit is what the traffic will bear—extortion. The ideal in public price-fixing for public utilities is still competitive price—if not actual, then constructive, hypothetical, and calculated in the best manner possible.

Amidst all the discordant clamor regarding the proper rate base and methods of estimating it, regarding the proper rate of returns, and regarding the nature and degree of authority intrusted to various public officials, there is substantial agreement upon this ideal of "fairness" and "reasonableness" found in the competitive price and rate of return. Lacking it, public price-fixing would be adrift without rudder or compass. The continued existence of a large area of competition in industry and agriculture is the necessary condition for the successful regulation of prices in the smaller group of public monopolies.

THE POPULAR TASTE FOR PANACEAS

We near the end of our study of those many ills to which the industrial body is heir, or has contracted through evil associations; yet we have not suggested as a remedy the popular panacea of another bottle of legislation. We confess that this is not quite in accord with the mood with which we began this clinic some years ago. The phrase, "there ought to be a law against it," comes trippingly from the tongue of every free-born American, who readily sees great virtues in a new law, as applied to the other fellow. Perhaps "there ought to be a law against it" in this case too, after time has shown that, when faithfully enforced, the laws already on the statute books are insufficient.

This is no time to weaken or amend the Sherman Act. The more we have studied it and the history of the ineffective attempts to enforce it, the greater has become our respect for its original simplicity, directness, and adequacy of wording for the purpose intended. The same must be said less emphatically of the Clayton Act, by which Congress sought to repair the havoc wrought in the Sherman Act by administrative bungling and injudicious decisions. Mr. James Bryce declared that the colonists of New England could make any sort of written constitution work, whereas the most ideal document of words is a dead letter in a nation whose citizens are unfit for self-government. So where and how could we begin, and how tinker with our present statutes to improve their wording? And when the repairs are made, are the new laws, all slick and shiny, to be handed over to the same agencies of non-enforcement and to be interpreted in the same manner? There is, after all, more hope in the slower but surer processes of education. Before the trust problem can be solved, it is necessary to clarify the purposes of the people and the economic ideas of the legal profession and of the courts, to bring all into accord with social needs. Our book, to this point, is an honest effort to contribute to these purposes. Our concluding chapter will indicate specifically how, under our present laws, the existing evils of monopoly may be hopefully attacked.

CHAPTER XXVIII

THE REMEDIES AT HAND

THE RIVAL VOICES

"WISDOM is knowing what is right to do next; virtue is doing it." The people have the political virtue to maintain free markets and the liberty of the trader when they know how it can be done. But they have suffered by divided counsels; they have been confused by evil counselors; they doubt, and halt, and waver. What is it wise now to do in policies of industrial organization and price regulation? Two extreme opinions compete for a hearing. The voice of those who have done most to violate and nullify our existing anti-trust laws, and to bring our traditional policy of freedom in domestic commerce well-nigh into an impasse, proclaims the necessity of further checking or completely abandoning that hard-won policy. The other voice, which has found expression in these pages, pleads for a sincere attempt to save the most precious principle in the system of private property—the commercial liberty of the common man. Almost we seemed to have grasped it; then it began fast slipping away.

MONOPOLY'S TOOL

Our main theme throughout this book is the basing-point practice, but in these later chapters the subject of monopoly in general, and of mergers in particular as a common means of attaining monopoly, have seemed to be crowding the basing point off the stage. However, the connection between the basing-point practice and mergers, and that of both with monopoly, is very close. Let us, therefore, see first whether, and how, restraint of trade by the use of basing points may be ended, and then see what situation that leaves with respect to mergers as a means of attaining and exercising monopoly power.

The basing-point practice is today the most common form taken by discrimination (though mild sporadic as well as cutthroat discrimination may often occur). It is an elaborate system of local price cutting and local dumping. All discrimination is a sign and exercise of monopoly power, whether attained by agreement (open or tacit) among otherwise independent sellers, or by complete proprietary merger of separate plants. True, the degree of monopoly power needed to make possible the initial acts of discrimination may be, and usually is, very small, but given a sort of fulcrum in local monopoly by reason of appreciable distance from the nearest competitor, and monopoly may use discrimination as a powerful lever to multiply further its powers. Let us consider now how a condition of market-price uniformity may be obtained, and the desirable results that must follow its attainment.

THE POSTED PUBLIC PRICE

Is the task of preventing discrimination in interstate commerce impossible? In fact, to put an end to discrimination is as easy as standing an egg on end when we know how. The sole necessary means for attaining a régime of non-discrimination is the requirement and enforcement of publicity for all prices in interstate commerce. Given a posted price, uniform to all at the announced place of sale and shipment of the goods, and the plan would be in large measure self-enforcing, and for these reasons: the public posted price, which alone is legal, will so clarify the rights of all buyers and sellers that their claims can be easily fixed and directly expressed. Once the plain policy of the law is made clear, a great force of law-abiding self-interest is enlisted to see that the law is enforced, buyers to see that they get the benefit of the posted price, and sellers to see that competitors adhere to their announced prices. This is the restoration of markets. In this direction, business, loosely organized in trade associations, has been groping by the adoption of so-called "codes of ethics" to prevent discrimination. This is a good aspect of trade association activity. Discrimination and secret prices have within very recent years been denounced by many associations as "unethical" and as properly to be restrained by voluntary action, but they are not denounced as essentially illegal. These associations have attempted an impossible straddle; the members have vainly hoped to escape the evils of discrimination by their neighbors while each member claimed for himself the right to discriminate, mildly and discreetly, when he pleased. And remember that the use of a basing point involves a tacit *de facto* conspiracy and a whole system of discriminations.

TRAFFIC LAWS AND COMMERCE LAWS

A non-discriminatory price system, generally and impartially enforced, may be likened to a well-enforced code of traffic laws which reduces the danger and loss from not knowing what the other driver is going to do next or who has the right of way at the crossroads. Think what would happen if drivers darted in and out, to right or to left, cut in on the others, and gave no signals with their hands, or by stop lights, or with horns, to signify their intentions, and if they did this at night without carrying lights, and if they were allowed to do all these things without regulation or penalty. That is a fair analogy with the chaos, injury, and loss that result in commerce where discrimination is suffered to be practiced in commercial dealings. The business world has just cause to complain against the evils of the present situation, but it has never seen clearly either the cause or the simple remedy.

A proof of the intolerableness, in free and orderly commerce, of basing-point and other discriminatory prices is found in this analogy with traffic laws. It would be impossible to retain the rule of the road to keep to the right while permitting each driver (or group of drivers) to decide for himself, if he pleased, to keep to the left. As it would still be legal to keep to the right, drivers of the bigger trucks, some veritable army tanks, would have it in their power at any time legally to crush any small car or to force it off the road by simply driving to the right, in front of it. As you cannot without traffic disaster, make it legal to drive either on the right or on the left side as each one prefers at the moment, so you cannot without commercial disaster permit individual choice between mill-base prices and basing-point (or other discriminatory) prices. To do so gives to the stronger party a big bully's control over the business fortunes of his smaller competitors.

Now mill-base prices are the rule in most industries. *They are
unquestionably legal.* They were the rule only a few years ago in
the very industries now following the basing-point plan, and even
there are always resumed when tacit conspiracies break down in
periods of stress. At such times we see the destructive power that
a dominant leader, a great horizontal merger, can exercise through
its legal right of resuming the plan of selling on a mill base at any
one of its mills that is in the sales area of some smaller competitor.
Equipment, sales, market areas, which have been built up during
years under the unnatural rule of basing-point prices, crumble into
ruin before such a sudden change in territorial price policies. Such
seem to have been the conditions in 1921 preceding the Bethlehem-
Lackawanna merger. If mill-base prices are economic and legal
(as they are) basing-point prices cannot be so at the same time.

BEHAVIOR V. INTENT AS TESTS

And here we may recall the judicial predilection to make intent
the essential mark of the violation of the anti-trust laws, rather than
visible acts. Intent is a far less simple and workable test than behavior. Anti-trust statutes, to be sure, are technically penal in
nature, and usually an intent to injure some one must be proved
to bring conviction under a penal statute. But has the construction
of the anti-trust laws not followed a false analogy? A law declaring every one who takes a gun in his hands to be guilty of man-
slaughter would practically prohibit the use of guns, and would
be silly if that were not its purpose. But some States have very
sensibly in the light of experience forbidden a person to point a
gun at another whether the gun is loaded or not. No intent to
kill or injure need be proved to constitute a misdemeanor.

Again, the traffic law requires that a driver stop when the red
light is against him. The traffic officer does not need to prove that
it was the driver's *purpose* to crash into another automobile, nor
does he wait to see whether the occupants of another car have been
killed before handing out a summons, nor does the judge next
day usually disturb himself about proof of these effects before
imposing a fine. To be sure, damage to property and to persons
gives grounds for other actions, civil and criminal, but the simple

offense against the traffic laws consists in heedlessly running past the light. Commerce laws are like traffic laws; they are, in essence, traffic laws regulating the behavior of traders on the roads of commerce. They make safer, and on the whole, despite occasional delays for individuals, they make swifter, the movements of commerce. What we need for a while in the enforcement of the anti-trust laws is less talk by criminal lawyers, and more traffic officers to watch crossings and to spot license numbers.[1]

BOGUS STABILITY FROM DISCRIMINATION

A claim put forward for artificial price control is that it "stabilizes" prices. As compared with a preceding period of chaotic local price wars, even a fair measure of price control by a dominant combination comes as a relief to nearly every one. If the preceding chaos were a state of real and lawful competition, and if (as is erroneously assumed) the only way to remedy it were by countenancing monopoly, that might be an improvement. But cutthroat competition is neither economic nor legal, and it can be ended by simply enforcing the law, not surrendering our whole industrial system in desperation to the slavery of monopoly. Moreover, the word "stabilize" (and the favorite synonym "rationalize"), in the argument in question, is deceptively used. What is meant is increase, not stabilize. Properly, stabilize means to reduce, or prevent, fluctuations, up and down, over a period of time. The monopolists succeed often in "stabilizing" (pegging) the artificial *basing-point* price for somewhat brief periods, but their efforts result rather in magnifying the extreme swings of the business cycle, as we have shown.[2]

STABILITY OF NON-DISCRIMINATORY PRICES

The short-time "stability" (in the proper sense) of non-discriminatory prices would be greater both to buyers and to sellers than is that of unsystematic discriminatory prices (contrary to the

---

[1] See further on the law of criminal intent in Appendix to Ch. XXVIII.

[2] Ch. XXV. As we write these words the newspapers report the meeting of economists in Cleveland, quoting the apparently unanimous judgment of those participating in the session, that concentration of industry amplifies rather than reduces cyclical fluctuations and increases rather than decreases cyclical unemployment.

view persistently fostered). Where unsystematic discrimination is practiced, finding the price presents a separate problem on each sale, calling for the constant expenditure of much time, thought, and expense by both buyers and sellers. A single uniform base price at each mill is no doubt more stable than sporadic discriminatory prices, as it is likely to be changed only when, in sum total, the conditions in the market area are such as to give the seller a motive to gain new marginal buyers or to retain old ones.

The price situation created by a uniform mill-base price plan for the sellers is far more stable than that of artificial basing-point prices, as a uniform mill-base price yields the same unit profit to the seller on every sale, whereas the so-called "uniformity" and stability of the basing-point prices is a deception, as they yield each seller the most varied net realized prices on the sales made at the same time as well as at different times.

NATURAL PROTECTION FROM FREIGHTS

The complete eradication of local discrimination would bring business competition into accord with the economic law of market areas. "Division of territory," when brought about by agreement, is illegally in restraint of trade, and usually unsound economically because preventing free competition in marginal territory. But the more normal division of territory that must result from uniform mill-base prices in the competitive sale of standardized products by locally separated plants is economically sound. Every local discrimination is an act of domestic dumping and is marked by all the insecurity and other uneconomic consequences to established trade that are such a just cause of irritation in the case of foreign dumping. But this sort of price cutting, ignorantly and recklessly done, unsettling to well-conducted business, destructive of established investments, wasteful of economic resources, and discouraging in the long run to enterprise and efficiency, the courts have declared to be one of the inalienable rights of private property. No doubt domestic "freedom of trade" in interstate commerce is the greatest economic boon of our Federal union, but this "freedom of trade" cannot wisely include freedom to the producers in any part of the country to "dump" their goods, at irregular times and in unpredictable forms determined solely with regard to their personal whims or fortunes of the moment. Yet this is what has been and is being done in fact.

The principle of justice is recognized in many railroad rate cases that each community within our borders is entitled to the enjoyment of its "natural" advantages of location and resources. Sound in economics, this rule, if consistently applied, would result in the best location of each plant and in its development to just the proper size to serve each market area most economically.[3] Without discrimination, the nation would be most efficiently served. The wastes of cross freights in standardized goods would be eliminated. Each locality and each enterpriser in his location would enjoy what may properly be called a "natural" fostering "protection" of freight costs, to which each citizen is entitled as an economic agent in a free state. Insuring to the enterprise of its citizens this domestic "protection" against the folly or the desperation of local price cutting should be deemed a function of the simplest police state, not a mischievous interference of government with private business. It is not "playing Father," as the propagandists of monopoly sneeringly declare, for the state to insure fair play and true stability in price policies.

DISCRIMINATION AND RUIN

What has been happening? Small enterprises and small investments, operating or newly started in areas where the previous high monopolistic prices would have given them an adequate profit even with their small and possibly less efficient plants, fall early victims to subtle discrimination. The countryside is dotted with industrial graveyards where rest and rust the slaughtered infant enterprises. In their tombs they were unable to prove "absence of good faith" on the part of their destroyers. Their ruin was no proof of their economic incapacity in a fair contest, but proof only of the financial strong-arm tactics of their competitors. Their gravestones are a lasting warning to the starting of new local industries, and a discouragement to all the motives of youthful enterprise that are not subservient to the greater financial powers.

No thoughtful spectator of the present territorial distribution of

---

[3] Observe that the false principle of "equalization of opportunity" is inconsistent with this one; see Ch. XXVII, section "Back to Fundamentals."

industrial establishments in this country can believe that it has resulted from the free play of economic forces. It embodies countless historic blunders in railroad rates, and the results of countless acts of industrial bullying and ruffianism in the form of local industrial price cutting. When the truth is recognized, the courts will be ready to condemn all local price cutting as "unfair competition," as "characterized by fraud, deception, and oppression." Open placarded prices may then become the rule in business. If discrimination in prices were ended, where would that leave the mergers, as regards both the enormous mass now in existence and the formation of others? These questions should be carefully pondered, not hastily answered.

"No discrimination without some monopoly," we have said; but it does not logically follow that there can be no monopoly without discrimination (though this may prove to be true practically). A monopoly may conceivably charge uniform monopoly prices, but practically this case rarely occurs, for discrimination is so much more profitable (i.e. charging each group of buyers "all the traffic will bear," instead of charging the highest uniform price "the traffic" will bear). In practical life, therefore, monopoly and discrimination appear like Siamese twins. No doubt in many cases neither could live without the other. Cut either away and the other must die. Remembering that all existing mergers came into being in a régime of local price cutting, let us, however, consider the possible and probable effects upon the more powerful mergers of outlawing all discrimination in the future.

MERGERS AND MONOPOLY

Prima facie, a merger of formerly competing companies is the most perfect, the ultimate, mode of stifling competition. Even the Industrial Conference Board, though viewing mergers with a kindly spirit, frankly declares—or admits—that

competitive conditions may be stifled, at least for a time, by the absorption of competitive concerns in a corporate merger . . . The form of corporate merger yields, as far as it reaches, the most decisive, the most complete, the most certain power over supply and over prices which could be obtained.[4]

---

[4] *Mergers and the Law*, pp. 148, 152.

Unquestionable; but why that timid phrase, "at least for a time"? Does not corporate merger also, "as far as it reaches," yield a power over prices that is never ended (are not corporations immortal!) unless by the long, costly, and uncertain process of the upspringing of new competitors, who, when their competition becomes troublesome, may under this same judicial policy be in turn acquired by the consolidation? Of this too there is no serious question. The really pressing question in each practical case of merger that has been presented to the courts is just this: how far does merger "reach" toward the attainment of monopoly?

In the cases in which this question has been presented to the Supreme Court, its hesitating answers have been in striking contrast to the confidence with which it has hit formal agreements between independents to affect prices. To the Court it seems always to have been an open question whether a merger, no matter how large, affected prices at all. Many have remarked upon the Janus-faced attitude of the Court in this respect. The developments in judicial decisions which followed so closely the announcement of the rule of reason in 1911 suggested to many minds a causal relation, an impression confirmed by their study of the decisions. As some see it, the patent monopoly (vertical) merger cases (Winslow 1912-13, Keystone Watch 1915, and United Shoe Machinery 1918) stuck a foot in the gates, the District Court's Steel decision of 1915 set them ajar, and the fiasco of the Steel dissolution suit (1920) finally threw the gates wide open for the consolidations to march through like a mighty army. As most men see it, the rule of reason caused the Court to sanction mergers, if in its judgment their monopolistic power is offset by advantages assumed to be passed on to the public. Some would go so far as to say that the Court ceased merely to enforce the law of Congress; it took unto itself the power and assumed the benevolent rôle in each particular case of deciding whether the net balance of public benefits offset the evils of monopoly. This explains the recent judicial rulings as effecting a change in the principle of the law. This view is held generally by the legal profession, and probably by a majority of economic students.[5]

---

[5] E.g., most of the writers cited in Ch. XXV; Watkins states the case with great fullness, *Industrial Combinations,* pp. 225-232, 253-262.

WANTED: MORE ECONOMICS

A different view is taken by other economic students well versed in this aspect of the law. Following most legal opinion, they consider "the rule of reason" to be an *obiter dictum* confusedly expressed in the Oil and Tobacco Cases, and they believe it to have been far less in place there than when used in the earlier well-warranted but futile attempts of the minority (1897, 1898, and 1904) to exclude railroads from the operation of the Act. But they accept at face value Chief Justice White's hint that the well-meant purpose was not to weaken but rather to liberalize the Act, by bringing within its scope all arrangements harmful to the public interest. By this interpretation, though the Act has been weakened since 1911, it has not been by the influence of the rule of reason, but by the inability of a majority of the Court, weak in its economics, to discover monopoly in specific cases where it was present. Witness the devious reasons, other than the rule of reason, for pronouncing the Steel Corporation guiltless of monopoly.[6]

There is this essential difference in point of law and in prospect between the two views: whereas by the first the principle of the Act has been modified by judicial interpretation so that a "reasonable" measure of monopoly may be tolerated by the Court, by the second the law against monopoly is unchanged in principle, the intention of the Court being to apply it impartially to collusions and to mergers. By the second view the Court's attitude toward merger is quite analogous to that toward the trade associations in the 1925 decisions, where a true understanding of the "restraint" in the basing-point practice would almost certainly have led to a verdict of guilty. The difference is that the judicial mind cannot readily detect the evidence of monopolistic intent or any monopolistic effect in the cases of mergers as they have been presented by lawyers void of economic training. This view is little more flattering to the Court than is the other, but is more consonant with judicial pride in adherence to precedent. Nor is the practical outcome to date very different under the one view from what it is under the other, but the second view holds greater hope of a future

---

[6] The author is indebted to his Princeton colleagues, Professors Dixon and Fournier, for a statement of their cogent reasons for taking this view.

alteration of the Court's practical attitude. It might be brought about simply if the Department of Justice made use of competent economic advice (which it has never made the slightest pretense of doing). The fault lies at its door for not better presenting to the Court the economic aspects of merger cases. The good will of the Court to suppress monopoly in every form is as far above suspicion as is its integrity.

Whichever view is accepted, every earnest student and citizen must be at times a bit bewildered about this matter. Whether the law has been modified in principle or merely the facts misread in respect to the economic results of merger, in either view, what the courts have believed were these results has powerfully shaped the development that we have witnessed. Prevailing opinions of the public and in business circles have filtered through the walls of the judicial chambers and have come to the Court through the testimony of numerous interested witnesses and the biased arguments in lawyers' briefs. Never has an economist been called to testify on this subject for the people, in a case that has reached the highest Court. However, of recent years it has been reported that a small brigade of lawyers has been busied in the Department of Justice, examining proposals of mergers which have been submitted by corporations—blind men in a dark cellar trying to read a strange language without learning the alphabet.

MR. EDDY ON DISCRIMINATION AND MONOPOLY

In strict theory it is possible to conceive of very considerable mergers (horizontal, let us say, to take the harder case) of manufacturing plants which would not result in monopoly power (or in an increase of it). But such an imaginary case is highly improbable to occur in reality.[7] Consider now the situation where an

---

[7] Start with one hundred plants equally distributed over the whole country; then let there be formed a merger of ten plants equally distributed, so that each merger mill had next to it and all around it several genuine competitors; or, going further, let ten mergers be formed each of ten mills so distributed that each had nine genuine competitors nearer to it than was any of its sister mills; under such conditions, competition might be as strong as ever. But things simply don't happen that way. It is usually neighboring mills, bidders in marginal areas that have been cutting each into the other's territory, that are merged. And here it is theoretically possible for the merger of but two, or of a few, mills, comprising, say, not over 5 per cent of the total national productive capacity, to yield a high degree of monopoly power in a certain

important merger gave one company a dominating influence in a certain region. The presence throughout this region or adjacent to it of even a few scattered truly independent mills can exercise a very considerable influence in maintaining competition. If it is true that a thoroughly equipped large single establishment is in general as efficient technically, and probably more so in the long run, than are large mergers, it follows, does it not, that it can survive under full and free competition with them? Its danger is not from the productive power (efficiency) of the mergers, but from their financial power exercised through discriminatory prices. Arthur J. Eddy, who knew the modern "trusts" in and out as well as any man of his day, and in certain ways was one of their shrewdest defenders (though he specialized on smaller "cartel" agreements), said frankly that the horizontal merger was "artificial," and was "for the purpose of controlling prices." And he quotes as expressing his own conviction the words he had heard from many independents fighting for existence against a trust:

we don't care how big the trust is or how many departments it operates in competition with us. We can take care of ourselves. On an even footing we can always get business away from it. All we ask is fair play.[8]

Here "fair play," as the context shows, means "not discriminating" by selling below cost while selling at a profit elsewhere. This testimony of independents and Mr. Eddy's own judgment are in harmony with our conclusions. The enforcement of the uniform mill-base price must put an end to the dominating influence of fear that large combinations hold over their neighbor independents. Ending discrimination would probably put an end to the uneconomic and subtly illegal merger movement.

Mr. Eddy was quite hostile to the Sherman Act as a whole, declaring it to be *"destructive* in *purpose* and *application"* (his italics). But it should be observed that his hostility to it was grounded in the belief that the law actually compelled cutthroat competition, that discrimination was not only permissible but neces-

region. Recall the discussion of this problem in Part II in the case of the Steel Corporation. The Bethlehem-Lackawanna merger is an outstanding example, leaving a great industrial region without any competing local sources of supply.

[8] *The New Competition*, p. 277.

sary to the competition sought by the law. But for this error, Mr.
Eddy's views on open price competition would have been largely
in accord with what we have shown to be not only the letter but
the true spirit of the Sherman Act, and of the Clayton Act as well.

MR. EDDY ON VERTICAL MERGERS

Mr. Eddy's keen eye detected in the perpendicular (vertical)
merger a grave possibility of danger which even the hostile public
had usually overlooked; that is, its power to sell the products of
one department (or factory or stage of the process) below cost (or
at less than a "fair profit") while "making its money" from another line, "more than recouping its losses from other departments." [9] This, it may be noted, is discrimination in goods, not
local discrimination. To prevent this, Mr. Eddy would have required every large "perpendicular" corporation to "segregate the
departments," essentially an accountancy process by which the
costs, prices, and profits of each department would be separately
shown.[10] This extension of the policy of publicity and uniform
prices may prove to be a necessary safeguard against a hidden
form of discrimination even after local discrimination is ended.
Mr. Eddy's proposal shows an insight into the inequality and bad
public policy of making mere proprietary unification of plants a
license to the component factories to exempt them from the operation of the laws of commerce, in whole or in part. Yet that appears
to be the result in some cases of the present *de facto* policy toward
mergers.

THE DOOM OF MERGERS

Here we come again to the basing-point practice. We have seen
much evidence that the basing-point policy is greatly facilitated
by the formation of a merger creating in an industry a market
leader. With the suppression of pools and agreements a certain
measure of combination became almost a necessity to provide a
means of announcing prices without having an easily detected
illegal committee of the industry. When at length the basing-
point method began, with the Pittsburgh-Plus case, to be ex-

[9] *Idem*, p. 267.
[10] *Idem*, especially Ch. XVII, pp. 227-228.

posed and endangered, a new stimulus appears to have been given
to further mergers. If the prospect and possibility of basing-point
discrimination had been taken away, it possibly would have taken
away the main motive for the formation of the Steel Corporation.
Still further, if the use of the basing-point plan had been revealed
to the Supreme Court even in 1920, would not the Court have
seen in it the evidence of restraint of trade which it otherwise was
unable to discover? Would not the slender plurality of four have
dwindled to a minority or have vanished? Imagine, if you can,
Justice Holmes voting as he did in that case if the basing-point
practice had been properly brought to his attention (or in the trade
association cases either). Our faith in the efficacy of posted prices
to restore the essential conditions of free markets makes us optimis-
tic even as regards the menace of mergers. They are not in economic quality the fittest to survive, and even those now existing
must shrink to their due proportions when put to the test of competition in a fair field with no favor.

THE FUTURE OF THE LAW

The personal integrity of our Supreme Court and its tradition
and settled purpose to maintain the industrial freedom of the
citizen are great national assets. It has been misled in its economic
analysis, but never intentionally has it betrayed its lofty office.
The Federal courts would have to reverse their earlier decisions
little if any in principle to alter profoundly the practical trend of
the law in this field. Wherever they could see an explicit agreement to raise prices, they have been ready to condemn it. But
they have failed to detect some of the plain signs of tacit collusion.
What is going to happen when the Court comes to a full appreciation of the nature and effects of discriminatory prices?

After all is said, grant that in certain cases, under particular
conditions, mergers may result in some real economies, and some
part may be passed on to the public. Would that justify a sacrifice
of the policy of commercial liberty? Public policy is determined
by the resultant of many influences. It seeks the greatest good to
the greatest number. The system of industrial liberty has virtues
—political, social, ethical—not measurable by the mere dollar

yardstick. It is not to be lightly cast aside, or sold for a mess of pottage.

THE PUBLIC FOSTERING OF FREE MARKETS

The Department of Justice long expended much energy in its blundering attempts to prevent business itself from making efforts to end the countless petty, concealed modes of discrimination in credit terms and in service. This was all on the wrong road. Rather, the regularization of such business practices and bringing them under public oversight is necessary to the attainment of truly competitive, non-discriminatory prices. In this there is a large field for the coöperative activities of the Federal Trade Commission.

The proposal to intrust to a board of public officials large powers to sanction monopoly and to *fix* "reasonable" industrial prices in interstate commerce is charged with political and economic dynamite. The analogy of such powers and such a policy with those of the Interstate Commerce Commission is misleading. The truly positive and constructive sort of service that can be performed by such a public authority as the Federal Trade Commission is the fostering and creating of open markets where traders in each line of products could and would meet to buy and sell goods fairly in free competition. Such a plan is not governmental price fixing. The individual (or corporation) should be left complete freedom in the choice both as to the price he shall post, and where he shall post it, whether at the factory itself, or at a warehouse, subject only to the condition that the price, wherever posted, shall be open alike to all buyers. The well-grounded public purpose of the medieval fairs and markets with their "merchant law" should be reasserted today, where under changed conditions and on a larger scale the same need cries aloud for fulfillment. Then, indeed, if enabling legislation is necessary to make such action legal and to force the unwilling seller to come in, it might be warranted. There is no need to fix industrial prices by law, but there is need to make possible the fixing of prices by the impersonal economic forces of competition and in accord with our system of private property.

The Supreme Court in one of its more inspired moments said

with unanimity of the State and Federal statutes directed against combinations:

According to them, competition not combination, should be the law of trade. If there is evil in this, it should be accepted as less than that which may result from the unification of interests, and the power such unification gives.[11]

[11] 197 U.S. 115, 129, National Cotton Oil Company v. Texas, 1904.

all good

ENDED—THE MASQUERADE

THE PARTING

WE HAVE followed the masquerader, monopoly, in his devious career for forty years. A habitual criminal, he is still at large, plying his trade at the expense of all honest citizens. We do not know whether he is now about to enlarge his activities and reap even greater booty, or is to end his days in disgrace behind prison bars. This, though, may give us some hope that he will meet the fate he so richly deserves: we have learned to penetrate his many disguises, and in his every gesture, tone, and bearing, we know him for what he is. So farewell, for the time being, Aristide. You are an interesting rascal, but the community will be well rid of your lying, thieving, hypocritical presence.

IN RETROSPECT

When we cast our eyes over the wide field of interstate commerce in the United States, do we see a system of free markets and competitive prices in accord with the ideal of Anglo-Saxon law? Do we find that, during forty years, the Sherman Anti-Trust Act and the later supplementary legislation have been so interpreted and enforced that industrial combinations and conspiracies having substantial monopoly powers have been impossible to form and to operate? Instead, everywhere we see the growth of little hindered combination of formerly separately owned enterprises. Everywhere we see systems of basing-point delivered prices in great industries, foreign and domestic dumping of products, and chaotic and, at times, anarchical discrimination in industrial prices, all convincing evidences of monopolistic powers. Not that the prices ex-

426

torted are unlimited—for neither are the powers of restraint. But in every direction the sale of the necessaries of everyday life is controlled by great monopolies to which the public must meekly pay tribute.

While all this is open to the eye of common sense and common observation, it would be impossible for the private citizen, being without large funds and police powers, to adduce the sort of evidence that satisfies the Department of Justice or as yet is acceptable to the courts. The most conservative financial journals apply such phrases as "honeycombed with monopoly" to the industrial situation and teem with items that fully verify the phrase. Yet our guardians of the law seem to know nothing about it. Must this chasm between common knowledge and common justice ever remain unbridged? There stand the statutes, hardly mistakable in their purpose and in their literal terms. Silently a change approaching a revolution in our public policy toward industrial monopoly has been in process, which many citizens are now hopeless of seeing checked or reversed.

THE UNEQUAL GAME

Must the American people meekly accept another conflict of justice involved in such a situation? The small firm or corporation, the single manufacturer, the millions of farmers, the small merchants, the multitude of individual citizens, are still subject to the laws and conditions of competition. The law is upheld in principle and enforced in fact against them in the sale of their goods and services. Competition is "the rule of the game," but some favored players "get off-side" and hold, and the officials somehow fail to see what is happening. What chance have their unfavored opponents? The score does not show which is the better team. It has come to look dangerously like one law for the great and another for the small, one law for the rich and another for the poor. The recently invented judicial maxim, "Mere size is not an offense," has come in fact often to mean that mere lack of size makes impossible the success of enterprise and efficiency.

A NATION DIVIDED

Lincoln said: a nation half slave and half free cannot endure. Neither can a democracy endure whose economic organization is monopolistic for the few and competitive for the masses. We cannot stand still. Either we shall continue to move in the direction of more, and more subtle, restraint of trade, or we must attempt by strenuous efforts to check that movement and turn it in the other direction toward equal economic justice to all citizens in domestic commerce. The issue involves more than mere tons of steel or dollars and cents; it involves ultimately more precious goods: national character and political and social democracy. As has been truly said, as mergers spread, the greater is the loss of spiritual independence in business, and more and more men chant in dreary unison the simple credo of the "yes man."[1]

ECONOMIC FOUNDATIONS OF DEMOCRACY

A great burden of proof is on those who would substitute for the competition of efficient independent operating units of industry in our capitalistic system, networks of artificial price agreements, and the ideal and practice of the vast financial consolidations, mergers of mergers far beyond the point justified by technical efficiency. Almost, by conspiracy of reiteration from powerful influences, this burden of proof has been artfully shifted. Unified control of prices under the attractive alias of "coöperation" is to take the place of orderly, regulated competition as the rule of the market. A chorus of self-interested propagandists has tried and almost succeeded for a time in making us believe that in this "new era" monopoly and not competition is the life of trade. In economics that is a midsummer night's madness.

The very institution of private property and individual enterprise may be at stake. While Russia under a proletarian dictatorship is trying a gigantic experiment, deliberately seeking to destroy individual enterprise and competition, are we, professing to base our political liberty and our economic organization upon these quali-

[1] Stuart Chase in *Harper's Magazine* for August 1930. An interesting symposium on "The effect of Industrial Combinations on Labor Conditions" was printed in the *Annals of the American Academy*, July 1912, pp. 3-59, which is even more pertinent today.

ties and conditions, needlessly to permit the very foundations to be destroyed? A "capitalism" without equal freedom of markets and of commerce is a system of hypocrisy. Political equality before the law cannot long survive the destruction of its economic counterpart, equal freedom in free markets. The choice lies between oligarchy and democracy.

APPENDICES

APPENDICES

Chapter III: LOCAL PRICE CUTTING—SAINT OR
SINNER?

UNIFORM BASE VS. LOCAL CUT PRICES
(PAGE 43)

The confusion of mill base uniform prices with local price cutting can be seen most clearly in the numerous instances of "price cutting" alleged by the defendants to have been initiated by an independent near Baltimore between 1905 and 1907 (described in Government's Brief Vol. 2, pp. 624-641). Here the independent followed what the Government (we think rightly) calls "the perfectly proper and natural practice of charging the Baltimore price with the freight added"; that is, it sold "at uniform net prices throughout its territory." Inasmuch as the policy of the Standard was that of "discriminating in price between highly competitive points like Baltimore and small towns" the result was, of course, that the delivered price of the independents at the small towns was lower than that of the Standard, and this is the so-called "cut price" which the Standard proceeded to meet by *real* local price cutting (discrimination) while discriminating against other localities by charging higher prices. Unfortunately, the only reply of the prosecution to this absurd claim was to point to testimony that the independents were not the first to "cut" prices, seeming thus to concede the claim that if such prior cuts had occurred, the independents would have been practicing the "unfair" local price cutting referred to in the petition. Though in several respects the prosecution's conception of the economic elements of this case was somewhat clearer and more consistent than that of the defense, yet here, as frequently elsewhere, it was quite as confused or mistaken, as is further indicated in the text following note 17, on page 43.

433

Chapter VII: INTEGRATION WITHOUT INTEGRITY

APPENDIX A: CONFUSION OF HORIZONTAL
MERGER AND INTEGRATION (PAGE 93)

In Judge Buffington's opinion in the District Court can be plainly traced the steps (and missteps) by which the idea of integration came to be confused and identified with that of the merger of competing plants, in the prevailing opinion in the Supreme Court. The first step was taken quite incidentally in noting the effect of more stable railway rates and the eventual abolition after 1900 of freight rebates.

When "under the regulating power of the government, freight stability was enforced, the steel maker's market was at once locally restricted, and his only way of overcoming the regular, stable, adverse freight rate was to integrate locally; that is, to erect or acquire other mills in the market locality from which freight forbade his heavy product entering. The embargo laid by freight on distant markets is simply a business fact, and . . . the steel maker was compelled to broaden his market by expanding his operations so as to manufacture in additional localities. Coincident with this tendency to integration," etc.[1]

"Integrate" here is evidently misused in the sense of "duplicate." The argument then goes off into a different question, that of the various qualities of ores, only to return soon to that of the integration movement before 1900 (to show the "natural" trend), in the discussion of which integration is hopelessly confused with merger. This confusion is betrayed by such phrases as "integration by consolidation," "the Federal Steel Company acquiring the Carnegie Company and thus integrating eastward" (p. 130); then plunging into the morass of confusion, Judge Buffington described the various consolidations before 1900 of duplicate plants in different localities in such phrases as these: "the principal tin-plate manufactories integrated by consolidation into the American Tin Plate Company"; "the American Steel and Wire was formed by a consolidation of all the leading wire product manufacturers"; "the National Tube Company formed by great concerns making various kinds of tubes and pipes"; "sheet steelmakers in large tonnage combined to form the American Sheet Steel Company"; "the American Steel Hoop Company was formed by the leading makers of hoops, bands, and cotton ties"; "In the same month we find the principal structural and bridge erectors and producers forming the American Bridge Company."[2] Every one of these is an example of

---

[1] 223 Fed. Rep. 126.   [2] *Idem,* pp. 130-131.

horizontal merger of competing plants at different localities, but is adduced to show the necessity of vertical merger (miscalled integration) of non-competing plants.

APPENDIX B: SMALL INDEPENDENTS THOROUGHLY INTEGRATED (PAGE 94)

Thus Judge Buffington describes admiringly the Bethlehem Steel Company and declares also that the Jones and Laughlin Company at Pittsburgh, even in 1901, was thoroughly integrated: "Going east, we find at Johnstown, Pa., the Cambria Steel Company, a strong company also thoroughly integrated"; at Youngstown, Ohio, is the Republic Iron and Steel Company, whose policy "like all other steel makers has been one of simply following the progressive and universal practice of integration incident to the development of the use of steel" (could this be said more sweepingly?); and there is the Inland Steel Company of Indiana, whose president was asked: "You are very well integrated, as you have stated?" and his answer was: "Yes, we did the best that it was possible to do" (pp. 68, 71, 74, quoting from Testimony Vol. 22, p. 9144).

"The proof is simply one-sided that they did not control trade . . . Take, for example, the last one formed, the American Bridge Company. During the years it has been a subsidiary of the United States Steel Corporation its business has increased 42 per cent. In that time, its competitors have increased their business 164 per cent. During that time the American Company has had the help of all the associated subsidiary companies of the Steel Company, it has shared all the economies of management, coöperation and financial help rendered by the parent company, yet with all these aids, its competitors have increased their business four times as fast as its own." [1]

What inference could logically be drawn from these figures? Judge Buffington thought they showed that the Corporation was *no more* efficient than the independents. But further reasoning on the same line would carry him to the conclusion that the Corporation, after all its "integration" (plus horizontal merger), was *even less* efficient than they—a view far nearer the truth than his belief that the giant merger was a necessity of progress.

[1] 223 Fed. Rep. 133.

Chapter VIII: THE GIANT WEAKLING

APPENDIX A: FALSE CONCLUSIONS FROM THE STATISTICS OF GROWTH (PAGE 101)

Judge Buffington said:

"They . . . show a strong trend away from any monopolistic absorption or trade-restraining control of iron and steel manufacture or markets of the United States by the Steel Corporation. On the contrary, these figures show a strong trend in that manufacture and market toward an even greater absorption thereof by the virile ,and growing competitors of the Steel Company." [1]

Of the comparisons as to percentage of the increase of various companies, Judge Buffington says that they afford "just ground for concluding that the steel and iron business of this country is not being, and indeed cannot be, monopolized by the Steel Corporation." Note the implication that if monopoly is not complete, or if it is a diminishing proportion of the whole country's business, it is not monopoly. Again of the comparisons between the Corporation's production with that of its competitors collectively, he says: "These facts and figures conclusively answer the charges of monopoly, and restraint in the home market." [2] This evidently was the settled conviction of all those other judges who upheld the Corporation. They accepted without independent analysis Judge Buffington's conclusions.

APPENDIX B: CONFUSION OF ABSOLUTE AND RELATIVE INCREASE (PAGE 104)

Judge Buffington said:

"During that time (ten years) the business of both competitors and steel company has increased very largely, but it is highly suggestive, indeed, conclusive, proof that the Steel Company had neither monopolistic control or power to restrain trade, since the proportion of trade increase was very materially greater on the part of the Steel Corporation's competitors than its own." [3]

Judge Woolley said: "The constituent combinations absorbed by the corporation were strongest at their birth. Their percentage of output and their corresponding control over their particular branches of the industry were greatest when organized, but diminished year by year in combat with competitors who entered the field against them, supplied

[1] 223 Fed. Rep. 67.
[2] *Idem*, p. 97.

[3] 223 Fed. Rep. 96.

with ample resources, equipped with modern plants, and unincumbered with obsolete or dismantled properties." [1]

By the way, what has happened to the great economies resulting from "integration" by the Corporation, thought to be impossible to any smaller enterprises? The independents now are described as leading on the road of economic "evolution," while the blundering and ineffective Corporation is encumbered with obsolete and dismantled properties. Truly a swift change in the picture.

Justice McKenna, after earlier citing the relative figures, speaks of them as if they showed an absolute decrease: "the Corporation declined in productive powers . . . The power of the monopoly . . . under either illustration is an untenable accusation." [2]

The reasoning of the Court involves the assumption (as major premise) that "a monopoly" (or any power to restrain trade) can exist nowhere, unless at the same time it extends everywhere; that a corporation has no monopoly power unless it increases its capacity in its comparatively restricted area at a faster rate than do all its competitors in the aggregate, in every other part of the country (or, with equal lack of logic, in the whole world). In truth, a very real measure of monopoly power might continue indefinitely to exist, and even increase in a limited area, while a great combination was decreasing either absolutely or relatively to any one competitor, or to all in the aggregate.

APPENDIX C: PREPOSTEROUS NOTION OF BOUNDLESS "MARKETS" (PAGE 109)

The testimony of this witness is in Vol. 25, pp. 11771-11774 of the Record. In substance it is as follows (somewhat compressed):

In his study of these industrial combinations, which began about the year 1886, the witness had given a good deal of thought to the question of the power of a combination to put its competitors out of business and had considered that question in connection with the steel industry. The conditions in the steel business are different than in a cigar store or a milk route. In the case of a milk route, for example, a business that is confined to a small locality, it would be a practical plan to put a competitor out of business by going into a local territory where he is doing business and selling his product within his special local market at a rate so low that in order to meet that low rate he must sacrifice his profits and sell at a loss, until he is driven out of business. That would also be true in the case of a local tobacco dealer. The larger establishment could sell at a low rate in his special locality, and with his small market he could

---

[1] *Idem*, p. 170.   [2] 251 U.S. 446.

be driven out, while they could keep up their profits by sales elsewhere.

In the steel business, on the other hand, the well-equipped steel producers in this country have markets that are practically general throughout the country for their various products. In consequence, any attempt to cut the price of that special product against a manufacturer would mean that the large establishment that attempted to force the smaller establishment out of business would itself be meeting losses on a much larger scale, on a scale proportionate to the extent of its sales, and under those circumstances it could not put the smaller producer out of business.

It would not be possible to make a drive at a particular competitor; in the production of steel in any well-equipped establishment it is possible for the producer to change his product from one type to another within quite material limits. So, if, for example, a cut were made in some special line of product, it would be possible for the producer to change his line of product to another one that was not attacked, so that in that way the larger producer would be forced to meet product after product to the extent of the change that it would be possible for the smaller producer to make. This, taken with the other, shows this also, that whenever there comes a lowering of prices in any one product or any line of products the country over, the large establishment is attacking not merely one, but he is attacking all of the different competitors, and any large producer that attempts to put a small steel producer out must try to put them all out. . . . He cannot fight one without fighting practically all of them, because, practically all the steel producers that have well-equipped establishments have markets the country over. For those reasons the fight could not be confined to a particular individual or a particular locality. He must fight all producers and all products, substantially. . . . And in all places. . . . The United States Steel Corporation has not the power to put out of business its competitors or any important one of them.

Chapter IX: BE GOOD AND YOU'LL BE HAPPY

APPENDIX A: THE MISUNDERSTOOD TESTIMONY ON COMPETITION (PAGE 115)

Judge Buffington went into this subject most fully and was most favorable to the Corporation, but the other prevailing opinions seem to be essentially in accord with his views, at least as to the period after 1911. Among other things he said regarding the independents:

"there is . . . affirmative testimony, . . . which, as it seems to us, constrains us to conclude that the prices of the product sold by the Steel

Corporation have been the result of the joint action of the law of supply and demand and of that vigorous rivalry which has at all times existed between the Steel Corporation and its competitors. In that respect
we have the testimony of the Steel Corporation's great competitors (and
of many others). The testimony of these men—and there is no testimony to the contrary—is that the iron and steel trade in the various
products of the Steel Corporation is and has been open, competitive, and
uncontrolled, and that all engaged therein have free will control in selling at their own prices." [1]

After making "typical extracts (of testimony) from varied sorts of
buyers, of varied sorts of products," Judge Buffington declares: "No
one can read these volumes of testimony and fail to be satisfied that this
great body of business men, scattered over all parts of the country, in
keen competition with each other in their several lines, is alert in seeing
that competitive conditions exist between the manufacturers of basic steel
products from whom they buy." [2]

Justice McKenna said on this point: "competitors, dealers and customers of the Corporation testify in multitude that no adventitious interference was employed to either fix or maintain prices and that they were
constant or varied according to natural conditions." [3]

APPENDIX B: ORACULAR EVIDENCE FROM FELLOW CONSPIRATORS (PAGE 117)

This testimony is quoted more fully in Judge Buffington's opinion
than anywhere else, chiefly pp. 82-85.

Youngstown: Competition with the subsidiaries of the Corporation
is active and energetic and vigorous, very at times. We sell to many of
the same people that they do. Severe.

Colorado: vigorous, independent and unrestricted so far as it affected
them. Has increased. More active.

La Belle Iron Works, W. Va.: "its market covered the entire country, etc. Prices not fixed in agreement." No price ever suggested by any-
body as agreed upon by any competitor. Keen. Competitors numerous.

Republic, at Youngstown: prices varied by size of order, etc; give
minimum prices to traveling men below which they shall not go, and
allow them to use their intelligence in getting all above they can; based
on cost.

Lackawanna, at Buffalo: Market covered practically the entire U.S.;
sold in competition, keen, aggressive; prices not fixed in agreement
with competitors, always independently. Prices both uniform and vari-

---

[1] 223 Fed. Rep. 82.   [2] *Idem*, pp. 88-89.   [3] 251 U.S. 449.

ant; uniform on rails, plates and shapes in some cases but not necessarily so. When so, followed "what they called the market price . . . the so-called market price." Price of steel rails at the mills tacitly understood to be $28. No statement ever made, in conferences with the president, "of a price agreed on with competitors."

Jones and Laughlin, at Pittsburgh: Competition unlimited by agreements as to prices. Keen.

Here is really every significant word and phrase, though they are repeated and recombined in various ways in the passages that were chosen by the Court as being so convincing to it. The vagueness of most of these expressions is, however, evident on closer scrutiny. Such words as "keen," "aggressive," "vigorous," etc., might easily be used of competition to secure sales, or by services, where price competition was entirely excluded by a follow-the-leader policy. Three of these six witnesses made no specific assertion that competition extended to prices. The others aroused suspicion by their merely negative assertions about prices: "no statement was ever made in conferences," or "no price was suggested as agreed upon." Such statements could mean anything or nothing to elastic consciences with some mental reservation or ingenious interpretation of the meaning of agreement (as in the case of the Gary dinners). The witness making the most positive statement (from Lackawanna) that prices were not fixed by agreement with competitors, always independently, at once virtually belies this by his statements about "uniform" prices and "so-called market prices." For the prices were neither truly "uniform" nor truly "market" but merely "so-called."

Chapter X: CAMOUFLAGING A CONSPIRACY

APPENDIX A: CUSTOMERS CONFUSED, ADD TO CONFUSION (PAGE 138)

The evidence abounds in such gratuitous inferences as these, all from one customer-witness: "We have always found competition. Very keen most generally. *I have never observed any indication . . . to fix prices.* [Italics in original.] We have always been able to buy on fair competition. I think we have always been able to get the benefit of fair competition." [1]

Others speak in like vein; to quote a few of many expressions: "There is competition. . . . So far as we know or can find there is no evi-

[1] 223 Fed. Rep. 85.

dence of price fixing between companies. . . . We believe there is genuine competition." "I never saw any evidences since 1904, etc. . . . We have always got the benefit of competition." "So far as I know we get the benefit of real and genuine competition." [1]

And so on, over and over again. Generally the courts are strict in holding fact-witnesses to statements of fact, but in this case these unwarranted expressions of personal opinions were simply taken as facts.

Further, many of the statements of these witnesses are a confusion of words, and no less, of ideas. In some cases it is fairly clear that competition is not meant to include times of delivery, service, and convenient nearness to the mill, but in other cases it is clear that these are included in the assertion that competition exists. Therefore, we are left in doubt whether these assertions that competition exists ever really mean that there is competition in price, and if so, of what nature it is.

A good deal of the testimony was apparently guided by questions intended to show that the delivered price quotations of different mills *on any one day* were slightly different, and hence (it was implied) competitive.[2] Sometimes that is what the answers seem to mean, but in many other cases "varying" or variant pretty obviously in the context mean fluctuating in time, e.g., "the quotations on rods . . . have been varying since 1904." Justice McKenna made one grand confusion of this kind when he cited the collective evidence of these 200 customer-witnesses as to different quotations on the same day as in direct conflict with certain figures compiled (for a quite different purpose) by the Bureau of Corporations purporting to show *the course* of steel prices during about a decade after the formation of Corporation.[3] The "prices" thus traced, moreover, were the "official" Pittsburgh-base prices, which were neither the delivered prices actually paid by most buyers nor the real steel prices received by the mills—whether corporation or independent plants outside of Pittsburgh. The significance of this fact, which largely destroyed their meaning for the purpose intended, was apparently not understood even by the Bureau of Corporations in collecting the figures, or by the Government counsel in offering them in evidence, or by the Court in commenting almost flippantly upon them.

APPENDIX B: JUDGES MIXED ON DATES (PAGE 140)

Observe among many examples: as unquestionable proof is taken the assertion of one salesmanager that *in the nine years* (1903 to 1912)

[1] *Idem,* pp. 86-87.
[2] See the same notion in the Maple Flooring Case, Ch. XVII.
[3] Opinion, p. 448.

of which he had intimate knowledge the competition had been unlimited by agreements as to prices.[1] Another swore to the truth of the statement that in the ten years (preceding 1912) in which he had been sales-manager, *at no time* had the price of any article been fixed by agreement with any competitor; and he reiterates: this is true of each and every article they have produced and sold in the market. Judge Buffington quotes this testimony (with other details) as if it were particularly impressive and conclusive, as showing both that no agreement ever existed and that competition was perfect, yet this same judge, the most lenient and complacent of all toward the record of the Corporation, declares in the same decision, his belief that in a considerable portion of the period covered by the witness's statement there was "an understanding about prices that was equivalent to an agreement" [2] and that "in actual effect prices were more or less maintained." [3] Two other Circuit judges (Woolley and Hunt) followed by the entire Supreme Court, were much more severe in their judgment of these actual and virtual agreements, yet all but the three dissenters found it possible in one connection to accept this ambiguous testimony as proving what, in another connection, they declared to be untrue. This analysis of the ambiguous quality of the assertions that competition did exist and that agreements did not, could be extended with like results to every portion of this testimony.

Chapter XII: SHARPSHOOTING AT A FORMULA

APPENDIX A: "NO SUCH ANIMAL" AS PITTSBURGH-PLUS (PAGE 169)

Counsel for the Corporation: "There has never been a time at any point in this case where we have admitted any such practice as is alleged and counsel [for the Commission] seems to state exists." [4]

"There is no evidence in this case that constantly the Chicago mills, or any of them, sell at any such things as the Pittsburgh price plus the freight. . . . any assumption to the contrary is improper." [5]

"It remains, of course, to determine whether there is such a thing." [6]

Commission's Counsel: "Assuming that they sell on the same basis as they quote." Corporation's Counsel: "I object, as containing an assumption contrary to the facts." [7]

Examiner: "You assume that the Pittsburgh-plus system is this sort

[1] 223 Fed. Rep. 85.
[2] *Idem,* 160.
[3] *Idem,* 161.
[4] Record 18070.
[5] Record 18020.
[6] Record 18021.
[7] Record 18051.

of a practice, that is, of pricing steel in such a way." Corporation's Counsel: "And selling, making actual sales?" Examiner: "Yes." Corporation's Counsel: "On that basis I object to the question on the ground that it contains an assumption contrary to the testimony in the record."[1]

In nearly the last portion of the brief submitted by respondent's counsel, they contended that no expert economic opinion regarding the Corporation's selling policy could properly be framed on the assumption that the method of selling employed by it was the Pittsburgh-Plus system (as defined in the amended complaint), for counsel submit that they have "demonstrated" that "this assumption was not warranted in fact."[2]

APPENDIX B: NON-ADHERENCE MERELY APPARENT OR INSIGNIFICANT (PAGE 171)

The Commission's analysis of 3,700 contracts of sales by the Illinois Steel Company shows conformity with the Pittsburgh-Plus delivered price resulting from the base price reported in *The Iron Age*, in 92.4 per cent of the cases (exactly or within 5 cents a hundred, i.e., $1.00 a ton); and its analysis of 3,709 contracts of different steel companies showed a like agreement in 89.2 per cent of the cases. In both studies the deviation was in excess of $2.00 a ton in only a trivial number of cases.

Corporation's counsel objected to grouping the cases (some 18 per cent of all cases) in which the deviation was not over 5 cents a hundred, with the 70 per cent which agreed exactly; and they claimed that "a very slight difference in price . . . is just as important in demonstrating that there is no hard and fast rule, such as the so-called Pittsburgh-Plus system," as if those variances exceeded a dollar. This claim of "just as important" is untrue, but those who compiled the statistics did not assume that the discrepancy was negligible if it really occurred. They showed that under the usual conditions, in the long periods when Pittsburgh-Plus rule was in force, the discrepancies were due to slight differences in the base assumed by different mills in the brief periods before and after price changes were announced in *The Iron Age*. This often necessarily occurred because the basing price published (once a week) did not accurately record for a few days the base actually in use. A striking statistical demonstration of this was given when a comparison was made between two long series of prices during the years 1906 and 1922, one of the Illinois Steel and the other of the Carnegie Steel

---

[1] Record 18053.   [2] Resp. brief, p. 143.

(both subsidiaries). As in the other studies, frequent divergencies were found by small amounts from the Pittsburgh equivalent calculated from *The Iron Age* quotation, but in such cases the Illinois price did agree exactly with that of the Carnegie Company, if there were no uncertainties as to kinds of goods, date of contract, etc., making exact comparison impossible. For a fuller discussion of these points and the figures, see the Commission's brief, pp. 156 ff., and brief for the Associated States, esp. pp. 15 ff.

Chapter XIV: CLOSE HARMONY IN THE BRASS

BASING-POINTS IN SALE OF NON-FERROUS METALS (PAGE 203)

Of the four most important non-ferrous metals, tin is the only one that is not mined in the United States and is the only one in whose purchase and sale the general conditions of competition have been pretty well preserved. For this we have to thank the open market in London, where tin from all parts of the world is freely sold. American pig-tin delivered prices are generally the London prices plus freight to destination. Thus far all attempts to control or to corner the London tin market have met with very meager success.

Copper, lead, and zinc, the three other most important of the baser non-ferrous metals, are all produced in the United States somewhat in excess of domestic consumption, and are pretty regularly exported in greater or less quantities. According to the principles of competitive price and the law of market areas (see Chs. XIX and XX), if their prices were not artificially controlled, the prices in all the markets from mine and refinery to the ultimate consumers would be regularly related by freight costs. This is not the case with these metals, and often the price relationships are actually inverted, plainly showing dumping, both foreign and domestic. Nearly all the ore production of these metals in the United States is in the west, but many of the refineries are in the east. The basing-point systems resemble somewhat that resulting in the south in the sale of steel under the Birmingham $4 differential base (and the present Chicago $2 differential base), being a multiple and modified basing-point zone system rather than a system of prices with a single basing point, such as was Pittsburgh-Plus before 1924 over the greater part of the country. The detailed description of the basing-point systems used in the sale of the different non-ferrous metals is a task that must be left to the technical expert. Various exceptions and changes from time to time complicate the subject, though the fundamental traits of artificiality, tacit collusion, manipulation of price, and restraint of freedom of commerce are manifest throughout. For the interested reader's information, however, the salient features of these plans are here briefly outlined.

Copper. Immediately after the post-war break in prices in January 1919, the basing-point system for copper was resumed. The country was divided into three zones: (a) west of Mississippi crossings; (b) east thereof as far as and including New York; (c) east of New York to Boston. The delivered prices to all (a) points were made the same as to New York, though the freight from refineries in Washington (Tacoma), Montana, and even Michigan was much less than to New York; the delivered prices to intermediate (b) points were ⅛ cent more than to New York; and the delivered prices to (c) points were the same as to New York, though the freight was more by 7½ cents per 100 pounds. This complex system of prices evidently discriminates most heavily against the buyers west of the Mississippi, less but very substantially in the (b) zone where fabricators, for example, at Chicago, Cleveland, etc., are required to pay imaginary freight all the way to New York and ⅛ cent per pound back from New York; and on the whole it favors the region east of New York in which are situated so many of the fabricating plants which of late have been increasingly integrated (financially) with the large producers. This whole practice, it would seem, would be assailable by an alert administration on the principles of the Pittsburgh-Plus decision by the Federal Trade Commission, as involving discrimination against fabricators and consumers in the west, and assailable also under the recent unanimous decision of the Supreme Court in the American Can–Van Camp case, condemning discrimination which restrains competition between concerns that buy the products.

Lead. The basing-point system of lead prices that has been in force since about 1899 is essentially the same as that for copper, though different in some puzzling details. Lead smelted in Nebraska is sold at the same price there as at New York, to which the milling-in-transit rate is 17½ cents a hundred ($3.50 a ton). At points intermediate between Omaha and New York, though the milling-in-transit rates thereto from Nebraska are less than to New York, the delivered price is generally a fixed arbitrary (differential) over the New York price. The smelting companies all make changes simultaneously in their selling prices.

If a broker or a fabricator could buy lead at Omaha, for example, and ship it to points east as cheaply as the pro rata part of the milling-in-transit rate on which the refineries ship, evidently the delivered prices would be something less than the present rates. But no, it is impossible to "beat the game." Without the milling-in-transit privilege the rate is 15½ cents ($3.10 a ton) from Omaha to the Mississippi crossings, and it is 35 cents ($7.00 a ton) from there to New York, a total of 50½ cents (or $10.10 a ton), being $6.60 per ton more than the milling-in-transit rate from Omaha to New York (and somewhat proportionally for the intermediate points). As practically only the refineries enjoy this milling-in-transit concession (or rebate) they are thus endowed with the essential power and character of common carriers, enjoying a special governmental monopolistic privilege of a rate so low that all others are excluded from the right to use the railroads. This result was all unintended and unforeseen, no doubt, when the milling-in-transit practice was originated in the days before monopolies and basing points.

This works out in practice as a system of discriminatory freight rates charged (retailed) by the metal producers to customers, whereas the rates the producers pay to the railroads are now non-discriminatory. The producers charge a higher price delivered to practically all points located east of Chicago and west of New York. For example, the delivered price of lead at Washington, D.C. (where the Government buys large tonnages for the Navy Department as well as for the water works of the District), is $1 a ton over the New York delivered price. As the milling-in-transit rate paid to Washington is actually 50 cents per ton less than that to New York, the producers net $1.50 per ton more on all lead sold to the nation at Washington than on that sold in New York and eastward. Similarly, they discriminate against Toledo, Cleveland, Cincinnati, Buffalo, Rochester, Philadelphia, Baltimore, and all the other cities of that intermediate territory. Such practices make a farce of the I.C.C. control of freight rates in this field, and of the supposed suppression of railroad favoritism and rebates.

Furthermore, the smelting companies buy ores from independent mines on a sliding scale fixed by the announced New York price of lead, less freight from the source of the ores to New York; whereas such of that lead as is sold to customers in the intermediate territory is delivered at 50 cents to $1 more, and nets them still more, by the difference of freights they pay and exact.

> "For ways that are dark and tricks that are vain,
> The heathen Chinee"—is not peculiar.

We make no attempt here to deal with the activities and policies of the Copper Exporters' Association whereby, no doubt, Mr. Ryan's wish to control prices abroad has in some measure been realized.

Chapter XVI: TRADE ASSOCIATIONS BECOME SUSPECT

CONFUSED NOTIONS OF ZONED AND OF AVERAGE FREIGHT RATES (PAGE 225)

Three briefs were filed for the appellees: the main brief (Walsh), a smaller one (Debevoise), and a third (Matthews) as *amici curiae*, filed by attorneys representing unnamed clients who were participating in similar association activities. The zoning system, said the defense, "was always in use, a long established custom" (Matthews brief, p. 91); yet examination of the testimony on which this assertion rests (e.g., Record, p. 70) shows that the witness was only blunderingly saying that before the zone system was adopted by resolution of the association, the delivered cost included the freight from the mill. "We are bound to have it [a zone system] because the farther you get away from the plant to sell goods the higher is the cost to get them to the buyer." He is talking about the normal gradation of delivered cost according to actual freight when sales were made on a uniform mill base, and not about what he pretends to be discussing, viz., zoned prices linked as in this case with an artificial basing point. Defendant's own main brief says that the adoption of a zoning system was first discussed in 1918.[1] In the District Court, Judge Carpenter was evidently tricked by this talk and by the misleading comparison which the witness made between this zone grouping of industrial prices and certain zone groupings of freight rates that had been approved by the Interstate Commerce Commission on transcontinental traffic. He remarked from the bench, "If a zoning system must be used at all, this does not show any more than the organic discrimination."[2] Thus he added a new technical term to the literature of the subject—"organic discrimination," whatever that may mean. The Judge then sought to elucidate his meaning by this further comment: "so that when you have zones, and approach the border, there are bound to be discriminations." He evidently is thinking of a mill-base zoning system, whereas in a basing-point zoning system discrimination in prices occurs not merely "when you approach the border" but everywhere on every sale, inasmuch as the net price of the goods figured back to the mill (or, what amounts

[1] Walsh brief, p. 36. [2] Record, p. 133.

to the same thing, the freight allowed, or absorbed) for any one buyer is either greater or less than that for most of the other buyers in the same zone. The good judge was all at sea, land nowhere in sight, without sextant or compass to fix his latitude or longitude. So [1] he trustingly declares that these "differentials" simply "equalize the cost of railroad transportation . . . were adopted after a thorough and intelligent investigation of freight rates from the base point to point of delivery and . . . after a fair averaging of those freight rates into the designated territory."

"Intelligent" and "fair," indeed! The real situation is grotesquely out of accord with the professed principle of the scheme, as counsel for the Government and the judges could have discovered had they properly analyzed the evidence. Within the basic first zone, freight rates averaged about 2 cents a gallon, but actual rates ranged from nothing at Minneapolis to 3 cents per gallon at Springfield, Mo., so that even within that zone the net price of oil involved grave discriminations among buyers, when figured back to the base. Observe that this is a sort of discrimination that was not present in the Pittsburgh-Plus case, in shipments actually made from the Pittsburgh base, where the Plus was always the actual freight. The reader may determine from the figures given below how "intelligently" or "fairly" the zone differentials really did equalize the cost of transportation.

The data used are those given in the testimony of an expert traffic witness for defendants,[2] given with evident reluctance as he realized what he was revealing. We have calculated the freight rate per gallon in each case by taking the weight of linseed oil to be 7½ pounds (the legal weight in every State which specifies this; see United States Bureau of Standard, report on Weights and Measures), or 13⅓ gallons per hundredweight. If an allowance is to be made for the weight of the container, this would change the absolute figures, but not the relative discrimination between and within the zones. The following table sets forth the essential facts as to the arbitrary differential, the average freight, the minimum and the maximum rates within each zone.

Zones	1	2	3	4	5	6	7	8	
Differential above Zone 1	0	1	2	3	6	7	8	11	cents per gal.
Actual *average* difference (plus)	0	1.24	2.9	3.5	4.0	3.0	4.5	6.6	"
Actual minimum *plus* in Zone	0	1.0	2.2	2.8	2.3	0.6	3.0	6.6	"
Actual maximum *plus* in Zone	3	1.5	3.0	3.8	5.6	6.0	6.6	6.6	"

[1] 275 Fed. Rep. 945, November 1921.   [2] Record, pp. 130-134.

Chapter XVII: THE INVISIBLE ACCOMPLICE OF "OPEN PRICES"

FAKE AVERAGES IN THE MAPLE FLOORING CASE (PAGE 233)

On shipments to Chicago the Cadillac rate used by all the mills was 24.5 cents; yet the true *average* from the seventeen mills was 19.8 cents, and from nine of them it was less, while from the two nearest mills (one at Menominee, Michigan, and the other at Oconto, Wisconsin) it was only 14 cents. These calculations are based on the figures given in the rate books of the defendants, as given in their delivered cost charts of May 31, 1922, shown in Government's Exhibit 35, Record, Vol. 3, pp. 328 ff., wherein it appears that each 5 cents on the freight rate amounts to $1.00 to $1.16 a thousand on the freight bill for 13/16" lumber, which is taken to weigh 20 hundred pounds. The actual freight received by the common carrier from the near-by mills was $2.80, the average amount the mills professed to be aiming to charge was $4.00, and the freight they collected from the public was $5.00; that is, the freight collected was 25 per cent more than the fake average, and 80 per cent more than actually went to the common carrier. Is that a negligible difference or close to the truth?

To take one other among many such examples: on shipments of lumber to St. Paul and Minneapolis the true arithmetic average rate from the seventeen mills would be 24.3 cents a hundred, whereas the Cadillac rate charged was 30 cents, while the actual rate from the two mills at Mellen and Phillip, Wisconsin, from which presumably many, if not all, of the sales would be made, was only 13 cents. Therefore the consumers in St. Paul and Minneapolis and all that region were paying $6 a thousand to get their maple flooring hauled from those near-by Wisconsin mills, while the *average* (the amount the Court deems "fair") was less than $5, and the actual freight from the mill was only $2.60.

Meantime another mill in the Association, far in the east, at Tupper Lake, New York, not included in the averages, apparently goes merrily on charging its inflated Cadillac-Plus and is never mentioned in the discussion. Happy is the mill without a history!

Chapter XX: THE ECONOMIC LAW OF MARKET AREAS

APPENDIX A: PROFITABLE WHOLESALE
AREAS (PAGE 292)

Under the headlines, "Wholesale areas found elliptical," and "Focus at shipping point," Mr. T. Hart Anderson, Jr., president of Anderson, Davis and Hyde, advertising agents, was reported in the New York *Times* of October 27, 1929, as saying that marketing research had shown that where the distribution of heavy merchandise in which freight charges play an important part is through selected wholesalers, previous conceptions of the area from which these distributors should draw the bulk of their business go awry. The statement continues:

"A study we are now making for one of our clients discloses that in this method of distributing merchandise on which shipping costs are high, such as furniture, pianos, rugs, etc., the area from which most of the wholesaler's sales volume is drawn is elliptical in shape. . . .

"In the ellipse the distributing center is always at the focus nearest the shipping point. If, for example, the goods are shipped from New York to a wholesale distributer in St. Louis, the latter place would be the focus. Fully three-quarters of the elliptical area, the boundaries of which are fixed by freight rates, the rail lines serving it and the location of other distributing centers, would lie west of the city. The northern and southern boundaries would lie about equidistant from it. This holds true of similar areas as far out as the Rocky Mountains. West of the Rockies water shipments to Pacific Coast points change the situation and the same is true of the Gulf States.

"The position of the focus is set by the uneconomic features of back hauling, or shipping goods back over part of the route they have already traversed. When back hauling over more than a reasonable distance is required to serve a retailer, he logically should be served by the wholesaler in the adjacent ellipse nearer the shipping point.

"The boundaries of the ellipse are not necessarily the boundaries of the area from which the distributer can draw business, but they do set the lines within which the largest and most profitable business can be done. In the study it has been brought out that the territory in which one Middle Western wholesaler is operating comprises twelve full states and parts of four others, whereas his elliptical, or logical, sales area should embrace but one full State and parts of six others.

"Analysis of the sales of this wholesaler brought out that this elliptical area, which equals about 20 per cent of the territory he has been trying to cover profitably, produces 85 per cent of his total volume. The remaining area has not yet been fully abandoned, but the wholesaler is gradually drawing his lines more closely.

"While the wholesaler in this case had not been satisfied with the business brought in from the outside of his ellipse, he had continued selling there because it was a good place to train junior salesmen, because he had always sold there and thought he owed it to the trade to continue, and because he also carried lines other than the one on which the analysis was made. When supplied with definite proof of the wastage of this procedure, he was somewhat astonished.

"The study has also brought out that in one big Middle Western city the business of the retailers is solicited by eleven wholesalers carrying similar or practically similar lines. The severity of the competition thus produced is not hard to imagine. Theoretically, only one distributer should operate there and he should be the one in whose ellipse the city is situated. That point probably never will be reached, however, due to friendship, price-cutting and other factors—aside from service —which still govern order-giving to some extent.

"The question naturally has come up as to how much business the distributer can expect to get from the elliptical area in which he is located. The study shows that in the counties immediately surrounding the distributing point he can hope to get about 75 per cent of the volume which our client feels should come from that area. The remaining 25 per cent is obtained by the client through direct sales to department stores and other retailers too large to buy through a wholesaler. In the outlying portions of the ellipse the distributer cannot expect more than 45 per cent of the volume anticipated by our client, due to competition with other distributers arising from overlapping of sales activities."

APPENDIX B: MAP OF WHEAT PRICES
(PAGE 293)

This map of local price differences is based on the data collected by the U.S. Department of Agriculture and presented graphically in a map published in February 1918 in Bulletin 594. The figures used were county averages of prices paid to farmers in the five-year period of 1910-1914 inclusive as compiled from some 30,000 township reports. In considerable areas in the arid regions of the west and in the southern and southwestern States little suited to wheat culture either no wheat is produced or but insignificant quantities, and from these areas no reports of producers' prices were received, and these areas were left blank on the original map. It may be assumed that the local price paid by users of wheat in these deficiency areas would be at least as high as that received at farms in the nearest adjacent producing area, from which it would have to be transported; and further that where the average producers' prices in some neighboring very large counties in the west differ by more than 5-cent intervals, the local prices in intervening areas are graduated between the two extremes (sometimes no doubt being even higher at points between). Therefore, in every case, the unreporting area has been divided into 5-cent bands of price and connected with the adjacent price-reporting zones. It must be observed, too, that as the Bulletin figures are county averages, the local price in some parts of the county would be higher than the averages and in other parts lower, and normally would be higher on the side toward a higher-priced county and lower on the side toward a lower-priced county. Multitudes of minor local differences of prices therefore are hidden in the statistical picture, being smoothed out by the averaging process, and in instances where local transportation is exceptionally difficult the real differences may be at times great. Many of the jagged irregularities shown on our map are the result of averaging the different local prices over such large areas, and doubtless the curves would be much smoother and more regular if actual local figures were used in place of these cruder averages. However, the picture presented of the general average large territorial gradations of wheat prices is both striking and no doubt substantially accurate.

Chapter XXI: DUMPING AND THE GENTLE ART OF SLOW MURDER

APPENDIX A: DISCRIMINATION, A RECENT LEGAL TERM (PAGE 300)

Discriminate (the verb) is derived from the Latin *discerno,* the fundamental meaning of which is to separate, with related meanings of discern, see, treat differently, and judge between, whence by an interesting coincidence came the word *crime,* as a thing adjudged. The word was used as early as 1628 in England (see examples in *Oxford Dictionary*) in the sense of "to make a difference in or between." The first example we have found of its use to mean treatment "in favor of one class and against another" is of date 1845 (example cited from an English newspaper by the *Oxford Dictionary*). After that date the use of the term discrimination and its derivatives became frequent in the discussion of tariff rates, taxation, and political treatment, but it extended very slowly into either legal or economic language relating to prices. The earliest legal citations of its use in the United States relate solely to railroad rates (this use apparently not before about 1880), and the term is very rare in the law in any wider sense as applied to prices before 1914, the year the Clayton Act was enacted. Various dictionaries of English law as late as 1923 do not include the term in any sense.

The first definitions of "discrimination" in the law follow the popular meaning: "the act of treating differently" (*Corpus Juris*, citing the *English Law Dictionary*); "treating one differently from another" (*idem*, citing Wimberly v. Georgia Southern, etc., R.Co., 5 Ga. A. 263, 266, 63 S.E. 29).

In its usual connection until after 1900 as applied to rates charged for freight, discrimination "consists of the single fact, without other qualification or exception, of charging a greater rate to the one person than to the other or others" (Houston and T. C. Ry. Co. v. Rust, 58 Tex. 98, 107). This simple statement becomes more or less decorated and elaborated by other phrases such as: "under substantially the same conditions as to time of shipment, destination, connections, and manner of transportation, and other details identifying the similarity of transactions" (U.S. v. Hocking Valley Ry. Co., 194 Fed. 234, 246; 1911).

Professor Hadley wrote in his work on *Transportation* (1885), pp. 101 and 108, as follows: "Some charges are made higher than others without any good reason for the difference"; and again: "A difference in rates not based upon any corresponding difference in cost, constitutes a case of discrimination."

APPENDIX B: DUMPING AND MONOPOLY
(PAGE 310)

In a recent excellent study of *Dumping: A Problem in International Trade*, the author, Professor Jacob Viner, being interested in dumping solely as an international problem, prefers to limit the term to discrimination between purchasers in different national markets. His choice seems to be influenced also by his evident belief that it is possible and usual in cutthroat competition and local price cutting for the prices to be uniform (*op. cit.*, pp. 1-3). This, however, is hardly conceivable and certainly is a rarity in practice. Although differing as to the minor matter of verbal definition, our views are in complete accord with Professor Viner's on the essentials of the problem. All that he says of "foreign dumping," in its economic as distinct from its political aspects, applies in principle, *mutatis mutandis*, to the domestic dumping we are discussing. Of the one as of the other it must be said that it "conforms with theoretical expectations" that "dumping on other than a sporadic basis was typically, if not invariably, confined to monopolistic producers' combinations." Undoubtedly true it is that "It is only to a monopoly that export dumping has attractions greater than those of moderate domestic price cutting" (*idem*, pp. 94, 95). This is as fully true if for the word "export" be substituted "domestic" and the price cutting be that done "at or near the factory." The general theoretical grounds for this conclusion are perhaps sufficiently clear after our foregoing study of the conditions of competitive markets and of uniform prices and will be further illustrated below. Professor Viner adduces inductive proof: "A study of the practice of export dumping by European industries offers no basis for doubting the validity of this reasoning" (*idem*, p. 95). He cites also America's foremost student of foreign trade, who has declared that "Sales at lower prices . . . to foreigners . . . for long periods and systematically . . . would seem to be explicable only on the ground . . . of monopoly" (F. W. Taussig, *Some Aspects of the Tariff Question*, p. 208).

APPENDIX C: FALSE NOTIONS OF NORMAL COMPETITION (PAGE 312)

H. B. Butler, a dealer in boiler plates, said: "There is another very curious thing about business, and it is human. . . . A man usually gets a better price for what he sells at home than abroad. Business that is at my door I think belongs to me, but I am willing to make a sacrifice to get a foreign market, because by that very process I reduce my cost at home. By a foreign market I mean a market outside of my natural territory. . . .

"Q. Is there no danger that [other sellers] may make an invasion into that territory on the same principle?—A. Yes; they do."—(*Report of the Industrial Commission*, Vol. 13, p. 493. 1901).

Mr. F. P. Fish, a lawyer of Boston, Mass., gave his views as follows to the Clayton Committee: ". . . Here is a legitimate effort which promotes sound competition. Take this case: A man, say, is in business in New York or San Francisco, doing business all over the country. In St. Louis some one starts a factory to compete with him and does business only in the St. Louis territory. To get business in that territory he puts his price below the price of the man in the East or the far West who can hold his trade near St. Louis only by meeting the cut price.

Now, under this proposed law the man in the East or the far West could not meet the price in St. Louis unless he would cut his price throughout the whole country, that is to say the normal healthy competition which will arise under such circumstances is forbidden. . . . it would be unjustifiable to hamper the other man who finds his business established in that territory attacked and who is willing to meet the local competition on the spot in the old-fashioned business way. His underlying thought is not in any degree to injure this new competitor except as such injury is inevitable in trade. There should be no law to hamper either in the natural fight for business . . . I think the effect of this bill is to stop legitimate competition. . . . This bill does not seem to me to touch cutthroat competition except, perhaps, in a few special cases; but it touches the every-day legitimate competition that you do not want to touch, in my judgment."—(Clayton Committee Hearings on Trust legislation, pp. 1508-10 1914.)

William H. Childs, president, American Coal Products Company, held the same view:

"Q. Let us assume that you have a factory situated in New York; you are selling your goods at a certain price at that factory. You propose to sell goods in Harrisburg, where a competitor of yours is located. I understand under your reading of this provision that you have got to sell those goods at a price at the point of shipment, plus the cost of freight. Well, if you have to do that, will you not give the man in Harrisburg a monopoly?—A. Absolutely.

"Q. And then, the only thing you can do to compete with him is to put a factory right alongside of him?—A. Exactly. This is the reading of the bill." (*Idem*, pp. 582-583. February 1914.)

The many business men who hold to views of which the foregoing are fair samples thus ignore (or deny) the possibility of the very real marginal territorial competition which can and must go on under a system of uniform market or mill-base prices without cross shipments into the competitors' normal sales territory

Chapter XXII: DISCRIMINATION, FINE AND SUPERFINE

APPENDIX A: DISCRIMINATION WITH INTENT TO CREATE MONOPOLY (PAGE 319)

State v. Bridgeman and Russel Company, 117 Minn. 186 (upholding the Minn. law of 1909). State v. Drayton, 82 Neb. 254. State v. Standard Oil Company, 111 Minn. 85. State v. Rocky Mountain

Elevator Company, 52 Mont. 487. Central Lumber Company v. S.D. 226 U.S. 157 (1912). The decision in the case last cited (the only one in the U.S. Supreme Court before the Fairmont Creamery Case) had been unanimous, the opinion having been read by Justice Holmes. He based the decision squarely on the ground that it is the right and duty of the legislature to decide what to do in such cases.

"We must assume that the legislature of South Dakota considered that people selling in two places made the prohibited use of their opportunities and that such use was harmful, although the usual efforts of competitors were desired. It might have been argued to the legislature with more force than it can be to us that recoupment in one place of losses in another is merely an instance of financial ability to compete. If the legislature thought that that particular manifestation of ability usually came from great corporations whose power it deemed excessive and for that reason did more harm than good in their state, and that there was no other case of frequent occurrence where the same could be said, we cannot review their economics or their facts."

The only words in the opinion referring in any way to "intent" to create a monopoly are these: "The Supreme Court [of South Dakota] says that the statute is aimed at preventing the creation of a monopoly by means likely to be employed, and certainly we should read the law as having in view ultimately the benefit of buyers of the goods."

The dissent of Justice Holmes in the Fairmont Creamery Case fifteen years later, strongly suggests that his own opinion and reasoning in the Central Lumber case would not have been different if the discrimination prohibited had not been limited in the statute (as it was) to that "for the purpose of destroying competition."

APPENDIX B: THE FALLACIOUS USE OF "UNIFORMITY" (PAGE 333)

The same fallacious argument about uniformity is contained in a book entitled *Portland Cement Prices,* written for the Cement Producers Association by H. Parker Willis, professor of banking, Columbia University, and J. R. B. Byers, instructor in economics, College of the City of New York. This book, pretentiously announced as "a scientific investigation of conditions in the cement industry," was published while the Cement case was pending on appeal in the Supreme Court (foreword dated February 15, 1924) and seems to have been widely circulated as a part of an extensive public propaganda. An effort was made in this book and in other literature circulated by the Cement interests to prove that the Pittsburgh-Plus practice (just then fallen into bad repute) was not followed in the cement industry. The public was never convinced, but, unfortunately, the Court was. The book was not offered in evidence (being too late for the Record), but is closely paralleled in briefs of defendants' counsel. It was reviewed by the present writer in the *American Economic Review*, Vol. 14, p. 649 (1924), and further in Vol. 15, p. 80. Other reviews, alike adverse to the theoretical contentions of the book, appeared in the *Journal of Political Economy*, Vol. 33, p. 107 (1925), from the pen of Professor Jacob Viner of the University of Chicago, and in the *Journal of the American Statistical Association*, Vol. 19, p. 547 (1924), by I. Lubin, of the Institute of Economics.

Chapter XXIII: MONOPOLY IN NAME AND IN FACT

APPENDIX A: EARLY USE OF THE WORD MONOPOLY (PAGE 335)

Aristotle (fourth century B.C.) in his *Politics* gave illustrations of its use as a financial device in the nature of cornering the market by one man, as that of oil presses, and of iron for manufactures (*The Politics of Aristotle*, Book I, Ch. 12, p. 30). It is believed that the word (*monopolium*) was brought into Latin by Tiberius (42 B.C.-A.D. 37), for when he used it in an address before the Roman Senate he apologized for introducing a new word (*Penny, Cyclopedia*, Vol. 15, p. 341). Its use in medieval Latin is reported by du Cange as early as the thirteenth century in the sense both of a public grant (the society having it, or the right itself) from the prince, and of "any kind of illegal conspiracies" by private acts—examples suggesting the object being to control selling and prices.

APPENDIX B: THE CASE OF MITCHELL V. REYNOLDS (PAGE 341)

A reading of the report of Mitchell v. Reynolds suggests that Chief Justice White put the cart before the horse. Judge Parker put the matter just the other way around, declaring that, if carried to the furthest extreme, the sort of "restraint of trade" he was talking about (which is not the sort Chief Justice White was talking about) might become a species of monopoly, not that monopoly was a species of restraint of trade. Moreover, Judge Parker made his statement not as a "classification," but merely as one of several special "observations

. . . useful in the understanding" of the distinction between "restraints general and restraints particular," *on the practice of one's own trade* (not the carrying on of commerce merely), with or without consideration. In that connection what he said was:

"1st. That to obtain the sole exercise of any known trade throughout England, is a complete monopoly, and against the policy of the law. 2dly, That when restrained to particular places or persons (if lawfully and fairly obtained) the same is not a monopoly" (p. 187).

Again (p. 193) Judge Parker, to just the same purpose of determining what limitation was reasonable in the interests of the seller and of the public, said: "It can never be useful to any man to restrain another from trading in all places, though it may be to restrain him from trading in some, unless he intends a monopoly, which is a crime."

APPENDIX C: EXCLUSION AND MONOPOLY
(PAGE 346)

Some but not all such cases relate to trade-union membership. In the Mason Builders Union Case, 169 Fed. 259 (1909), it is first said: "the thing which is essential to monopoly—concentration of business in the hands of a few." Then it is said: "members of the unions cannot be said to be monopolists when any qualified bricklayer can join a union." This seems to imply that a union enrolling all bricklayers would not be a monopoly, or have any monopoly power in bargaining, if it was an open union. The following additional cases seem especially to stress the purpose or action of excluding other persons: The American Biscuit Case, 44 Fed. 721 (1891); Fenotipia v. Bradley, 171 Fed. 959 (1909); The Reading Case, 183 Fed. 427 (1910); U.S. v. Whiting, 221 Fed. 466 (1914); Patterson v. U.S. 222 Fed. 599 (1915).

APPENDIX D: COMPETITION V. MONOPOLY
(PAGE 350)

Justice Holmes' statement in his dissenting opinion in the Northern Securities Case was quoted by counsel for the defendant corporation in the hearings on the Standard Oil Case in the Circuit Court as if it were in entire agreement with the words cited from the Whitwell Case, 125 Fed. 462. See Rosenthal Brief, Vol. 3, p. 624. But Justice Holmes' words were: "According to popular speech, every concern monopolizes whatever business it does, and if that business is trade between two States it monopolizes a part of the trade among the States. Of course the statute does not forbid that. It does not mean that all business must cease." (193 U.S. 406, 1904.) Here Justice Holmes is going no further than Judge Jackson, not to the lengths of Judge Sanborn. He is not sanctioning the use of monopoly as a proper synonym for competition in the legal sense, but rather is referring to this as a merely popular usage, impliedly absurd for legal purposes. Perhaps he had in mind the very opinion of the Circuit Court above quoted, which had been announced little more than a year before, in 1903.

Chapter XXIV: MERGERS MULTIPLY IN JUDICIAL SUNSHINE

APPENDIX A: SIZE OF ESTABLISHMENT (PAGE 354)

There are few statistics bearing directly upon mass production. The average number of wage-earners per establishment (in factories and hand industries together) was 7.8 in 1849 and 10.4 in 1899. Thereafter hand industries ceased to be reported. The number of wage-earners per factory averaged 22.7 in 1899, and 43.5 in 1927, nearly doubling in 28 years.

Industries differ greatly in the tendency to concentrate in few establishments. The ten industries leading in horse power per establishment (in 1925) were copper refining, iron and steel smelting, steel rolling, locomotive building, cement manufacture, sugar refining, paper-pulp making, zinc smelting, lead smelting, and the manufacture of rubber boots and shoes. "Every instance is an industry of elaborate technical processes and vast machinery." "There is a close relationship between the number of wage earners and the amount of horse power in the various industries" (*Recent Economic Changes*, p. 178). Only 7 per cent of all manufacturing establishments had a product of over a half million dollars. Only 8 per cent of the factories had over 100 workers each. Only one in 200 had over 1000 workers, though this is our usual mental picture of the typical modern factory. The smaller factories, outside of a few industries, show a remarkable persistence. Indeed, between 1914 and 1925, among the 321 industries reported, the number showing a decrease in the average number of wage-earners was slightly greater than the number showing an increase (*idem*, p. 172). Further, between 1919 and 1925 the number of these industries averaging more than 100 workers per establishment actually decreased from 77 to 70. While there was a reduction in the number of establishments in the smaller groups, there was "a tendency to concentrate about the group centering at 20 workers per establishment . . . the extremes moving in toward the middle" (*idem*, p. 170). A study of costs in baking indicated that "plants of a size below the largest may have somewhat lower cost" (*idem*, p. 189). "There appears to be a size that is most efficient" (*idem*, p. 190). The Federal Trade Commission's studies of bakeries, flour mills, and various branches of the petroleum industries "do not show significant net economies of large operation" (*idem*, p. 194).

One difference appears constantly in the figures relating to average comparisons of large and small establishments classed by value of product (either less or more than a half million dollars): although the value of the product per worker is about 63 per cent higher in the group of larger factories, yet there is no appreciable difference in the rate of profits in the two groups. The larger factories have more costly equipment per worker, while the smaller factories expend relatively more for wages. There is thus a constant shifting and selection to find the size of establishment and sort of equipment that is best fitted to each industry in each market area. Long ago it was said that "division of labor is limited by extent of the market." Every business is in a very real sense a zone business, and evidently in many kinds of production a plant of moderate size is large enough to attain all the technological economies that are profitable, and beyond that point growth meets the increasing obstacles of overhead costs and of freight zones. For a completely standardized product, the tendency would seem to be for some one plant to "get the jump" on the others in attaining the maximum size economically fitted to its market area, and thus become a local monopoly. But every lack of standardization, and every individualization or appeal to personal tastes and fashions, tends to retard and prevent such an outcome. Rise of local monopoly power appears to be more closely correlated with standardization of products (steel, cement, non-ferrous metals, coal, oil, foodstuffs, etc.) than with mere size of establishments and extreme use of machinery. Probably weight relative to value (and wide separation of plants, necessitating long shipments) is also a local monopoly-fostering factor. Local monopoly power appears most marked in industries of highly standardized products such as petroleum, steel, non-ferrous metals, sugar, and cement, combined with great relative weight and extensive use of machinery. Compare, with these, cotton and woolen textile industries, conducted in large factories with much machinery, but patterns little standardized, freight not so great a factor of delivered costs, and little monopoly emerging.

APPENDIX B: THE WINSLOW CASE (PAGE 362)

No doubt the Winslow Case has been erroneously used as a precedent, as likewise the later decision on essentially the same state of facts, the United Shoe Machinery Case (247 U.S. 32, 1918). Sometimes overlooked are two peculiar and essential features: (1) that all the machines brought under one ownership were patented, as the Court said, "making them a monopoly in any case," and (2) that the various machines admittedly "did not compete with one another." These features are of the very essence of the opinion read by Justice Holmes, making the 1913 decision at most an extension of the monopolistic power conferred by patents (a grave danger, to be sure), and secondly, applying only to vertical mergers of non-competing industries, not to consolidations in general. This distinction is observed in *Mergers and the Law*, p. 89. Justice Holmes' remark, "The disintegration aimed at by the statute does not extend to reducing all manufacture to isolated units of the lowest degree," is completely surrounded by context implying that the statement is made regarding vertical merger only, and not unqualifiedly of merger in general. The subsequent 1918 decision was by a divided Court of 4 to 3 (Brandeis and McReynolds not participating), in which the minority (the same three, Day, Pitney, and Clark, who dissented two years later in the Steel Case), strenuously contested these concessions to patent monopoly and vertical merger. In a suit against the same company, brought later under the Clayton Act, a District Judge ruled (U.S. vs. United Machinery Co. 264 Fed. 138, March 31, 1920) that restrictive and tying clauses were illegal, and this opinion was affirmed by the Supreme Court, only Justice McKenna dissenting (258 U.S. 452, April 17, 1922). But this did not dissolve the merger or override the decision of 1918.

Chapter XXV: THE DOUBTFUL VIRTUES OF MERGERS

FALSE REASONS FOR MERGERS (PAGE 376)

Though presented by indirect phrase as the product of "scientific research" (Preface, p. vii), this book does not come in a guise that commends its conclusions to unbiased judgment. There is no pretense that in final expression the report represents the conclusions of the Research Staff. "The conclusions expressed are those of the Conference Board as a body," an impersonal responsibility on a controversial question of public policy, widely diffused among a group of business men, all connected either by financial ties with consolidated industries or by close personal ties with those who are. Even such members as gave careful study to the evidence would not compose an impartial jury before which to try such an issue. The case is hardly better with the Board's "advisory Committee on anti-trust laws and their enforcement." Of the thirteen members, eight are business leaders and two are lawyers distinguished for their defense of large corporations. No trace of active participation of the two academic members or by the more liberal attorney are to be detected.

What statistics in this report are offered to prove that consolidation has been actually the cause of lowering prices more and faster than has independent enterprise? (*Idem,* pp. 136-150.) Sixty industries are divided into three groups: A, those in which there have existed, since 1910, strong consolidations; B, weak consolidations; C, no noteworthy consolidations. It appears that by index numbers, the group averages of prices (selected dates) of the three groups compare as follows:

Groups	1900	base 1913	1925
A	115.3	100	148.5
B	91.6	100	150.4
C	90.4	100	196.5

The statistical result may be thus stated: Before 1913 prices in A tended actually to decline, while prices in C rose rapidly and in B somewhat less so. Since 1913, prices in A have risen least, B but little more, and C most of all. The Board then draws from these facts this quite unwarranted conclusion. It says:

"The purport of this result is manifest. It suggests that corporate combinations have exerted an important influence upon costs of production, tending to reduce them. . . . Industrial concentration has acted as a check upon the upward movement of prices induced by an altered currency situation. . . . [If] mergers have brought about quasi-monopolistic returns for themselves and for the industries in which they produce . . . their high profits have been obtained, not through boosting prices, but through lowering costs . . . The inference is not only reasonable, but unavoidable, that the factor (tending to hold down costs in group A) has been industrial consolidation." (Pp. 145-147.)

Such an inference of the causal effect of mergers in reducing prices is utterly unwarranted. It confuses statistical concomitant with cause.

As matter of the commonest knowledge, confirmed by statistical studies, unit establishments tend to be largest in industries where machinery is most advantageously used, and in turn mergers, as a very general rule, have occurred in industries where establishments were already largest and tending to grow larger. (See Appendix, Ch. XXIV.) Conversely, small units persist best in industries where relatively less machinery and more labor is required per unit of product-value. Since the War, it has resulted from several generally recognized causes, including restriction of immigration, speculative prosperity, and organization of labor, that wages have risen relatively higher than general commodity prices (as shown by index numbers). The recent great technical improvements in factories are of course such as yield the larger results in lowering prices in the predominantly machine-using industries—whether in merged or in independent units. These combined influences sufficiently account for the divergent movement of prices in machine-using (hence merged) industries as compared with others, without the flattering tribute to mergers. The Board has thus reversed the causal order of explanation. Technical, mechanical advancement has preceded and been the occasion for the formation of consolidations, rather than the reverse.

The greater development of research in the larger companies in the last very few years, so strongly stressed by the I.C. Board, is not demonstrated to be a peculiar virtue of consolidation. Indeed, in 1929 a well-informed steel fabricator who was a witness for the Corporation in the dissolution suit and smiles about it now, expressed strongly to the writer the opinion that nearly all of the advances in alloys and practical metallurgy since the formation of the Steel Corporation were due to the enterprise of the smaller independents. The Corporation did not undertake research work seriously until some twenty-eight years after its formation.

Another innocent oversight in this supposed proof that "mergers have tended to keep prices down rather than to keep them up" (*idem,* p. 149) is, as our readers are well aware, that industries in which there are dominant mergers are those in which the basing-point method of prices has been most prevalent. But the basing-point quotation is not the true price at which goods are sold at the mills. The steel quotations included in the price indexes are Pittsburgh base prices, whereas buyers of steel at Chicago and western mills have had to pay much more; for example, when $30 was the quotation, the price at the Chicago mill was really about $37. The statistical procedure of taking basing-point quotations as real prices is crediting monopoly with its own misdeeds.

Monopoly exacts "plus prices" and then is praised as a social bene-factor because it is assumed to be charging the base prices. The basing-point practice explains also the smaller degree of seasonal (average monthly) price fluctuations found in consolidated relative to uncon-solidated industries (*idem*, pp. 150-167), which leads the Board flat-teringly to impute to mergers the virtue of "stabilizing" prices. The Industrial Conference Board comments with surprise on the fact that "in several instances there occurred absolutely no change in price for a number of years" so far as the records show (*idem*, p. 158). But it is not surprising that when basing-point prices are artificially pegged the base quotations are "stabilized," although actual realized prices have been dancing an Irish jig.

Chapter XXVIII: THE REMEDIES AT HAND

THE LAW OF CRIMINAL INTENT (PAGE 414)

The familiar legal maxim, *actus non facit reum, nisi mens sit rea* (no crime without intent), is subject to various interpretations or qualifications. (See *Corpus Juris*, article "Criminal Law," p. 74, to which other page references are given below.) In certain more serious crimes, as murder and robbery, *specific* intent to accomplish a par-ticular purpose is an essential element without which no conviction can be secured (p. 80). But "upon the ground that every one is presumed to contemplate the natural consequences of his acts," negligent per-formance of a duty may render the person liable (p. 75). The legisla-ture may forbid the doing of an act although the intent of the doer may have been innocent, as frequently in statutes in aid of the police power of the State (p. 76). When such a legislative intent appears, one who does the act cannot escape liability by showing mistake of fact (p. 86).

To make proof of specific intent *to destroy* a competitor necessary to convict of discrimination in interstate commerce is to assimilate a commercial regulation with laws against robbery and murder rather than with mere police laws, or with traffic laws, where it properly be-longs. To require proof not only that a discrimination occurred but that it was not "in good faith to meet competition" is to make con-viction for charging a discriminatory lower price practically impos-sible, though it now, fortunately, has become possible to convict for charging a discriminatory higher price. See above, Ch. XXII.

INDEX